**Also by E. W. Count**
The Hundred Percent Squad

# COP TALK

## TRUE DETECTIVE STORIES FROM THE NYPD

# E. W. Count

WITH A FOREWORD BY
**William J. Caunitz**

POCKET BOOKS
New York  London  Toronto  Sydney  Tokyo  Singapore

POCKET BOOKS, a division of Simon & Schuster Inc.
1230 Avenue of the Americas, New York, NY 10020

Library of Congress Cataloging-in-Publication Data

Count, Ellen.
    Cop talk : true detective stories from the NYPD / E. W. Count with
a foreword by William J. Caunitz.
      p.  cm.
   ISBN 0-671-78336-X
    1. Crime—New York (NY)—Case studies.  2. Criminals—New York
(NY)—Case studies.  3. Detectives—New York (NY)  4. New York
(NY). Police Dept.  I. Title.
HV6795.N5C68  1994
364.1'09747'1—dc20                                93-48588
                                                   CIP

First Pocket Books hardcover printing September 1994

10  9  8  7  6  5  4  3  2  1

POCKET and colophon are registered trademarks of
Simon & Schuster Inc.

Printed in the U.S.A.

*For the widows and children*

Some of the most skeptical New Yorkers in law enforcement and publishing believed in this book from the beginning and lent their expertise and support: All my thanks to detectives Al Marini, Tom Scotto, Jack Healy, Tom Sullivan, and Jack Donovan, and to Dominick Abel and Bill Grose.

For the original inspiration, special thanks to Lieutenant Jack Doyle.

An editor is a writer's best friend . . . thanks first of all to Dana Isaacson, also to Sarah Ferrell, Lynne Bundesen, Philip Friedman, Karen Anderegg—and to the Sisters-in-Crime group: Marissa Piesman, Eleanor Hyde, Lita Lepie, Bernice Selden, and Diane Ouding.

Someone answered every research call or question, no matter how compulsive or obscure. Thanks to detectives and bosses . . . Bob Cividanis, Ray O'Donnell, Bob Nardoza, Steve Davis, Tim Byrnes, Katy Stanton, John Hartigan, John Mullally, Scotty Jaffer, Pat Barry, Ray Pierce, John Monahan, Lee Van Houten, Lenny Lemer, Charles McGowan, Sam Skeete, Ted Theologes, Steve Weiner, Paul Murphy, Joe Chimienti, Al Wong, John O'Brien, Vito Aleo, Charles Butera, Evrard Williams, Mike Sheehan, Pat Picciarelli, Gene Crimmins, Bob McKnight, John Furey, Ed Norris, George Pagan, Ken Carlson, Ron Waddell, John Russell, Bob Louden, Bill McCarthy, Ellen Hale, Matt O'Brien, Bill Tomasulo, George Terra, Jack Walsh, Pat Brosnan, John Fleming, Richie Dillon, Al Flores, Ron Cadieux, Jeff Timmerman, Ken McCabe, Andy Rosenzweig, Bill Seidenstein, Felix Marquez, Jean Di Gennaro, Fred Elwick, and Luis Llanes. Thanks to all the Manhattan DA Public Information staffers and to prosecutors Bill Hoyt, Pat Dugan, Eric Seidel, Armand Durastante, Tom Wornam, Dan Castleman, David Shapiro, Greg Lasak, Andy Zwerling, Brian Coad, and Chuck LaBella . . . and to Mike Mannion, Pat Clark, Kate Cosenza, Anton Matejka, Sam Maull, and Hal Davis.

Heartfelt thanks for indispensable support to. . .Helen Gheraldi, Laura Burke, John Davis, Jackie McKee, Susan Thomas, Deborah Brissman, Yael Schuster, Jim Weikart, Debra Robertson, Lynn Lenker, and Cummington Community for the Arts.

And to all the narrators in the pages to follow, thanks for sharing your reality. I'll never be the same.

# CONTENTS

You become a cop so you can watch the parade from the front. Detective is even better because you don't have to be in uniform to watch the parade.

—Detective Captain Frank Bolz

There's people that have magic. Whenever they work, things happen. An example of magic is, you could have an informant and the informant tells you that a bank is gonna be stuck up. The informant tells you where a stolen car that the people are gonna use to stick up the bank is parked. You find the car. You sit on that car for three days. Nothing happens.

I relieve you for coffee break, for lunch; I'm there twenty minutes. They come, they stick up the bank, and I wind up making an arrest or getting involved in the situations. You find that this magic goes hand in hand with being competent. But there are plenty of competent people that don't have the magic. It's just unexplainable.

—Detective First Grade Steve Weiner

# FOREWORD

*Cop Talk* is a first-rate collection of detective "war stories" that captures the realism of detectives working cases in the urban slime pool called New York City.

E. W. Count's book is so real it made me feel the sweat coursing down a detective's back as he comes to realize he has just killed a perp in a gunfight.

E. W. Count paints a large canvas with bold brush strokes that have it all, from the frustration of detective squad work, to the spine-tingling fear of a Bomb Squad detective defusing a live one. E. W. Count allows the reader to be in on the opening moves of an Intelligence operation and brings you along on every step of a Narcotic Division sting against a major drug lord.

Reading this book resurrected memories of my days working cases in the 75th Detective Squad. I remembered the boring attention to detail that each case demanded and the endless tedium of sitting on a plant and the shocked disbelief of seeing a hard-worked case go out the window on some arcane legal technicality.

I came away from reading these accounts with the same sense of shared camaraderie that I felt when I was a detective.

*Cop Talk* is direct evidence that E. W. Count knows all about the inner workings of the NYPD's Detective Division.

William J. Caunitz
June 10, 1993
New York City

# INTRODUCTION

*Hell's Kitchen, Fifth Avenue, Radio City Music Hall, Times Square, Rockefeller Center, Madison Square Garden, Broadway, the theater district, the waterfront. . . . The Sixteenth, where I worked as a cop. Maybe the precinct slept for an hour a night.*

A generation and a half later, the old Sixteenth has been renamed twice, its boundaries redrawn—and its charisma reincarnated. Today the legend goes by the name Midtown North. But back when Officer Al Marini, a Queens kid with no cops in the family and no "hook" in the job, managed to find himself a foot post in the neon-lit center of the world, it was still the Sixteenth. The original gent painted on the huge Camel cigarettes billboard puffed perfect smoke rings over Times Square, as if to certify that this was the city that could run rings around all the rest.

The Sixteenth epitomized the glamour of the Big Apple, and the precinct had its share of the grit too. Midtown detectives, Al Marini quickly discovered, were lords and masters of the world's most glamorous grit.

*I didn't know any detectives well, but every arrest you had to bring upstairs to the squad. The detectives had to print the suspects for you. Cops didn't print in those days, and it was a big mystery.*

*Maybe there were three hundred homicides a year then, the*

1

*early and mid sixties, and every one was reported. A clown from the Ringling Brothers Barnum & Bailey Circus was killed—famous thing. And maybe three weeks later—an arrest by Midtown detectives. Gee, how the hell did they do that? To this day, friends of mine will ask, "How do they do that? That thing is solved!" The mystique. . . .*

Oklahoma sheriffs come to New York to collect a suspect in a cross-country murder; Scotland Yard investigators come seeking evidence in an international jewel theft. Before the visitors leave, they're apt to go bouncin' with their New York counterparts, put away a few beers, and soak up at least a few of their hosts' favorite stories. Stories of bad guys and good collars, of victims famous and anonymous. From the murdered circus clown, the murdered Mafia godfather, and the murdered brother-in-law to the violated child, the battered prostitute, and the defrauded grandma—New York detectives work for the world's most diversified menu of victims.

*How did you do that?* Even Scotland Yard wants to know. In the chapters to follow, New York detectives from Coney Island to Harlem answer the question in their own words. (Certain names and identifying details have been changed.)

"If you have something missing from a crime scene, you often have the cause—the motive, of the crime." Joe Ryan, Midtown detective, was around for the clown murder caper; a typewriter, Ryan remembers, a gift from the clown's wife, was stolen from the scene, and "that was the start of the right direction." Ryan's partner, the late Georgie Barrett, reached out to his street network. Look in the Harlem pawnshops, he was told.

"They traced the typewriter," recalls Al Marini, "and the whole thing broke." Dazzled by the Midtown detectives, all this kid wanted was a piece of the mystique. The time came when he got it.

How do you get to be a detective in the city of cities? Back when Al Marini started, Plainclothes was the standard route out of uniform and into the Bureau. After four years in "Clothes," you usually went to a detective squad, working bona fide investigations with your police officer's "white" shield, as the silver-color badge is known. Then, finally, you got your coveted, envied NYPD detective's gold shield.

Or, "If you made page four of the *Daily News*," Detective Joe Ryan says, "you had your shield." Shortcut to glory. Ryan was just twenty-four in the spring of 1953 when his robbery collar hit the *News*, and, in NYPD jargon, he got made.

Collar or no collar, kid, to get made you gotta have that *hook*—someone to put in a word for you. In the seventies especially, when the city almost went broke and almost nobody got made.

**Detective Second Grade Dennis Roberts:** One midnight in 1977 I was riding along with Ricky Duggan. We were goin' down the E. L. Grant Highway in the Four-four in a marked radio car, and I saw this guy on the corner. Ricky, I don't know where I know that guy from, but I know he's wanted.

We stopped, got out of the car—and he ran. He had a bag on his shoulder, a paddle bag. Back then, everybody was playin' paddleball. He dropped the bag, ran into an alley, and got away. We finished up at eight in the morning, and I went home. And then I remembered.

That night when I came in to work, I brought *Spring 3100,* the NYPD magazine, a two-year-old issue. I says, Ricky, 'member that guy last night? Look at this—this is him! "That *was* him!"

Street name was Blackie—Luis Martinez. Wanted for homicide in Manhattan. I got in touch with the Sixth Homicide Squad, Freddy Cappetta, the detective that got me going in my career.

Every day I would drive around to the paddleball courts in the Four-four Precinct. Behind Yankee Stadium, there's a big court, and one day there was Blackie playing paddleball. I was with a sergeant, me an' another guy, Jimmy Coba. I told the sergeant before we got out of the car, If this guy tries to escape, run him over.

We went in, and I just grabbed him and threw him on the floor, and we handcuffed him.

I called Sixth Homicide—We got the guy! Freddy came up. Frist time I ever met him. He didn't take the credit; he could've said, "Well, I went up and got this guy—" He introduced me to his boss, Herman Kluge. As a result, they brought me down to meet the police commissioner, Mike Codd. Between that and a couple other arrests, I was able to get into Plainclothes.

Freddy wrote a letter for me, helped me a lot. He was in the Homicide Squad apprehension team; very, very well known detective in Manhattan North. He had many, many informants, had a great rapport with the community. I wound up working with him as a detective in the Barrio, East Harlem. Any homicide I ever worked on was solved when I was with Freddy. People could call him up, and we'd know half an hour after the homicide who did it.

Hey, you got the shield! You still got a lot to learn, kid.

**Detective Evrard Williams:** I was twenty-three, and everybody else in the squad kinda resented that, and they thought I was a spy for Internal Affairs. I was pretty much left out. They didn't know what to do with me, and I didn't know what to do.

Al Jackson was in his early thirties. Short, kinda thin, didn't look much like a cop. Very, very cool. Always a big car. He started introducing me to people, and we started working together, started hangin' out. From Jackson I learned that "Just the facts, Ma'am, just the facts"—that shit really didn't go across very well in Harlem. I would watch the way he'd do things. He would talk to people and make them feel like people. I found out you get a lot of results that way. Very smooth, very quiet.

Get to the range and practice—you never know when you'll have to use that .38. One thing is sure, though; from day one, you're gonna have to talk to people. And if you're a New York detective, you're gonna keep talking when the tour's over. Among themselves or in other comfortable company, detectives tell what they've seen on a good day, how they saw it, what they did about it.

**Detective Tom Ullo:** Five or six other couples and everybody was just sittin' around; they all wanted to know little police stories. I would tell the funny stuff. But I never liked givin' people the impression that there is not a difficult side of bein' a detective and seein' other than just funny things.

If you start to tell somebody who's family or a friend, Yeah, I was at a certain incident, some kind of tragic thing, you could see the change in their demeanor. Sometimes you wonder whether it's disbelief—"Impossible. How could you do that?" Or, "How could you *see* that?" "How could you be involved in somethin' like *that*?"

Like goin' to the medical examiner's office and seein' what's done there. It's an experience you'll never forget. You go to the ME's office and see what the final outcome is of some human being that an hour ago was walkin' down the street, and now they're just—inhuman. That you can never explain to anybody.

**Detective Patrick Early:** The night I met my wife, I was at a party with actors in a regional theater. They did *The Mystery of Edwin Drood*—my best friend and his wife were in it, and they introduced me to my wife. At the time, I was a "ghost" in Manhattan North Narcotics. I had to work the next morning, I'm drinking soda, and I'm in the kitchen getting more.

Two of the women at the party find out I'm a cop; I start tellin' a few stories. Next thing you know, I had half a room full of people. "Whaddaya do in the City?" I'm a detective. My future wife thought it was kinda cool I found out *later*. . . .

I was at the World Trade Center that Friday right after it went. They needed detectives down there—part of our job is to help with the identification of the dead and the injured, and the notification. So they mobilized Manhattan detectives on an "all available" basis.

Later that weekend I went to a small party. One guy was talking about how great the FBI was and how they were handling this Trade Center thing. Someone said, "Well, y'know—Patrick was there."

The guy was astounded. I said, Let me explain somethin': feds do not investigate homicide. We had five homicides in the First; it's the First Precinct's responsibility to clear them. It is a joint investigation.

Even though I am a bit of a ham at times, I was a little embarrassed. It ended up being like the E. F. Hutton commercial. Everybody stopped. I was just givin' 'em some basic facts—it's *not* Croats or Serbs. 'Cause bein' a detective, I was right there at the command post.

You're a *New York detective?* Your reputation invariably goes before you when you go out of town on business, even on vacation.

**Detective Second Grade Tony Lombardo:** Most of the time I tell anybody I meet that don't know who I am—I'm a truck driver. This judge was sitting in the cabanas on the beach in Puerto Rico, and sitting alongside was a pseudo-gangster from Court Street, Brooklyn, who wanted to buy a lemon ice from the vendor at the hotel we were at.

Now, I knew who the guy was, the pseudo-gangster, because he let me know the day before that he recognized me and that I wasn't a truck driver. We were standing by the water and he says to me, "You look familiar, you sound like you're from New York." And I says, Yeah, and you sound like you're from Brooklyn. So he says, "Yeah, what do you do?" I drive a truck. "Yeah, well, I'm on the piers."

The next day he tells me, "No, I remember who you are now. You locked up my brother." This person also says, "Well, my brother deserved it, y'know. You didn't do nothin' wrong."

He proceeded to borrow five dollars from the judge because the vendor couldn't cash a fifty-dollar bill. He didn't know who the judge was—a human being in a bathing suit—

and he says, ''Gee, could you lend me five dollars? I'm in the hotel also. I'll give it to you later. They won't cash the fifty.''

The judge gives the five dollars. I'm sitting there; if I could only tell each one of them who they are, what they are, they would both have colitis. These little things, this is what makes life go on. Two innocent parties—here's a guy removed from his criminal element; here's a judge relaxing off the bench on her beach chair. It's a small world. It's a funny world.

You can't, as they say around here, make this shit up.

# 1

# FAMILY ALBUM

## Crime Scene Photos

A nondescript Saturday afternoon in May. "It's already a disaster—" says Crime Scene detective first grade Gerry Donohue. "Five in forty-five minutes." Five bodies. One in Manhattan, three in Queens, one in a nearby Bronx schoolyard. The tour has begun.

Donohue, six foot one, wears glasses, looks as mild as the day. He has investigated more than five thousand homicides in over twenty-five years in the NYPD. Donohue and his partner lug toolboxes and a camera case across the drab traffic circle to where the blue-and-white Crime Scene Unit station wagons are parked. They pile their gear in the back of a wagon and go.

Five floors up in an anonymous office building, commanding officer Lieutenant Donald Stephenson's window overlooks the traffic circle with the fancy name Fordham Plaza. Parked smack in the middle, the one remaining Crime Scene wagon looks poised for takeoff. "You can't really plan for the activity [of this squad]," remarks Stephenson. Can't predict the twenty-six-year-old male black shot dead in the Bronx school yard, the male Hispanic roughly the same age dead in Harlem—even if you can guess that the shootings are drug related.

Love-related violence happens often enough too, but you didn't exactly count on this lovelorn Queens boy killing his girl today, and the girl's new boyfriend. And then himself.

Unique in the Bureau, a CSU detective is guaranteed to handle at least two hundred dead bodies a year. It's still a sought-after unit. The imposing six-foot-four Lieutenant Stephenson has his own take. "This is a glamour assignment? Standing ankle-deep in blood, breathing aromas associated with death that are penetrating and lasting—you don't get them out of your clothes." Bottom line: "You have to be a little eccentric, I guess—more so than other specialists."

Lieutenant Stephenson, who is black, describes his "basic ghetto cop" background—on the streets and in the detective squads of the South Bronx and Harlem. Now he supervises the specialists in physical evidence, tangible clues that help the field investigator who's talking to people "know within the first hour of the homicide whether you have a liar on your hands or not," as one veteran Crime Scene guy put it. Stephenson's detectives uncover the hard evidence defense lawyers would rather not have to argue with. Variations on "We got your prints at the scene" are commonly followed by a plea bargain.

It's said a killer will either leave something at the scene or take something away. This something is what Crime Scene detectives attempt to isolate as they sketch the scene, measure it, ferret out shell casings and spent rounds, dust for fingerprints, collect samples of hair and body fluids for lab tests, expose otherwise invisible marks to laser light, and—perhaps the squad signature—take relevant photographs.

A long shelf in the squad room holds black looseleaf notebooks thick with eight-by-ten color crime-scene photos. For these "family albums"—shown by Gerry Donohue at the NYPD's renowned homicide course and wherever squad members lecture—only the bloodiest and most grisly shots are chosen. When candidates come up to the squad for interviews, the sergeant is usually occupied for the moment. "Here," he says, handing over one of the black notebooks. "In the meantime, take a look at what we do." Some candidates withdraw then and there.

"How do you do such a morbid job?" Crime Scene detective Tony Amplo used to ask his father when Anthony Amplo, Sr., worked there. Now he knows: You do it because you're concentrating on your mission as an investigator. And you're not alone—you and your partner function as smoothly together as partners in a radio car. Of course, when you're "up," you're the only one who handles the body. The "family albums" illustrate the squad's pride in their ability to withstand the horrors they routinely confront.

The younger Amplo never really considered a career other than the PD. His first detective assignment with a Brooklyn squad felt made to order. Then one day he happened to drive his partner up to Crime Scene for an interview. "The CO at the time, Lieutenant Guiney, knew me since I'm a little guy: You want an interview too? I'll take you," Lieutenant Guiney said.

Amplo Senior had recently moved on, but his son wasn't sure he was ready. "When my dad was here, all I understood was, you're touching dead bodies. People say it's ghoully . . . But now I understand it. Sure, it's a dead body, but somebody's been killed, and we want to find out who did it. We're not looking at just a dead body. We're looking at bullet wounds. We're looking at Was the person shot in the front or the back? Close up? To me, it's not morbid."

Eccentricity aside, do you need a scientific bent to get into "Forensics," as dinosaurs still call the unit? "A hook," cracks Detective Liam Ahern, referring to the influential friend who makes The Phone Call recommending you to the CO. A hook to get you a morbid job like this? "It's nice up here, believe me." He's tall too, broad shouldered, sandy hair. What's nice? "The people."

Stephenson says it's essential—and hard—to find the right people. The Crime Scene burnout rate is quite high, he adds.

The three bodies out in Queens present no mystery. The lovelorn boy left an electronic suicide note, an audiotape. The car where the young couple died must get the fine-tooth-comb treatment anyway—what if somebody else recorded the tape?

Street maps of all five boroughs plaster one wall of the squad room. Wherever an act of homicidal violence occurs, the scene will be processed by one of the CSU teams. Another squad room wall has neat rows of what look like studio portraits—fifty Crime Scene alumni photographed by Gerry Donohue.

Starting at two P.M. Saturday, four teams of two detectives work this double tour. Too few; at this rate, CSU has manpower enough for only the big ones: homicide, rapes, child abuse. You can be so busy that you simply travel from one scene to the next without returning to Fordham Plaza until the tour ends at eight Sunday morning.

"We just got the East Side Rapist," Tony Amplo gloats. "This rapist comes in the fire escape, and she does her best to talk him out of it, single girl. He talks to her for about three or four hours, somebody from Special Victims told us. And he has a few glasses of something to drink. He does rape her and leaves. But he *touched* something—a glass. And mugs. That's our dream."

Detective Chris Fortune is one of Crime Scene's three women detectives. At five foot nine and a half, she can stand up to the squad's commanding male presences, and to the job. "I didn't think I'd be able to handle Crime Scene, but my sergeant in a previous command said why don't you give it a whirl? I'd never really had that many dead bodies to deal with in my career. He said, 'No, I think you can handle it.' He must've known me better than I knew me."

Her degree in forensic psychology was hard won—she studied part-time for a decade. Even so, she sometimes thinks seriously about retiring after fifteen years to exploit another talent, cutting hair. But then she thinks if only she could get into Detective Ray Pierce's Criminal Assessment and Profiling Unit, "I'd stay forever. You'd have to throw me out."

In Crime Scene, "You see so much, you end up forgetting a lot. At least I forget a lot," Fortune says. "You just have a little spot in your head that you put all that stuff and all those memories in. I never think about them again. Some guys here can remember cases years down the road. I won't. I don't know if that's good or bad, but it's gotten me through."

Today's first job is still fresh. The scene, near the Hunts Point wholesale food market that supplies the City, is a footbridge high over the Amtrak tracks, where, Fortune says, prostitutes recruit customers. She and her partner were looking for evidence of child abuse involving a boy of eleven or twelve and a relative, probably an uncle.

"The uncle banged the boy's head against the railing a couple of times, gave him multiple injuries—the kid was conscious, apparently—and then sodomized him. We heard the kid's in bad shape."

After photographing the scene overall and taking specific shots requested by the case detective, they collected a jacket, possibly the child's, with possible bloodstains—still viable evidence if the night's rain had not washed them out. Searching further, they found blood and hair, "probably the kid's when his head was being banged against the bar." Fortune is optimistic that they got enough "to sink the guy. He's gonna have to plead guilty; he's gonna go away."

No self-respecting big city police department would be without specialized crime scene investigators today. In New York City, the sheer volume of suspicious deaths makes NYPD Crime Scene detectives the expert's experts. When the work comes too thick and fast, the lieutenant is out there too, "attempting to reconstruct from the evidence what happened before our arrival. . . ."

---

In 1967, looking down the road toward high school graduation, Steve Egger saw himself going nowhere. He didn't have a high enough academic average to apply to the city university. Trained in commercial art, he guessed he'd get some kind of job. For the time being, he just rode the bus to school, day after day, as usual.

Until the day, the story goes, when his father, a retired cop, stopped the bus—and changed the course of Steve's life. He drove Steve to the place where the City was giving the test (since abolished) for a new job, police trainee. As a trainee, you could start down the road to becoming a cop even if you were still too young to be one. (At the time, you couldn't be sworn in until you were twenty-one.)

"Two months later, I was saying 'I do . . .' " And instead of being handed his diploma at graduation, "I was workin' the switchboard in the Six-nine."

Back then, the Photo Unit made all the department charts (today civilians do such tasks), and the unit needed someone with lettering and drafting skills. From Photo, you could get into Crime Scene. Once Egger got to CSU, he stayed nearly fourteen years.

CSU felt like somewhere. "I was motivated. I went back to school"—for an undergraduate degree in forensic science from John Jay College of Criminal Justice, followed by a master's in education. At John Jay, he minored in math. He can put two and two together.

New York detectives call the ability to add two and two crea-
tively "making your own luck." You don't necessarily need a steel-
trap mind (sometimes you can be too smart for your own good and
defeat luck). Detectives with average intelligence regularly make
their own brilliant luck. But concentrated brain power can certainly be an asset.

Egger, a Brooklynite of German extraction, and his CSU partner, Tony Lombardo, an Italian-American from Manhattan, com-
plemented each other's dispositions, but both were demon workers. Lombardo claims Egger is "the only real blond in the Police
Department." If Steve Egger reminded the squad of Joe Palooka,
this was a version with aviator glasses and a college education.
Though he's not a prizefighter like the cartoon character, Egger
keeps his six-foot frame in fighting trim.

He would one day become the Detective Bureau's computer-
technology coordinator, but as a Crime Scene detective, he was
already using his own mental microprocessor, systematically stor-
ing odds and ends for the moment when Chance might appear—
then suddenly putting two and two together in a way that Conan
Doyle would die for.

*Tenacity.* Before the deductive fireworks comes the quality that
can keep you processing a crime scene for twelve hours straight,
that when you ask yourself "What's wrong with this picture?"
keeps you looking till you find out. Meanwhile, in the back of your
mind you know the case will take months or years to get through
the criminal justice system, and you can wait that long to find out
your work has been validated.

There are some exceptions. A precious few times in Steve Egger's
long Crime Scene experience, he scrutinized the "picture" in front of
him . . . he analyzed it . . . And what a rush—"That's it! In *hours,* you
broke the case."

### Detective First Grade Stephen Egger:
### Blood Simple

I've had homicides that involved everything from strangulation and hanging to
chainsaws. When you've seen that and seen how people mutilate one another, you just

have to look at it that "this is an inanimate object." You have to repress all your emotions so you can deal effectively. You have to come in totally unbiased, whatever you feel. Once you come in with a biased attitude, you're finished. Your investigation's gonna lean towards that biased attitude; you're gonna overlook something that you should have seen. And you'll be embarrassed later on.

We look at the physical evidence and the known information. If we have conflicting stories, we'll try to take each story and see if we can substantiate the information given. If we can't, we let the detectives know there's something a little funny about this, and you may want to pursue this area further. We try to give them as much ammunition as humanly possible.

There was a homicide in a bar—a peculiar bar. To give you an idea of how tough the neighborhood must have been: you had to be buzzed in. That was the first time I had to be buzzed in to a bar. And the bartender was shot. Money was missing from the register. When the detectives got on the scene—nobody. Everybody left. They had this total mystery.

We showed up, and the case detective comes over and he says, "Listen, we don't even have anyone to talk to." Even the glasses on the bar were totally gone. Everything. The place was clean. It wasn't that much time afterwards.

There was next to no lights. I take some photographs, and I go over, and I start looking at the bartender, and I find a hard material. Little granules of very hard white material. What is this? When I started to open up his shirt, I saw this white material on him. So I take some and I put it into an envelope to send down for evidence, and I'm looking at it.

I look at his wound; he's shot once in the chest and he died. And we're looking around—I don't see any blood or anything else. How'd he get here? I start walking around the bar.

Finally, a detective comes back: "One of the women outside says, 'Well, I was in the bar. This guy came in and shot him, and afterwards, the bartender walked around the bar.' " So I start looking at the other side of the bar—I begin seeing some blood. Mind you, real dark wood; it's on dark wood.

I start examining everything. I said, This is inconsistent with what went on. There's too much blood—but no blood on the body: the *perp* has to be hurt. The bartender was a boxer, they find out; maybe punched the perp in the nose. That's what everybody was thinking: he punched him in the nose. No, there's something wrong with this.

Then I start taking a look at some of the blood around, and now I go out. It had rained. I start walking; all of a sudden I see a couple of splatters of blood up on the side of a building. Now I start looking on the sidewalk, and I see the very faint remnants of blood. Kept walking around the corner toward the park. I said, The perp shot himself. I'd be willing to bet he's shot in the left hand. Take a look at one of his fingers.

So they put out a call to the hospitals. Meantime, I get the radio car; we put the headlights on, take the spotlight, and now we're driving up on the sidewalk, and I'm followin' the blood trail. Across the street, into the park; a couple blocks away in the middle of the park, it ends.

This is about two hours later. All of a sudden, the detectives come over. "We got someone who said he was in the park and he was 'shot during a robbery.' " What? "Yeah, the guy says he didn't turn over his money fast enough, so the robber shot him in the finger." I said, Left hand? He said, "Yeah."

He's the one! Most people are righties: you'd hold the gun in your right hand. . . . The bartender was struggling with him, probably punching the shit out of him. And so he probably pulled out his gun, and trying to hold the bartender off, his left hand was out—and he shot himself through the finger. It turns out the hard material is what I thought—bone.

They did a quick background check on him. The park where we followed the blood: on the other side was his sister's apartment. They called her up. She let us in; we found a rag with blood on it. But she wasn't talking.

We know she knows—she can ID him, but she won't. This was long before DNA testing. We had to wait. . . .

Her daughter got arrested later for prostitution. They told the mother, we're gonna take her for prostitution unless you tell us. And she says, "That's him."

The whole case broke in about four hours. Broke wide open. Must have been spring or fall, because it wasn't too cold. But it had rained and washed a lot of the blood away. So I had to walk sometimes like forty, fifty feet to pick up the blood trail again. Like a bloodhound.

———

Detective Hal I. Sherman is a chubby fellow with horn-rimmed glasses and trademark red python boots who spends his leisure hours under water, scuba diving, or on some playing field or other. He is also a wily sort. Back when he was a narcotics undercover, at a time when a vial of crack normally cost ten dollars, he'd appear on the set unshaven and turned out like a homeless person. " 'I only have twelve, I know it's fourteen dollars. I'll come back tomorrow.' They figure if you want it to be more money than it really is, then you can't be a cop.

"Or you could say, 'Oh, I have this girl downstairs. She'll do the right thing if I give her some crack. I don't use it, I'm buying it for her. I'm not gonna try any with you here.' They would say to themselves, Well, It sounded plausible."

As an undercover and an investigator in the war zones of northern Manhattan and the Bronx, Sherman was bound to collect some scars. Not too many dealers were inclined to just leave all the profits behind and go peaceably to Central Booking. Sherman's two years in Narcotics translated into fifteen layups in the hospital. What turned out to be his last confrontation was with a crew of Jamaican traffickers.

"When I made the buy, I told the backup team just to give me two minutes and then come into the building, because I knew the Jamaicans would flee. The backup team went down the block— four guys who all looked like cops in a four-door car in a Jamaican neighborhood—and somebody raised up the dealers.

"I thought my backup team was entering the building, so I go: *Police, Don't Move!* I got jumped. I was fighting one of the guys— he had partial control of my gun, and we were fighting back and forth while somebody else was kicking me in the ribs. I couldn't shoot the person because this was during the change of school hours, there were kids in the hallway.

"He was pointing the gun at me, pulling the trigger, but I knew how to stop the mechanism. A minute and a half, but it seemed like an hour. We both had to go to the hospital.

"A lot of other people got a lot more hurt—I had two friends in one year killed in Bronx Narcotics. I realized, maybe I don't want to do this much longer. Crime Scene, here I come."

An upsurge in drug murders that year—1987—made the CSU bosses look for people with Narcotics experience, Detective Sherman says. "When I came to Crime Scene, there were eighteen detectives here who were cops before I was even born. They really wouldn't know hiding places or drugs, certain material used to cut drugs, certain paraphernalia. They might just overlook it in a homicide, whereas I'm trained from a different era and a whole different background."

In Narcotics, Sherman took surveillance photos; earlier, as a cop in uniform, he'd conducted burglary investigations, dusting for prints. He also knew mayhem firsthand, and now he had his gold shield. How could you prepare, though, for one horror show with eighty-seven innocent homicide victims?

### Detective Hal I. Sherman:
### Happy Land

Around four A.M., four-thirty, we're in the back room, watching TV. Couple of guys were out there typing, doing their thing; I was in the back. The phone rang and we thought it was a prank call because we don't go to fires normally and somebody calls up in the middle of the night—"There's forty people dead in a fire." You figure, no way.

"I'm telling you, there's a fire, and it's terrible, terrible!" It was almost like the radio broadcast from the *Hindenburg*.

My partner goes on the phone; he says, "What do you mean a fire there? You have any information—? Get all the information; call us back in five minutes." He decided to just let everybody know. "Finish your report because we're outta here and we probably won't be back for quite a while."

Made two pots of coffee, and the phone call came back in. Now they said there's fifty people dead in a fire. They really weren't sure of the cause, but it was a firebomb or an incendiary device. We called up our commanding officer, all the people that needed to be notified. We emptied out the entire storeroom and put it in the car. Polaroid film, evidence bags, gloves, flashlights. We suited up in the coveralls, firemen's boots, and the construction helmets—fire can make the roof fall apart.

Happy Land social club is on Southern Boulevard; I'm not sure of the cross street. It's a very, very wide street—it's gotta be at least two times as wide as Broadway is in Manhattan. In the middle is an island with a park, with benches and a monument. There's a school nearby.

When we got there, there was still about fifteen or twenty pieces of fire apparatus. And by now, a sizable crowd forming. The crime scene was the building, but outside there was a temporary morgue—about fifteen bodies on the sidewalk with sheets over them. Those were people that were on the first floor, closest to where the fire began; they were burnt pretty well.

We instructed the patrol supervisors that the scene should be moved outward, we wanted the entire block. We closed off from the park area over to the building line and both sides of the street.

People on the first floor were the ones that were burnt. That was a pretty roaring fire. The paneling had, what they call, "alligatored"—blisters were forming. There was some chairs and tables left, but for the most part, that's really where the fire was.

Heat rises, the smoke rises. The second floor, there was minimal, minimal damage. Out of the eighty-seven that died, approximately seventy died of smoke inhalation up there. They really didn't even feel it. It takes less than a minute for the smoke to affect you. I've been told it's almost like when you go into hypothermia, where you just get very tired, you don't even realize that anything's happening, and then you just go right out of the picture.

One of the main problems we had was, because it's a dance, a lot of the women didn't have identification on their person. They had it in their pocketbooks. When you're dancing, you put your pocketbooks against the wall—so we had people's identification on the perimeter of the room. Now we have seventy bodies.

Some people panicked, I would imagine. We found jewelry on the floor, we found clothing. By the time we finished, there was something like thirteen hundred items vouchered. At one point we saw a man with his arm around I guess his girlfriend. Almost like a loving gesture. One area, there was just bodies piled on top of each other.

The real hero of the whole place was the DJ. He ran out, could have escaped without getting hurt at all, and he ran back in and started flipping the light switch on and screaming Fuego! Fuego! Fire. People just didn't react. They thought he was kidding or something—there was no fire up there, so they didn't see it.

There were a few people who did escape. He escaped and he had third-degree burns all over his face. His whole body was—we didn't expect him to make it at all. He could have just ran out and probably not have had anything happen to him, but he decided to come back in. He thought it was his responsibility. He was really something.

You have to start doing some thinking, quick. The mayor was there; every chief in the department was there. Buildings Department, Health and Welfare, every sort of agency you could imagine.

The Fire Department and the Police Department in the past had always had some sort of rivalry. Everything was put aside and we worked great. It should be a model on how well agencies can work with each other when need be—they always should—when really need be. The fire marshals would help us out with their equipment; we'd lend them our equipment. Really a perfect, perfect working condition. The cooperation between agencies was really something remarkable.

Our office had to document everything. Instead of making eighty-seven families go through the morgue and look at everybody, we took two Polaroids of each person's face. That way, it's a little more humane and a little less interpersonal. You can flip through the photos and find the person—instead of looking at eighty-seven bodies.

There was about eight of us. Each team had a different chore to do. Two guys took all the photographs. Two of us took all the measurements, down to the last inch of the place. We handed all the property out in large bags. We had to go through every pocketbook in order to try to find identification, phone books—people to call. Clothing to ask relatives about, Did anybody have . . . ?

It was mainly family people there. Hondurans. There was a big soccer club. Absolutely no drugs and no guns recovered. It was after hours; people went there for a party, I believe. There was drinking but no gambling, no drugs. Some people lost as many as six or seven in a family, and being that they were predominantly Honduran, it was the whole community. They lost seventy people out of their small community.

It's something you can say you certainly will not forget. Seeing all those people and having to examine them. To look for wounds, to see just what happened to them.

At one point it was determined that it was a jealous person who had done this. We knew it was a homicide, and in every homicide investigation, you have to perform all these tasks in order to document what is happening. To prove what happened and to show the severity.

We had to dig through all the rubble, take out eight to ten garbage cans just of soot and dirt, because samples would have to be sent to the lab to be examined—to try to find accelerant. The accelerant was later determined to be gasoline and hydraulic-jack fluid, I believe by the federal Alcohol, Tobacco and Firearms lab. We recovered a fingerprint on the gasoline container.

The state police brought in dogs. One was a "human" dog, a dog that was supposed to check out the scents for human beings. We also had a dog there for accelerant. At one point, one of the dog handlers came out and we said, Are you done? He said, "No, he's gotta blow his nose." I thought he was kidding. I said, All right, show me this.

He takes out a handkerchief, and the dog blows his nose into the handkerchief, because the whole time he's goin' *sniff sniff sniff,* he sucks all the ash up in his nose. Here's a guy holding a handkerchief, and the dog is blowing his nose into it.

If you only pick out all the death there, it really is a bit overwhelming. At a time like that, you have to try to pick out some amusing things, if you can call it amusing. Otherwise, you would really lose your mind.

This was the largest fire—the Dupont Hotel fire was, I believe, ninety-two killed—the largest mass murder in the continental United States. (The Dupont was in Puerto Rico. It was over a labor dispute, I believe.) There were news trucks—it was all over the world. We heard reports from as far as Paris, France. It's always a little frightening that you're doing stuff that everybody all over the world hears about. The next day, everybody's in the paper: That's the back of my head! I can tell!

We'd worked twenty-nine hours straight that day. You'd think everybody would run right home, but we all just sat in the back room—just trying to compose yourself. It's over; let's just sit down and relax for half an hour, an hour, because otherwise . . .

The other agencies, they were all offered counseling. "You saw all these bodies, and you couldn't save them." But the Police Department? "Well, you guys are used to this." There's nobody gonna tell you that they just examined eighty-seven bodies and it didn't faze them in the least. There's no switch you can just turn on, turn off: I'm going home, okay, turn the emotion switch back on. It doesn't work like that. If anybody says so, they're mistaken.

We documented all the happenings . . . probably close to two hundred pictures at least, fingerprints and accelerant samples, and thirteen hundred pieces of personal property that was recovered—and none of it ever went to court.

They don't want the evidence to be in because they don't want people to see it. It makes you more empathetic with the victims and less empathetic with your perp. It was pretty much the only move they could make. "Well, we admit that Julio Gonzalez lit the fire, but we just say that he wasn't in control of his mental capacity."

He's been found guilty. Eighty-seven people died, but it's still just one crime, one act, and all he can do is twenty-five-to-life. I don't think if he came out, he would survive.

———

Suppose you catch a violent crime and you've got no witnesses, no notion at all whodunit. Or you've got a classic whodunit with a whole set of possible suspects. If you're enlightened—or at your wit's end—you want the scene of such a crime to be analyzed for "behavioral evidence." This process, now called criminal investigative analysis, was first known as psychological profiling.

In the fall of 1983 Detective Raymond Pierce, another John Jay College alumnus, caught a homicide that would put him at his wit's end. Three years as a detective in Brooklyn's murder capital, the Seven-five, had given him experience you couldn't get in twice the time in most squads. He'd also been a uniformed cop there, then a field training officer, and then in plainclothes on Anti-Crime patrol—a decade altogether in the infamous East New York precinct.

He definitely knew how to "track somebody, collar somebody, put 'em in a headlock. . . ." But now, when a young intern's wife, an X-ray technician, was found in the bathroom of the couple's garden apartment—strangled, the ME said, and suffering from multiple stab wounds—Detective Pierce had yet to address "the criminal mind—what motivates somebody to commit the crime."

The bathtub-cum-coffin was overflowing with water and blood. Jewelry was missing from the apartment. If that wasn't enough of a mess, Detective Pierce had more than a roomful of possible suspects: he had an entire City housing project right across the street, pretty close to a thousand people. "The feeling was that it was a kid from the project that broke in—it was a burglary that went bad, or whatever. But we didn't have forced entry into the apartment, meaning that the victim would have had to admit the killer. And because she was a street-smart person, I didn't think she would open the door for a kid that time of day unless he had a very good reason to be there.

"Except, I didn't *know*."

He had heard about the FBI's psychological profiling capability several years earlier. "When I got stuck with this investigation, I decided to use it. We never found out how many people in the project had prior arrest records. The profile arrived before then, and now I had something documented. That's how a major agency is: 'Okay, something's on paper; this is someone else's—we can nail *them* if they're wrong. We'll go with it.' "

Pierce received the FBI profile in 1984. His murder suspect, FBI experts posited, was a male white over six feet tall, who lived in walking distance of the crime scene, had been in the apartment before the crime, and was of similar educational background to the victim. Only three males had been in the couple's apartment; Pierce was able to eliminate the husband and the wife's father.

The third male lived next door. A medical colleague and friend of the husband's, he had been a frequent guest in the apartment—but attended neither the couple's wedding nor the wife's funeral. Persuaded to take a polygraph test, he failed spectacularly, but Pierce had only circumstantial evidence to follow up with. It was time to confront the suspect with what he had, and the two men skirted the issue during an interview.

" 'Yeah, well, you probably found out that I didn't get along with her. That I hated her, but I would never kill her.' After two-and-a-half hours, he asked for an attorney. The next day, he left the hospital and moved to another state."

The suspect's interview tape at least left no doubt in the family's mind who committed the murder. The case showed Ray Pierce how useful a profile could be. The following year, he applied for a fellowship to the National Center for the Analysis of

Violent Crime at the FBI Academy in Quantico, where he immersed himself in interesting cases for eleven months.

But early on—"The first time I got the keys to the office, I went and read my case of the doctor's wife to try to figure out how they determined that profile. It took a good four or five months before the light finally went on and I saw how that whole process evolves into a description of the individual based on the forensic and the behavioral evidence at the scene."

Pierce, who received his master's degree in forensic psychology in 1992, says a personality "signature" can be observed at the scene, "and those characteristics are then developed in the profile. If you're the investigator, among the people that you're looking at, you'll recognize, for instance, the guy that prefers to work with his hands rather than in an office, that can't handle wearing a shirt and tie to work every day . . . I still don't know the person's name, but I know the type of a person that should have committed that kind of crime."

As the Detective Bureau's one-man Criminal Assessment and Profiling Unit, Ray Pierce goes from squad to squad, consulting with detectives all over the city. Because of his FBI training, he is also a resource for other agencies around the northeast. He can rarely stick around long enough to know the outcome of a case, but seems not to need closure. "Every detective likes an interesting case, and that's all I get now are interesting cases."

Carmen, a single mother, and her two teenage daughters, Dina and Elena, had been out to Thanksgiving dinner at relatives. On the following day, a school holiday, the older daughter was murdered at home.

*Boyfriend-girlfriend thing* is New York detective shorthand for a romantic dispute that turns homicidal. Attractive sweet-sixteen, murdered on a day off from school—you've got to look at boyfriend-girlfriend.

### Detective Second Grade Raymond Pierce: The Jewel Box

The younger daughter stayed over with the relatives; Carmen returned that night with Dina, the sixteen-year-old, to their apartment in a lower-middle-class Brooklyn neighborhood.

Carmen left about seven the next morning for the beauty parlor where she worked but returned home for lunch shortly after noon. (She'd come home for lunch anyway, but particularly this day because Dina was at home.) That's when she found her daughter, apparently violently stabbed to death.

Detective Ed Ayling located a boyfriend and two other boys that Dina and her other girlfriends would hang around with after school. The boys were the most likely suspects, sixteen and seventeen years old. They were all off from school too, and they had all been at the house before.

Ed Ayling centered on those three, and when he wanted to question them, they were fairly open in their answers. But he still felt that they were holding back information, so he approached them with the possibility of taking a polygraph exam. The good counselor in the school said, Of course you don't have to take a polygraph test, so don't. Don't cooperate with the police—and further, get an attorney. Good advice, having their welfare in mind—and a complication for the detective. Are they deciding not to take a polygraph because they're guilty? Is the advice just an excuse not to take it?

Detective Ayling's problem was, Which one of the three kids did it? Now, many of the cases I receive, it's not that easy—out of the *entire population,* who did it? I reviewed the case, and as I always do, I kept asking him for more information. And more, and more. Finally, he said, "I've given you everything I can think of."

There's got to be something more.

The house really wasn't disturbed. There wasn't any forced entry; she would have been killed probably between nine and eleven or so, in the morning. It appeared that she had been sexually assaulted.

The next day in autopsy, that was discounted. No sexual assault. I thought she was stabbed to death—she was in fact strangled to death and then the stab wounds were applied after.

Now, I'm working with my forensic knowledge and my behavioral training, but I'm also a product of my prior investigative training. What's going on here? What's similar? What can I draw off of my own investigative experience?

"I didn't think it was important—" Ed Ayling said, "the only thing I can possibly think of that I haven't told you is that the victim's mother is a lesbian."

Well, that *could* be important. A little bit different behavior than I had anticipated, a mother living with two girls. . . . Can you tell me, does—?

"No, no. Rarely does she have any groups of people over. She's seeing one woman that she's been seeing for the last ten months or so, and she describes it as a very stable relationship. The other child and other people in the building describe the mother as a terrific mother. There's nothing negative there."

It's not necessarily something negative, it's just telling me something about her lifestyle, which, depending on where she goes and the kinds of people she meets, might elevate the risk here.

"What does that have to do with these three kids that we're looking at?"

At this point, I'm not really looking at them. There's something else going on. Carmen's lifestyle might have given someone else access to the apartment. You have an attractive young sixteen-year-old who winds up being murdered and it looks like it's a sexual assault, but you don't have any semen. A male could assault her and not ejaculate, of course. It's also possible that you could be dealing with a woman.

I had to discount the boys. There were some other indicators. Dina and Elena shared a bedroom, and they had a big jewelry box, cardboard, kind of a cheap kid's jewelry box. All the drawers had been removed, and they were placed just so. Carefully.

Now, you look at something like that, the way they were placed—the person piled one on top of the other and then took everything out. At sixteen years of age or so, I'd seen the jewelry box in my parents' room—but I don't think that if I'd just brutally killed someone, I would've been able to take the time to take those drawers out and then stack them neatly there. It made me think maybe we have someone a little bit more familiar with a jewelry box, that would go right for it.

And they had minor, minor articles of jewelry, nothing really of value. So why would someone take the time to take all that? Because it looks like a burglary. We're dealing with staging now. Would a kid have to do that? Well, a kid would be after the money. So we're probably looking at someone who'd go straight to a jewelry box, wanting to stage the crime. Someone that's employed—that doesn't really need the money.

I gave the detective a profile of a *female* Hispanic. A woman between the ages of twenty-seven and thirty-five years old that would know the mother and the victim, would have been in the residence many times. No forced entry. Dina opened the door for the person; she was doing a jigsaw puzzle when the person came in and the television was still on.

Victim information is very important: She was a sixteen-year-old who enjoyed swimming and had great upper body strength; a terrific athlete. So you're talking about a strong, agile teenager. And nothing disturbed in the house. The jigsaw puzzle was still in front of the TV, partially assembled.

In the profile I also said that the killer would be in tremendous physical shape. Probably attend a health club; work out several times a week, if not daily. The victim was just grabbed, taken down, strangled, and then stabbed. And I said there's a strong possibility that the killer would have been in the military, although women only represent a small part of the military population.

We were able to determine with the help of the ME that she was probably taken down from the back and strangled—more or less what you would see in a war movie. That's consistent with basic training in the military and going on to another job in the military, not infantry. You wouldn't bother taking a person down from behind and then go around the body to stab her. They go right through the back, stab the person initially, and take them out that way. So I felt strongly that the killer may have been a veteran.

A couple of other things. The height, which is usually pretty easy to call with a woman, except this victim was kind of tall, about five foot seven, I think. I said the killer was under five foot nine.

Detective Ayling was amazed when he got that description because he was looking at sixteen- or seventeen-year-old boys. But the crime scene showed too much sophistication. Not necessarily criminal sophistication, but someone who had been around a while. Experience and knowledge of certain articles. The ability to respond in an intelligent manner, deal with a lot of stress right after the killing. That's what she was able to do.

The case progressed. He found her—wound up identifying the current girlfriend of the mother as fitting the exact pattern. I think she was thirty-one. The motive that seemed to evolve was that she hit on the girl. Came there, knew that Carmen would be gone, knew that either one of the girls would be there. We're never gonna know—Dina probably threatened to tell. The absence of stab wounds in her nightclothes indicated that the killer probably got her as she was changing clothes in the bedroom. Walked in on her.

Everything fit the profile except the woman didn't work out in a health club. Never belonged to one. It turned out that she worked at a factory on a loading dock. That's where we got the good physical condition. And she was a former WAC.

Interesting—but no conviction. She refused to talk. Time had passed. . . .

Profiling is used to give the detective direction, but it's not sufficient for an arrest warrant. You can't just say, "Based on this information, this type of person should be arrested." This type of person should be *interviewed and investigated*. Ayling did a tremendous job; followed her, caught her in numerous contradictions. But it was all circumstantial; the DA wouldn't go for an arrest.

What happens? The mother and surviving daughter are made aware—and hopefully there won't be a recurrence with that family.

———

To the NYPD detective, skepticism comes naturally—and gets honed when you're paid to use it on suspects, witnesses, alibis. Often enough, you use it on each other. Just because a psychologist happens to be a fellow detective doesn't mean a Ray Pierce is immune to the skepticism freely accorded psychologists by NYPD squads. Even a Steve Egger can end up in a contest for who has the most jaundiced eye.

## Detective First Grade Stephen Egger:
## Cobwebs

The Fire Department had been called for a fire in an abandoned apartment. They went to put out the fire in the bathroom, turns out there was a body burning in the bathtub. Three o'clock in the morning, Crime Scene showed up and took their photographs. The apartment was totally unlit, couldn't see anything. They examined it with the high-powered flashlights; they found some blood around. No other real evidence.

Next morning, the squad goes up and they find in the closet—typical closets, about two-foot square or so—they find blood splatter in the middle of the floor and blood splatter on all the walls up to about a foot and a half, all the way around the door. And you could see where the door was slightly ajar—the splatter even came out through the door. So they called back Crime Scene. Another team comes and they examine it, and they can't figure out what exactly transpired. There's inconsistencies there.

I had gone up to the command on another street homicide. And I happened to know the squad commander, Vernon Geberth (author of *Practical Homicide Investigation,* a famous text). Anyhow, he said, "Steve, you gotta take a look at this. This is really interesting. We can't figure it out. You have to come take a look."

The first thing, we have even blood all the way around—there's no missing splatter. The body could not have been standing up somewhere: it had to be hanging. There were little tiny splats all the way around, and you can see where it was dropping for a while in the center. You take a look and there's cobwebs around the top of it. That means the body couldn't have been hanging *in there.* So I said, the only thing: It has to come from the apartment above.

That's when they told me, Listen, they let us in; we looked at that; there's not an ounce of blood. I say, fine. With that, I take a look where it's consistently falling. Whatever it was, it didn't move for a long period of time.

I get a chair, prop it up, and I take my flashlight. There's two black marks in the ceiling maybe about six inches apart. I take my flashlight, and I hold it up to each one of the black marks, because first off, I know plaster is notorious. It will allow puddles to accumulate above, and it will only seep in one little tiny area. And blood in plaster will look black, especially when it picks up other stuff in it.

I just hold my flashlight up to one mark and then to the other. I hold it up to the one, let it drop down, lo and behold, the mark is right above where it was dripping. I photographed the mark, and I take out my trusty knife and I scrape a little off, and then you can see it's a little red. Based upon that evidence, they went and got a search warrant. "You sure of this?" he says. They're shaky.

And I say, Listen, I guarantee—when we get Emergency Service in, when they saw through that floor, open it up, there's gonna be so much blood, we'll be able to give you a transfusion.

Once we got into the upstairs apartment, that was it. There's blood over here, found blood over there, ballistics damage here. It was all over the apartment. When they opened up the floor, it was loaded with blood underneath. Loaded. That was it. The woman broke.

This was a drug deal—deal went bad. The night before, while the kids were watching TV, the husband kills one of the people involved in the drug deal. They put the body into the closet and it sits there and it drains. Blood hits the floorboards, goes down . . . all the way down.

The perp waits till like three in the morning, and he drags the body down, puts it into a bag. Puts it in the bathtub in the downstairs apartment. Who's gonna know, right?

They clean up upstairs, did a good job of that, and then they set the body on fire. When everybody showed up, everything was totally cleaned up.

Once they sawed up the floor, they asked the woman to come over—"We wanted you to see what we found." She knew we were gonna take everyone, so I guess she was trying to get out from under now. She gave it up.

Those are pleasurable moments, when you can add something to an investigation that helps break it wide open.

## Partners & Bosses

**Detective Sergeant Tom Duffy:** I had a lot of unpleasant memories. I had nightmares on a couple of cases. One of these cases was a double murder and a suicide. A couple had separated, but the judge said the father could have custody of the two children on weekends, even though he had a mental problem. My detectives called me down to Borough Park. The first thing I saw in the corner was a steam-riser pipe with the husband hung there, and underneath him was a little boy of six years old hanging there dead. I was at the kitchen door, and I said, Where's the girl, for Christ's sake? The detective said, "Under your left arm, Sergeant," and on the doorknob to the kitchen was a little girl, four- or five-year-old, hung.

I saw that, I just lost it. I went outside, threw up. I had nightmares. I can't even talk about it now. It was probably the worst thing I've ever seen. It just bothered me. What bothered me worse is one of my best detectives, Richie Payne, super detective, and unbeknownst to me—I had been sending him out in a rotation order, in order of calls—he was getting a lot of child murders. When I sent him out to this, this was the straw that broke the camel's—I mean, he was disrespectful to me. He talked to me like I couldn't believe. That's not Richie Payne.

Anyway, he got me the next day. He said, "You can't send me out to these kids' murders. I have kids of my own. They're seven, eight, and that day I was shook up because of that one." I said, Richie, I didn't understand. Now I'll filter the jobs and you won't get any child murders. 'Cause it bothered him. But it bothered me—I had nightmares on that one for a long time.

# $2$

# MY FIRST BIG CASE

A generation apart, Gennaro ("Jerry") Giorgio and Joyce LaMorte shared the same ordeal—working their first big cases in a fishbowl. High-profile cases, by definition, are worked with peers and bosses looking over your shoulder. Not to mention the entire city.

Both detectives were nudged into the job by friends, but Giorgio came to it with more confidence. When he was appointed in 1959, the NYPD was a man's world. When LaMorte came on in 1981, it was still a man's world—and, not so surprisingly, it remains a man's world. Women, now fourteen percent of the NYPD, occupy a niche, with varying degrees of comfort.

Giorgio seized control from the start, literally picking his perps off the Wanted posters and stalking them on Manhattan's Upper West Side. From her rookie decoy days out in Coney Island, LaMorte's cases always seemed to choose her. When it came to their first major investigations, both ran true to form.

Divergent in personality and style, the two detectives neverthe-less used a common weapon—improvisation. Both got results.

*Improvisation:* offense, defense, and holding action, all rolled into one, invaluable with witnesses as well as with suspects. All good New York detectives are good improvisers. Beyond that, NYPD detective talent is as individual as personality. But when you're working a "heavy case"—especially a *first* heavy case—

under the scrutiny of the bosses and the media, improvisation is critical.

You improvise by instinct.

By the seat of your pants.

The Street is your coach, sharpening that vital sixth sense.

You put yourself in the perp's place: where would you go?

Drop a couple of hard facts to someone, and they'll think you know the whole story. . . .

Often, you do all of the above.

———

A first grade detective now, Giorgio has twenty-five years in the Detective Bureau, thirty-two years on the force. He took the police test "on a lark," when a friend put up the five-dollar application fee. Because he came from mob-ridden Greenwich Village, the NYPD made a federal case out of his background investigation. Nearly two years after passing the exam, he entered the Police Academy, curious, indeed, to know what all the fuss was about.

A tall, self-described "obsessive-compulsive" with nice brown eyes and a sweet smile, Jerry Giorgio looks mild-mannered enough to make a bad guy stop worrying. Born and bred in Manhattan, he has never worked another borough. "They try to send me somewhere else, I'll pack it in." They won't. Thanks to the friend who paid the five bucks for his police test, some of the Big Apple's biggest cases—the "Waldorf Murder," "Murder at the Met"—fell into the right hands.

One day in 1967 Giorgio noticed a robbery suspect being fingerprinted in the station house. The suspect's face looked familiar to the cop—from a Wanted poster. The guy was being sought in connection with the ambush, months earlier, of a police officer. That was the day the chief of detectives decided that Jerry Giorgio belonged in the Detective Division—since renamed the Detective Bureau.

Before his first year as a detective was over, noteworthy cases, mostly homicides, began to have his name on them. One of Detective Giorgio's first major collars, however, was a rapist.

## Detective First Grade Gennaro Giorgio:
## Sixth Sense

In 1967 I got transferred to the Twenty-sixth Squad, my first detective assignment. The squad was in an old station house on 126th Street. I think they had condemned the building ten years before. They always give it to the police after they condemn it. The place was really a rambling wreck, but it had a lot of class to it.

We had a rash of rapes on the City College campus over a period of about six months to a year. The perp would grab them on campus, sometimes take them up to a rooftop. It put some pressure on us. The college was all upset.

I think four out of the five women were students. One was a nurse from Columbia Presbyterian. She had to be in her late thirties, early forties. She had a child who was sixteen or seventeen. She was going for her masters or something. He grabbed her off the street, took her into a college building, and raped her.

I had another complainant. The rapist impregnated her and gave her gonorrhea when he raped her. She was eighteen years old. I interviewed all the rape victims—we didn't have the Sex Crimes Squad then—till I got what I felt was a mental picture of what this guy looked like. I asked the lieutenant, Why don't you give me a couple days. I'll wear soft clothes, shorts and sneakers, and just walk around the area.

Some kid just stood out. Sitting up on top of a mailbox—one of those big, humongous, khaki ones that they leave the mailbags in—and he was just watching all the girls go by. Then he got off the mailbox and started to follow them. And I followed him.

I was just out there by myself, making observations. He did no overt act, nothing that really stood out, just following this girl. He turned and saw me—he would change his direction anytime he saw me. I had to get into my car and drive away, watch him from a couple blocks away. Finally I said, there's something about this kid. There's just *something* about him.

Most cops have that sixth sense. If you're a good street cop, you'll pick it up. Mine may be a little more developed than others. I don't know what it is. Maybe it's vibrations, I don't know. I will look at an individual—the guy will walk in, and I'll look at him. I try not to do this, because you could be a hundred percent wrong. I'll talk to a guy for a half hour and I'll walk out. I'll say, this guy's dirty as they come.

I was looking at the description I had gotten: the rapist had a protruding Adam's apple. I think two of the five women described a long neck and a protruding Adam's apple. But they all made him older. They all made him like nineteen or twenty.

So finally he's out there with some friends, and he's doing karate on the street. I pull up. I flash my shield and I said, you three guys get in the car.

"Hey, man, what's the matter?"

I said, Just get in the car. A little old lady was just mugged, and you fellas fit the description.

So they knew they hadn't mugged anybody. Okay, they got in the car. And I bring them in, hold a lineup. I had done this once before in this case. Brought in a guy that fit the description, and brought in complainants—and they hadn't picked him out.

My sergeant says, "Y'know, you're gonna wear these complainants out." I said, Sarge, I'm telling you, this guy just gives me . . . He just raises the hackles. Something wrong about this guy.

I bring in three complainants and they all picked him out. It was him. I took him in the back; I sat him down: Empty out all your pockets.

"Whatsamatter, Officer?"

Might've sounded like a racist statement, I said, Seems that you have a yen for white girls. He's black and all the women had been white. And he looked at me, and he said, "Man, them girls wanted it." Got a full statement from him.

So we got him for five rapes. And we had just received a letter from the mayor's office, saying What is being done about all these attacks? That day that we got the letter was the day I made the arrest.

I think we had four identifications. The fifth woman would not identify him—extreme liberal. Her husband was studying to become an attorney. He came into the grand jury with her. I'll never forget it.

At that time they had specific people assigned to the grand jury to present cases; it wasn't each DA presenting. Blue ribbon juries, hand-picked juries—they sat forever. The system was different. The assistant district attorney, ADA Walsh, interviewed the complainants, and she got to this young lady. "You gonna go in and tell what happened?"

"Well, as I understand it, he's been identified by the other women."

"Will you identify him also?"

"If you have three or four cases against him, that should be enough." She had been raped and sodomized, this gal. On City College property. Right in the school itself. He'd taken her up to one of the empty classrooms.

Her husband steps up. "You can't force my wife to do—"

Walsh says, "Now, just a minute. Your wife was raped and sodomized by this animal. And you're telling me she's not going to go in and testify?"

"Well, that's right. That's her right. She can choose."

Walsh turned to me, and she said, "Jerry, if he opens his mouth once more, I want you to arrest him for interfering with governmental administration." The guy looked!

"I understand you're a law student?" Walsh says. "You'll never become a lawyer when I get finished with you."

He just walked away. The wife went in, most reluctantly, I think.

The young girl—my complainant? Her father was coming to court with a gun. He was gonna kill the kid.

He pleaded guilty. I don't know how many years he did.

———

A generation after Giorgio took the police test on a lark, a friend of Joyce LaMorte's lost interest in his NYPD application and tossed it her way. Intrigued, she filled out the form. When she scored ninety-seven on the written test, her motivation soared. She haunted the Police Academy gym to train her five-foot-ten, celery-stalk body for the physical.

To succeed in the NYPD Detective Bureau, a woman needs the kind of verbal "contracts" the men of the Bureau have always made for each other: strategic phone calls to the right CO to get a friend into the right squad. Women also need luck, guts, and talent—ideally, at least twice as much of each as men. Divorcée Joyce LaMorte, who arrived at police work by chance, turned out to have everything she needed.

After only eight months on the job, friends sent her for an interview with Brooklyn Senior Citizens Robbery. She wanted a decoy slot but was told five-foot-ten was too big. She looked her age—twenty-four. "They said, 'You're supposed to be an old lady? No.' And then they gave me a shot at it." The sergeant said if she got herself mugged in a month, she could stay. If not, back to patrol.

Tour after tour, she put on the disguise: stage makeup, eyeglasses, long coat—even a fake humpback. And, "I stooped. Stood in a plié position for hours. You get strong thighs."

The deadline had passed. She was living on borrowed time when a Coney Island mugger finally fell for her old-lady act.

From mugger-bait she advanced to investigator on senior citizen robberies. Next came a short stint in "The Big Building" (one of several nicknames for headquarters), lecturing on felony cases to other cops at the criminal investigation course and the sergeant's course. Deserting the palace guard, she soon returned to the field with the Brooklyn robbery squad.

From her vantage point in the war-zone precinct that houses

Brooklyn Robbery, LaMorte looked forward to a Manhattan assignment. When she got one, it was in the First Squad, a few blocks from City Hall.

Like any detective, she dreaded the news of a cop shot. Like most detectives, she dared hope that when, inevitably, it did happen, the case would be hers. At age thirty-one, three months after she made it to the lower Manhattan *quartier* of "artists, models, and Robert DeNiro," LaMorte caught the case of a lifetime.

## Detective Joyce LaMorte:
## Confidence

I was working alone that night. Maybe it was destiny—my number was up. Eddie Norris called me (he was covering Manhattan South). "What are you doing?"

I'm bored, Just typing a couple cases up.

We went to eat. "I hope it's quiet," he said, " 'cause I got a cold."

Well, I don't feel good either. I think I have the flu—my throat feels sore.

It's amazing how you can feel so sick and then get this adrenaline pumping in you that'll keep you up three days at a clip.

I had just come back to Manhattan, to the First. Extortions, bad checks—that's what you get down here. I worked with a guy who has three and a half or four years in the squad, hasn't had a homicide yet. We only do about eight a year, on the average, and it's usually the Oriental youth gangs, people found in trunks of cars. Things like that.

I was here about three months. We had just finished dinner, and we were on our way back. Lieutenant Norris's beeper goes off—My beeper goes off. So we know whatever it is, it's in the First. He said, I'll make the phone call.

*A policeman's been shot.*

He jumped back in the car, and we sped down to Rector Street subway station. There was blood from one end of the train to the next. Apparently, when the bullet hit him, it ricocheted and cut the jugular vein in the neck. His body was already removed to Bellevue. From the amount of blood and chunks of tissue, we just knew he was dead.

My first homicide and it's a retired cop! There's at least fifty bosses there. All kinds of brass. Transit police, people from our job, and everybody was nervous. I'm like, Oh my God, I'm not even sure if they're gonna let me keep it; I'm the new kid on the block.

Lieutenant Norris said, find your best witness, grab him, and go back to the precinct; everybody'll follow. I found a young guy, Richard Grant, about twenty-eight years old, male white, who had been on the downtown Broadway local, and he was harrassed earlier by this person.

Richard was very good. He described the guy: male black, approximately twenty, twenty-two years old. Perp turned out to be twenty-four, but he looks young. About six foot, thin, wearing a ski-type jacket, three-quarter length.

The guy kept saying to this witness, "You work and I don't, and I have nowhere to live." So the paper plays up *Homeless Man Kills Retired Cop*. My witness told me, "He's not a homeless guy—he was dressed pretty neat." He was just obnoxious. He kept tusslin' with Richard, wanted to go in his briefcase. Finally, Richard stood up and said, "You wanna fight? Let's get this over with."

Richard Grant was with another witness, Jimmy Shu, and they were both coming from work. They were on their way to Staten Island.

"Don't make me have to kill you," the guy says. And he kind of sauntered away. He came back about three or four times, just taunting him, just annoying him. Unfortunately, when it didn't go too well, he went to Irwin Rutman, the retired cop.

I'm in the middle of doing this interview in my boss's office. Now everybody comes back. Everybody. Packed house. So I'm standing there with all these men. Chief DeMartino looks over at me, and he's, like, whispering too loud, *"Who's this woman?"*

"That's the detective that has the case."

So it was very scary, very interesting. It was emotional to say the least: he was a police officer. And they let me keep the case, which was a big plus for me. I called my boss at home, and he came in. We had guys come in from Brooklyn.

Transit had picked up two guys that fit the description a little bit, and we had to bring all the witnesses up to the Sixth Precinct because they have better facilities. We did some lineups that didn't pan out. We were up all night. I don't know what time I got home. Six in the morning or something, and I came back at eleven.

When you catch a homicide, you usually work with a Homicide Squad detective. The whole squad was with us from September to December, because we just kept getting hit. We had a guy found in the front seat of his car, shot in the head. We had the three Vietnamese kids in the parking lot—the triple homicide—and then of course, my case. I worked with Joe Brandefine, and I was very fortunate to get him. He *knew* Mr. Rutman— it was very peculiar.

The Rutmans raised four fine sons, one better looking than the next. All bright young men. And this man worked, like three jobs, to put all the boys through college. He was coming from one of these jobs that night. Horrible.

We set up a hot-line number. We kept a log book, and any call, no matter how crazy or retarded—we just logged everything. There was always someone on that phone. We got a lot of tips out of that book. Unfortunately, a lot of them went nowhere.

We couldn't keep Richard Grant after that night 'cause the guy was getting married in two weeks. He had so much to do, and we were really gonna use him a lot.

First we took Jimmy Shu to the police artist, and he made up a sketch, which was pretty good. We rode the ferries, took posters down to subway stations—put them up all over, just hoping we'd get some calls. Which we did. Took us all over the city. From the night of October 29 to December 11, we were all over the city.

No holidays last year—didn't have time.

Later, we took Richard Grant to every CATCH* unit, tryin' to find this guy—Staten Island, Brooklyn, Queens. The unit has photograph files: perpetrators according to their age, height, so on, and the crime. There's thousands and thousands of photos. Negative results.

Somebody said, this guy's getting off the bus at Port Authority; he's a dead ringer for the guy you're looking for. We staked out Port Authority.

A tip led us to The Bronx.

A tip led us to Staten Island, to a guy by the name of Barry, and I was all excited.

This was only the second week in November—early on in the case. We had another witness, Dexter, who went out to Staten Island CATCH and picked out a photo of this Barry. Now there's *thousands* of photos down there. Richard Grant picks out Barry—a different photo! So now I'm saying, this is him. I feel it. This is the guy.

We get Barry, and he keeps saying, "I didn't do it. I didn't do it."

He didn't do it. We put him in lineups. Nobody picks him out. The best we get is Dexter: "Yeah, I think I saw him on the train."

But Dexter, is that the man who shot Mr. Rutman?

"No, I think he's the other guy."

Some people said the shooter was with another guy, and other people said he wasn't. It was just frustrating. We had to bring Barry back home. Then there was another Staten Island fellow. This guy was very cooperative. It wasn't him. He didn't fit the description. He was too short. He had an alibi. I'm starting to believe I'm never gonna find the person that did this.

We weren't getting any more hot-line calls.

I had already notified Crime Stoppers 'cause I wanted to do a "New York's Most Wanted" segment. They rushed it. We filmed the reenactment in Brooklyn at the Transit Museum. I had to do my bit: go on camera, speak for about ten minutes. I'm not one for the press or talking to people, but I'm a little psyched about this. I'm thinkin', Well, now we're gonna get a lotta calls.

Lieutenant Norris is on the Meir Kahane case. The Homicide Squad was taken away,

*Computer Assisted Terminal Criminal Hunt

everybody except for Joe Brandefine. When they left, it was like—you missed them. You wanted these guys to be with you all the time. They are great. Very helpful.

I was working till six or seven that day, a little bit later than Joe. I went back to the office. The phone rings: it's Mike Paul, a detective I know from Brooklyn. And he says, "Joyce, I don't know what this is worth, but there's a guy here, a neighborhood guy, Jimmy Lincoln. He was always in trouble, but now he's kinda straightened out, and he gives me a lot of information. Lincoln says the guy that did this homicide is his sister's boyfriend."

*Really?* I said, I'll be right over.

I called the captain. Do you mind if I get some overtime? He said, No. I said, I'll do it for free; I don't care. So I grabbed a few people from Homicide, and we went over to talk to this Lincoln.

I'm interviewing Lincoln, and he's very evasive. He's talking like this ghetto language I kinda understand, but I don't really. "The deal is . . ." and he just won't verbalize what's goin' on. He's driving me nuts.

Just tell me what happened. I don't want to play games with you.

"All right, Miss LaMor*tay*."

He had just come back from Jamaica. (He was in jail in Jamaica for some kind of pot bust. Of all places! They smoke spliffs this big, *he* gets in trouble. He's a nice guy, actually.) So when Jimmy Lincoln comes back, a friend of his tells him that his sister was watching the news and she got all hysterical. "Shaborn did that!" They were showing the cop's family, and the sister, Frances, realized what he had done 'cause he had told her about it.

Frances tells this friend of Jimmy's—some local drug dealer, so of course he doesn't want to deal with the police. Won't talk to me. Everything is, like, thirdhand information.

Jimmy tells me the guy's name is Shaborn. I said, that's a nickname. Nobody can look at a brand-new baby and say I'm naming you Shaborn. Jimmy says, "I only know him by Shaborn." But he gives me an address—St. John's Place. He gives me the apartment number, gives me who he lives with. So I felt very confident. I knew he wasn't lying to me, or at least he really believed this was the guy.

I went back to the office that night. The guys from Homicide were still working. And there was really not much I could do, but they suggested, they said, we'll take Jimmy over to BCI* and try to find a photo of this Shaborn. They did. Jimmy was very cooperative. He was good.

He was supposed to call me the next day, and I come in early in the morning, pumped up. This is it. I beep Joe, and he calls me right back: "What's happening?"

---

*Bureau of Criminal Identification

We got a good tip, really good. We have to go out to Brooklyn.

He says, "I can't—I'm on the Gotti collar."

They're gonna get John Gotti! I'll take care of this, I said. I'll see you tomorrow.

I'm waiting for the phone to ring and I'm waiting and waiting. I'm getting nervous. I'm calling the number Lincoln gave me and nobody's answering. Now I'm lookin' for my friend Mike and he's at the range. Call the range, I don't care where he is, pull him off the line, get him on the phone. Nobody could find him. Finally Mike called me back.

What happened to Jimmy? You know him better—does he play cute?

"No, but maybe he's confused."

If you can, please tell him to call me, otherwise we're just gonna take a chance. We'll go out to the house and just try to talk to this guy. I don't want him going to North Carolina or something.

I spoke to the bosses, couple of guys from the Homicide Squad. We decided we were going to talk to his girlfriend first, see what we could get out of her. That was supposed to happen at nine in the morning.

I'm in the office early, before eight. I'm alone. The phone rings and it's Jimmy Lincoln. "Oh, I thought I was supposed to call you *today*—but I got good news for you. The boy you're looking for is in the Fifth Precinct with my sister. He was locked up for robbery last night."

I never felt so elated in my life. It was better than sex. My heart's pounding. I beep Joe: Hurry up, wherever you are.

He's on his way from Staten Island. "I'm going through Jersey 'cause the traffic's bad."

Hurry up!

We went over to the Fifth and Shaborn was gone. He was already in Central Booking. He was arrested with his cousin, Tywan. (These are real names. His name turns out to be Shaborn Esquillin.) And this young lady, Frances Lincoln. Three of them are locked up together for robbing a Chinese man with a fake gun, like a musket. It was a nice collar, but nobody realized who this kid was. Had I not gotten the call, he would've been through the system, got out, and that would have been it.

They had just recently changed Central Booking—they lodge the women someplace new, so I have to find out where she is. That's my game plan: talk to her.

In the meantime, we go to Central Booking—I gotta look at this murderer. I go over and I thought, ah, he looks a little dark. Everybody's laughin' because they know I'm getting cold feet. Four or five times, I was so psyched and I thought it was him. Now I said, well—possibly. We'll see what happens.

We sent two other guys to get Frances. We put a chair in the bathroom, and we put Shaborn in there with a cop. I had a lot of trouble with this at the trial—it's an office, but it's also a men's room, a locker room, because that's the way this old precinct is. I'm waiting for Frances to show up. She comes in and Joe said to me, "I want you to do this."

You want me to do it?

"You do it," he says. "Let me see how you do. If I think you need help, I'm gonna jump in."

She was charged with robbery. She also told me she had a crack problem and she was possibly pregnant with Mr. Esquillin's child. I said, I'll speak to the DA, but you're gonna be in jail for Christmas. Do you understand that?

"I don't want to talk about the robbery," she said. "I was read my rights, and I told that cop I'm not talking about the robbery until I see an attorney."

I said, Do you want to see an attorney now? She said, "No. But if I have to talk about the robbery—"

I want to know about the homicide.

She rolled her eyes and now I know she knows. I feel good.

"What homicide?"

Your boyfriend—Shaborn? The cop? October twenty-ninth?

Her eyes are dark.

I know he didn't mean to do it, I said, but you have to tell me. If we find out that you know, you're gonna be in trouble too. You want to think about it?

"Yeah."

You hungry?

"Yeah." She wanted a sandwich, cigarettes—whatever. We order lunch.

I continue the interview and she starts crying. She said he came home that night, "It was right before Halloween. I don't know the date—"

October twenty-ninth?

"Yeah. And he was very upset. He asks me to go to the bodega with him and he told me, 'I killed somebody. I shot the guy on the train. Tried to take his bracelet, he got up, pulled out a gun, and then I took the gun and shot him.' "

That's what he said to you?

"Yes."

What did he do with the gun?

"He threw it on the track and a couple days later, he went back and got it."

Thank you, Frances, I said. You're gonna feel better about this.

I put her down the hall in another room, and I go—YES! I start screamin'—tears in my eyes. I've never been so happy in my life. 'Cause now I *know* it's him.

Now I couldn't wait to talk to him. What would be her motive for making up this outlandish story? I asked her what he did with the coat he was wearing the night of the homicide. She said he gave it to his aunt that he lived with.

I brought him in, sat him down. Do you know why you're here?

"About the robbery—"

It's not about the robbery. I'm gonna ask you some questions about a homicide, but I'm gonna read you your rights first.

I wasn't doing anything to screw this up. You wanna eat?

Whatever he wants. I order some food. In the meantime, I start talking to him. What happened on the night of October twenty-ninth?

Hemming and hawing, "I don't know what you're talking about, man. I *really* don't know what you're talking about." He kept insisting.

People in your neighborhood already told me you did it, how's that? What if I tell you what you did and where you went? How you ran off the train?

He was very frightened of getting beat up by cops, starts crying. "Please don't let them hurt me."

I guarantee you that nobody is gonna lay a finger on you. Nobody.

He was under the impression that it's like the old days when they hung people out by their thumbs. Joseph and I were doing this interview together. We assured Shaborn we just wanted to find out what happened. He was very vague about it. I think he lied a lot, but he did give me a confession. He said he had been drinking. He drank a pint of White Rose and decided to go see his girlfriend. Not Frances—his girl Corinne Gray. In The Bronx.

He got on the train with his cousin, Tywan, headed uptown—which is interesting, because there was a string of Transit robberies that night. It's my guess that he had done quite a few. What do you do? Go uptown, then get back on the other train, come down, and finish up the night. And that's what he did. But he told me he changed his mind 'cause he was too drunk. So he decided to come back down to Brooklyn.

He remembers Richard Grant. He says, "I went over to some white dude. I ask him for some money—he got nasty, cursed at me. An older guy got on the train, sat down. I went over to him." Words were exchanged apparently, but nobody heard the conversation, and then Shaborn tried to grab Mr. Rutman's bracelet.

The broken bracelet was still in the train, but I didn't know if paramedics broke it. I couldn't prove that Shaborn actually got it off—nobody could testify to that, which would have been perfect.

Mr. Rutman starts gettin' up. He had his gun in his waistband. He must have been unsteady—his knees are still bent—and Shaborn had the better of him. Grabbed the gun: "I pointed the gun at him, and I must have shot him, 'cause I heard a shot."

I said, Well, did you pull the trigger?

"Yeah, I pulled the trigger."

Okay, what'd you do after that?

"Then the doors opened and I ran off the train."

According to all the witnesses, the doors were already open. He's saying he had to kill him because he was scared. Every other witness says they ran off the train when they saw him get the gun. They were afraid he was gonna shoot *them*.

And he claims that he fled: ran down toward the World Trade Center, threw the gun in some bushes on West Street and Vesey Street.

We searched. The captain was on his hands and knees, literally beating the bushes. We were all in the bushes. We had Emergency Service in the bushes on Vesey Street. Didn't pan out.

Frances said he told her he threw the gun on the tracks. The gun was never found.

Before I start writing down his statement, I went outside—there's a few of the guys in the squad. I said, He did it! He said he did it! I was so elated. Then I called Mr. Rutman's wife. She dropped the phone; she was crying, "Are you sure it's him? Are you sure?"

"Yes, I'm sure."

"Did you get the gun?" That was her second question. "I would hate for someone to get shot with Irwin's gun." A real cop's wife. At one time she was a secretary in the ME's office, before they had tape recorders; she used to handwrite the autopsies. I think she took the job because it offered her the same hours as his, and they could be off together.

Everybody loved this guy. I had about fifty phone calls—you always do with a cop, but these were friends that knew him for years and years. I felt like I had the burden of the world on my hands, I really did. I wanted so badly to solve this. I can't believe it's over.

At the press conference, Chief DeMartino said, "Stand here by me, stand by me."


The judge kept postponing the sentencing. The courtroom is taken or he had another case. Unfortunately, I wasn't there. A very good friend of mine, a retired detective, sent me a dozen roses, "Twenty-two to life—great job."

It was the greatest case I'll ever have. I'll never top it. I was honored by the Nassau County Shields; I brought my whole family and Joe. We were like the stars of the show. It was really touching. A couple hundred men stand up and clap. I didn't know whether to cry, smile, laugh. It was great.

I always wanted a homicide. I wanted to be a real detective. To me, those are the real guys. I was one of the real guys.

## Partners & Bosses

**Detective Joyce LaMorte:** Shaborn made up a few stories at the trial. He has to. He's trying to save his life now. He's goin' away forever. He said he was threatened by one of the detectives who had "grayish hair. Joyce's partner." "If you don't give us the story, we're gonna kill you—" some nonsense. So Joe has to come in.

I had this same defense attorney on another case in Brooklyn, a rape case. He didn't like me then; likes me even less now. He gets Joe on the stand. "Do you ever do anything to alter your appearance, Detective Brandefine?"

"Well, let me think about that."

The judge is getting a little testy. "Do you alter your appearance or not? That's the question."

"Your Honor, as a matter of fact, I do. I use Grecian Formula Forty-four every six weeks or so to cover my gray."

And now the judge says to him, "Does it really work, Joe?"

I wasn't in the room, but I wish I could have been in the room. I'm in the witness room and I hear them laughing. The whole jury was laughing. That's the type of guy this guy is.

**Detective Second Grade Joe Brandefine:** When nothing happens right away, the Police Department loses interest; it goes—Well, when the next thing hits the press, yours is old news. A perfect example is, about a month later, Meir Kahane got killed. They took everyone out of the Rutman case, they even told me I had to go up there.

I grabbed the sergeant and I said, With all due respect, Sergeant, I'm gonna do what you tell me. But we gotta put things into their proper perspective here. You got a radical up there who's dead, they know who the killer is already and they have the killer. Here you've got one of our own, and we don't really know who the killer is right now. Why are we stripping this case bare? He said, "You're right. You can stay here."

And the next day I grab the inspector, who's a friend and I said, Not for nothing, this isn't right. "What do you mean?" What do I mean? We're down here with three people now. He sent us more people to work on the case. . . .

But Joycie and I worked seven days a week. We had some good times, some sad times. If I got tired, she'd say, "Come on, we'll stay another hour." If she got tired, I said, Come on . . . We always stayed the extra hour.

When you get involved in cases like that, you tend to say, Let's go have a beer and talk about it. She'd say, "What are we gonna do tomorrow?" I said, Don't worry, we'll go another route tomorrow. We'll find a way. Just don't give up hope. And she never did, and neither did I. Neither did the captain. Captain Kelly was real good—always believed we were gonna catch the guy. Not many other people really thought we were gonna catch the guy. He said, "Whatever you need, whenever you wanna work, don't worry." We were out canvassing and needless to say, everybody wanted to go canvass the topless bar—except Joycie. It was right near where the train had stopped. Myself and I don't know who else went in and asked all the patrons, asked the guy, asked the girls, asked everybody if they saw anything. We were talkin' to the guy and he wanted to give a reward of a thousand dollars, which was real nice. We told Joycie.

We went back and met the guy in his office, away from the bar, a day later. And he said to her, "You know, if you don't need this job, you can always work in my place."

**Detective First Grade Ed Kelly, Jr.:** With the young people in the sixties, I used to hear, Oh God, they're all on drugs, they're goin' to hell, it's all bad. Well, I had people like Jerry Giorgio come on board. These guys that I had, that I broke in, they weren't lazy. They'd work harder, they were all good people.

Right after they broke up the Borough homicide squad, they sent me to the Fifth District and that's where I met Jerry. I knew he was gonna get first grade detective someday. He was intelligent, fearless, had an inordinate amount of common sense. And he was a gentleman. He wasn't trying to knock anybody over.

# 3

# FACTS OF DEATH

―――――――――

"Imagine your mother getting killed—" Rows and rows of detectives in the NYPD homicide course get the grim message from Lieutenant Patrick Barry: "You got four days to solve it."

More than a few of the hundred-and-fifty detectives in the big lecture hall have worked homicides for years, but they're attentive anyway. The intensive two-week course is a hot ticket, by invitation only, and you get a chance to hear from some master craftsmen. The waiting list is as long as the St. Patrick's Day parade. In New York City, you can never know too much about murder.

Lieutenant Barry doesn't need to stand at a podium to pass on what he has learned. "He gets down with us—" said a new detective when Paddy Barry commanded the prestigious Nineteenth squad, "and gets his hands dirty."

Especially in homicide—the ultimate investigation—experience is the best teacher. You jump in after the senior guy and learn your trade. Psychologist, magician, salesman, mechanic, actor, priest. With murder cases pouring into the City's squads at the average rate (in the peak year, 1991) of six a day, you better be efficient. Sharpen your time-management skills, Paddy Barry exhorts, so you can get the most out of those four days.

Some experts claim you'll be more successful if you bond with the victim, but NYPD detectives are skeptical. Most homicide victims, they feel, are agents of their own death, after all. Except for the kids. You dwell on the "baby case" long after others are forgotten. "Baby Hope," detectives called the little girl, aged three to five in the ME's estimate, whose body was found in July 1991, crammed into a picnic cooler. Nobody had ever reported her disappearance. Two frustrating years later, Jerry Giorgio and the rest of the Three-four Squad celebrated a funeral mass and buried her, but they haven't given up hope yet.

At the other end of the victim spectrum: "When somebody kills the scoundrel on the block," says Lieutenant John Doyle, "nobody minds." The lieutenant retired out of Manhattan North Homicide with more than thirty years in the Bureau—half of them commanding homicide squads.

Folks don't rush forward to help solve what Lieutenant Doyle calls the "public service homicide." You can hardly hope to mobilize the community to help find the assassin of a José Yepez. An Upper West Side drug dealer, Yepez had a habit of ripping off the competition and selling their wares—a habit that made him highly unpopular with all but a handful of cronies. And if the cronies had information that would help the cops catch their pal's drive-by killer—the Two-four Precinct detectives didn't exactly hold their breath.

But, declared the squad CO, Lieutenant George Pagan, "we're not gonna have Dodge City around here." He assigned the case to Detective Felix Marquez and the D team—who followed a partial print and came up with a perp.

Solving murders is a job, sometimes easier than it looks from the outside. Detectives in the Bureau talk about "grounders"— easy cases to solve—but, hey, it's easy when you know how. The opposite of a grounder? In New York detective-speak, the homicide without witnesses or leads, with few if any clues, is called a "mystery."

New York is the high-profile, high-tension Hollywood of police work. NYPD detectives, especially homicide detectives, are envied for their celebrity, admired for their talent. Sure, success depends in part on your ability to reason, inductively and deductively— but only in part. The most brilliant reasoning is not likely to make the collar without motivation and ego strength for backup.

*Ego.* You gotta have it to keep you upright at the horror-show crime scenes, to keep you afloat in the daily sea of paper, to help you do a convincing I-know-more-about-you-than-your-wife-does number on a suspect. An ace homicide detective's ego is, fortunately, a match for an ace defense lawyer's ego.

An offshoot of ego no doubt, a firm belief in your own moral authority helps keep you on track when the odds seem to favor the other side. Juries and judges don't unfailingly agree with a detective's view of the facts; that only strengthens your convictions, at the same time as it breeds cynicism.

The lack of a death penalty in New York State compounds the cynicism—after all, City detectives typically believe, shouldn't murderers get as good as they give? But cynicism isn't all bad; it's a perfect filter for the revelations of suspects and witnesses.

*Motivation.* Pride motivates; so does sympathy. If you sympathized with every "DOA"—an expression cops use as a noun, when they mean a corpse and, by extension, a victim—you wouldn't last long. When a child is murdered, though, even the New York public hurts. But nobody hurts like the investigators who live with this death and know its every ugly detail.

For detective bosses, especially, the big picture is a big motivator. Nothing thrills a commanding officer like the strategy of the chase, the game plan he or she puts together with the input of the squad. Especially when the plan works.

Along with ego and motivation, a New York detective's survival kit includes the ability to see the funny side of homicide. You develop this ability as a police officer in a radio car, hurtling from irony to tragedy and pathos and back again, or you won't survive on patrol.

But now you're a detective with a murder on your plate. Working the case is slower, deeper, more painstaking. The victim's wounds, his address book, and his grieving survivors, all are part of your job. You rely on humor more than ever—your own and your partner's too.

In the end, all of a New York detective's survival skills don't count for much without luck. You try to be receptive. Do all the legwork your case calls for and more, because you never know where you'll run into some luck—and the more experienced you are, the more likely you'll know it when you see it.

———

Detectives usually pick up their knowledge of the job from their peers and their bosses—Chief Joseph R. Borrelli was already a boss himself by the time he had to learn the craft.

"I never read any handbooks," insists the chief, who came up through patrol all the way to captain before he ever commanded detectives. "All I read was some of the technical stuff on what kind of tests you could perform to bring up latent prints, and all that kind of stuff."

Did the pipe-smoking Borrelli also sample the fictional exploits of that other pipe-smoking sleuth, Sherlock Holmes? The familiar profile among the images of various famed detectives on the chief's office wall would lead you to think so. And after all, like Holmes, Borrelli is lean and beaky; at six feet one, he's an inch taller. Once he played minor league ball (first base) for a New York Giants farm team. Now he golfs and tools around Long Island Sound in a modest-sized cabin cruiser.

Then-Captain Borrelli had been in the Police Department for fourteen years, but only a week in the Detective Bureau, when Officer Timothy Hurley was killed in the One-o-three in Queens in 1974. And responsibility for solving the police officer homicide was all his. On the advice of his chief, he addressed himself to the horse's mouth: "I sat down with Kenny Bowen, the sergeant, Joe Lyons, Jack Sephton, who was an old-time detective—sharp detective. I say, Hey, I'm not a captain. I'm just a member of this team."

No one was exempt from Borrelli's grilling. "What are you doing?" he'd ask the Crime Scene guys. " 'What can we get out of that? Can you do this?' They'd look at me. 'What are you crazy, Cap? Can't get fingerprints off that!' 'Oh—'

"Typing . . . I was doing everything. I was a captain and they were very polite. But that's how I learned. We ran with that case and made it." Going on two decades later, Borrelli's satisfaction hasn't dulled at all. The perp was Martin Settles. "They locked him up in Atlanta, Georgia." (Settles was convicted of the officer's murder, but the conviction was reversed on appeal. Rather than face trial on robbery charges in connection with the original Queens incident, Settles pled to robbery second degree.)

After five-and-a-half years "out there in Queens," the Brooklyn native knew all those detectives by their first names. "I knew Queens—but since I've become chief of detectives, now I know what everybody's doin'." He is eight rungs up the ladder from his Indians, squad detectives in seventy-five City precincts, and in such specialized squads as Homicide. Borrelli flips through his mental file; "the cases we didn't solve" rush to mind. But he is proud of the triumphs, especially "any case with kids."

Ten-year-old Jessica Guzman was the last of five young victims who disappeared mysteriously from a mostly Latino area of The Bronx, apparently abducted, between June 1989 and October 1990. All lived in the same bleak southeastern part of the borough known to residents as Castle Hill. Like the first four, Jessica had the life choked out of her and her body was dumped in a secluded spot off a highway. After a weeklong search, her body was discovered on October 17, 1990, and the investigation gathered momentum.

The murder was a cause célèbre. A black mayor, David Dinkins, was highly sensitive to minority constituents' doubts that the case would get the full attention of a police force that is still about three-quarters white. Detectives and bosses were mobilized, from both the NYPD and the New York City Housing Police.

"It's personal," most would say about their motivation. The mayor was beside the point; they owed it to Jessica. As they learned more about the suspect, says Bronx ADA Edward Talty, they recognized the signature methods of a serial killer. The NYPD's chief of detectives kept close tabs on their progress.

Over a nine-month period, the Jessica Guzman task force—twenty detectives at peak strength—followed a paper trail as far away as Texas and kept the crime lab busy analyzing microscopic evidence. They put together a mostly circumstantial, yet convincing, case against livery cabdriver Alejandro Henriquez, age twenty-nine. From Chief Borrelli's bird's-eye viewpoint, though, getting the goods on the self-possessed, self-styled entrepreneur depended first of all on sociology and strategy.

## Chief of Detectives Joseph R. Borrelli:
## Nobody Was Talking

This Guzman case—a great investigation. Not only because of the investigative effort. The game plan, that's what the key is.

The detectives were being truthful when they said way back that Henriquez was a "suspect," because his name popped up two or three times. Interesting, but he wasn't a suspect. They were doing a lot of things, just the investigative efforts, in the beginning. Then they started pullin' in these other homicides that looked similar. There were a series of meetings going on. He starts poppin' up in some of these other homicides.

When the other investigations were pulled in and the name popped up, then the feeling was, hey, there's more to this than meets the eye. But he was totally cooperative, comin' in, talking to us. In the beginning, he looked like the best witness if we ever solved the case. Then the detectives became cynical and all—suspicious.

He had a lot of dealings in the neighborhood. People weren't talking. Perhaps they were fearful of him. So the game plan was, We gotta get this guy, get him on *something*.

In an intensive investigation, we found this robbery in Manhattan that he had committed two years earlier. We worked that case, got him arrested for that. Got him off the set.

Piece of information comes in. Now we go down to Jersey—we found out he was involved in a sexual abuse case down there. The Jersey authorities come up; they lodge a warrant on him.

Now people say, jeez, they got him in for robbery and sex abuse. . . . A little bit more information comes. . . . We do a little investigation in Puerto Rico; we come back with *more* information. And that's how the whole case evolved.

Henriquez used to rent cars, loan cars out; he had a whole lot of different things that he was doing up there. One of the cars we traced down to Texas; Tyler, Texas. Processed it—came up with some fibers that matched! That's a heck of an investigation.

The investigation was good. But I think the game plan and how that evolved, that was even better. The plan was, Get this guy on something—get him off the set, and then maybe people will talk to us. That's exactly what happened.

That's an intimate knowledge that detectives pick up of human behavior. The greatest sociologists in the world are New York City detectives. I'm a sociology major. It was easy for me. You understand people, you understand relationships, you understand what goes on in these subcultures.

You try to utilize that intimate knowledge. Like they knew his reputation in the neighborhood—pretty tough character and this kind of stuff. They knew people were afraid to talk with him still on the street—through all his machinations, people were making a living with him. So once he was off the street, they no longer had any obligation to him. That's how that all came about.

How do we proceed? Who do we target? Every investigation has some sort of a game plan. This is after you've gotten all the basics in. You get some sort of a direction and you're startin' to look. Sometimes you're just floundering around for months. You just don't go and grab this guy, go and grab that guy. You may *do* that, but it's "let's talk to *him* first because he might . . ." That sort of thing.

Sometimes you put a game plan together and it falls apart. This particular case, it worked well.

Indicted for Jessica's murder and two of the four others in which he also was a suspect, Alejandro Henriquez was convicted of three counts of murder on August 28, 1992, and sentenced to three consecutive terms of twenty-five years to life.

---

The drive-by machine guns that killed drug dealer José Yepez in 1992 felled three crossfire victims too. Relatively small-scale mayhem compared to that created by some mass murderers, but arguably a product of the same mentality. Forensic psychologists draw sharp distinctions between the mentalities of the *mass murderer* and the *serial killer* whose death spree takes place over time.

A decade before the Yepez murder, Detective Bob Doyle of the Two-six precinct and homicide task force detective Jim Varian hooked up to try to solve a couple of .38 caliber shootings in Harlem. When their six-week investigation ended, the partners collared Manhattan's *first* serial killer—a "disorganized type," a psychologist would say—opportunistic in his timing and choice of victims.

In the Manhattan Area Task Force office in December 1981, Varian heard about violent felons and felonies all over town, but the new terms *serial murder* and *serial killer* weren't yet in circulation. Varian and Doyle had not been briefed on the latest FBI psychological profiling techniques; nor had Bill Kelly of the Three-four or John Worth of the First Precinct—but the detectives noted a trademark pistol-to-the-head MO in a spate of homicides. The list of similar killings soon grew to four, and counting.

Varian had first worked the December fifth murder of a part-time actor in northern Central Park with Detective Jerry Smith of the Central Park Squad, but before the investigation really got rolling, Smith went on vacation and Varian found himself teamed with Bob Doyle. Varian had fourteen years in the Bureau, and Doyle about half that, but Doyle was conscientious and thorough, Varian heard—and reliable.

"You don't want somebody who, when it gets a little hairy, he's gonna go out to check the parking meter or something," Varian says. "I worked with a cop like that. We would get a gun run in the basement; he would go up to the roof. Said he was cutting off escape routes."

If Bob Doyle played himself in a movie version of the case, the handsome detective would be a box-office draw—except he's too retiring ever to do any such thing. A real choirboy type, says ADA Patrick Dugan, who prosecuted the case. Dugan says he immediately liked the choirboy and the street-driven go-getter. Seemingly mismatched, the pair turned in a well-coordinated performance.

When Jim Varian was assigned to help with murder number one, he was looking at retirement after twenty years of top-drawer police work. Good thing he wasn't called on for an encore to the investigation that ensued. From the arrest (January 13, 1982) that he and Doyle pulled off in a stifling, pitch-dark basement apartment under a Harlem church, to the perp's confession to all the killings they'd been investigating—plus that of his roommate and a few others no one had even reported to police—Varian couldn't imagine a more dramatic finale to his NYPD career.

### Detective James Varian:
### The Same MO

The body had been found that morning in Central Park. One gunshot wound to the head. His wallet was on the ground, but his money was missing, no credit cards. A dog walker found him.

Jerry Smith from Central Park Precinct briefed us on the case, and he took us up to the location. We stood out there that Saturday night, talking to people walking through the park. They see anything? Hear anything? We came up with nothing.

The next day we found out that a Volkswagen had been parked around there for two days, and that it was the victim's roommate's car. The roommate reported James Weber missing and the car missing at the same time. Mr. Weber had been using the car to go back and forth to work. That's how we identified him, 'cause he had no ID on him at all.

We also learned that he was an actor with the Light Opera of Manhattan, on the East Side. They were doing *Babes in Toyland*. He had worked Friday night. Friday night/Saturday morning he got shot. He parked the car in the circle in Central Park and walked up to a burnt-out building which is a known area for homosexuals to hang out.

The roommate was a nice man. Very concerned. Almost crushed when he found out Mr. Weber was dead. He helped us as much as he could—giving us bills and credit slips, and whatever.

Monday morning I got on the phone and notified all the chiefs of security of the credit card companies that the guy was a homicide victim and asked them, Don't cancel the cards. We want to see who's gonna use them. Put a priority on it: if a charge comes in, we get notified right away. (A lot of times when you use your credit card, if that account is okay, the company's not gonna know it was used for two or three days.)

We got word a couple days later that someone used the card down in the Village. We went down, Jerry Smith and myself, two or three times to different stores and interviewed the clerks. They gave us a description of the people: three or four blacks, all males. And they showed us the types of articles of clothing they were buying.

We're riding back uptown in Jerry's unmarked car, which had a Fourth Division radio in it. A 10-13 came over: "A uniform holding three." No violence or anything, but you never know what's gonna develop—if he's holding three and one of them gets hinky, now the cop has a problem. So before they can get hinky, you're there and you just make sure they don't.

I think we made one turn and we were right there. A rookie cop has three prisoners on 72nd Street and Amsterdam Avenue. The store owner comes out screaming, and the cop grabbed 'em—now he doesn't know what the hell to do with them. The kid had just come out of the Academy. I think he had six hours in the street, and he had two homosexuals and a transvestite that had been shoplifting. Couple of radio cars responded, and we brought 'em right up to the Two-o squad.

We're there kiddin' with the kid, the cop. On the street we didn't notice, 'cause they all had their outer jackets on. When they took their jackets off, I'm looking at these shirts they're wearing: exact same shirts that we had just looked at. Exact same shirts. I say to Jerry, Look at these things! And he's goin', "You're right."

It was a plaid-type shirt, heavier than a dress shirt but lighter than a flannel shirt. Melvin had on green plaid, Lew had on blue plaid. Nice-looking shirt, long sleeve, expensive looking.

We split them up, started talking to 'em. No, they didn't kill anybody. They don't know anybody; they don't know nothin'.

Tell you what's gonna happen to you, I said—You're gonna get charged with homicide. And I told them about the homicide in the park. (I didn't think they had done it; they weren't that physical. If they ever heard a gun go off, I'm sure they'd go under the table.) But they had *some* connection to it, because they're wearing the shirts that were charged on the credit cards. They had some information that we could use.

They wouldn't talk to us. We kept 'em separated, and I said to Jerry, We just gotta keep hammering. They gotta give us something.

What we did is we switched: he went to one guy and I went to the other, found a couple of discrepancies in what they had told us. Then I said, Well, I told you what I'm gonna do with you. We're gonna hold a lineup. We're gonna bring the people from the store up here.

I took 'em into the lineup room. I showed 'em the whole thing: You're gonna sit in here with your partner, and when the girl says, *That's the guy that bought the shirt*, I'm placing you under arrest, and I'm gonna charge you with homicide. Because you used that guy's card.

"I didn't do it! I didn't do it." Then Lew says, "Mink was the guy"—the guy who gave them Weber's credit cards. Okay. They met Mink in the billiard parlor or pool room on 42nd Street and he had an American Express Gold Card. The guy tells me, "You don't screw around with American Express. They try and give us double time." That's what he heard, so he tore that card up and threw it under the train on the way downtown.

I go and get Jerry: You talk to this one now, and let me see what happens with the other one.

So we go back in and I drop the name "Mink." Your buddy told me, you might as well tell me the whole story also. He corroborates everything Lew was saying to me. Tells us where they met. Mink was one of the guys with them when they went down to buy the stuff. Melvin didn't know the fourth guy—"a friend of Mink's." He hadn't seen Mink in a couple days. They gave it all up that night.

I called the DA's office. I explained to them that we had a homicide and that these two individuals had information about it, but were under arrest for shoplifting. Pat Dugan was the covering DA at the time for homicides in Manhattan. He came over and interviewed both guys. First time I met him. Usually, if I don't know the party, I'll ask somebody, and Pat had a very good reputation for being thorough and fair. He didn't believe the two guys had anything to do with the homicide either.

Now we had to find Mink and see what he could tell us, where he got the credit cards. We turned the two fellows back over to the cop and told him that we'd see him in court in the morning.

The next morning I went to headquarters where they have the Modus Operandi room and the nickname file. I worked the name "Mink" into the nickname file, and we had one hit. Michael Winley.

I had about four copies of Winley's photo made up and went right over to court, into the holding pens, and brought out my two friends. I had other photographs with me and I just stuck Winley's picture in the middle. They both picked him out: this is Mink.

Now we know who we're lookin' for. Or we figure we know who we're looking for. I pull his arrest sheet. I think it was mostly boostin'; may've been a little drugs in there. Find out as much as we can about him. Areas he hung out in, known associates. We also checked to see if maybe he's on probation or parole. He wasn't.

Because we were the Task Force, we were assisting the detectives in all the Manhattan squads and, during the course of all this, other stuff started drifting back into my office. John Worth was up from the First Precinct one day. He had the homicide down there of Stephen Glenn Hassel, shot in the head and the apartment set on fire. He told me Bobby Doyle had a similar case up in the Two-six: Edwina Atkins, a prostitute and lesbian, shot in the head and the apartment set on fire.

John and Bobby had the bullets compared in the two cases—they match: six lands, six grooves with a left twist in the barrel. So I says, Hey, I got a guy shot in the head. We call Ballistics up, ask them to check—now all three bullets match! That's how I got hooked up with Bobby Doyle.

Doyle and I are working our two informants, Melvin and Lew, telling them we want to find Mink. They talked about Magic Cue Billiard Parlor, on 42nd Street. We had that place staked out for a couple of days, but we couldn't come up with him.

We had the two informants out on the street as much as we could get them out there to look for him, ask questions where he's at. "They wanna do some business with him," the word would flash around. If they got good information, they were gonna walk on the shoplifting case. But when we left them on the street, they'd get locked up again for shoplifting someplace else. One guy went right into Macy's. . . .

We go up into Harlem and talk to some of Mink's associates, people he'd been arrested with before. When someone gets arrested, they're allowed to make a phone call. That gets logged on the arrest sheet. You keep track of these things and then you go back.

A female up there told us that Mink was living with a guy named Nicky. We asked her about him; she gave us just a physical description and that he was living with Mink. But she also said that Nicky supposedly had known Edwina Atkins. Bobby mentioned the name because Edwina was his case. We thought that was strange about Edwina knowing this Nicky. We couldn't put it all together.

Then I found out Bill Kelly in the Three-four had a homicide, Heriberto Morales, up on Haven Avenue. Guy was shot in the head, and then a Christmas tree was set on fire in the place. Detective DePasquale from the Task Force was assisting Billy on the case. They were in the office talking about it, and I'm there doing other things, and I hear about this thing.

So I gave Sal DePasquale my Ballistics number and they called upstairs to the lab. The problem Ballistics had is the bullet hit a lot of bone in the Morales head and they couldn't give a positive on it. It was very similar. They believed it came from the same gun, and if they had the gun, they could give it a positive match.

We believed we had somebody for four homicides. The three guys who were killed were all homosexuals. The girl was a prostitute, but she was a lesbian—maybe she and the killer moved in the same circles. And all four had been shot in the head.

We had a meeting with the Task Force, everybody that was involved in the case, and the DA's office. Pat Dugan was there with two or three people; my lieutenant, Tom Power, was there. When we ran Nicky through the nickname file, there might have been twenty or thirty Nickys, but nothing matched up with the physical description we had, so we were concentrating on Mink. Our job was, if we located one of them, to put him under twenty-four-hour surveillance until we put the two of them together.

Mink had an outstanding warrant on him. I got copies of the bench warrant and put one in the case folder. (Once I had seen the warrant, I didn't have to have it on me; I just have to be able to lay my hands on it in the near future.) So we started again looking for Mink. We finally got a phone call from our two little friends out in the street. They had information for us.

Bobby Doyle and myself met them on 43rd Street and Eighth Avenue, and they told us that Mink was supposed to be living with a guy in the basement of a church opposite a Turkish bath. They have no idea where. Yeah? And who gave you this information? This is just street talk.

They wanted two hundred dollars apiece and all sorts of guarantees that they're not gonna go to jail. I told them go out there and work some more.

All of Mink's addresses and his activities were either in the 42nd Street area or up around 125th Street, Mount Morris Avenue, in that area. I met Bobby one morning up in the Two-six and we started driving around near Mount Morris Park. There's a couple of Turkish bathhouses up there. There's also churches across the street. We did stop into local post offices and check if they knew the name Michael Winley. And we just started knocking on doors.

The snow started to fall. January '82—I don't know how much snow fell that day, but I know there was a blizzard going on.

We were around Madison Avenue at 124th Street. I'm looking across the street. The park is right here to our left. There's a Turkish bathhouse over here and a Pray-to-God church on the right. And there's an old man outside shovellin' the sidewalk. We were actually looking for the postman who had Madison Avenue to see if he knew the name. There was nobody out in the street, so that's why we even stopped to talk to the caretaker. And the situation was there. The Turkish bath, the church. We got the car double-parked, and I get out.

Do you know Michael Winley?

"Yeah."

It just seemed like we were in a movie now. This is unbelievable; we said—You know where he lives?

"In here."

Bobby parks the car. We go down a couple of steps underneath the front steps of the church and in towards the rear. This was eleven-thirty, twelve in the morning, and it was dark in the corridor. There was a lone light on at the far end.

The caretaker was going right back through. We were coming in out of the daylight; my eyes didn't get accustomed at first. I could see his shadow going down the hall, but that's all. The old man hits the door and says, "This is his apartment." Nobody answered.

I just said, Oh, shit. That blew the surveillance. There was nothing we could do but eventually go into the apartment.

He says, "There's somebody home." I said, How do you know? He says, "Well, when they go out, they always put a padlock on the door, and the hasp is there but no padlock."

Okay. I knock on the door. No answer.

We checked out the apartment from the outside to see if there was any way anybody in there could get out. There was two windows in the apartment, heavy bars on the outside and inside, heavy drapes. You can't see into the place. No light showin' out.

The caretaker couldn't tell me the last time he heard or saw anybody in the apartment. We checked with the fellow in the front apartment, and he hasn't heard anybody in there. He says the guys who live in there burglarized his apartment. Then he tells us to be careful. Why? He says he's seen both guys carry guns.

The caretaker says, "Oh, yeah, they're always carrying guns around." I said, Where do they carry them? He says, "They stick 'em right in their waist, and they walk in and out of the house with the guns. One time I saw them carrying a long, rifle-type gun." Oh.

We're sitting in this little hallway for a while, trying to figure out what the hell to do. I didn't want to leave the apartment door and neither did Bobby. Sitting in the car wouldn't have done us any good 'cause we don't know if anybody was in the apartment, or if there's any other means of getting out. I didn't want to take any chances.

The caretaker told us the owner of the building was a reverend who worked over on 125th Street. Bobby stayed by the door while I ran over and asked the minister about Michael Winley. He knew his family—very religious people. Michael was a super guy until he brought home this friend who was living with him now. They haven't paid their rent in a couple of months, and the reverend's a little mad.

I said, We may have to go through the door, and that's when he gave the key up. He said the caretaker had a spare. He'd had a lot of complaints about Winley from other neighbors.

When I went back, we got the key from the caretaker and the layout of the room. We can't do anything now, I said—have to get some backup in here. I called Lieutenant Power from the phone on the corner, and Tom says to me, "Do you know what's going on out there?"

Tom, I'm standing in a blizzard. Yes, I know what's goin' on. He says, "There's nobody in the office—I have nobody I can send up to you." I said, Okay, I'm gonna call the Two-five Squad, have them send over one of their teams. He wanted to know why we didn't set up the surveillance instead of going in.

I told him I couldn't, and I didn't want to get into a long discussion with him because Bobby was standing alone in the corridor. I said, I'll talk to you when I get back.

I called the Two-five; I tell 'em we have a warrant; we're gonna make an arrest. One of the detectives who came over was Bob Bowens, a big black guy. He probably could have played linebacker someplace. He and I had worked the Robbery Squad. He's got a lieutenant with him from the Two-five. They were the only guys in the office at the time.

When I told the lieutenant we were looking for Michael Winley who's a suspect in four homicides, the lieutenant wanted to see my warrant.

I said, It's in my file down in the office. He says, "Well, you don't want me here." And he says to Bobby Bowens, "Bring me back to the office." Bobby takes him back. He grabs an Anti-Crime guy to come with him.

We're all in the corridor. There's not much room for anybody. We found out the room was only about ten by twelve, a small bedroom. The caretaker knew of a chest, a dresser, a chair, and a little closet in there. And the bed. He had described where the bed was, as best he could recollect. The door opened in, from left to right. The bed was behind the door.

I put the key in the lock and turned. It sounded very loud, the lock goin'. We had banged on the door a couple of times. Police— Open up— No response at all. I turned the knob and started to push the door open. It opened maybe an inch or two, then stopped like something was holding it from the inside. I started exerting some pressure and it slowly started to open.

Down on my hands and knees—I get hit with a blast of hot, sweet air. It was like the exhaust from a boiler came out of the apartment and hit me right in the face. I sat back on my haunches.

I could hear a creeping sound, like paper. Later I found out it was vinyl crinkling up. I start pushing the door. I'm getting this sound and I'm getting a lot of resistance. I got the door open maybe twelve, fourteen inches, shined the flashlight in.

As I panned the light down the wall, I could see clothes hanging up in a closet at the far end of the room. I couldn't see anything on the floor. I knew the bed was to my right, I'm trying to see part of it, at least. I couldn't—I didn't have the door open far enough.

I'm still down, but I rolled to my left side and put my foot on the door to get a little more leverage and started pushing. I had my gun in my right hand. By using the foot, I'm also a little bit back from the door. I finally got the door open far enough so I could see the corner of the bed. I could see the full closet now, clothes hanging in it. Still no sound in the room at all. I get back on my haunches and I said to Bobby Doyle, I can see the bed; I got a closet where the guy told us. I don't see anybody.

I hadn't stuck my head into the room and I didn't want to. I got back on one knee and I kicked the door some more—I could see maybe an eighth of the bed. I quickly dropped back to my haunches: I see a foot! The shoe was black, pointy toe with laces. I sat there for a minute.

Bobby wanted to know where the foot was. I said, It's on the bed, straight up. I think he said, "What do you want to do?" I hesitated—I'm gonna go in. I'm just gonna swing around the edge of the bed, put my light on. Just watch my back, 'cause I don't know how many people are in there. He said he was ready.

"*Police*—We're looking for Michael Winley. Answer us."

No answer. Back on my haunches. The door is open that much now that the other fellows in the hall with us could hear. The foot hasn't moved. This toe pointing right toward the ceiling. I'm saying to myself, If the foot is straight up, he's not laying over the bed with a gun. You're only talking three, four feet—but he's not turning, aiming. He's gonna be shootin' blind if he does shoot.

I knew I just couldn't creep into the room. I had to be movin' in case he did have a gun, to make it a tougher shot. I get down into almost a three-point stance, like a football player; flashlight in my left hand, the gun in the right. I said to Bobby, We're gonna go now. And I waited a second or two. I hit the door with my right hand. Nothin'. I was waiting for a shot to ring out.

Another second or two, I jumped into the room and threw the light onto the bed. The beam caught this fellow laying on the bed with his hands across his chest, eyes closed— but I knew he was awake because the eyes were flickering.

*Police! Don't move!* In the beam of my light I could see a knife stuck in the wall. All he had to do was go for the knife. He never moved his hands! I'm right at the foot of the bed. I walked to the side and my foot came down on a metal clyinder object. I thought it was the barrel of a gun.

I said, I know you're not sleeping. Who are you?

He opens his eyes. "I'm Nicky." We knew Nicky was our shooter's roommate. Holding the light on his face, I have the gun barrel pointing at his chin and I tell him to sit up. I took him off the bed, handcuffed him, and put him over by the closet.

There was a weapon in the wall, maybe a weapon under my feet. What about the .38? I couldn't see anything else in the apartment because it was pitch black. I said to him in the dark, Where's the gun? He says, "I have no gun."

When I got him over to the wall and put the cuffs on him, my head hit the drawstring hanging from a ceiling light. I pulled and it was like a floodlight. The place just illuminated. You're momentarily blinded.

We saw we had a bed, a little portable bar, a dresser, a chair, a radiator up full blast. And the closet in the corner. The wall had the knife in it. I said to Bobby, I think there's a gun on the floor on the left side of the bed. It wasn't a gun; it was a blackjack. Which again, he could have reached. I asked him, Where's Michael? He said he didn't know.

Where's the gun?

"I don't have a gun."

I looked under the mattress, didn't see anything. I lifted it up from the foot of the bed and put it back down. Bobby's on the right side of the bed. "Jim, I think I have something here." A green string with a loop on it coming out from underneath the mattress. Bobby pulled the string and he could see it was a shoulder loop. He lifted the mattress and came up with a sawed-off shotgun. You hang it on your shoulder, underneath your coat; you just whip it right up, and it's a very dangerous weapon. In a room that size, it would just blow a wall out.

I said to him, Is it loaded?

"Yes."

Bobby said he didn't know how to unload it. I left Nicky on the wall and unloaded the shotgun—there was one round in the chamber. I safeguarded the gun by sticking my handkerchief up into the barrel. I asked him where Michael was.

"I don't know." We put Nicky in the hallway with Bobby and the two guys from the Two-five.

We looked in the closet, under the bed, behind the dresser, behind the chair. There was a Bible open on the portable bar; he had passages underlined in red. I picked up the Bible, a spent shotgun shell casing, and the padlock. I left the knife in the wall and the blackjack on the floor. We secured the room with their padlock and kept the keys.

"Nicky" was young, twenty-one. Fairly good-looking guy. Brown skin, clean shaven. Nice complexion. Guess he was about five eleven, six foot. He had a nice build on him.

Weighed about one-seventy, one-seventy-five pounds. When he talked, he didn't sound like he had a New York accent. He had a nice diction—it was like he was educated. And he didn't seem upset or rattled at all. I've locked people up that were cryin' or pleadin', It's not me, It's not me. He had none of that. Just went along with the flow, like it would get taken care of later. No problems at all going with us.

He was wearing dark pants; believe he had a black shirt. He had a black overcoat and he wanted his "gangster hat." It was a black, wide-brimmed hat, Al Capone era. Like felt. We got the gangster hat and put it on his head. We had the shotgun, and him. The fellows from the Two-five were gonna stay until Crime Scene came, in case Michael showed up.

It took us an hour and a half in the snowstorm to drive from 124th and Madison Avenue to the squad at 20th Street and Second Avenue. I asked Nicky in the car what's his right name. He told me David Bullock. I advised him of his rights, and I says, I don't want you to talk to me and I don't want to talk to you.

We got back. Lieutenant Power was all upset that he didn't have anybody to send us. He was apologizing up and down. I called the DA, Pat Dugan.

Pat got annoyed that we didn't wait and get the two of them. I said, Pat, we didn't have a chance to. You gotta trust me on this one. He was upset. He says, "Call me at home tonight after you talk to him. Let me know what happens."

We called a couple of the bosses to tell 'em Nicky was in. That was all we knew—Michael's friend Nicky. We had the guy sittin' in our locker room by himself. Handcuffed, sittin' at the table. We left the door open, just let him sit in there by himself. I put the Bible on the table in front of him.

After about twenty minutes, Bobby and I went in and sat down with him. We introduce ourselves. We took the handcuffs off him and told him we wanted to talk to him about Michael. He's talkin' how he met Michael, how he and Michael were living together. They weren't lovers, but they lived together. They did have sex together, but they weren't lovers, that's the way he explained it. He would give Michael credit cards, whatever he found, and Michael would know how to turn 'em into dollars.

I guess we talked for maybe about an hour. He was strokin' us. He didn't wanna get into any kind of details. We just had the impression he was lyin' to us. I asked him how long Michael used the name Mink, and he seemed surprised that we knew the street name. "You guys know a lot."

We said we know a lot more than we're telling you. We want you to tell us what's going on. And he still wouldn't open up to us. We asked him if he wanted something to eat. He said yes. We got him something to eat. Every time we went in to him, we advised him of his rights. He says, "I got no problems. I didn't do anything."

We told him he was under arrest for the shotgun.

He's telling us his life story. As a child, they sent him up to Pius XII Camp up in Chester, New York, which is down the road a little bit from where I live. He started to smile.

I said, Did you like the country?

He said, "Yeah, it's a nice area, but they didn't like me up there."

Why was that?

He used to put Clorox in the goldfish bowl and watch the fish die. He said they got all upset at the school because the goldfish were their pets.

I asked him why he got up there. He said his mother had caught him hanging his younger brother out the window by his heels because the kid brother had taken something of his. At that point, she thought he was in need of supervision.

We took another break. We believed those two stories that he had told us, but we didn't believe too much more. Bobby and I are trying to get our act together. We did give him a couple of bits and pieces hoping that he would expound upon them, but he didn't. We don't want to give him everything we know. We went back in the second or third time.

We were kind of at a dead end when I opened up the Bible that was on the table. This your Bible? I see you got passages underlined. Do you have favorite passages?

"Yes, I do."

I said, Tell me some of 'em.

"An eye for an eye and a tooth for a tooth." He's tellin' me that he's gonna get back at somebody for doing him wrong.

Oh, okay, I said. But do you know the passage in there that says, Thou shalt not kill?

He says, "Yes."

Well, Can you tell me the difference between the two passages?

He couldn't. Or he didn't want to, or whatever. I asked him for another passage, and he said, "Do not covet thy neighbor's wife."

I said, Oh, that's a good one. Do you also know Do not steal?

"Yes."

I said, Do you steal?

"Not really."

He mentioned a couple of passages; I really don't remember which other ones. I said, Do you also know the one, Don't lie to the police?

He says, "Yes."

I looked at him quizzically, Oh, you know that one?

"Yes."

I says, I think it's time you stop fooling around and start telling us what's going on.

And he just said, "Where would you want me to start?"

We had that shotgun. I said, "Tell me how many shootings you were involved in."
He said, "Ten."
*Ten* . . . Let's go with the first shooting.
"Well, I iced that guy in the park."

So began one of New York City's classic murder confessions, narrated in precise, chilling detail by a young man just turned twenty-one, who realized his first time out that he was good at murder—and enjoyed it. ADA Patrick Dugan and the district attorney's videotape unit subsequently taped a formal Q & A with Bullock that would become celebrated in the genre.

A few days before Halloween 1982, at a hearing before Judge Burton Roberts in Manhattan Supreme Court, Bullock's attorney lost a motion to suppress the confession. Then at the judge's behest, Bullock recited the macabre story in open court, as the usually blasé courthouse press corps scribbled down quote after shocking quote.

Then-*Newsday* reporter Gerald McKelvey says he and the *New York Post*'s Mike Pearl listened from seats in the jury box. "It took almost two hours to go through the whole thing," recalls McKelvey, who had heard a couple of cases with public confessions, but "never anything like that."

Unlike reporters excited by the prospect of inch upon column inch of bylined newsprint, McKelvey says, Bullock stayed cool, cooperatively answering questions from the bench. Then he coolly pled guilty to six counts of murder second degree. A month later, the court sentenced him to six terms of twenty-five years to life.

Versions of the taped Q & A have been seen on a French TV news magazine and studied by numerous U.S. law enforcement agencies. Highlights of the transcript—including Bullock's revelation about what happened to Mink—are found in Chapter 11, "True Confessions."

———

Like police officers everywhere, New York cops often say they took the job because they like working outside. Some, like Long Islander Tommy Lane, originally had their sights set well beyond the city limits. Lane says he was always a "farm boy." The farm boy had an extended career as a homicide detective. Today he is a cattle farmer with a goodly supply of campfire tales.

Lane's father, typical in this respect of City cops, chose to raise his kids as far as possible from the streets he worked. Thomas Lane, Sr., worked some of Manhattan's meanest—in the Two-five—East Harlem. "He was a famous cop there," says the son, "made some tremendous arrests."

Lane Junior, who looks as average as his name sounds—five feet eight, a hundred seventy pounds, brown hair, hazel eyes—spent the early years of his police career working midtown Manhattan gay bars in the plainclothes Public Morals Squad. He started in the fancy Seventeenth, noted, among other things, for the United Nations, the Chrysler Building, and Sparks Steak House, where, in 1985, John Gotti would rub out godfather Paul Castellano.

As a detective, he later put in for a transfer to Queens to be nearer "the farm," but the closest he could get was a precinct near the Manhattan side of the Triborough Bridge—the Two-five. There, he spent the latter half of his career, mostly investigating the murders of prostitutes and other not-so-good citizens. Several such fatalities per week were not uncommon.

These are homicides that don't put you in front of the TV cameras, but Tommy and his last partner, Jack Freck, got off on their own fine-tuned sense of the right source, the right question, the easy-if-you-know-how solution. Freck, a few years younger, went on to one of Manhattan's two elite homicide squads: Manhattan North.

Detectives on the verge of a "media" arrest hope for an assistant DA who'll appreciate their work and put as much into the case as they have—literally do it justice. "DA shopping" by detectives is frowned upon, but who is more devious than a detective bent on justice. You could, for instance, just happen to pick up your perp on a night when an assistant you know and trust is on the DA's rotating homicide call.

In more routine cases, however, the luck of the draw determines which ADA you end up with. But whether by choice or by chance, it's the prosecutor who'll try the case, not you—so once a case reaches the prosecutor's desk, he or she calls the shots: Bring in this additional item of evidence. Pick up that witness, no matter how many crack houses you gotta hit to find him.

At some point in the career of a seasoned detective comes a prosecutor with a far-out wish list. On just such an occasion, Tommy Lane and Jack Freck set out earnestly, diligently, to get the goods.

### Detective Tom Lane:
### Teeth Marks

The Two-five is made up of blacks and Spanish; Spanish controlling the southern end and blacks the northern end. Three or four hotels in the fairly small precinct were used by prostitutes. One day, a black girl was found stabbed to death in the Saint Something-or-Other, Fifth Avenue and 125th Street.

Me and my partner Jack went in. The registration card had a Spanish name on it: Marian Diaz, or something like that. The clerk described a Spanish girl going into the room with a black guy—but the dead girl is black. So there was a little confusion to start out with.

We ran around the area looking for all the known prostitutes. We're interviewing and we come up with a Spanish girl who says, Yes, she was in that hotel with a black guy. He was unhappy with her or somethin', and she left.

We went and spoke with the victim's friends and found out that the john came back down to the street, made an offer to this black girl, and they went back upstairs. But they never changed the registration card. So that's where the confusion came in.

Since this Spanish girl had the best look at the john, we bring her into the squad. Her boyfriend comes floating in, who's a raging alcoholic. We're goin' through mug shots of guys in the precinct, and the boyfriend says, "I'm an artist—I'll draw a picture from her description." This guy is totally whacked out. We're all laughin': Mr. Potato Head drawings?

Anyway, he draws a picture from her description, and he did have a little artistic blood in him. He drew the face of a black guy, and she says, That's the guy. It's like, unbelievable.

We put the word out on the street that if anybody sees this guy around, to call us. Nobody's seen him 'cause he's not a local. We put up posters with the boyfriend's sketch.

Two or three months go by and one of the girls calls during the day tour. We weren't working yet; we came in at four. She said the guy was on the corner soliciting. It's a

Friday in the summer. Two of the detectives on the day tour went out and grabbed him and brought him back to the squad.

When me and my partner came in, he was there.

My deal with interviews was you would go in and talk to the guy but not about the crime. You talk to him about his family. About his interests—whether it's sports or something else. His religious convictions. We would spend quite a bit of time on these things. Say he's religious, believes in God. Then that's what we would home in on. That would be his weak spot.

This particular guy was religious, and I think he loved his mother: two things. So we went on about going to heaven, clearing your name, and all that. What would your mother think of you? These kinds of things.

Finally, he confessed. He says he's from Jersey and he came into the big city. He wanted a girl. He solicited a girl up in our precinct. They went to the hotel room and for some reason he didn't like her, so he brought her back down.

Then he goes out and solicits this black girl, takes her to the room and she's giving him oral sex. She clamped down on him and demanded more money. It's a fact!

So in a rage—he had a knife handy—he stabs her to death. And then he leaves and goes back to Jersey.

We arrested him, of course. The DA comes up and we tell her the story. "Oh, my God, she says, he may have a viable defense there! I want you to go down to Bellevue and have him inspected for teeth marks or any kind of scars, even though it's a couple of months later. And have a picture taken, in case this comes up in the trial."

So me and my partner bounce down to Bellevue, I guess around midnight. Ever been to Bellevue on a Friday night in the summer? I mean, gurneys are lined up around the block. People are sittin' there with axes in their heads. Really busy night.

We go in and the triage nurse comes running out. "What do you guys want?" I tell her the story.

"You're crazy! You're nuts! What are you, wacky? This is Friday night!" She ran up and spoke with a couple of doctors who threw us outta there.

The second humorous part of the story—that sketch that the boyfriend did who never saw the john was better than any photograph you'll ever see. It fit him to a T.

Perhaps Tommy Lane's DA had a crystal ball and foresaw the "rough sex" defense that would one day be innovated by Robert Chambers's attorney in a case that became nationally known as the Preppy Murder. Like Lane, Detective Sergeant Wally Zeins, who became part of that famed investigation, never wanted to be tied to a desk.

Prey to acute *shpilkes*—Yiddish for "ants in your pants"—
Wally Zeins says he chose assignments exciting enough to dispel
the *shpilkes* by "tranquilizing" him. Deep undercover work, for
instance.

The NYPD now has about three percent Jews. Zeins says that's
up from when he came on in the early seventies. Then it was one
percent. For one of his early cases in the Brooklyn's DA's Squad,
the bearded, prematurely gray Zeins played a Hasidic landlord.
Another time he was known to members of the Gambino crime
family as a hood named Michael Simon.

*Shpilkes* has prompted him to seek out other unusual assignments—the Hostage Negotiator Team, and for a time, Nightwatch.
This squad of seven or eight detectives are often the first detectives
at murder scenes.

Even though the midnight-to-eight A.M. hours make it a "terrible" tour, Zeins enjoyed covering the whole city and he liked the
responsibility. "If you have a heavy-duty homicide, you get your
chance to really go out and see what you can do. It's like being the
mini-chief-of-detectives." Is the implication that "heavy duty" is
treated differently? "The unidentified person or the derelict or the
decomposed body, you're still gonna do the same."

The case that called out the Nightwatch Squad before the sun
came up one summer day in 1986 was definitely a heavy. The
"Preppy Murder" had begun in Dorrian's Red Hand, a Second
Avenue singles bar in the Nineteenth Precinct where victim Jennifer Levin was last seen alive with her killer, Robert Chambers.

In the Nineteenth, many a homicide is page-one news—on Park
Avenue, Madison, or Fifth, in the fashionable East Sixties, Seventies, and Eighties, anything less than a safe neighborhood is judged
a scandal. And when someone who lives or plays in the Nineteenth
Precinct meets a violent death, more often than not it is a scandal.
The same day that Sergeant Zeins's Nightwatch detectives began
investigating eighteen-year-old Jennifer's death in Central Park,
she became a celebrity.

Nightwatch detectives are like nocturnal moths, gravitating to
the glaring light of disaster. Their stay may be brief, yet their
paperwork is a crucial part of the case record. The sergeant signs

off on every DD5 report: "When your name's on the bottom of those fives, you've got to be sure that everything's right."

On August 27, 1986, about the time Manhattan's early joggers hit the street, Nightwatch sped to Central Park. What the squad confronted there was a murder mystery worthy of a fiendish author determined to confuse matters with as many red herrings as possible. But tragically, this was no fiction.

### Sergeant Wallace Zeins:
### Sunrise in Central Park

It was about six-forty-five. We were notified by the dispatcher of an apparent homicide in Central Park, located behind the Metropolitan Museum near the obelisk monument. At first I thought, oh, it's gonna be a gay homicide, because most of the homicides that I've responded to in the park are homosexual assaults. I learned in Nightwatch, if there was ten or more stab wounds on a person, almost always the perp was a gay.

We had a very interesting group of people in the squad. Very eclectic. Very seasoned, knew what they were doing. And very humorous. You have to have a degree of humor to deal with tragedy for eight-and-a-half hours a night.

As soon as we got up there, this uniformed sergeant from Central Park came running up. He said he had this great crime scene all cordoned off. Body's over there by the trees, he said. He had information that a car came up and went off the wrong way, brown Oldsmobile or a Nova, and he had a partial license plate. I immediately went on the radio and called in a description to all the bridges and outer crossings from Manhattan. Tire prints from the "brown car" were analyzed. Months later we found out they came from a police car assigned to Central Park precinct.

Usually when I get to the scene—look, think, do a complete 360 and look around, especially if it's an open field. You got a very large crime scene; there's a lot of things you might see. Behind trees, you're gonna find many things that might be part of the homicide that really aren't. You might find another pair of bikini underpants because someone else was *shtupping* behind the bushes. You may find cigarette butts—you may find that they belong or don't belong. You don't even know yet if the person smoked or not.

There was a video camera on the museum exterior for security. I assigned a detective to go in there and see if we could rewind the tape from the time the call came in, to the present. It turned out that the camera wasn't working.

When we come on the set, the first thing we do is grab anyone who's in the area.

The first to come through that day was a bike rider. Later we interviewed a lot of joggers. Robert Chambers supposedly sat on a bench and watched the cops! I don't remember seeing Chambers around there and neither did my detectives.

We went on to look over the body. A young girl, she was very physically fit, nice body, torso. She really was battered. The black and blue and all the hematomas didn't settle in yet. They were starting to swell when we got there. A scooter cop came over and was saying she looked like someone he knew from 86th Street. We started a team to canvass up there.

We never touch the body until Crime Scene gets there. You don't want to disturb any physical or circumstantial evidence. We didn't go into her pockets—let them do the physical search. When they came, I immediately had them bag the hands—put paper bags on the hands—because a lot of times, victims scratch and they get skin under the fingernails. Robert Chambers had scratches all over his face, and he said his cat did it. Could've been a lot of physical evidence under her fingernails, matching up with Chambers' skin.

Then we went through her pockets. She had a Citicard. She took out a hundred-and-something dollars that night. A card saying she worked at the Seaport, at Flutie's. There was a photo driver's license. We found an address book.

But the thing that really shocked me: I really thought she was much older when I saw her laying on the ground, but she had this card showing that she had just graduated from high school (one of the private schools on the Upper West Side), and it just took me aback. I kept saying to myself, How are we going to notify her parents that their child who just graduated high school is dead? Words can't explain it. I wasn't even a parent then, but I kept saying to myself, How are we going to make this notification?

Crime Scene had a Polaroid camera. I photographed her and I gave a photograph to all the investigative teams I sent out.

I remember calling Chief Voelker, telling him, I think we got a heavy, you should get down; calling the zone commander, Captain Luisi, and advising him that I think this is a highly visible case, we'll get a lot of play on this one from the media. And calling Manhattan North Homicide—they started at eight. I had my people notify the commanding officer of the Central Park detectives.

When the ME came, we had to form a circle around her, because there were news cameras rolling, construction workers nearby. It was just so sad—she really took a beating. Chambers really beat the shit out of her.

When the day tour began, Manhattan North Homicide picked up the investigation of Jennifer Levin's death. "The homicide squad was about a year old, and everybody was gung ho," says

John Mullally. "Lieutenant Doyle picked hungry guys—the hunters in Manhattan North." Mullally, in his fourth month wearing a gold shield, was definitely gung ho.

Another hunter was Mike Sheehan, a charismatic detective who had grown up ahead of Chambers in the same Upper East Side neighborhood. In a TV movie about the "Preppy Murder," Sheehan made his acting debut in the role of Doyle, his boss in Homicide and before that in Two-four Squad. Sheehan has since done quite a few turns in television and big-screen movies, but hasn't topped his portrayal of Jack Doyle.

The squad delved into the dark side of the preppy killer's background and followed Levin's path to her tragic and brutal death at his hands. Mullally, later a sergeant in Manhattan South Homicide, says the Chambers case is among the biggest he worked on in Homicide.

### Detective Sergeant John Mullally:
### The Squad

When I came on for the four-to-one tour, it was "all hands to Central Park." We got the rundown from the sergeant, Mike Ryan.

Chambers was already sitting there in the cramped interview room at the Central Park station house. Myself and Marty Gill were sent by Lieutenant Doyle to pick up Jennifer's girlfriend Betsy, down in Chelsea. By this time we'd heard Chambers's first story: he had left Jennifer outside Dorrian's; she had gone across the street to get cigarettes. That's when Robert "went home and never saw her again."

Betsy told us Jennifer didn't smoke.

No matter how smart a guy is, there's always something—once you catch him on something like that, you have him. We went back to the station and sat in while Joe Brady did an interview with Chambers. Brady's been around awhile—he worked on the Albert Anastasia hit. Mike Sheehan was Brady's partner.

Around seven or eight P.M., Lieutenant Doyle came in. Jack Doyle is like a Barry Fitzgerald kind of character. He's an older guy. Never raises his voice. You'd run things by him and Doyle would—I never saw him send a guy in the wrong direction. Never. Great guy. Great guy to learn from. Great experience just to see him in operation.

I was watching him with Chambers. He used a priestlike type of thing. He got real close to him. "Listen, I have sons at home your age—" he says. "Sometimes they do things that they are ashamed to tell me about. Once they do tell me, it's a relief. They cleanse themselves." He does the whole father-confessor thing.

He knew he was the lieutenant running the investigation. When he walked out, Chambers is startin' to go. Doyle was really a catalyst. Detective MacEntee from Central Park caught the case. He came in and took a statement. Marty Gill was next, then Sheehan—and the guy went in about five minutes.

We kidded about who broke the case. Marty had a big part. Everybody did their shtick to get Chambers to give it up—Doyle had the ability to bring out the Catholic guilt. The whole scenario took about eight or nine hours.

Various infractions of prison rules have added more than a year to Chambers's five-to-fifteen-year sentence for manslaughter.

———

The slaughter of a ghetto grandmother and the murder of a privileged teenager in one of the City's best neighborhoods should get equal justice; so believed an aggressive homicide prosecutor, William K. Hoyt, Jr. Bill Hoyt headed Manhattan DA Robert Morgenthau's Homicide Bureau in the 1980s. The detectives who worked with him shared his notion of justice and brought in bulletproof cases. Hoyt won everything he tried. He likes to talk about the exploits of detectives Ray Brennan, Jimmy Rodriguez, Joel Potter, Tony Krassas, Jim Killen, Mike Burke, Terry Quinn, Jack Donovan.

Like Hoyt, Jack Donovan fought in the Marine Corps, where they teach you to stand straight. That here-I-am Marine Corps posture sends the right message both on the street and in the courtroom. Hoyt tells about a murderous drug gang—over fifty strong at their peak—that all but owned the streets of Harlem. The Vigilantes did at least nineteen homicides. In the five-year stretch from 1984 to 1989, Detective Donovan helped ADA Hoyt convict five members of the gang. All five are serving life sentences.

At forty-five Jack Donovan had won the NYPD's highest honors, the Medal of Honor and the Combat Cross, and had attained first grade. He retired in 1990 to manage a family pub. The sociable business suits him, but he misses the job he left—especially, he says "the challenge."

Poker-faced with regular features, fair and blue-eyed, Donovan began going gray at fifteen. His almost-white straight hair is cut rakishly—a foil for the poker face. The sense of humor, dry and sneaky like a well-made martini, is a prime asset in the pub just as it was on the street.

Donovan, the youngest of three brothers, now has four boys of his own. If any of them wants to step into his shoes, their dad hasn't heard about it. "I never glorified the job at home." He sounds a little sorry. "They don't know much about my cases."

Several Vigilante murders went down in the Two-eight, where Jack Donovan worked for eight years. The precinct covers sixteen square blocks—five-eighths of a mile—sometimes described as the armpit of Harlem. In 1972 the squad handled a record hundred and twenty-seven homicides, Donovan says. In 1982, the year he got there, the homicide tally still was over eighty.

The squad boss let him choose his murder cases, Donovan says, and he solved fifteen to seventeen a year. There's definitely no perfect crime, he contends: "Somebody made a mistake—you just have to be persistent enough to find it." Detective Donovan was busy chasing Vigilantes in 1987, but not too busy to hunt down the punks who killed Harlem's favorite grandmother. Whodunit was soon clear enough; bringing Mary Harris Caroline's killers to justice took longer.

### Detective First Grade Jack Donovan:
### The Two-eight Is Murder

There are people living in the precinct, old-timers, that were there before all the drugs and the trouble. Mary was one. When you work Homicide in Harlem—years and years of one drug dealer assassinating another—you don't come across a helluva lot of victims that everybody you talk to speaks highly of. I got very involved in this case emotionally, because the people are good people.

Members of the church Mary belonged to marched on the precinct. Church groups very seldom got together with the Police Department, because they were afraid of repercussions in the community. But this woman was an exception to everything.

Mary was a grandmother that tried to raise a family in a tough area. People would go by, they needed a dollar, she would lend it to them. She never said no to anyone.

She was kinda cute in that to support herself she sold bootleg booze on the weekends—pints of whatever you needed. She had a miniature liquor store in her house on 115th Street, but she wasn't licensed to sell it. You could get a jug on Sunday even if you didn't have money. People paid her when they got their checks. She wasn't strictly within the law, because she sold the booze illegally, but she was a good person. Everybody knew Mary Caroline. She had a restaurant in the basement. Either Christmas Eve or New Year's Eve, she fed everybody on the block for nothing.

Now, all of a sudden she turns up missing. A lot of people are upset about it. Her friend Ezra Garbutt is gone too. Originally it's a missing person case, but everything looked to me like there was foul play. I think most of the people knew right away that it was a murder—a double murder. They're all pointing to Coco, her older grandson. But everybody backs off—they're terrified of the kid. He has a history of violence.

Mary Caroline, she's the kind that doesn't go anywhere or do anything unless she tells her tenants, who are also her friends. Most of them aren't paying rent because they don't have the money, but they're her friends, so they're living in her house. (It's a four-story building, probably three or four apartments on each floor.)

Mary's friend Ezra lives there. He tried to make out like they were boyfriend-girlfriend, but the family always denied it. He wasn't just the plumber everybody thought. He was addicted to the numbers and he was a gigolo, bilking women of their money. But he didn't have any left because he gambled all of it away. Came from the West Indies somewhere. Very dapper man. When he wasn't working, he always had a suit on.

He owned a plumbing van and two cars. Every morning he would take one of the cars or the van and this fella George the Bookmaker would move the others for the alternate-side-of-the-street parking. George lived at the house too. An oldtimer. He stands at the front door every day. Has the newspapers—maybe ten *Post*s, ten *Daily News*—and people come by in the morning: they get the paper; he takes their action for the day. This is his life. He can generally be found in front of the building.

A Wednesday night in March, Mary goes to visit a sick friend in New Jersey. Coco, her grandson, comes looking for her that night with his buddy Efram. Everybody knew Coco wasn't allowed in there. He pushed Mary around a couple of times, and she finally banned him from the building. All of a sudden he shows up out of the blue.

Nobody trusted the grandson; nobody liked him. Real bad attitude. He was in his early twenties, I'd say—twenty-two, twenty-three. Big guy, six foot four, six foot five, strong. I think probably a little crazy. Efram Meralla was also a big guy, six foot one, six foot two, but Coco had kind of a power over him. Coco could tell him to do anything, he would do it. Would go as far as getting involved in this murder. Whether their intentions at the time were murder, I don't know—but they were looking to take control of the building, make a drug factory out of it.

Mary's not there when Coco and Efram arrive, but Ezra is. Coco gets him into the house and they kill him. Shoot him, wrap him up in black plastic bags, and take him out. A man named Matinda Evans, who used to date Coco's mother, is on the scene with the other two. What the hell's this fifty-two-year-old guy doing with these kids? Well, they promised him Ezra's van. He helped transport the body—we have witnesses seeing him carry out this package. The van has pipes in it, plumbing equipment. People see them empty out the pipes. They put Ezra in the back and drive out of the block.

Now, every Wednesday night, Ezra plays cards with some guys in the basement of the barbershop up on Lenox Avenue—all the old-time players. He doesn't show up there, so they're looking for him, these Damon Runyon characters. Everybody assumes he's with Mary because both cars are gone. Then Mary comes back. Where's Ezra?

Later on that night, Coco gets into Mary's again with Efram. Coco tells him, "I can't kill my grandmother. You gotta shoot her." She was bendin' over, giving some milk to the kittens, and *Boom!*—the guy goes ahead and shoots her. They take her up to The Bronx.

Things that aren't normally done in any investigation were done for this one because of who Mary was. Forensics came back a number of times for photographs, for fingerprints. We did a whole layout of the building, a model. Not that she was a big, wealthy movie star. She was a good person caught in the middle of Harlem. She probably belonged there forty years ago, but she certainly didn't today.

The whole family is involved with the investigation. The father, the grandfather, the mother, the grandsons—Coco and his brother. It's quite a cast. I had a folder for all the players—notes on every person, cross-referenced with the DD5s. And if I could, a photograph.

James Caroline—Mary's ex-husband, Coco's grandfather—an old Harlem character, owned a candy store up on 145th Street. I think eventually he got into a little hanky-panky himself. When Mary marries him, he's got all these screwed-up daughters from another marriage. But these days James Caroline is up in Rochester in the middle of the woods; this old Harlem character, living on top of a hill in—if it was made of logs, it would be a log cabin. No heat in there except for a fireplace. Couple of beat-up cars outside. We couldn't even get up there in the winter; the car started sliding down the hill.

James's stepdaughter—Coco's mother—is a drug abuser, been arrested for selling drugs, did some time. But Mary takes her in, helps raise her kids. (I don't know where the father was.) They all wind up jailbirds, but the two older ones have a lot of love for the grandmother. They looked up to her. Very upset that their stepbrother killed Mary.

Her ex-husband, James Caroline, it's alleged, told his oldest grandson, Coco, that the 115th Street house is his—he had all the inherited rights—which he denied ever saying. But Caroline didn't know he'd lost the house in the divorce proceedings, or that Mary willed it to Katherine Everett, her goddaughter.

When somebody gets arrested, we ask for somebody we can call. In Harlem they'd give me the godmother, like it was their mother. In my home, we exchange gifts at Christmas with our godchildren, and that's pretty much it. In Harlem, the tie is real strong. Anyway, after Mary won the house, she willed it to her goddaughter. This was a surprise to the family.

———

Now, Ezra Garbutt's gone, his van and his cars too. Everybody says the grandson who's not allowed in, showed up—so the cops are looking for Coco. When he goes there again the next day, they bring him in. Efram too.

Both of them give statements: They were up in Syracuse. They met these girls, and they spend some time in a motel. Coco goes with this girl to the grandfather's cabin. Efram has to go back to the City to his hospital job.

Eventually Coco gets caught at the building again with the keys, is taken to the precinct. Yes, he admits he was there. His grandmother "gave" him Ezra's Maroon Cadillac. Coco claims he returned it. Meanwhile, he has it parked a couple blocks away—"Ezra is fiine." But everybody knows Ezra's missing, the grandmother's missing.

Now Coco takes off with the car to Mama in Albany. We know where she lives. We got the police looking for the car, and sure enough, the detectives in Albany catch him—he's washing the trunk of the Cadillac out with a hose. We tell them to impound the car. We call the DA's office, and my partner, Bill O'Hara, and I go up and bring it back.

The case happened in March. Early April, I receive a phone call from Coco's younger brother Rudy about where the bodies were. I had a little more experience than the detective that had the case. I gave him the information, and he wrote it in his notebook. Later on he made sergeant and got transferred. At the trial he had to go on the stand and say why he did nothing. "I had made sergeant and, you know, I forgot about the investigation." Defense counsel said, "Wait a minute. Donovan gave you information in April, you didn't get promoted till June."

We got the car, but we're working other homicides. At least four or five months after the initial missing-persons reports were filed, I get another call from Coco's younger brother, in jail on a rape charge: "You gotta help me out."

Why should I help you out? You never helped me out on your grandmother's murder.

"I told you guys where the bodies were."

We checked that out, I said—the bodies weren't there.

"Well, you better check again, the bodies are there."

I asked the boss if I could take over the investigation, and we went from there. Up to The Bronx, looked over the area—nothing visible. I made a phone call to the Forty-first Precinct: Did you find a body at a lot on Fox Street?

"Yeah—the body was burnt." And the day after, they had found a body in the Fortieth Precinct. Both victims burnt, and both shot with the same gun. Two hours after I was given this information, I have my two missing persons.

The Fire Department found two bodies in the South Bronx, one in a lot on Fox Street on March 25 and another in a lot by a high school on St. Anne Avenue a few days later. The bodies had been set on fire. The first descriptions the ME's office gave of the bodies didn't match that of the missing persons.

A lot of other reasons why they weren't connected to our case at first. In Manhattan they knew we were looking for two missing people; The Bronx didn't know. It's one city, but it's so big, and the amount of crime is so vast—you're arresting uptown criminals uptown. You don't go downtown, and you generally don't even know the detectives from Manhattan South.

Now we had to have the bodies exhumed by the Medical Examiner's office. They were buried in Potter's Field—you track them through the plot numbers. It's early fall by the time we got the bodies out. Positively identified them through dental records.

You almost couldn't tell whose body was whose. Looking at a picture of Mary, you could tell the way she combed her hair. She had it in a bun in back—you'd see that outline. Other than that, they just looked like two big pieces of burned chicken.

If you have the physical evidence in a homicide, you need the suspect. You have the suspect, you need the physical evidence. You need a lot of luck, a lot of time. . . .

We locked up Efram, but we couldn't find Coco. We tried Efram for one murder—Ezra's—and lost. I had a perfect conviction record till then. I found the girl that Coco went up to the Syracuse motel with. Helen was a reluctant witness in the beginning, but she testified at Efram's trial. We lost.

We were getting a lot of information from the goddaughter, Katherine, who knows the Caroline family, Coco's mother. Knows the mother is no good. I'm working close with Katherine, but the case is going on a year old when I finally get more on this Matinda Evans.

He owned a printing shop up on 125th Street. We're looking all over 125th Street for a printing shop—it's upstairs, over a bakery. We have different locations where he lives, hit a couple of those spots. He's moved. I had somebody that was good with a computer getting Motor Vehicle information on the guy. We come up with a house in Hempstead, Long Island. Now I'm excited.

The tour's over. I leave work, have to stop at my brother's first. I live on the North Shore, but I drive to Hempstead on the South Shore, and I drive down this guy's block. Can't believe it. I'm shaking. Hidden behind two other cars in the driveway: the plumbing van. I park and I sneak down the block on foot. And here it is, the van—with the *plates*. I couldn't believe it. Intact.

I got permission to pick Evans up, but we didn't have enough to arrest him. So after I brought him in for questioning, he fled.

When we found Coco, we tried him and Efram for Mary's murder. I had to get Helen back, our witness; I tracked her down through the welfare rolls. Now I had to convince her to come to the second trial: face Coco, her boyfriend or whatever. She really sunk him.

I just couldn't swallow it—Coco killing his grandmother. He felt that he had a right to the building, to her money. I'd say he killed Ezra out of jealousy, because Mary was taking care of him. Coco is the kind of guy that you'd be talking to with a hot cup of coffee in your hand, and your coffee would go cold. That's what he was like.

This investigation and the trials lasted over two years. A lot of waiting. A lot of legwork, trips to Rochester to the grandfather's house, to Albany to the mother's—the mother was hiding him. A lot of trips to no avail. Until that one when I brought Coco back, and I told him—"I can retire now. 'Cause I swore I wouldn't retire until I got you."

I made that promise to Katherine and the people from the church. Coco and Efram both got twenty-five-to-life.

Matinda Evans was never arrested, never tried. To this day, he's in Africa or wherever. If nothing else, his life is miserable because he doesn't know I retired. He knows through the grapevine, I'm sure, the other two guys got life—and he still thinks I'm out there, looking for him.

## Partners & Bosses

**Detective Ed Kelly, Jr.:** Homicide was a borough command covering all the precincts in Manhattan; when I first started in '58, it was Manhattan East. So six years on the job.

Boss told me, "Look, kid. You think you're a pretty hotshot detective."

I said, Well, I'm here.

Says, "It's gonna take me about five years to make a good homicide detective out of you." And he was right. These guys had a wealth of experience. Very specific, homicides are. You have to form a rapport and liaison with the assigned homicide MEs and the homicide DAs. Three in the morning, you're the ME on duty, I knew your number. I'd call your home and send a radio car to pick you up. Same with the DA and the stenographer, if I needed them. We got to know each other.

And we knew what we were looking for. The regular detective: he's like a general practitioner; he's doing everything. I know what it's like down the road, going to court, testifying in a homicide case. I know what's admissible, what the DA wants to hear and what he doesn't want to hear.

# 4

# RIP-OFF CITY

Detectives of the Queens Robbery Squad work out of a station house in Forest Hills, one of the borough's prettiest and most affluent sections. Bill Toner had what his partner Bob Flanagan calls "a real good eye" for robbery and sex-crime patterns. More than visual, that "eye" might also be described as detective's intuition. To spot the patterns, you compare the narratives written by uniformed cops on their complaint reports ("61s"). "Toner would pick up things that someone else might not," Flanagan says. "I learned from him."

One winter evening in the squad room, Toner interviews a mugging victim—an older woman, accompanied by her husband. After listening to the woman's account, Toner thumbs the color-coded master file, organized by perp's physical description and by "MO," looking for a likely suspect in the mugging. The husband, a retired gentleman in a camel's hair coat, watches and listens. He and the detective agree that computerizing all this data would certainly speed up an investigation.

The year was 1981. Bill Toner and two other Robbery Squad detectives had just recently been assigned to set up the elaborate file of robberies and sex crimes that Toner consulted that evening. By browsing through it by hand—free-associating, in effect—the pattern specialists used this master file to identify crime patterns all over Queens and to help detectives narrow the field of suspects in a given incident.

Toner doesn't recall an arrest in the mugging of the retired gentleman's wife, but the story nevertheless has a surprise ending. No more than four months after the squad room conversation, he says, NYPD robbery investigation was "centralized." Both Flanagan and Toner remember hearing at the time of an anonymous million-and-a-half-dollar gift received on behalf of the department by Police Commissioner Robert McGuire. Before long, the first robbery computers appeared in squad rooms.

By now, every precinct is on the network—called CARS, for Computer Assisted Robbery System. CARS helps make a good eye for crime patterns even better—but you need more than bells and whistles to catch a New York City thief.

In a homocide case your best witness is dead. In a robbery or grand larceny you can interview the victim. A computer will never have what it takes to overcome a survivor's trauma and discover useful information about the crime. Psychological insight, compassion—that's where a good detective comes in.

In a city where a single square-mile precinct (the Four-six, in The Bronx) can suffer some three thousand robberies a year, you probably avail yourself of any technological edge that's legal. Maybe even a psychic, if you happen to have one around. And especially if his or her hunch is the same as yours. Technology of the more conventional kind is a great asset to detectives in constant combat with every kind of rip-off artist, but there's still no such animal as a pure techie NYPD detective. Pattern hackers like Bobby Flanagan and Bill Toner confronted the perps on the street long before they ever accessed them on a computer.

The victim who's just been mugged at knifepoint or gunpoint is in no position to know or care that the law defines this terrifying crime not as larceny or burglary, but as robbery. If convicted of armed robbery, thieves do more time—a lot more, if they're making a career of it—than they do for rip-offs without a weapon. Robberies in New York City are investigated by RIP (Robbery Investigation Program) detectives, so if you're in a precinct squad, you're left with larcenies and burglaries. Boring? Not necessarily, as Detective Dave Carbone found out.

"In the ghetto," says Carbone, "people sometimes don't realize what crime is. A crime to us can be an everyday affair for them." Carbone of the Seven-five Squad is talking about the sprawling Brooklyn ghetto known as East New York—a neighborhood that often leads the city in homicide complaints. East New York thieves no doubt consider themselves charitable if they leave a victim in possession of his life.

Dave Carbone came to the Seven-five Squad in 1988, at age thirty-four, as a "white shield." Starry-eyed, it would be fair to call him, and shocked to get assigned to the precinct he wanted. "Originally, they told me 'No, you have to know somebody.' This place here was a busy house; they couldn't take an average guy.

"I picked three of the busiest houses to go to 'cause I liked to be busy. Luck of the draw—I didn't have any hooks, nobody made any phone calls for me. My name just popped for the Seven-five." A dream house where the detectives are mostly too busy to stop for a meal. "Yesterday, I was up at seven in the morning, I didn't get home till two in the morning, and I started here at eight again. Last night I had pizza for dinner. That's all so far. No breakfast, no lunch, pizza last night, and I haven't eaten yet today."

In most Manhattan squads, Carbone would have to clip that brash little brunette ponytail he sports with his flattop haircut. Maybe he'd get away with the stud earring that competes with the twinkle in the blue eyes, but he'd surely have to decrease the carat count. Old-time New York detectives wore diamond pinky rings— times change. You still see pointy Italian slip-ons on the feet of guys with a lot of time in the job; Dave Carbone's generation is into pointy cowboy boots.

Carbone's sergeant, Mike Race, looks like your normal detective boss—blond hair cut normally, a signet ring bearing a miniature sergeant's badge. "My father worked in the Eightieth Squad as third-grade detective, second-grade detective, first-grade detective. When he got made sergeant, the squad members chipped in and bought him a ring. When my father died, I got it." The badge is numbered. "We all have the same number, my father, my brother, me."

Race was born a few blocks away from the Seven-five station house, grew up there, and has worked most of his career there. "I saw Before and After. In the fifties and sixties, you had eight murders a year, ten a year. If you look at all the canvass files, the interviews, you see 'Rabbi Teitelbaum,' 'Mrs. Shapiro.' All the old names. That's gone, ever since the birth of crack.''

Not quite gone. The names persist in the cemeteries that cross the border from Queens into the northeast corner of the Seven-five. "Miles. Acres. Huge. It's massive." Union Field Cemetery, Mt. Carmel Cemetery, Salem Field Cemetery, Beth-Olom Cemetery, Mt. Neboh Cemetery, Mt. Judah Cemetery, Cemetery of the Ever-greens, Cypress Hills Cemetery, Mt. Lebanon Cemetery.

Cemeteries haunted, of course—by thieves.

Caretakers do make the rounds every day, but it's tough to notice everything, Sergeant Race says. The vast graveyards are the richest in the state, he believes, if not the country. In the mid-eighties, "Millions of dollars worth of Tiffany glass from Salem Field mausoleums were being shipped out to the West Coast from here. Art collectors would buy it and keep it. Not auction it off, 'cause you can't. It's all numbered, stenciled with someone's name on it, so it's very easy to trace."

In 1991, says Carbone—new plunder: "Two cops on patrol went past a junkyard and saw a whole bunch of bronze plaques from the mausoleums, and it turned out to be a pretty big case for them."

"They found fifty-four; we went back, we found more," adds Race. "The guy's like a fence." A junkyard fence, to be exact. Carbone explains: "In his confession he told us he was paying let's say ten cents a pound to these crackheads—most of 'em were white crackheads. They would go into cemeteries, tear off the plaques. Let's say they brought him ten of 'em. These things weigh thirty-five or forty pounds each, you're talking a lot of weight, and at ten cents a pound, a lot of money for a crackhead. He turns around and sells it for maybe twenty-five or thirty cents a pound, so the fence was making money for doing nothing."

Exactly what the guy figured he was doing—nothing. Definitely nothing wrong. "That's not the point: you 'didn't do it,' " Carbone lectured. "We didn't care whether you 'did' it. You knew where they came from and you just continued buying to make money off dead people. Call a cop and say, 'Listen, these guys are stealing this shit out of a cemetery.' He didn't think he was doing a crime. Sick thinking.''

Get into a suspect's motives, as Carbone does. Establish, as he does, a working relationship with witnesses from any layer of society. If you can't, all the technology of the twenty-first century won't help you catch a thief in Gotham.

### Detective Dave Carbone and Detective Sergeant Mike Race: Skullduggery

**Detective Carbone:** We were getting a rash of mausoleum break-ins that same year, in the spring and summer. They would go into the cemetery at night, break open the steel grate doors, and break open the crypts. In the mausoleum you usually have four crypts on the sides and two in the ground. They'd break the marble facing where the name is etched in. Then they rip the coffin out of the slot and let it fall to the floor. Sometimes it broke open, sometimes it didn't.

It's an old Jewish cemetery, and back then, they had the sealed coffins. They made 'em airtight, vacuum sealed so the bodies didn't deteriorate as fast as normal. Believe it or not, now the bodies look pretty good.

Most of the time they would take the coffin outside 'cause you couldn't see in there. And they would either stand the coffin up, dump the body out, or just reach in and tear the head off. There was five separate incidents where we had parts stolen from five different crypts. Five heads, two hands, and two feet.

We start an investigation on it, and we end up getting a call from Queens, two or three minutes from here, that said there was people into Santería—voodoo stuff—it was getting pretty big. Cemetery's on Jamaica Avenue where most of these people were hanging out. The cemetery was close. Hop, skip, and a jump. Go get a piece and take it home.

We started doing surveillance work, talking to a lot of people out there. We had plainclothes cops in the cemetery at night. They caught a few people, not stealing or anything, but a lot of people just cut through. I would never cut through there, but they did. It was weird.

Those plaques had nothing to do with our case. We were worried that investigation would scare the people that were stealing the skulls. We were building a case up, and this made us hustle even faster.

We were doing a lot of spade work. Going out to Queens, canvassing, interviewing a lot of people. We give out a lot of cards: "Don't talk to me here, call me later." One person called me later.

We talked for about an hour on the phone, and she got me onto like five different people that were doing Santerías. She had heard through the grapevine that they were the ones stealing the body parts. She gave us a description of one guy, a male Hispanic, about five foot seven. Always wore a bandanna on his head, but he had no eyebrows. He shaved 'em. And he had no expression on his face. She didn't know his name. A lot of nights, me, Mike, and Al Smith, we were sitting out in Queens looking at certain areas to see if we could see this guy.

Then through some of her friends, she was able to get a name for us. We started checking the background on this Matías Frías, and I was able to get turned on to his girlfriend. He was a homeless type of guy. He slept in the cemeteries, behind a supermarket. Park benches. A cardboard box in the cemetery. And he was sleeping in his girlfriend's hallway, 'cause the mother didn't let him in. We couldn't sit on one spot. He could be coming from anywhere in Queens—Richmond Hill.

He used to walk her to school. We staked out her house every single day, and this took a couple of weeks, just sittin' there for eight, nine hours. Walking around. We either just missed him, or they never came home—she used to stay out with him. To hear her story, it was pretty horrible. Sick girl. She was in love with him. That was the whole thing it came down to: she was in love with him.

I knew most of his hangouts now. When he wasn't at the girlfriend's house, there was like seven different spots. You can't spread yourself seven different ways, so we would spend an hour here, race to another one, just to race back again. We were running this whole area, hoping that he would show up or just lay down.

Finally, one day we get a homicide early in the morning, me and Mike, after we worked the day before. I took the guy down to Central Booking; we charge him with murder. I get back and the phone rings. It's this girl informant of mine. She says, Listen, he's out in Queens now, in the shopping mall, riding around with a security guard. She had told us once before that he hung around this guy in that mall. He was twenty-one and homeless. They had nothing else to do; they just hung out together.

We went flying out there, and sure enough, we see a security guard; we pull up and we take him out of the back of the car. He's like buggin'. We cuffed him. We took the girlfriend back too.

He was a little nervous at first. After about two hours of talking to him, he started telling us what was going on. Then we got to the girlfriend, who started crying and told us everything. She knew he went to the cemetery one night, tore some mausoleum open, tore the guy's head. He took it home, boiled it, and he skinned all the skin off 'cause he wanted a clean skull.

He walked around with it one day. Had it in a backpack, went to his girlfriend's school with it. After school, he waited for her. He'd play basketball.

They had an argument another day, so he took the skull home, put it on her stoop, and did a voodoo thing in front of her house. She got mad at him.

The next day he walked her to school. He started playing basketball, and he took the skull out 'cause he wanted the skull to watch him play. He put the skull at the end of the basketball court and someone must've called the police. When he saw the police cars coming, he ran off. Left the skull there.

During her interview, we asked her, How could you fall in love with the guy? He stunk from sleeping in garbage. She says, "He's really gentle to me and nice, and he's lovable." Plus she was pregnant by him. She said, "He never did nothing to me. The only thing I didn't like, that night we made love in the graveyard on top of the mausoleum, but he wanted it, so I did it." She was a few years younger. She was of age—it wasn't rape.

Her mother didn't like him, so she had a conflict. When she wanted to see him, she had to leave the house. She wouldn't come home for two days, and she was pregnant. She was a little girl, really confused. And the baby confused her more. The mother said, "Listen, she's pregnant. She's not eating, she's not washing—you can't have that." Her mother was very nice.

When she got out the next day—we didn't lock her up—we turned her in to Bureau of Child Welfare, and we tried to get some help for her. Worked out pretty well. Supposedly, they're back together again. We tried to explain to her, You don't need him. He's goin' to jail. Be safe. Get healthy for your baby—the whole nine yards. We had the mother come down here because she wasn't talking to the mother that well. We did like a counseling type of thing. It was nice. At least they left together crying and happy, where before all they did was argue. I felt sorry for the girl. She was torn, confused, and pregnant.

**Sergeant Race:** Great show for Oprah.

**Detective Carbone:** We go back to him, and now I'm talking to him again. He gives up a little bit more. Mike comes in at this point: "Do you think you can take us to the mausoleum?"

**Sergeant Race:** He mentions the name of the mausoleum. I said, wait a minute, that name's not on our list. We had a list of every mausoleum that was broken into with the heads taken. And he's telling us the gentleman's name whose head it was. So we thought we'd get the key from downstairs, 'cause they were doing the night surveillance of the cemeteries.

**Detective Carbone:** Mike knew the names. Mike says, "How the hell did you know the name?" He goes, "I hang out in there every night." Mike says, "You hang out?"

"There's about sixty of us in there. The Red Hoods." They pray in front of the mausoleums or the graves before they do whatever they gotta do.

We're goin'—*Wait a second.* They have candles. They play tag and hide-and-seek. He had sex with his girlfriend on top of a mausoleum because he thought that was erotic.

**Sergeant Race:** He thought that would be like the ultimate high.

**Detective Carbone:** He says, "I can take you to it." What do you mean, you can take us to it? "I know it like the back of my hand." Okay. Three-thirty in the morning and it's dark and we're tired; we've been up for about two days. We are tired. We put him in the car. Me, Mike, and Smitty. And we have him in the backseat.

It's very windy. One of those creepy nights. Spooky. Windy. It was in July, but it was windy and it was a *cemetery.* We chase murderers every day; okay, we're going in here. We open the gate. Mike drives in.

He goes, "Whoa, go down this road here." We go down the road.

"Make a left at Snake Road." He had names for every road that we were on. There was the Attitude Tunnel—something to do with an attitude or a spiritual thing. It's an underpass, but to them it was a tunnel. You went through this tunnel and it was supposed to transform your mind, I guess, into voodoo—I don't know.

"Go up past Snake Mountain." It was a big mausoleum, but at night, with the trees and the moon there, it looked like a castle. "Snake Road to Snake Castle."

Mike makes a right and we go down this hill. We're goin' down and all of a sudden, this guy jumps out of a tree right in front of us. Well, my heart—!

Mike's got his brights on. It was hard enough driving 'cause it was pitch black. We're trying to find the road and this guy jumps! We go, *AAAAH!* We're out. I get my gun—

He just disappeared. He looked around and went *WHAM* into the dark. It was like, Oh, man. Could not believe it.

**Sergeant Race:** He tells us, "That's one of the Red Hoods." They hang out in the trees, and they play the games.

**Detective Carbone:** After about five more minutes of driving—'cause he takes us way into the back—he takes us right to the mausoleum.

**Sergeant Race:** There's the name! The name's on the outside of the mausoleum. This guy is telling the truth.

**Detective Carbone:** We come back in the morning, make a phone call to the cemetery guy. I said, This was never reported—this was a different one. "Yeah." Now there's media outside like you would not believe.

There was nothing on the list with that name, so we thought maybe Frías was just nuts, he picked the wrong one. He's going, "I'm tellin' you—I picked it out." He tells us exactly what he did that night.

We're not gonna argue. He had no expression on his face. If you just look at him, he looked like he was dead. He didn't laugh. He cried, *later.*

So we're sitting there talking. He says he meets three guys, and they want to go play in the cemetery. A normal night for them—pick up some beer and go to the cemetery; they start meeting all their friends and running around.

He had a new voodoo ritual he wanted to try out. He said he wanted to smoke the skull. By *smoking,* I mean like Scooby Doo on TV. Scooby Doo, they put the head over an open fire and the smoke comes out the eyes and the openings. He's "smoking out the spirits."

Frías and a helper broke into the mausoleum, but it was too pitch black in there again, so he put the coffin outside under the moon. They broke the coffin open, and they stood it up, and the body fell out, flat. The helper claims he didn't want to touch it. Later I arrested him too. According to him, Frías goes over to the body, puts his foot on the shoulder, and rips the head off. Grabs the head and rips it, puts it in a bag, and off they go.

They go back to his mother's house, in the backyard. He gets some kind of a heating thing. They get the water, and he takes a toothbrush he has in his bag, and he starts scraping it clean. Brushing it. Picking off all the hard skin that's stuck to it. He needed a clean skull.

Frías's mother was heavy into Santería, that's where he learned it. When we started doing the investigations, we were finding a lot of chickens hung in the park. I was trying to get a guy locked up right over here on Jamaica Avenue because he was selling chickens. You don't have to ask what they use it for. You knew, 'cause every time you'd go in the park early in the morning, you'd find circles and a pentagram, the chicken hanging over it, and you'd find the blood. But there's no law against selling chickens.

**Sergeant Race:** Four thousand dollars they'll pay for a human head, twenty thousand for a whole body.

**Detective Carbone:** Frías was saying they would pick on the freshly buried ones 'cause the ground wasn't as hard. They would actually undig it, open it, and then redo it—you would never notice. I find that hard to believe, but that's what he said they did. We could never prove it.

After another hour or two of talking with him, I said, Well, listen, you're in trouble. You just can't do—

"Well, what did I do wrong?" In his mind to go into a cemetery and steal somebody's head is not actually breaking the law. "But I didn't do nothing wrong," he says. "They're dead. They're not using it. I didn't take any jewelry." All through the night. Then we finally told him he was under arrest, and that's when he started bawlin' and cryin'.

He gave me the first name of the helper, so we're hittin' the streets. Really wasn't too hard, 'cause we started mentioning the first name, and people said, yes, he lives here, he lives there. I talked to the mother and I told her what happened. She called about four hours later and she said she would have her son ready for us during the week. They wanted to get some advice.

July 31 we picked up Luís Sanabria at his house with his mother, and we brought her back with him. He gave us somewhat of the same story; he kind of just let himself out of it a little bit more. He didn't want to say what he did because he was embarrassed. Finally, he said that he really didn't want to do it, but he did it anyhow. We ended up locking them both up.

We made the front page of the *Post* and *Newsday*: "SKULLDUGGERY." It was on every single major channel. Mike did a press conference. I get a call a month later from Queens. I think it was from the One-o-five. "Listen, you had that skull caper over there?" Yeah. He said, "You want to come out here?"

I said, Well, what for? "We found a skull—" I said, What? "You'll never believe this. This guy has a private house. He hires a guy to trim the bushes. He's trimming the bushes and there's one of the skulls sitting in the bush. When he looks down, he sees the skull and freaks out."

We recovered one of the skulls out there, and they're still trying to match it. It takes that long.

**Sergeant Race:** Problem is there's no one to match it to. You can't get dental records from half these families—people buried like a hundred-something years. Instead of a coffin lid, they have glass.

**Detective Carbone:** One woman looked very good. They broke it open and took her hands.

**Sergeant Race:** Once you break the glass, it just ruins it and then she'll fall apart.

**Detective Carbone:** Most of the bodies were pretty good.

**Sergeant Race:** I think he was dead for seventy-five years, the person we charged Frías with stealing.

**Detective Carbone:** He gave us indications that it wasn't the first time he did it. He was charged with burglary, larceny, criminal mischief, body stealing, and opening up a grave (that's against the health laws). In the end, he pled to attempted burglary and was sentenced to six months.

The person's family was totally distraught. They just could not believe that someone did this. They were very grateful to us that we got the guy, but to know that your loved one's laying there is hard enough. To know that someone did what they did, the way he did it—tore it off, and just left it like it was nothing—was a shame. The family was very thankful. It was nice.

———

Night-vision scope
Night-vision binoculars
Jet Ranger helicopter (NYPD #7)
24-volt battery searchlight
Fluorescent paint
Ballistics 101 know-how . . .

Not exactly the makings of a late-model techno-detection saga? Okay, but even in New York, even today, even a run-of-the-mill bag-of-tricks such as this would normally be out of the reach of a plain-vanilla neighborhood detective. And we aren't even talking today. We're talking a moment when the sixteen-inch RCA television was the popular ideal of high-tech. The late 1970s. A detective had his five-shot .38, his typewriter (usually manual), and he could sign out a walkie-talkie from the precinct radio room. He was based in what for a time was called a police detective unit (PDU), not the more glamorous-sounding "squad."

Then or now, such a detective would hardly be messing with an authentic mob hijacking scheme—mob rip-offs were (and are) reserved for specialized squads. And he certainly wouldn't be setting in motion the whole wingding shebang that made this such a memorable caper. Complete with a detective by the name of Marty Mak who really knew his way around a tractor trailer.

It all happened, nevertheless, for Detective Bob McKnight of the fifteenth district robbery squad in Queens, for no more obscure reason than that he's a-good-with-people type—a phrase detectives use when they mean street psychologist. He also has an innate talent for doing the right thing.

To start with, McKnight, a Brooklyn native, had to find the One-o-two—in fact he had to find Queens. When he became a cop (after two years in Sanitation while waiting to be called by the police force), he patrolled Brooklyn for thirteen years. Three days out, he knew he wanted to be a detective, and when, so many years later, he finally got the shield, he didn't fool around. At this point on his career path, he'd made a classic move—to Narcotics, Manhattan North Narcotics, at that. Harlem.

By now, though, the drug trade had spread to what had always been the Safe Borough, and the brass wanted to put an experienced

Narcotics detective in every Queens squad. Off went McKnight on his odyssey. . . . "It took me about an hour and forty-five minutes to find the One-o-two on 118th Street." Harlem it wasn't.

Soon the big, affable detective felt at home in the rinky-dink precinct with its unremarkable mix of commercial and residential districts. Everything suited him except for the Jamaica Avenue el "going through there all night long. We were right off the avenue, maybe half a block down. And that train would pound through. They all had one square wheel."

If somebody came up to see a detective, it didn't have to be anything life-threatening for McKnight to pay attention. When McKnight first got out to the One-o-two, a kid named Joey came by about "a little scrape—really a bullshit type of thing." Typically, McKnight just followed normal procedure, letting Joey know how any New York City resident can serve a summons on any other and take the person to court. But in Joey's eyes, normal procedure took on the proportions of a miracle, and he talked as if the detective was his savior. All things considered, Joey was not about to forget the detective's name.

### Detective First Grade Bob McKnight:
### Night Vision

I guess when Joey was between a rock and a hard place—"Hey, let me go and see my friend and see if he can get me out of this one too."

He had gambling debts. The people that he was in debt to were bookmakers and they were starting to pressure him. They knew he worked in the trucking industry—offered him a deal to hijack a high-value-load truck. He would bring it to a diner in Queens, where they would take the driver out, either tie or handcuff him behind the diner, then take the truck to Long Island, where they would empty it. Joey didn't want to do this, so he came to me, and we set it up where he would "go through with it."

He later called me from some restaurant in Brooklyn, East New York. "Hey, Bob, they gave me a piece." A small .22 under-and-over derringer.

Okay, I said, do you recall the serial number on it? "Wait a minute, let me look." Don't take it out! Don't take it out of your pocket! He took it out. Somebody seen him. There was a radio car parked outside and they arrested him.

By that time, we knew the One-o-six was a little too small with the size of the job that was developing. We had gone over to the DA's office in Queens, and we were working out of there. I quickly got a sergeant and Gabe Leone, the assistant DA that was working with us, and we zip over to the Brooklyn precinct. They already had him booked; they already had the gun vouchered. The whole damn bit. We had to get the *Brooklyn* DA to get the arrest voided.

When they gave Joey the gun, they told him, Okay, we'll meet you back at a certain spot. They were gonna make final plans. They had given him fifteen bucks to get into a gypsy cab and go back. Now the kid is gone three hours; he's been arrested. We have to invent a story. . . .

I took the gun over to Ballistics in Manhattan. They took the firing pin out and got the powder out of the rounds, and I come back to Queens with it. Now Joey has gone back to meet these guys, but where's the gun? "I got it hidden," he tells 'em. What the fuck d'ya mean, you didn't bring it? Why?

Kid had a lot of balls. So he says, "Hey, big wiseguy. You get me a cab; the guy don't even know where the hell I'm goin'. 'Where the hell's the thing?' I got lost for two hours." That's the story we concocted: he got lost. And they had an accident—another car hit 'em.

Anyway, that went over, and they finally decided they were gonna hit this freight yard the following night. Joey was gonna have on a stocking mask, go over the fence. He was gonna get the spot starter, the guy who would take the trailers to load and put them in certain spots in the yard where they would be expedited to go out on the road the next morning.

We decided, okay, we'll let the whole thing go, the only difference being, we're gonna have a detective driving. We went through the cards to find out who could drive a trailer truck—we picked out Marty Mak. And Joey with a gun that was useless; about eleven ounces of iron, that's all it was.

Of course in the truck it was nothin' but a lot of stale air. We had to have something that would give it weight, so it was loaded with pallets. At that time, sixteen-inch televisions were the rage; this was supposed to be a load of sixteen-inch RCA televisions. The people in this trucking outfit—they were great, they went along with it.

The powers-that-be wanted a helicopter to be in this. The trailer they were gonna hijack, I had gotten on top of it with my partners, Jim Lane and Jack Fitzsimons, and we painted a big, fluorescent stripe down the middle. I also put a twenty-four-volt searchlight on top, with a big battery in it. Our detective who was gonna drive, he was gonna turn it on before he got into the cab.

The next night, we have everybody alerted. We have Communications—big truck. We have chase cars. And we're all in the DA's office waiting on a certain time to start this ball rolling. The wiseguys told Joey what time they wanted him to hop the fence. Once that was done, with Marty driving the trailer—and sitting next to him, Joey the informant in a stocking mask, who's supposed to be the crook. Marty has a walkie-talkie with him. Plus, of course, his own gun.

I was out doing something, and I come back and everybody's looking at me. I'm looking, What the hell's the matter? "You're in the helicopter." I have to go out to the Marine Air Terminal at LaGuardia: The helicopter meets me there.

We get up in the air. We're about two miles from the freight yard where they're gonna get the trailer. We get a call to pick up a guy at the 34th Street Heliport! Now, this deal is ready to go down. I get on the radio, This is ready to go down—

"They want the night-vision guy over there with you, with the night-vision scope and all that stuff." We got about eight or nine minutes. Can we make it back and forth? Pilot says we'll make it.

We were in the Jet Ranger helicopter. Never forget it—it was number seven. We go shooting across Queens, across the river, through the Twin Towers, zip, we land at 34th Street. The guy gets in, we take off, and go back.

Joey's orders from the wiseguys was to get the truck and go to a certain rest stop by the Long Island Expressway, and they would stop the truck, get the driver out, put another driver in, and go from there. The overt act, that's what we had to wait for, and of course, if they physically took our guy out of there, that would be the overt act. But we didn't know how many guys would be involved in that, the taking out of the driver.

Joey calls: last minute change. They're not gonna take the driver out. They're gonna make him drive the truck all the way to the drop, which was good for us. Everything seemed to fall our way in this one. Sure enough, Joey pops over the fence, sticks the gun in the detective's nose, he says, Hiya! And they take off. They're playacting now. He takes the truck out of the yard, and they head out on the Long Island Expressway.

We have the Communications van linking the portable radios. We have about nine cars in chase: Lane and Fitzsimons in one, we had a truck, an ice cream truck, a whole armada. They'd be ahead of him, they'd get off at different exits, come back on. It was good. Really had time to set it up. We had two or three ADAs with us, the bureau chief, Queens detective commander Eddie Dreher, Robbery Squad lieutenant Jack Doyle—and me.

I'm about a thousand feet over their head. The bad guys wouldn't make us because we were maybe a half a mile away, but with the binoculars, the night-vision stuff, it was really good. It really worked out. I was glad we picked this guy up. I'm watching the light, it's beautiful. Everything's fine. We go all the way out to Exit Fifty-three on the LIE, someplace out around Dix Hills. Nice area.

We see these two cars. One is moving up, giving instructions, yelling up to the driver or to Joey. As soon as they move out, Marty Mak gets on the walkie-talkie. "They want us to follow them . . .'' Now we have to wait on the overt act, because the guy'll say, Hey, I didn't do anything.

Finally, just before we get to Exit Fifty-three, I'm looking down at the passenger side of the trailer truck and I see Joey stand up in the trailer and pee out the window. Real cool, real cool. It was in the fall, and it was brisk. He sat down again, rolled the window up. Now this big black car pulls up alongside and Marty the driver says, "Okay, they told us to get off at Fifty-three and go into the rest area.'' That's the overt act.

My job was to come down and block off the eastbound lane of that rest area with the helicopter so they couldn't get out until a chase car got there. Lane and Fitzsimons were gonna cover the other end in their chase car. Finally, the trailer's pulling in. One of the big plans that we had, how are we gonna get rid of the driver and our stoolie without having to lock them up?

I had a shotgun; I'm supposed to fire in the air. . . . The helicopter's landing. I jump off. I think I'm on the ground, but I'm not—I'm up ten feet. I go right on my ass. I land on my feet, but I go down on my knees. Now Marty Mak and Joey are running. They're at the fence. They're goin' over—

Stop! Police! *BOOM.* I let go a blast of the shotgun, and they "got away.''

But now we got three bad guys. We round everybody up, and we were gonna go back to the DA's office in Queens. "Hey, what am I? What?'' "Whatsa matter? I didn't do nuttin'!'' "Hey, what are you, crazy, or what!'' Two bad guys were in one car, and the other one was in the other car. "Who? Who's dis guy?'' They "didn't know each other.'' "Who's he? I don't know him.''

Anyway, I have to fly back in the helicopter, 'cause there's no room. I'm waiting. Our guys come back, and our car pulls in. They take our informant in the car and they get him away. Marty drives the trailer truck back.

Everything went good there. Now we left in the helicopter startin' back. We get up in the air, the pilot says to me, "Hey, Bob, we're low on the go stuff. We can't make LaGuardia.''

What the hell do you mean, we're low on the go stuff? The windshield wipers go *whooop,* going slow because it's icing up. I said, Where the hell are you gonna go?

"We're gonna have to stop off at Kennedy. We'll never make it—''

Don't even tell me that!—that we're never gonna make something! Just do it and don't say nothin'. So he does. We stop at Kennedy. We load up with fuel and back to the Marine Air Terminal.

In the DA's office, now they got one bad guy over there, one guy there, and the other guy, the driver of the car, here. They're not talking to each other. We're filling out the arrest cards. We're taking one collar, the DA's squad is taking one, and Marty Mak, the driver. I keep calling him Marty, so I gave him away. Good man. Good detective. A lot of balls too. He done a hell of a job.

Anyway, I'm sitting there typing with my two fingers. The guy that's in the car alone—I'm doing him. And he says, "Could I call my wife?" Yeah, all right. I dial it for him.

Your husband would like to talk to you.

"What do you mean, where am I? I'm in the DA's office in Queens! Why am I here? I don't know why I'm here! I didn't do nuttin'. I'm on the road, goin' home." Goin' home, he says. He lives in Brooklyn. He was goin' out the ass end of the Island.

"All of a sudden I'm surrounded by cops. Throwin' guns in my nose. I'm arrested with two guys I don't even know, I never seen before in my whole life." Going on and on about a trailer truck. He's talking about three minutes. I said, okay, Vinnie, hang the phone up. "Awright, awright. Listen, I'm gonna go now."

Now, the two guys who were in the other car over there. They don't know this guy. They claim. One of the guys, the passenger in the other car, says, "Hey, Vinnie, lemme talk to her." I'm making believe I don't hear this.

"Wait a minute, your brother wants to talk to ya." He hands him the phone. So they don't know each other, but they're brother-in-laws. That's the way it ended. We locked 'em up, and the high-value load was safe.

I got the car radio on going home; I hear a news report about the cops and the "high-tech odyssey." But it's two in the morning. Nobody heard it except me.

———

" 'Those guys over there are looking for a victim—' " de Stasio's Street Crime Unit partners coached her; "I would have never been able to spot that because I was new."

The plainclothes team was patrolling the edge of Central Park in an unmarked car. "Get out right here," the partners told her. In another unmarked car, riding with the sergeant, a *Daily News* reporter researching a story about a Street Crime decoy.

"I walked down Central Park West towards the two guys, and sat on a bench," recalls Maureen (de Stasio) Ayling, small-boned and sweet-faced. "I was just dressed like myself—dungarees. I was just me," Irish/English/French/Dutch/Native American/German Maureen. "About twenty minutes later, the two characters came right over to me. Do I have the time? So I told them what time it was. The one guy had his hand in his pocket. He picked up his jacket and pointed through the pocket; he says, "Come with us. I have a gun."

De Stasio had all the backup in the world that night, but the main reason she felt safe: "I knew they didn't have a gun. That's when I knew I was good for this job. 'Cause I deduced that it wouldn't have taken them twenty minutes to approach me had they had a gun." Psychology as much as deduction.

They tried to drag her into the park; de Stasio figured they wanted more than her handbag. "Even though I had all those backups, some of them in the park, I wasn't going—" In seconds, the backups converged.

"That was my very first time I got mugged. The funny part was, these two characters leaned against the other car and the *News* reporter heard them plotting and planning the whole thing."

De Stasio came on the job in 1968 expecting to patrol and found herself, like the rest of the handful of policewomen, on matron duty with female prisoners. The only way out was to volunteer to "fly" every chance she got.

Any detail, off she went, dressed in the distaff uniform with skirt and carrying her gun, as mandated, in her shoulder bag. (Today civilians take care of the prisoners; female police officers wear pants uniforms and holsters.) De Stasio worked a lot of the era's political demonstrations, dealing with rowdy women demonstrators—"sometimes more rowdy than the men." The only place she ever patrolled was Washington Square, Greenwich Village, the City's political protest hub in almost any decade, but especially in the 1960s.

Twice she interviewed for Street Crime—crash course in the worst of New York streets. The second time, in 1973 after five years as a matron, she made it to the unit. At first, the men gave her a wide berth, but de Stasio was happy just working "in the whole five boroughs and only in high-crime areas. No safe areas." She loved working violent street crime, period.

Deployed as a decoy in a Brooklyn neighborhood during a manhunt for a rapist, "I got robbed twice. You can be looking for a rapist or robbery condition—When you're walking around some neighborhoods at night, you do become a victim. Somebody was going to get mugged anyway, so we got them." If you've been a decoy, maybe *only* if you've been a decoy, you really know how a victim feels, a psychological advantage you may choose to suppress.

Street Crime trains more than your eye—also your detective's intuition: "You could spot a potential crime before it happened. You could spot a victim before that person actually got mugged. We would often save somebody from really getting hurt.

"I had been mugged off duty before I had any street experience. In a way I did want revenge, yes. I thought to myself, what a horrible predicament to be put into."

De Stasio trained in Street Crime for seven and a half years. There were so few women, they didn't give you a steady partner. About thirty-two people in a squad, eight squads total, maybe one female per squad. "You would be riding with certain teams and you would really work your way through the squad." Learning something from just about everyone. "Ultimately they all accepted me."

Women are more numerous now, fourteen percent of the NYPD, and a like percentage of the detectives. "A woman that does a good job, and there are many who do, is appreciated more because men don't expect it."

What's a woman up against on the street? "I found out a long time ago, when I first went to Street Crime. You just can't get out in a bad area, for instance, and say *please*. Three of us did this car stop. No license plates on the car; the trunk lock was punked out— So we stopped 'em. I had the driver. I told him, Put your hands up. He paid no attention.

"My two partners, they each had somebody. One looked over: 'You heard her! Put your eff-in' hands up!' The guy did, right away. I said, Oh, I got it now. You can't make everything a request. From then on, although I left out the 'eff-ing' as much as I could, there's times when I had to say it. You got somebody that's running with a gun in their hand, I say, Drop your gun or I'll blow your eff-in' head off. That's the way it has to be." She has never yet had to fire her gun, however.

Awarded her shield in 1981, de Stasio spent five months in Brooklyn Sex Crimes—and then came Central Robbery. "As soon as I heard about that, I applied. I was very lucky—I was accepted.

And I'm still there . . . . It's very diversified work, what we do. Very. It's never boring. The only thing I don't like is my typing, but you have to do your reports." She may sound a bit wistful about never having worked a homicide, but she has made a vocation out of robbery.

One day she IDs a pair of robbers in a shoe store stickup, but she's not interested in solving "that one crime. When they're doing it, I want to get them on a lot. So I go back to Bill Curley, the computer man—Billy, here's what I have. See what you can give me.

"He came up with about eight cases that all looked similar, and they were all in the same basic area. Six-three, Six-nine, Six-one—the precincts all border each other. All good areas, where bad guys would like to come in and do some stickups. Relatively safe areas, where there's a lot of commercial establishments. Where people feel safe. . . .

"I just like to go out and grab these guys. The more cases we get on them, we can seal them in. Even if Detective Curley gives you twelve, if you only get four hits out of twelve, now you know this bad guy is goin' away. All you have to do is get your photo hits. That's all. Then you run the lineup.

"Once we finish with them, these guys are not gonna be on the street for a long time. They're probably not gonna go to trial, but I like it when they do because we have good, solid cases on 'em. But generally when they have so many charges, they want to plea bargain it out. Even plea bargaining on four or five armed robberies, you're not gonna walk out the door like you would on one. That's why I like where I'm working."

Revenge? Could be.

### Detective First Grade Maureen (de Stasio) Ayling:
### Gold Cadillac

I did a year in Queens Robbery and then I came over to Brooklyn. The squad was already familiar with these two individuals who were taking cars off the Brooklyn Bridge or the Manhattan Bridge in the middle of the night: Arthur Campbell and his wheelman.

They were really slick. They would wait till they saw a good car coming over. They weren't just looking for a car like mine, a Nissan. A Lincoln or Cadillac—somebody with money. As they saw the car comin' up, they would put the barriers out. Police barriers—I guess they were there for construction purposes. Right across the street. It was an excellent trick.

Generally, it was a man driving, with his wife or on a date; lot of times on the weekend, three or four in the morning, when people are coming home from these kind of outings. Now, the man would get out and move the barrier. Next thing he knew, he had a gun to his head. They not only took his wallet and his jewelry and his wife's pocketbook and her jewelry, they also took the car. It was a really good scheme. The people are left there with nothing.

If it's a good car, they'll use it over and over, not necessarily for pleasure, for jobs. They'll put it in some nice, secret spot where they know nobody's gonna find out it's stolen. These two were holding on to a gold Cadillac. That particular car was used in a homicide in Brooklyn—young couple in a lover's lane. Two guys with the same description as the guys that we were lookin' for came up to the couple's car, and they blew the guy's head off with a shotgun. The female could never testify because her mind snapped, and that was it for her.

However, other witnesses that were in the lover's lane in cars described the gold Cadillac. Without anything else to go on, now we knew it was them.

I arrested one of the guys on a simple, gunpoint robbery: *Give me your coat or I'll kill you, I'll blow you up.* He took the victim's sheepskin coat. We showed the victim photos 'cause we had a feeling it was them. Of course, you have to do a photo array, but we could almost tell. Guy picked him out and he was arrested for that crime.

Billy Behrens, my ex-partner who's now off the job, he really was very enthusiastic when I first started working with him. This was '83. Behrens had arrested one of these guys, Campbell, for robbery prior to that, and his partner, George Johnson, had arrested him prior to *that*. Every time the guy got out, he just kept doing it again. We no longer had cases on him and his partner—ours were finished—but somebody else in our squad did.

So now there was another pattern, and two other detectives had cases, two separate detectives. Because we knew how vicious they are, even though it wasn't our case, we decided to hunt for another car they were using. We knew by the way that car was taken that it was them. We beat the bushes and we found it in the Seven-three Precinct, at Rockaway and Livonia. It was behind the projects in a lot where there's many cars. This is what I mean—they hide their cars like that and keep using them.

We informed our bosses, and we sat on the car for three days. Around the clock too. They put the whole squad on it. One of our cars was in the lot; the rest of us were on the outskirts. And we all had radios, naturally. (We had shotguns also. The Robbery Squad, years ago, did carry shotguns because of the things that you get involved in.)

Three males approached the car, and as they were getting into it, our team in the lot radioed. My partner and myself pulled in as quickly as we could, but our people in a van pulled up and Campbell's car rammed into the van. Campbell and the other guy jumped out and took off before we could even get close enough.

They ran into the project, where we knew they had family ties. The next morning, Sergeant Moore—greatest guy too—he was really annoyed. He hadn't been working the night before, but he said, "Why weren't you out there until five or six in the morning trying to look for these people?" But, boss, they didn't know it was us who was following 'em. That's why we didn't want to knock on doors.

Campbell had very much to fear from the Robbery Squad because we were so onto him that if he knew it was us chasing him, you wouldn't see him for a month. He would be goin' to Queens again, 'cause he had contacts in Queens. Well, was I ever right!

We're driving right down Rockaway Avenue, and I said to my partner, Is that . . . ? and I couldn't get the words out of my mouth. Behrens threw the car into park, jumped out, and just grabbed him. It took ten people to put cuffs on Campbell. My partner was not a little guy, and I'm not little. He's strugglin'. We knocked over the newspaper stand. We had no time to radio for backup. There was one big cop, and then all kinds of rookie cops; it was like a whole gang—I don't know where they all came from, but they were there. Rockaway and Livonia is a bad area. Really took ten, and the guy's not that big.

He was cryin' in the car on the way back. He didn't get hurt or anything; nobody got hurt. And he really wasn't trying to kill us. He just didn't want to get put in because he knew what he was gonna pay for. He didn't have his gun on him, unfortunately. I wish he did have it, 'cause then we would have got that gun off the street. He was just out to go to the store.

But had we knocked on that door the night before, he would've been gone in the wind. When we came in with this guy in cuffs—!

Campbell had also approached a young kid and his girlfriend in Queens, him and his partner. The partner was always the wheelman. The kid took one look at them—he was gonna come on this job, by the way, he was waiting to be called—and he said to his girlfriend, Run! She runs. Campbell gets out and puts the gun on him: Give me your wallet. The kid didn't resist. He was smart—you don't resist when somebody has a gun on you. Gives him his wallet.

With that, Campbell turns to get in the car, then he came back: Give me the chain. So the kid gives him the chain. And then he shot him for nothin'. This is what a vicious guy he is.

Once we got him, we gave him to Queens; they put him right in the lineup. Queens and Brooklyn Robbery had the same CO anyway. You always exchange information 'cause very often our bad guys are theirs and the same with Manhattan. Thieves don't have any boundaries, especially vicious guys like this.

They did a fantastic job in Queens, and naturally, my partner and I had to go on that case, because we were the ones that apprehended him. That was my best thing. That guy is gonna be in for more than fifty years. He's the guy that put the contract on the judge in Queens. From his jail cell! He had won some suit, some kind of a civil thing. He really did get ten thousand dollars, and he really put a contract on that judge for sending him away for all that time. True story. The judge was getting all sorts of protection.

The sad part is, the second guy, the wheelman, nobody could ever ID him because he always stayed in the car. We knew who he was.

To Detective Joe Pepe, nothing was more fun than bugging the wiseguys of La Cosa Nostra (our thing) in Little Italy, and Pepe got to do it in more ways than one. John Gotti et al. had their thing, and Pepe's thing was them. A bachelor into his thirties, living alone with his widowed mother, for a long time the detective didn't do much else. Pepe was a top member of the Manhattan DA's squad for a dozen years, and he could have just gone on and on, but a new captain came in—and they didn't hit it off. He transferred to Queens Robbery, close to home.

"I was down when I got to Queens Robbery—I mean, emotionally, psychologically," Pepe says. "But I hooked up with Billy Dwyer, and he had that type of personality that I bounced back again." He arrived with a hotshot-from-Manhattan sort of reputation. When an armored car stickup happened, the bosses laid the tricky case on Pepe and Dwyer.

The stickup looked to Pepe like an inside job. But then, by chance, he got sidetracked by the mysterious homicide of a little girl. The detective assigned had reached out for a psychic from Virginia, Ann Gehman, who showed up earlier than expected. Pepe was the only one available to meet her plane.

Opinions about psychics varied in the Detective Bureau. Pepe himself was a virgin when it came to psychics. He and Ann Gehman rode around Queens, visiting different parks that might have been the scene of the little girl's murder. They kept riding; what she said impressed him. Finally, he asked, "Can you work two cases at once?" Like an armored car stickup.

"Do you have anything I can touch? Money bags or any photographs?"

Pepe gave her the photo of the big four-wheel-drive armored vehicle. Touching the picture, she related what she saw—a scenario, complete with a New Jersey license plate clue, that jibed with Pepe's theory of the case. She knows the guards by name, Tito and Juan, sees them planning the job, gives directions to a location—then describes the heist of so much money, "they can't even carry it!"

Joe Pepe knows the take was a hundred-and-sixty-thousand dollars in quarters, dimes, and nickels from a bus line. "Joe, they have some kind of a wagon that they're bringing up the money into this apartment." There's a female accomplice: "Lisa or Lydia. When you find her, if you put *this* much pressure on her, she's going to confess." Ann Gehman assures Joe Pepe—Guaranteed, these two guys did it. Pepe rushes to tell his lieutenant.

"That fuckin' psycho—" The boss seems unimpressed. "She's a nut. Joe, you're taking the easy way out. Go find the real robbers."

Pepe broadens the investigation, but it always comes back to the guards. He tries to catch Tito, the driver, on a detail about the "holdup guy." The trap works less than perfectly. All that stolen silver, Pepe figures, has to wind up in slot machines. "Have you ever been to Atlantic City?" he asks Tito. Negative, but Tito's facial expression gives him away.

Joe and Billy Dwyer stop at his house again another day. On a table is Tito's credit card bill. The bill surfaces in Pepe's possession, tells the name of the San Juan hotel where Tito relaxed one week after the robbery.

The detectives proceed to The Bronx to see Juan. While waiting in the car for him to return, they're caught in a gunfight that Gehman foresaw, though she was unable to positively identify participants. "Billy and I jump out, and we're shootin' it out. There's a guy lying there dead—shot three times in the stomach, just like she said."

After a night of grueling paperwork on the shootout, the detectives are back at Juan's. A girl opens the door: "Lisetta, Juan's sister-in-law."

"I look at Billy, he looks at me. I grab her and I throw her against the wall. 'You're under arrest. You and your brother-in-law stole all that money.' "

"No. I only helped them move it."

"Where to?"

"We brought the money here." Lisetta told them Tito had picked up all the money four or five days after the faked stickup and converted it into bills in Atlantic City.

The detectives locked up Tito and Juan for larceny. Robbery, Pepe notes, "is the use of force; also you can't rob yourself."

Lisetta admitted disposing of the guards' guns in a plastic bag wrapped in a towel, tossed from the Willis Avenue Bridge. The divers "came up with all kinds of guns, but not their two. There was enough air in the plastic bag to keep it floating for a while— the tides were very heavy.

"This jury found one guard guilty and one guard innocent. Don't ask me how. Tito walked.

"I just saw him downtown near City Hall about two weeks ago. I looked at him. 'Do you have any of that money left? You had a good lawyer; you beat it.'

"No way. The lawyer took all the money I had."

"Well," I said, "you start with nothing, you end with nothing."

———

I ♡ NEW YORK. If the feeling's not mutual, watch out. It's easy to slap a slogan on millions of everyday objects, from takeout coffee containers to shopping bags schlepped by bag people—but New York can still be the most heartless of towns. Not even the church poor box is sacred to the thieves of Rip-Off City. East Side, West Side . . . Manhattan lowlifes are never above overturning the fragile world of an elderly person and leaving him or her with nothing to live for.

"When a senior citizen becomes the victim of a violent crime, many just become shut-ins, and they die a lot sooner than they would have. That's my own feeling," says Detective Sergeant Mike Gerhold who led the Manhattan South Senior Citizens Robbery Unit in the early and mid eighties, toward the end of his long NYPD career.

Starting out in Harlem in 1963, he developed an immediate

appetite for his job. "When you came out of the Academy in the old days, if you went to a real shithouse—there was very, very few of them then—the best part was, you learned at an accelerated rate. What I learned in three years at the Two-eight in uniform, other guys took twelve to fifteen years to learn out in Queens. I loved to make arrests. Back in those days when people cooped, rather than coop [lie down on the job] I would be on a rooftop looking for somebody selling junk or something. I just loved the work, and after only a short time I went into the Bureau. About three years."

Gerhold confronted a lot of savagery in almost three decades in the job, but what he saw in the six years he commanded the Senior Citizens Unit often haunts him. "We had a Hispanic guy downtown who used to get elderly Chinese people in the elevators and practice karate on them because they couldn't fight back. They were a live victim where he could practice chops, he could practice kicks. Horrible.

"And the hardest thing in the world is to get a senior citizen to make a report. An elderly Chinese—forget it, there was no way." Asians are terrified that contact with police will bring repercussions, but Gerhold drew a crowd of three hundred Chinese people to his one-hour crime prevention talk, given through an interpreter. Before his promotion to sergeant in 1973, he had earned second grade in a Brooklyn squad, and now his definition of detective work came to include speaking to seniors groups all over downtown Manhattan—warning them of current criminals and prevailing scams. There's really no such thing as a new scam. The old ones are just repackaged, like detergent.

To staff his Senior Citizens Robbery Unit, the sergeant looked for investigators—including the "white shields" in training to be detectives—blessed with the patience to stand up and address a group that didn't hear too well and the presence not to mortally scare the elderly audience while alerting them to the karate choppers, as well as to the psychological predators—like Brenda Ford. A phenomenon of the early eighties, Brenda's pattern spread over two boroughs and six precincts; her ill-gotten gains, Gerhold says, added up to about thirty-five thousand dollars.

"If she could, Brenda looked over her potential victims. If she saw them on the street and she could follow them and get into an elevator with them, fine. She *picked* people—the older, the better. As slow moving as possible. If they had glasses, the thicker the glasses, the better. She really preyed—she knew her victim well. This was her life.''

Quietly, with a charming smile, Brenda would discover whatever of value remained to you. And steal it.

### Detective Sergeant Mike Gerhold:
### Brenda Ford, AKA Brenda Ford Wolfe, Brenda Jenne Wolfe, Brenda J. Moore, Tyesna Ford Dae, Lynette Blackwood, Brenda Johnson, and Brenda Lynette Smith

I was getting copies of the 61 reports sent up to the squad. All serious felonies involving senior citizens, not just physically serious but felonies where they affected the quality of life of the person. Now grand larcenies to me were serious, because as I would look at some of these larcenies, I saw that somebody was getting into their apartment through guile and cunning and was ripping off their life savings. A lot of the seniors didn't believe in banks, and they had their money carefully squirreled away in places that they would never expect somebody to look.

Looking at some of these 61s, I saw that the same name appeared. "Mrs. Schwartz" appeared as a person who worked for the housing office. The perp would tell the senior to "contact Mrs. Schwartz to see if their property had been recovered." Some of the uniformed cops in being very, very thorough in the preparation of the complaint would put this down. For the most part these were petit larcenies and grand larcenies from the home.

We started canvassing, and recanvassing, talking to the victims that had reported the crimes. They gave us a young woman described by some as female white, some as female black, some as female Hispanic, some as possible gypsy, European origin. And she was always described as very, very polite, soft spoken, sweetheart of a girl, butter wouldn't melt— Her age ranged anywhere from late teens to maybe her mid-thirties. She just was there.

The more we dug, the more we asked, Did it happen to anyone else? Well, here it happened to the woman across the hall, but she never reported it because it was only fifty dollars. We talked to Housing 'cause a lot of it happened at projects on the Lower East Side; they told us they had cases in Queens too. We contacted Queens. We asked them to read us their 61s . . . "Mrs. Schwartz." I said, Holy shit, what have we got here? Is this like a huge ring?

By and large she used the same particular scam. She'd knock on the door. She would usually have four dollars in her hand, four singles for the most part. "Excuse me, Mr. So-and-so, I believe this is your money." This was the opener.

"My money?" One of the things that she did was always try to create confusion. People would react, "What do you mean it's my money?"

"Well, we think we have a guy down in the housing office that robbed you or burglarized your apartment," words to that effect. Now, from having money in their hand, they are being given a jolt of "I've been robbed?" She was very clever—there was like from a high to a low, and then she'd say, "But look, we have him, we have some property—could you just please check and see if you are missing anything."

Their hearts are racing and the seniors would let her into the house. They are certainly not going to turn away a girl that just gave them four dollars, so they let her go in. Only one guy turned her down. She had the four dollars in her hand, and the guy opened up the door and said, "Yes, what do you want?"

"I believe this is your—"

"Yes, it's mine," and he closed the door.

But usually they would escort this young lady into their apartment; and when they did that—usually there's a knickknack stand in the hallway, or from the kitchen table— she would always take somethin' and put it in her pocketbook.

She picked somebody that was very slow, remember, poor eyesight—usually followed them to where they were looking to see if their valuables were still there. Now she knew exactly where the valuables were kept. Sometimes she'd look in a mirror to see into the bedroom and then step back out. Now the senior, totally relieved because the valuables were there, would come back out and tell Brenda, "No, you must have the wrong person. I have all of my stuff."

The senior is feeling good again, and Brenda would come out of her purse with the wallet or a knickknack, house keys. "Well, he had these on them. Are you sure these aren't yours?" Now the senior was devastated again. Really clever.

"Oh, I can't believe that!" The senior was totally convinced that in fact this guy had my wallet, he had to be in my apartment. They just were totally blown away.

And she'd say, "Look, I'm sure if the guy has your property, we will get it back for you. Let me dial Mrs. Schwartz." She would dial and hand the senior citizen the phone, which again was clever because she actually put the senior in a position where the senior is going to stay on that phone to find out if the property is there. While the senior was waiting for Mrs. Schwartz to pick up the phone, Brenda would say—Could I use your bathroom a second?

Oh, sure.

Into the bathroom supposedly, but right to where she saw the senior check for valuables. Whether it was under the carpet or wrapped up in underwear or wherever the money was. She would be back in a minute, and usually the senior would say, But there's nobody answering.

Okay—hold on to the phone; I'll run down and get them to pick up. The perfect escape because the senior is still holding on. And if you think about it, it's sort of simple but how much psychology was involved: the ups and the downs and the mood swings of the seniors. Gluing them to the phone. Then she would disappear. Gone.

She picked buildings where there were tremendous amounts of senior citizens, like 282 Cherry Street, where we finally collared her. You have to utilize manpower really efficiently. My unit at the time had anywhere from ten to twelve men. Sometimes I'd have guys come in earlier to relieve guys. It was tough. You'd have people going to court. You might have five or six guys working at one time. Sometimes you might only have four.

But 282 Cherry Street, for whatever reason—we looked at fifty-something addresses from Stuyvesant Town all the way up to the Tenth Precinct, all the way around the horn to the Lower East Side—282 Cherry Street. When you start plotting these things on a map, putting your little pins in, 282 Cherry Street was the only place I think there was at least three. I think she hit it a fourth time, and I said, Fuck this, that's the building we're gonna sit on.

I put one guy, Michael O'Connell, who wound up making the arrest, in a recreation room on the first floor. I put a guy in the park in the back, and myself and Mike Brennan were out in the traffic sitting in a parked car where we could observe people coming towards the building. I had another car just ridin' around. We did this day after day, and we plotted the days and we plotted the times; we had a pretty good idea when.

Stakeouts are the most boring things in the world. They're demoralizing. It's like a needle in a haystack. How are we going to get this girl? Especially when you don't know if she's white, plaid. What are you looking for? This is crazy. In police work you have to be lucky, I think sometimes, more than good.

So we're sitting there. I just happened to get a car coming by with two of my guys in it, and I stopped, and I was leaning out of the car and we see, almost simultaneously, a girl walking across the open area, approaching 282 Cherry Street, and we look at her. We couldn't tell if she was Spanish or black and we're looking at her.

And as she's approaching the building she's got keys in her hand and she's waving to somebody in a window and she's talking. (It's really amazing how clever she was.) So we just watched, and I wonder if she looks anything like that girl, but naturally this girl lived there because she's talkin' to somebody at the window. We are like sixty, seventy-five feet away, but she's talking and she's going into the building, keys in hand, and we don't think about it.

Within a minute, Mike O'Connell, who's in the rec room, sees the girl press buzzers. Somebody buzzes her down, she enters, but a couple of other people also buzz, meaning that she probably hit a whole bunch of buzzers. He's looking through the rec room doorway. Now, this is the girl that approached the building with keys in her hand. She approaches the elevator door, opens up her pocketbook, and takes four dollars out of her wallet.

He says, "Fuck this, this is too much to be a coincidence; what should I do?" He starts to call us on the radio; she gets into the elevator and goes to the fourth or fifth floor. He sees what floor it stops at; he's gonna go up there after her. Just as the elevator comes down she's standing there, and he grabs her and she gives a big, "What are you grabbing me for?" and this and that.

By this time we are now responding to the building. We are only thirty seconds outside and we come in. He grabs me on the side. "I'll tell you what I got—"

She's screaming, "You've got no right to do this. You're doing this 'cause I'm—" You know, all this—"What do I look like? You have no right to treat people this way."

He says, "Look, I saw her take out the four dollars."

Now, I'm thinking to myself this is the same girl that was talking to somebody at a window and had keys in her hands. She explains that to us later. Anyway, we say, "Where were you going?" She says, "I was going to visit somebody on the seventh floor." That's not where she went. We know she's full of shit, and it's going on and on, and now she's trying to be a little cooler. "I went to buy some pot. There's a good friend of mine sells some pot."

They go up to the apartment on that particular floor, and there's an old lady who lives there. There is nobody sellin' pot there.

We got her for criminal trespass, which is probably the best tool that the Police Department has. If somebody will press charges when somebody doesn't belong in the building, at least you have an original charge. We now take her back to the station house. She's full of shit. Back in the station she's very uncooperative. This girl was like steel. She wouldn't bend, break. "Have your fucking lineups."

Of all the cases that we had with her, it's amazing how many people right off the bat, because of failing eyesight or an inability to even travel to the station house, couldn't, wouldn't come and make an ID. Six hours later we finally got what we thought were maybe nine or ten good complainants, including a guy who got ripped off and chased her but never caught her. As a matter of fact, unfortunately, he testifies in the grand jury, leaves, and outside on the sidewalk has a heart attack and dies.

Five or six of our ten complainants are able to make a pick, and so we've got her for grand larceny. Now that we've got her and she's ID'd, she starts talking to us about this and that. She's giving us these cases.

Jeff Schlanger prosecuted some of our cases before, so we got Jeff involved, and she now proceeds for about ten hours to run our fuckin' asses off. At the time we grabbed her, there were murders on the Jersey Turnpike. She "knew" who did the murders; she "knew" where the guns were kept. . . . Jeff could go on for hours about how she jerked *us* off. She was a little wacko but very, very clever.

We were getting search warrants. We had Emergency Service in Brooklyn. This is the night of the day we locked her up. Jeff and I were yelling at each other, we were so hot over this. "Ah, she's jerking us off. She's full of shit." "No, there's got to be something to this."

It was wild. She had us going at each other, and she had us breaking into a house where we almost killed a woman with her two children sitting on the couch. Guys from Emergency Service with shotguns. She said the guns were in there but "they are not gonna go without a fight." Sent us to an innocent house. Her information was so accurate on different things, but she just had a vivid imagination that went with it.

Anyway, that was Brenda Ford. Many of the victims in their seventies and eighties, failing eyesight.

Most of the 61s said she was light-skinned black, and we started to go with that, but we really didn't know until we got her that she was a black. (We were thinking gypsy because the senior citizens dealt a lot with gypsies. They rip off the senior citizens all the time.) We did get her fingerprints on some of the notes when she wrote down, *Call Mrs. Schwartz.*

We find out that Brenda is an escapee from I think North Carolina. She took off and she owed six years. We worked out some kind of a deal where Brenda now has to go back down there and Brenda goes down there never to be heard from again.

About two or three years later, I'm looking at a 61 and it's for grand larceny. I'm looking at the body of the thing and it says the complainant was told to contact Mrs. Schwartz. I said, I don't fucking believe this; this is incredible. We go to the DA's office and try to find out where is Brenda Ford. A lot of this is happening up in Harlem housing and they got all kinds of 61s and, yeah, Mrs. Schwartz all the time.

Brenda Ford is nowhere in their system down south. She walked away again and she's back doin' it again. This time the Housing cops grab her. We have pictures of her now; we know who she is, and it's as clear as a bell as opposed to the original investigation. But she just walked away from her time in North Carolina for whatever she did, and she's back here in the City doing it again. She may be out doing it right now. So if somebody tells you to hold the phone and talk to Mrs. Schwartz—forget it.

A lot of times when you were a detective and you had a case and the case went nowhere, negative results, you closed the case out. Sometimes you'd remember it if it was a particularly heinous crime, or something really stuck out in your mind about it.

But with the senior citizens, you always remembered how grateful they were when you were able to do something. Because even it was going to be negative results, maybe you got them money, maybe you got them food, you got their locks changed, you might have gotten a peephole put in their door. It was fine when they could climb up on a chair and look out, but now that they are a little bit bent over, they couldn't climb on the chair anymore. You were able to get Housing to put a new peephole in the door. You didn't think about it. It was automatic, all part of it. A multifaceted job. It was very rewarding.

There was always something to keep you going. Always people that want to rip off seniors.

———

Betrayal—the ultimate rip-off—leaves you with nothing more to lose. In one form or another, betrayal is a detective's daily portion. It's your job to win the bad guy's trust to the point where he betrays himself. Then you offer a chance to break his fall: Help us help you—betray your partner, your boss. You hope you can trust the DA to back you up. To avoid being ripped off yourself, you must anticipate each link in the endless chain of betrayal.

A fallen hero of course is the most despised villain—the farther you fall, the bigger the headlines in the biggest, most spiteful of cities. When you're dead, you're dead; disgraced, you're still walking around.

In the subculture of evil, success is ripping off a cop. "Big major drug dealers want to have bad cops working for them," says a former IAD detective. "They set it up. You have the good guys working for you, you write your own ticket. That's what corruption is all about. It's sad. And that's why you have an Internal Affairs Division." No longer a division, NYPD Internal Affairs has become a bureau, bigger than ever.

The same surefire gotcha technology used by the law to catch a bad guy lets the underworld test a good guy—and reveal him in the act of failing the test. That freeze-frame is forever—the rip-off you did to yourself, from which you don't recover.

### One-time Internal Affairs Investigator:
### Vouchered Property

The dealers give "integrity tests" to cops. One way is putting out drugs—say, a hundred tins of cocaine or heroin—leaving a couple thousand dollars in cash, and having the cop come in there and arrest a person.

When you get arrested, they give you a receipt for your property—what they vouchered. The officer writes out the voucher: a copy stays with the property; a copy stays at the desk in the precinct; the perp keeps his copy. . . .

The bad guys are all set up with their own hidden video and they videotaped the count: cash, drugs. Now they compare—and that's the way they nail the cop who vouchered less than he found there. The cop's on the street; they know what he looks like—he arrested them. They go look for him. *Hey, it's Monty Hall! We're gonna make a deal on our side now—you're gonna work for us.* And that's basically how it happens. Doesn't happen often, but it happens.

### Partners & Bosses

**Detective Lieutenant Jack Doyle:** When the informant "Joey" came in, he told Bob McKnight he wanted a hundred dollars for the tip—today; or that's the end of it right there. Remember, a hundred dollars then was like two hundred or three hundred now. McKnight told me what Joey wanted, and he said he happened to have a hundred in his pocket. It was Christmastime, and he was goin' to get an electric train for his boy.

We had a new procedure for reimbursement—more complicated. This was a completely legitimate expense, and we went round and round, got the money back down the line. After Christmas. But the point is, if McKnight didn't hold off on the electric train for his kid, there wouldn't've been a case at all.

# 5

# KIDNAPPED!

Snatched in Brooklyn in May 1987 by a very sophisticated, organized Colombian cocaine crew and openly killed, a young drug dealer was the first kidnap fatality in New York history. When the abduction of José Varela, age twenty-three, ended in his death, police attention focused on the City's latest illicit growth industry: kidnapping.

Even though most abduction victims are anything but innocent and thus undependable about reporting the crime, NYPD detectives worked two hundred and forty-four kidnappings in 1992—almost half the number worked by the FBI that year for the entire U.S. (The comparison is for federal fiscal year 1992: October 1991 through September 1992.)

Some professional abductors make a nice living by targeting successful drug dealers and taking them for all they're worth, but it's not the kind of high-volume kidnap enterprise developed by Asian nontraditional organized crime mobs—the Fuk Ching (Young People of Fujian), for example. While this vicious gang readily kidnapped to collect drug debts, abducting smuggled Chinese nationals was a wholesale business. Allied with smugglers in China ("snakeheads") who collected deposits from immigrants on fees of about thirty thousand dollars, Fuk Ching thugs in New York would then snatch the newly arrived illegals to extort the balance from their families.

For every suburban industrialist or Manhattan fashion executive kidnapped for millions of dollars, *scores* of illegal Asian aliens have been held in Chinatown and in more obscure Asian neighborhoods for small stakes. A hundred and fifty thousand dollars is high, according to Major Case boss Lieutenant Joseph Pollini, who directs NYPD kidnap investigations. Despite the disappointingly hard facts of life in the promised land for most of the would-be Americans, illegal immigration, according to TV news reports during the mid-1993 grounding off Queens of the illegal immigrant ship *Golden Venture*, is a three-billion-dollar-a-year business.

Well before the *Golden Venture* incident, Major Case detectives had worked kidnap after kidnap resulting from Asian immigrant smuggling. Suddenly the long-standing problem spilled into the media spotlight as the crew of the grounded tramp steamer forced some three hundred Chinese nationals overboard to struggle through the surf toward Rockaway Beach. Ten drowned.

Asian families almost never cooperate with police for fear of retaliation—depriving kidnap detectives of the control they must have if they are to recover victims alive. Two fatal abductions got 1992 off to an ugly start. In one of them, "Things weren't materializing at the rate the perps wanted. The victim was shot once in the head and thrown out in the middle of a Queens street," says Lieutenant Pollini. "That's what we're faced with."

In 1972, Joey Pollini was three months into his undercover Narcotics assignment. At least once a week perps had tried to rip him off. Then, sprawled in the dark hallway of a Brooklyn tenement, conscious of the sudden steely chill that is "a knife to my neck, I shot the first person through my coat pocket—and fortunately I had a backup gun. . . . Ever since, I normally carry, like, two or three guns with me." And ever since, pals call him Joey Guns.

On-duty NYPD detectives weren't mandated to carry semiautomatics until mid 1993, but the Major Case squad already had received special handgun training. "We were one of the first in the department's nine-millimeter trial program, because when we go on kidnappings, most perpetrators have automatic weapons and it's a little difficult with a five-shot weapon to go up against them."

Chinese gangs in the kidnapping and extortion industry are "somewhat cowboys in nature," Pollini says. "They don't do things in a well-organized way per se. But they are starting to get more educated. The older the gang members, the more responsible to the organization they get; they seem to be gaining strength, becoming more violent." In their use of violent tactics, Asian gangsters are often compared to Colombian crews, who were ultraviolent to start with.

The Asian gangs remind Lieutenant Pollini of the Neapolitan mob around the turn of the century, the Camorra, or Black Hand. "The Black Hand started out victimizing their own people—store owners—through extortion. They gained more funds and moved on to drugs and other things. . . . Then they moved out to prey on others in the population." Illegal Asian aliens who came of age in the early nineties function not too differently from soldiers in traditional organized crime, Pollini suggests.

The lieutenant has testified before the U.S. Senate on Asian organized crime, but more than blue-ribbon panels, media coverage of the *Golden Venture* episode seemed to heighten government concern about Asian organized crime—in time, perhaps, to suppress it before it can mushroom, Italian-style.

In an ironic kidnapping incident, the notorious Ghost Shadows of Chinatown actually called the cops one winter night in 1992—the first time, Lieutenant Pollini says, "a criminal gang came to us for help." They needed to be rescued from another gang, a bad Colombian crew in Queens, because when the Shadows "purported to sell ninety-eight thousand dollars worth of brown heroin to the Colombians, one of the Chinese gang took off with the proceeds, leaving the rest behind. The Colombians held them for ransom.

"The Chinese called us because there was no way they could come up with the money, and they knew that their people would be killed. They weren't really sure after all the problems they had imposed on us whether we would actually come to save them. But, of course, we don't distinguish between good and bad victims, we just go out and do what we have to do."

After the Varela homicide in 1987, responsibility for kidnapping investigations shifted from precinct detectives to the headquarters Major Case Squad. Pollini's assignment was to systematize all procedures and techniques, and train detectives in the new systems. With a command post in place, field teams fan out to do surveillance, while "inside" detectives closely monitor contacts between the victim's family and kidnappers.

The troops were run through drills. "No one knew it was gonna happen, and then all of a sudden we'd put in a call, 'Someone kidnapped!' Now we scramble. We made someone a courier, someone the victim. They would know it's a drill, but we would do everything just to make sure we wouldn't make mistakes when we went out on the street." Pollini feels prepared, "even if the President gets kidnapped. That's what the inspector says, we're always ready in case the Cardinal gets kidnapped."

In the meantime, the NYPD experts train neighboring law enforcement agencies, as well as local FBI agents, Pollini says. And they handle the snatches generated by the kidnap industry. Lieutenant Pollini can call on any of several hundred kidnap task force investigators, on duty or off, to work "twelve hours on and twelve hours off, seven days a week, around the clock."

Chances are good that you'll be called away from your family on a holiday and very good that they won't see you on the eleven o'clock news, either. Still some detectives feel the excitement of a kidnapping investigation is more than worth it. (Of course, the overtime pay doesn't hurt either.)

Lieutenant Daniel J. Kelly, longtime CO of the Queens Homicide Task Force, worked many kidnaps with his detectives. "You do a homicide lead by lead by lead—" he says, "but with a kidnapping, it's like you're playing ball, right then and there." Kelly has a bulldog look around the mouth, isn't given to a lot of smiles. A kidnapping case is "more fun than anything else," admits the lieutenant, almost smiling. "I'm playing against you; you're playing against me—"

"We became quite adept at it," says Detective Steven Weiner, who retired from Queens Homicide about the same time as Kelly. "My Steve Weiner—" Kelly calls him, "detective first grade. He's about this big," meaning not that big. He's tall enough, though, in the Paul Newman mold. Kelly, slightly ruddy, has straight, dark hair. Weiner is fair with sandy-color wavy hair. High contrast, but both men come across the same: smart, serious, tough.

They honed their game on numerous drug-related snatches by Queens-based Colombian gangs. "We would use those as the maneuvers," Weiner says. "And we told headquarters, You don't have to stage anything—we'll use the drug kidnappings."

"When you're making some other apprehension," Kelly explains, "you set yourself up a plan, the plan works, you get the guy—it's all over. But in a kidnap, now you're working for two things, the perpetrator and the victim. That's why it gets so much attention; it's happening now—you have to move on it." Few perps who could bow out would play against Kelly, whose reputation went before him during thirty-two years as a detective and a leader of detectives.

Until the creation of the kidnap task force, kidnappings were handled from the precinct where the crime happened, with Major Case as backup. Before 1987, when, for example, an incident occurred in Queens, Lieutenant Kelly set up shop in the precinct of occurrence. He relied on a radio, a telephone, and a single board with his famous three-by-five cards listing all the relevant data and detectives' assignments. He remembers the hours of tedium, and the seconds of tension: "You're callin' a lot of shots from what you're getting. You're tellin' me A, he's telling me B. I have to make a decision. Such a challenging thing. . . ."

Now the local precinct squads back up Lieutenant Pollini's kidnap task force, which runs investigations from a given borough office. "They'll have a war room," Kelly notes. "Half a dozen easels all around. It's grown from say one desk, to maybe three. Because it gets complicated." The complexity, Kelly says, is what makes a kidnap fun to work—a good contest against bad adversaries. In the eighties, Kelly's detectives engaged in ten to twelve such contests per year.

On another plane altogether is that rarity detectives call a "legitimate" kidnapping: innocent victim, usually not famous, usually from a hardworking family that's rich only by the kidnappers' wishful standards. Perhaps once in your career, you help reunite a law-abiding family with a child in jeopardy.

### Detective First Grade Steve Weiner, Detective Lieutenant Dan Kelly, Detective Mike Kelty, Detective Lieutenant Joseph Pollini: The Real Thing

**Lieutenant Kelly:** We had just finished a drug kidnapping over Thanksgiving that ran for ten days. My Steve Weiner was working Christmas Eve, 1987. He's our in-house Jewish fellow. He works every Christmas for me. He'll do sixteen hours—whatever has to be done so that somebody can have off.

Now, this guy is a good detective, made a lot of good arrests, a lot of homicide arrests. Very heavily involved with Colombian drug murder investigations. He was deep undercover before he even became a detective. And he said, "I was never so satisfied in my life." To hear that come from him, I knew he really sincerely meant it.

**Detective Weiner:** The desk officer in the One-o-eight received an anonymous phone call from a female. He calls me in Homicide. There's an ongoing kidnapping of a youth in the One-twelve. That's all he's got.

What would someone in the One-o-eight Precinct know about a kidnapping here in the One-twelve? I thought that was unusual. I said, I'll be covering tonight and tomorrow; I'm doing a double. If they call back, see if you can get any details, get a call-back number.

We went through all the missing-persons cases, and we came up with one from that afternoon. Silvina Casinelli, thirteen-year-old reported missing by her parents. Then when the cops went to the apartment, they weren't allowed in. The parents said the girl had returned. That jumped out at me—they weren't allowed entry. Kind of peculiar.

I tried to get in touch with the sergeant who signed the missing-persons report to see if he remembered. Or the cops, to see what was the problem—how come you didn't get into the apartment? You're a cop; you should go in there and see what the story is.

About fifteen or twenty minutes later, a couple comes in. The female says the daughter of a friend of theirs was kidnapped; she wouldn't give me any further information. I explained that if we're going to do a job, we have to have some facts.

She says, "The kidnappers told the parents 'If you tell the police, we're gonna kill your daughter.' " (The parents didn't know what to do, so they called this longtime friend.)

I understand your allegiance to your friend, but if you really are a friend and if you're really concerned about the child, you have to cooperate with me. As a matter of fact, is your friend a doctor?

They looked at me like I had a crystal ball, "Yes. A doctor."

Okay, give me the name.

"No—"

I said, Is it Casinelli?

"How do you know?"

I explained about reports of missing people.

"I don't know what to do. I feel like I betrayed them."

No, you didn't betray them. I'll tell you what I want you to do. Go back and reason with the parents. Tell them to contact me. If I don't hear from you within a half hour, I'll take an unmarked car, park a couple of blocks away, and walk over.

**Lieutenant Pollini:** This kidnapping was set up by the maid that used to work for the father. She was terminated, and as a result, she and her boyfriend proceeded to abduct the daughter.

**Detective Weiner:** Half an hour passes and I don't hear. I call up Larry DiTusa, a sergeant in the One-o-seven. It's Christmas Eve and all the squads were down to either no men or one guy. Like, one guy would work the bullshit cases and if anything major came in, they would notify us in Homicide.

Forty-five minutes later I still didn't hear from the parents, Larry and myself went over. It was an apartment house off 110th Street by Continental Avenue, Forest Hills.

The father was a psychiatrist and his specialty was counseling parents who had a traumatic loss in their life. Usually a kid that had leukemia, or something happened to the child. He would counsel the parents. Now it came full circle.

I knock on the door and a voice answers—the mother. She doesn't open up. It's the police, I tell her, and we're just checking on a report that she made.

"Oh, no, no. My daughter is home—that was a mistake."

I would like to speak to your daughter.

Naturally, she couldn't produce her daughter, but meanwhile I'm in the hallway: *I'd like to speak to your daughter.*

"No. My daughter's sleeping," or some excuse.

Okay, go wake her up. It's Christmas Eve and I don't want to make a scene here, but I'm not leaving until I get into the apartment. Unlock the door.

I'm in the doorway for about twenty minutes and finally I tell them I'm going to notify the neighbors that I have to come in through the fire escape. I hear the locks unclick and I push in the door.

I see Marta Casinelli and the couple that came into the One-twelve—she had an embarrassed look on her face. She blurted out to Marta, "Before we came here we went to the detectives."

Look, don't blame her—I sit down with Marta. They did you a favor. I tell them I've been a detective for twenty years, on homicides, etc., I've been on the kidnap team and not to worry. Just tell me about your daughter.

She wouldn't give me any information. "You'll have to speak to my husband."

Okay, where is he?

"He's in the bedroom." I walk into the bedroom and I don't see anybody. I said, Am I in the right bedroom?

She points to under the bed.

After about ten or fifteen minutes of trying to speak to Dr. Casinelli, I go back to Marta: You think you can handle this by yourself but you can't. What's gonna happen is you're going to get a series of phone calls. They're gonna give you instructions. Could be today or it could be over the next two days or even longer, I tell her, but these people have to make contact with you and one way to catch them is electronically—a trap on the phone.

**Detective Mike Kelty, TARU:** When there's a necessity to identify the source of calls, the Technical Assistance Response Unit is contacted through Major Case, and working closely with private communications companies, we identify the actual instrument and the location.

**Detective Weiner:** The mother refuses to let us trap the phone. Doesn't even acknowledge that her daughter was kidnapped. I go back into the bedroom and try to negotiate with the father. Back and forth like a Ping-Pong ball. We must have been there about two hours, easy.

Another friend of theirs knocks on the door.

Who is that? I say.

"Well, that's my friend Maria—"

She's carrying a bag. When she heard I was the police, she held on to that bag. I went over and introduced myself and took the bag. In it was fifteen thousand dollars. Then I called up the Borough and I told them we have a legitimate kidnapping, but there's a problem. I can't get consent for the trap. They won't cooperate.

"Okay, leave it," I was told. "Just go home. It's probably a drug kidnapping," 'cause they had a Spanish name.

I'm not goin' home until I get the information. This kid is kidnapped. Then I explained to Marta Casinelli again what's gonna happen.

"I'm from Argentina"—she said, "I have a masters in psychiatric social work, but even though I'm educated, I'm from the old school. I will not go against my husband."

It's one thing if you let him make a decision when he's rational. His decision may be wrong, but at least he gave thought to it. You cannot let him take responsibility for your daughter now because you will never see your daughter again.

This went on over four hours. Finally, she told me that at eleven o'clock in the morning Christmas Eve, her daughter was supposed to go to a friend's house and had to stop on the way at a bank within walking distance. The friend called, like twelve-thirty: "Where is she? Did she leave?"

**Lieutenant Pollini:** She was spotted by the maid, called over to the car, and at that point they pulled her in and took off with her.

**Detective Weiner:** It was Christmas Eve day. Before the father left his office, he had called Mrs. Casinelli and told her he received a strange phone call—Silvina had been kidnapped and they would give him instructions.

He came home maybe two o'clock, and they tried to retrace Silvina's steps—see if she made it to the bank. There was no indication that she did.

Then the family received two or three more phone calls. "We have your daughter. We want—" I forget what the ransom was. Some ridiculous number for a kidnapping. Something like they started out at thirty thousand dollars or fifty thousand and worked down, and they got fifteen thousand.

I called Borrelli, the chief of detectives, and my boss, Lieutenant Kelly. Kelly first— he was in charge of kidnapping in Queens. I said, There's only Jews working. I do this to you every year. Guess what? I'm doin' it to you again—and I told him, This is real. All that bullshit drug kidnapping we've been doin', that's all maneuvers. This is the real thing. I know you're going to *love* this, but you better get in here.

Before I left, I took the mother aside. I promise you I will get your daughter back. You made the right decision. She was still reluctant to cross her husband.

**Detective Kelty:** When you get a beep like that on a holiday, you know that everybody you need to make a successful operation go—all the senior individuals who are manning various stations—are always gone. You have to work with someone that may not have the knowledge you really want.

Naturally, we make a test call to make sure that the system is working, and then when the inward-bound call came, we were able to identify the source areas in Brooklyn. We kept people at the command post in the One-twelve for further operations but sent surveillance vans and other support people to the vicinity of the phone in Brooklyn.

**Lieutenant Pollini:** We brought in fifty detectives for this particular case, on Christmas Day. Picture how happy everybody was. But we weren't really taking too many chances because it was a thirteen-year-old girl, a legitimate kidnapping. We do treat each kidnapping with the same severity, more or less. But this one was a little bit different.

**Detective Weiner:** I came back about nine o'clock in the morning. By that time a second flurry of phone calls had come in and a drop was supposed to be made. Once you get permission to put up a trap, now you have an inside kidnap team. The inside team just stays with the victims—they monitor the phone calls and try to comfort the family. Pollini from Major Case was the inside guy.

**Lieutenant Pollini:** Whoever the kidnapper is going to converse with—the husband, the father, whatever—we drill them and tell them what to say and what not to say.

Because we feel a person was killed in '87 because the father negotiated with the kidnappers on the phone and he didn't know how to talk to them.

The biggest job in the residence is to keep the person that's gonna talk to the kidnappers at an even level psychologically on the phone. Because you have a tendency to be very hyper at points, to get very exhausted at points—and when you get hyper, you have a tendency to get angry. If you get angry and lose control, they'll probably kill the victim.

Then, sometimes, they get really subdued, and somehow you seem to lose interest. Now, they know you're losing interest and that can also prompt physical harm to the victim. So your job is to keep drilling the script into the person. "If he says this, you say this; if he says this, you say this." And that comes from the experience of doing it before.

**Detective Weiner:** The drop was supposed to be made at Alexander's Department Store on Queens Boulevard, and they instructed Dr. Casinelli to walk from his house and down Queens Boulevard. By this time, he was totally composed. It's a pretty big walk, about a mile and a half, two miles from his house, but it's like a bullet, straight down Queens Boulevard.

**Lieutenant Pollini:** Queens Boulevard is a relatively large street with little commercial establishments. There's very few people on the street. We observe the contact with the kidnapper, and we start to do an extensive surveillance. We had the FBI with us on that day because we utilized their aircraft to do surveillance, and we had the FBI surveillance team out there too.

**Detective Weiner:** We know what the perp looks like. He's a Spanish guy and we've got a description of him. Black hair, dark complected, maybe five foot eight to five foot nine. He's wearing black pants and a black leather jacket, and we've got a description of his car, which was a real shit box.

We were in the chase cars now. I was with Sergeant Reilly. We're opposite Queens Boulevard, and we have the observation point on Alexander's. We see Dr. Casinelli walking down towards Alexander's. At the corner there's a traffic light, and all of a sudden a bus—no matter how you make plans, the unexpected always happens. Not that we knew what was gonna happen, but just as we got to that corner, traffic backed up, and there's a bus in front of us so we can't see.

Lenin Rios was the perp's name. He's in an old, beat-up car, and he was first at the traffic light. He yells in Spanish, "Throw the bag in the car." Then he takes off. One of the other teams saw what happened, and we start following this car.

Anytime there's a kidnapping, even if it's a drug kidnapping, we get our own band on the radio, our own frequencies—this way, anything that comes over the air is only relative to the kidnapping.

Reilly was driving. I was the recorder—you talk on the radio; you put over what the perp is doing. He was really driving erratic.

**Lieutenant Pollini:** He started to make all sorts of turns and moves, so we dropped the surveillance, only because we didn't want him to know we were there. We'd paid the required ransom; we more or less let him go. We later found out he wasn't making all those turns because he was trying to shake surveillance; he was lost. Didn't know how to get back on the highway.

**Detective Weiner:** We were always maybe ten minutes away from him, because he would go on the Long Island Expressway and we would be on Queens Boulevard; then we'd get on the LIE, but there were other vehicles. We were always just five to ten minutes behind, but in a car that's a lot.

**Lieutenant Pollini:** Earlier in the day we determined that the origin of the calls was a phone booth in Brooklyn, around 17th Street and 8th Avenue. Once we dropped the surveillance, we went back to that area, and we started to do a grid search, checking the blocks up and down.

**Detective Weiner:** TARU says they were calling from a Brooklyn exchange. Five or six chase cars are proceeding. About fifteen minutes later they tell us, Go to the Sunset Park area, because one of the phone calls came out of a public phone in a subway station over there.

**Detective Kelty:** A phone on a subway platform in a deserted area, an inconspicuous out-of-the-way place. (People seem to always feel comfortable with a phone they've used in the past. Either that or they know it works, so they go back and use that phone again and again.)

When we arrived in Brooklyn, we decided to set up a field operations point approximately three blocks away from where the phone was. We pulled up with the department cars and vans and trucks and equipment, and we used the parking lot of a gas station that was closed 'cause it was a holiday.

You would stick out like a sore thumb if you were police. We had to set up discreet surveillance on the location, which required a little bit of "technical expertise" on our part—a detective dressed up as a maintenance worker for the subway system. He went through there taking a look around and doing "maintenance" things, and then followed the individual out of the subway arcade area.

**Detective Weiner:** We're riding around Sunset Park, and Billy Clark stops the car 'cause he had seen the drop. What you do in a kidnapping, you try to put the drop in something that can readily be seen so everybody can see the drop being made. It was in a red and green plastic shopping bag. Billy spots Rios leaving a bodega and getting into a car. As soon as he gets into that car—it was under an el—he takes off like a bat out of hell and then he stops in the middle of the block.

Other units are—they're not chasing, but they're trying to follow as best they can. He's driving again, still erratic; now he comes to a cold stop. They're following him for maybe ten minutes. He'd make U-turns and go up a one-way street.

Reilly says, "Y'know what—let's just stay on this block." We're just driving around, not trying to follow him. "When he stops, then we'll see what happens." As it turns out, we picked the right block. We're parked and all of a sudden we hear they lost him.

But then he comes down our block, stops in the middle, and jumps out. Now I get on the radio—Blue base unit: We have him. He's double-parked. He's out of the car. Nobody come down the block!

We start heading slowly over, and there he is. He's talking to a female, and there's a girl holding on to the female. Like clutching her. We had photos of the kid. She was gonna be a model and this was for her portfolio. Professional photos and she's all made up—she looked like about eighteen years old, we have her age as thirteen. I tell Reilly, Jesus Christ, I can't make the kid—she looks about twelve. I can't tell from the picture.

**Detective Kelty:** We were west of where that house was and one of our surveillance vans watching the house, and when we saw the kid come out, a female was with her.

**Detective Weiner:** I get out of the car, and now he comes down the steps, gets in his car, and takes off. Reilly starts to follow him. He had a radio too. Reilly tells the other units, "Okay, I'm on him—" and they all take off.

Now Rigo Garzona got out of one of the cars. He was taking a smoke. I go over to him, Rigo, we're gonna stay on this house because he was talking to a female and there was a kid holding on to that female and I don't believe in coincidence. I can't tell you if that's the kid or not—but let's see what happens.

We stayed out there for maybe twenty minutes. Now the door opens and the female walks down the steps with this kid dressed like a refugee—babushka on her head, all bundled up. The woman is holding a white plastic shopping bag.

We don't know how many perps are involved. We'll follow 'em down towards the end of the block, and then we'll take 'em. If there are other perps lookin' out the window, they won't see what we're doing.

We let 'em go three quarters down the block. I tell Rigo, You speak to her; I'll speak to the kid. We separate them on the street. I ask the kid, What's your name?

"Carla."

Rigo talks to the older female in Spanish. She tells him whatever name. "This is my daughter. We're going to my cousin's house for Christmas Eve."

**Lieutenant Pollini:** At that point, they were going to take the girl to a place and execute her, basically because she knew who her abductors were and they didn't want to take a chance. They had the ransom; they were going to kill the victim.

**Detective Weiner:** I tell the kid, I'm a friend of your parents. I'm the police—I show her my badge. If you don't want to tell me your name, that's okay, just tell me where you live. She starts to give me her address. She's, like, in a daze.

I get on the radio and I tell them to send a radio car; we have the victim. Bring her back to the One-twelve and the hospital.

**Detective Kelty:** At the set we happened to have cellular phones, I remember. Not everybody had them yet. They put her on the phone right there in the middle of nowhereville in Brooklyn and called the parents just to tell them the girl was safe.

**Detective Weiner:** As soon as we put her in the car, Rigo and myself take the woman and go back to the house. I get the keys from her. She had told us that she lives on the second floor and that there was nobody in the apartment.

Rigo is on the steps and as I'm keyin' into the outside door, the door opens. The perp, Rios, had come back! I saw him and we walk into one another. There's a little lobby and I grab him and I know he shit himself. Now, I'm rollin' around on the floor with him. Other units come to assist, and we put the cuffs on him.

We go upstairs and he tells us that it was just the two of them, that there's nobody else. When we go into the apartment, on the couch is the red and green shopping bag.

Doing homicides for twelve or thirteen years, you're always there after the fact. The victim's family always feels that they want the arrest and that somehow that's gonna make things better. Until the arrest, that's how they really feel. It doesn't change a thing. You feel good that you're gettin' these mutts off the street—but it doesn't change anything for the family. Now they have to contend with He's dead and it's over. It's like, anticlimactic.

Here was one of the few times it was before the fact, before the kid is murdered. It was proactive rather than reactive. If I could've bottled that feeling—'cause it only lasted about three seconds—but, if I could've bottled that feeling. . . .

**Lieutenant Pollini:** That was more or less everybody's Christmas present, that we got the girl back in one piece.

**Detective Weiner:** Four years pass and I haven't seen her. We all go out to holiday dinner—the family and ADA Debbie Stevens and me. Silvina is all grown up. After we eat, as we're leaving she says, "What can I do for you?"

I tell her, Do me a favor. Somebody saved my life and I always call around the time that it happened. Thanksgiving. All I want from you—(I don't care if you don't call me during the year) around Christmas, just call me. Let me know how you're feeling. Let me know you're all right, and you'll feel better. Because every Christmas, you're gonna get a queasy feeling.

# SPECIAL SQUAD 3

---

I was sworn in all by myself with the chief clerk. He put my
police officer's shield in my left hand. I raised my right hand; I
took the oath of office. He took the shield out of my hand, he
put it in my envelope, sealed the envelope, and placed it in a
big safe in his office. And that was the first and last time I ever
saw my white shield.

—Detective First Grade Jack Godoy

The revolutionary 1960s picked up steam in the City. At the
time, the NYPD maintained an intelligence-gathering arm for organized crime, and one for political threats to public safety—the
Bureau of Special Services. BOSS (also known by the acronym
"BOSSI") aimed to infiltrate suspected extremist groups of the left
and right and was looking for credible undercover operatives to
match with the targeted organizations. BOSS talent scouts—including Watergate figure-to-be Tony Ulasewicz—combed the lists
of police recruits and checked their applications.

Winnowing several thousand young men, mostly in their twenties, they leaned toward higher test scores and lower profiles—if
you had come to New York City from somewhere else, all the
better. Sometimes college helped—the unit was investigating a lot
of college-educated political activists. Military experience often

was helpful—someone who knew his way around guns, for instance, had a definite edge with extremists.

But consciously or instinctively, the bosses zeroed in time after time on a certain political innocence, a blank slate. Strongly held views might get in the way when an undercover tried to spout some party line. Also risky, however—for everyone—was sending political innocents into any of the era's ideological lion's dens. Some came away confused, others tormented, but only one out of over a hundred is known to have turned.

Once your name was selected, a boss—usually *the* boss, Lieutenant Barney Mulligan—would telephone to ask whether you'd be interested in a secret undercover assignment with the Police Department. If you wanted to know whether you'd be investigating drug traffic, he'd say definitely not. What about corruption—fellow cops? No. Otherwise, you heard no details before your interview. Some candidates were interviewed several times with months between.

If you got through your interviews successfully, you underwent your physical and medical exams separately from any other applicants. When the rest of your class entered the Police Academy, you did not. You were not to be exposed to any police information or habits of thinking that could betray your true role when you infiltrated a movement. Nobody was to know you and you were to know nobody but your bosses. As far as anyone other than your closest relatives was concerned, you had lost interest in the police and were looking at other careers.

I had to meet a guy who was gonna be on the corner of Spring, a couple blocks from headquarters. He was gonna have *Life* magazine under his arm. I got there whatever time it was—he came over to me and said I was to follow him into headquarters, fifteen feet behind him. Not to stop at the desk, they knew I would be going in with him. That's what I did. We went to the chief clerk's office. . . .

—Detective First Grade Bill Clark

You entered the police brotherhood without benefit of brothers in a chilly, unceremonious rite witnessed only by one of your detective bosses. His presence was appropriate, for as this under-cover solo flight of yours continued, the bosses in the control tower, so to speak, would be your only link to the secret reality of your mission.

The feds' intelligence exercises of that era had nothing on the secrecy of NYPD Special Squad 3, or the fearsome isolation you felt as an "operator." That was the word in the NYPD, rather than operative, but the cold you went out into was at least as cold and the ice where you stepped, at least as thin as anything the feds experienced.

> The undercover unit never gave you any inkling of what you were to do, no script. Sink or swim. The reason they never gave you a script: if you memorized the script, it would be unnatural. You went completely on your own. What that meant was they had more washouts than successes, but the successes infiltrated to the very depths.
> —Detective First Grade Steve Weiner.

Special Squad 3 members knew their parent was BOSS, but little of the history of intelligence in the NYPD. Forerunner of BOSS in the first years of the century was the Italian Squad, formed to combat Neapolitan immigrant mobsters of the Black Hand. In a decade the name changed for the first but not the last time, to the Radical Squad, or Red Squad, as it came to be known, which was an overt unit.

But as early as the 1930s, there had been covert agents, as well. "In the new undercover squad, we copied quite a bit from 'Special Squads one and two,' " says Theodore Theologes, retired detective second grade, who was one of the undercovers' handlers. "Just before and during World War Two, they had people working in defense plants to spot any espionage or acts of sabotage." Under-covers also worked the draft riots of the Kennedy years.

The undercovers of the 1960s and early seventies never even knew their unit's official name. Their bosses only talked among themselves about "Special Squad Three." This new generation's mandate was nevertheless clear enough—to counter perceived subversive and violent designs on the City by gathering intelligence among suspected political extremists. But day to day, the novice undercovers would have to invent their tactics as they went along.

The NYPD unit was the most sophisticated of undercover operations, says Jackie Godoy, a Latino detective who stayed under about six years. By comparison, "the feds, who used informants, basically—they never used their own personnel for undercover work—looked like they were back in the Model T Ford days. They even met on a weekly basis with Lieutenant Mulligan, at his convenience, at his location, to be briefed on what was going on and where certain individuals were."

BOSS made sure the squad's internal security was tightly controlled—fortunately, because one undercover turned. "The only one that we know of," Ted Theologes says. "We put him in with this embryo group that became the Black Panthers, and he became philosophically involved with them—emotionally?—I don't know what it was. But he started informing on us. He would tell us what was doing with them—and he would also tell them. . . .

"We would have everything under lock and key, labels on some of the stuff, but it wasn't what it really contained. We knew what it meant, but no one else would. He thought he could figure that out and he wasn't too good at it. But when the FBI arrested this leader down in Philadelphia, they came up with letters from my guy showing that he was a turncoat, a double agent."

The squad had a couple of offices, one for meetings, another where the undercovers would type their lengthy reports in triplicate each week. When the turncoat came to light, "we had to kibosh him, and we had to move out of that office real quick." He was allowed to resign from the NYPD—and became a cop in the Virgin Islands, Theologes reports in incredulous tones. But, in fact, most of the undercovers in Special Squad 3 did well for themselves.

Before joining the police, Jackie Godoy had worked in banking, an industry where he knew non-WASPS couldn't advance. Not only did the Police Department pay better than any job the BOSS undercovers had previously held—they got cash overtime in the field and expense money too. And later, prestige.

"In June of Sixty-six, I was on the job about eighteen months," says Godoy, whose undercover activities included teaching street Spanish to leftwing radicals at the Free School. "I got a phone call, 'Congratulations!' What? 'You've been promoted to third grade detective.' I said, How much more does it mean? 'So much.' Thank you!"

Three years later, another phone call: Congratulations, you've been promoted to second grade! "My basic concern—how much more in the goddamn pay check? Later on, I realized the prestige. Not then. When I got out in the field and played cops and robbers, I realized how nice it was and important it was. Not only being a detective, but being a second grade detective in less than five years."

Undercovers whose work prevented radicals from lobbing Molotov cocktails around the City or blowing up the Statue of Liberty were awarded the Medal of Honor. But mere good performance in this unit meant that the gold detective shield and promotion to grade could come a lot sooner than if you worked somewhere else in the department. Getting promoted twice while you were still in the unit was a big push. Several of the undercovers retired as first grade detectives. A couple of others are still with the Police Department as ranking bosses—lieutenant or better.

Blacks and Hispanics joined the NYPD and Special Squad 3 "to better themselves," says Ted Theologes. "We all did." But some of the unit's black undercovers say the treacherous, high-stress assignment may have stunted careers or personal growth.

As usual in the NYPD, the undercovers' promotions to third, second, and first grade detective were at the bosses' discretion—until a lawsuit established a mandatory promotion timetable unique in the department: third grade after two years, second after six, and first after ten. Yet unlike the protected civil service ranks of sergeant, lieutenant, and captain, a detective's gold shield is always on loan—and so is the prestige that comes with it.

For many of the undercovers, however, especially whites, detective status seems to have been reward enough and career enough. Some even stayed beyond the twenty-year mark when they could have retired fully vested. But a black undercover who advanced to the rank of lieutenant regrets that their undercover experience didn't encourage most of the blacks in the unit, who were college-educated, to become "chiefs instead of great Indians. They never saw the Police Department as an organization they would like to rise in."

Because the bosses didn't want the undercovers studying material that could make them think like or sound like cops, promotion exams were forbidden. When the ban was lifted, there still were bureaucratic hassles; of those who finally took the sergeant's test, few succeeded.

> At that time it was [Mayor] Lindsay's Silk Stocking District, the Seventeenth Precinct. People wondered how the hell did I get there. There were no blacks, and suddenly this detective was here. "Are you from IAD?" For months, nobody would speak to me.
>
> —Detective Leslie Hinds

When you came in from the cold and attended the Academy at last, your classmates, of course, had not yet earned *any* shield. Your gold shield was envied—even suspect. Where did you really come from? When you joined a squad, you could even be ostracized.

Psychological stresses affected every undercover, regardless of race or background. You contended with fear of discovery and fear of being attacked by unwitting police. But even more, if you were married, and most were, the anxiety about the effects on your wife and kids of what you were doing kept your stress level booming.

When you surfaced, you needed "some sort of a psychological debriefing to bring you back to the real world," says former undercover Leslie Hinds, and nobody disagrees. But " 'stress' was not invented yet in the Police Department," says Steve Weiner, who was asked years later to critique the unit he had served.

Ted Theologes and his partner counseled by instinct and best intentions. "You had to be like a priest and comfort them, a brother, a father, whatever they needed. They went through a lot," Theologes says.

I wouldn't want to see another guy go through what I did. I really wouldn't. Maybe because I feel that they may not have my tolerance, so to speak. I wouldn't want to see one of the guys go through what I did mainly because of the pressure, the stress, and nine times out of ten, the nightmares. Because you do this, and you're gonna have nightmares.

The guys that are out there now doing UC work in drugs, they're gonna have bad dreams forever. Especially if they get involved in real deep cover. They're gonna have bad dreams forever. I think it's the tension and the danger. The acting part—I guess we all got a little bit of ham in us. But the tension and the danger—what you put your family through.

You don't want to show fear, but you're afraid. You even try to say, Well, I ain't afraid for myself. But you're afraid for yourself; you're afraid for your family. You've gotta come out looking over your shoulder. Certain places you don't go that you would like to go. The bad guys hang here and somebody might recognize you. It gets to be a little touchy.

—Detective Gene Roberts

Ted Theologes's partner was Detective First Grade Anthony T. Ulasewicz, later of Watergate fame. "They were like our handlers," says Jackie Godoy. "These are the guys that guided us, that instructed us, that got us out of jams such as being arrested on demonstrations. They were our guardian angels, shadows, followers, godfathers, whatever you want to call 'em. Their primary concern, naturally, was everybody's safety. They would never put you in an unsafe situation unless you were properly covered and coached."

Detective Gene Roberts, who eventually became known for his undercover role with Malcolm X and later with the Black Panthers, says he and the Watergate figure-to-be "got to be very good friends. Tony was the best first-grade detective in New York."

Not a few of the "godsons" of Tony U., as they called him, became respected first graders themselves. Steve Weiner, for instance, had taken the police test at his father's urging but didn't know what he wanted to do.

"It was 1969. Beatles. Drugs. Long hair. Everything was changing. Also at this time, a large antiwar movement was just starting to take a foothold. I get a phone call from Lieutenant Mulligan, and he tells me that he has a special unit—and he says, would I be interested?

"The white movement at that time was predominantly Jewish; it was predominantly college-educated and wealthy. I fit two out of the three. And most important, I didn't look like a cop."

In 1969 and 1970, Weiner infiltrated the Crazies, the Yippies, and ended up "in a cell of the Weathermen. It was like being Walter Mitty. It was living a double life. And I was actually living and seeing history unfold. I wasn't predisposed to like these people or not like these people. I didn't know anything about the Police Department, so I didn't think like a cop. I was just there, like a camera."

He was there when the Weathermen talked about killing for their ideals. They considered targeting two activists who had been unmasked as undercover cops, Weiner says.

He and Jackie Godoy both went with the movement to Chicago for the 1968 Democratic Convention. "We got up to Evanston," Godoy recalls. "We set up our little place to stay and we were commuting revolutionaries. We'd jump in our station wagons every day and head down the Drive along the lake. Park our cars and go and do our thing. I think I'm in Abbie Hoffman's book [Steal This Book]—there's a picture of me up there in the demonstrations.

"Some of the demonstrators from the New York City area—the Mark Rudds, Students for a Democratic Society group—were very radical. One of the suggestions from the SDS group was the taking over of gas stations and unleashing the fuel into the sewer system underneath the Cow Palace, where the convention was being held, and then setting a match to it, which would have created quite a blast, to say the least.

"One of the BOSS guys had followed us out there, and he had to stay for that whole week, sitting in the hotel room waiting for a phone call if we either got jammed up or we came across any information. I passed this thing along as fast as I could. I feel that's why the police acted the way they did—because they knew something like this was planned, which never came out in the press. Never been published."

Godoy had first interviewed with BOSS in the early sixties. They grilled the Cuban-educated applicant who had played ball with Raoul Castro about his feelings for Fidel. When the handlers were satisfied that he'd be loyal to his job, they were pleased. His Cuban connection could easily pave his way to leftist circles. Or maybe the NYPD would use him to infiltrate the anti-Castro right.

Too old at nearly twenty-eight to infiltrate younger groups, "especially after Jerry Rubin or Abbie Hoffman—one of those two nuts—said, Don't trust anybody over thirty," Godoy became a mainstay of Veterans and Reservists Against the War in Vietnam. The seven-year veteran of the Army and the Army Reserves celebrated "Stop the Draft Week" in March 1966 at a demonstration in Central Park. He burned his honorable discharge (a convincing copy).

"As any good Boy Scout knows," Godoy was quoted in the *Times*, "an American flag must be burned whenever it becomes dirty or unserviceable. Our actions in Vietnam have made my honorable discharge paper dirty and unserviceable. It must be burned."

Bill Clark, now a detective first grade with Queens Homicide, was recruited for BOSS and expected to find himself with a bunch of antiwar college kids. He ended up in the White Panthers, support group for the Black Panthers, hobnobbing with Zayd Shakur (Tom Coston), a minister for the Black Panthers party. "The Panthers later went into the Black Liberation Army. Shakur was killed when Joanne Chesimard killed the state trooper on the Jersey Turnpike."

Outside the 1970 trial of the Panther 21 in State Supreme Court, Manhattan, undercovers Weiner and Godoy joined the Crazies' uproar—while inside, three black BOSS undercovers who had infiltrated the Panthers took the stand. The Black Panthers were violent conspirators, testified Gene Roberts, Ralph White, and Carlos Ashwood.

Their testimony went on for months, detailing planned precinct bombings and department store bombings. The defense derided the outcome—little damage, few injuries. The Panthers must be nothing but pussycats meowing about killing cops. The jury,

like the demonstrators outside the courthouse, supported Lu-
mumba, Shakur, et al. Not guilty.

Only as the seventies wore on, when the Black Panthers turned
Black Liberation soldiers, would the toll of police officers maimed
and dead lend tragic weight, after all, to the testimony of the black
undercovers in 1970.

———

"We want you to infiltrate Malcolm's group," Gene Roberts remembers the bosses eventually telling him. "No problem," would have
been the reply most characteristic of the soft-spoken former sailor
with the light-coffee complexion. Ten to one he said exactly that.
When he first went undercover, he had just got married, his wife
was pregnant.

Malcolm X was mostly a name to Gene Roberts, and the Muslim
leader was away on his pilgrimage to Mecca when Roberts got to
know the organization. The group learned about his Navy training
in both martial arts and first aid. Soon they had themselves a self-
defense teacher and a medical officer. No problem.

Once Malcolm returned, Roberts became one of his "security
people," which is how the two came to be photographed together
in the Audubon Ballroom on February 21, 1965. The stark image
catches Malcolm's bloody form on the Ballroom stage, Roberts on
his knees, bent over giving mouth-to-mouth respiration.

In the bedlam of the assassination, Roberts had knocked down
one of the assailants. He had tried to keep Malcolm alive, and
afterward, in the black activist universe, doors opened readily. He
"bounced around various other groups—Progressive Labor Party,
Mobilization for Youth. They would always say, 'That's the guy
that gave Malcolm mouth-to-mouth.' "

He was a hero—until the Panther 21 trial revealed he was a
cop. In 1989 Malcolm's wife, Betty Shabazz, told a Newsday
reporter Roberts "helped murder" the minister.

It was through Black Panther Charles Kenyatta, a former aide to
Malcolm, that Roberts got hooked up with the Black Panther Party.
"The next thing I know, I'm under for about five, six years."

He stayed under until the Panthers' arrest and his own arrest,
staged for their benefit. BOSS sent Roberts and his family out of

town for a period of weeks. When he came back, he did his first stint in a squad room—the BOSS office.

### Detective Gene Roberts:
### Faces

We had photo files of most of the Party members. I'm in the office goin' through pictures, familiarizing myself with faces that I hadn't seen in a while, and I run across pictures of a couple people from Oakland.

One night my godfather was at the house, and we get this knock on the door. I look out, then I open the door and this guy asked for a Carl Russell.

As soon as he said "Carl Russell," it struck me, because that was *his* name. The guy in the picture and the guy at the door were the same. So I said, No, no, no, I think you got the wrong number, and closed the door. I didn't say anything to my wife because I didn't want her to get upset, but I told my godfather, Hey, I know this guy. This guy is an enforcer from Oakland.

When I closed the door, I looked through the peephole. He walked away. He looked back at the apartment and then he got on the elevator and left. My godfather said, "You gonna be all right?" I said, Yeah, I'll be fine. No problem.

### Detective Gene Roberts:
### Deep Cover

You gotta put yourself into it. My parents got afraid because they thought I had flipped over and really had become what I was portraying. Because I kept an attitude. I played the role when I was working and I kept a facsimile of the role when I was home so I wouldn't slip.

Couple of times they asked me, "Did you change?" I said, No, I'm still me, but I'm just trying to stay alive. So if you hear me come out of my mouth with something, don't get upset. Like I said, I'm just trying to stay alive. I used to tell 'em, I got a little girl that likes to see her daddy come home. And that was my attitude. Tried to keep my game face on.

I did it by being me for one and being them for two, and trying to blend the two together. Trying to keep my personal feelings away from my job feelings and my job feelings away from my personal feelings. Because I knew that if I slipped and said the wrong thing at the wrong time, I was goin' to go. All of them were armed.

I came on the job in sixty-four, didn't start carrying a gun until latter part of sixty-eight. I told my supervisors, Things are getting tight. They want everybody to be armed. What am I gonna do? "Don't worry about it. We'll give you one, and it'll be all right." I told Party members that my brother-in-law brought the .38 from Texas.

Leslie Hinds is an attorney in general practice today, concentrating in civil law. At twenty-seven, he was "Gene's replacement in the organization that he left when he went with Malcolm." He won't name that organization today because, he says, "they're still alive and well." Back then he was a Freshman, as it were, and getting educated fast.

Tapped by BOSS after writing a top-drawer police test, Hinds was then a mix of innocence and experience. True, he had four years in the Air Force behind him, but it happened that he enlisted after Korea, got out before Vietnam, and never left the U.S. Checking out the NYPD brass at demonstrations, the rangy six-feet-one-and-a-half recruit knew right away by their rank insignias who was a "major" and who was a "colonel" and who a "general."

Why would such an easygoing type of fellow join the police force, anyway? He had a family, and ambitions to become something. "I did it for sheer economic reasons, I was never into that mode of 'macho man.' " He was also "totally apolitical"—perfect for BOSS's undercover unit.

Ironically, perhaps, "it was only thanks to the Police Department that I became politicized. I was like a sponge and I had an opportunity to take in both sides and evaluate." Like so many in the unit, he traveled undercover far beyond the city limits and "saw so many things." For instance, the Chicago police: "I knew what their attitude was.

"On a subsequent visit to Chicago, I met Fred Hampton. Later, Fred Hampton and many people in an apartment he was in were killed by the Chicago police. We made a visit to the apartment, this particular group I was with, including prominent attorneys, and we did our own investigation."

Leslie Hinds saw "innumerable bullet holes through the wall, like a 'Bury My Heart at Wounded Knee' kind of scene." And that disturbed him, that among other things. For instance, the Vietnam War issue. "There were two sides of that. The side that the magazines and the newspapers would let us see, as opposed to the other side that was smuggled out—that you would see through the groups I was infiltrating. I said, something's definitely wrong."

In the course of his evaluation, "I made my own decision. I didn't believe what the department was doing was correct. As far as politics, as far as Vietnam, as far as from A to Z! So I said, I don't want to be a part of this."

The bosses gave him "a long vacation to think it over, and what I did during this vacation, I drove cross country. I took a month and a half, two months, to see the country, and when I came back, I was firm in my belief. I said, You're wrong—and I got out from undercover."

Once he was assigned to the squad room, a much-loved top boss, the fatherly Inspector William Knapp, invited him to sit down. "He brought me in his office, we talked, and he thanked me. And I said, *Wow*. He said, 'I understand what the heck you're going through, I really do.' " But Bill Knapp seemed to be the only one. The just-surfaced undercover felt "totally screwed up. I didn't know whether I was coming or going, I really didn't."

He still regrets the lack of some competent help, back then, in easing his psychological reentry. Otherwise, despite mistreatment by uncomprehending Police Academy instructors, "I have no complaints against the Police Department. I wasn't forced to do anything. When I asked to stop, I was allowed to stop. And then a contract was honored: twenty dollars an hour. . . ."

Detective Hinds gave the job twenty years, one month, and nineteen days. He worked Bronx Nightwatch from midnight to eight for years to finish law school. But it's safe to say he never had a learning experience to rival the time undercover.

### Detective Leslie Hinds:
### Fuck the Trucks

I don't remember the year, but I was with the National Committee to Combat Fascism, the NCCF. We were going to a "Fuck the Trucks Demonstration" against *The New York Times* for their "yellow journalism." We were gonna do something to the trucks and they wouldn't be able to deliver the papers.

I was just supposed to be counting leaflets. We had tons of leaflets prepared, and I was given a shopping bag to carry them. Never looked in the bag. When we got to the demonstration, there were a lot of police officers and they searched my bag. In the bag was a smoke bomb. It was in a canister, say about six inches tall by maybe five inches in diameter, olive green.

"Oh, my God, he's got a bomb!" Needless to say, they ferret me away into the back of a truck, where I was searched and interrogated.

The Police Department had just gotten a *retroactive* pay raise. We were not paid by check; we were given cash—I had a lot of money on me. I was accused of being paid for attending these demonstrations. And I had the bomb, so I was a mass bomber.

I was bounced off the wall of the back of this truck and called all kinds of names. It was in the winter; I was wearing a brown full-length leather jacket. I had a head cold, so I had Coricidins in my pocket. They said, "You're a junkie too!" I was arrested.

I couldn't say a thing about who I was; I just looked. . . . At that time, the expression was "pigs." Cops were pigs. I said, You know, you're acting like a pig.

*Bang!* They'd hit me again.

But you don't know what the hell's going on!

*BANG!*

The same night, Abbie Hoffman and the Yippies had climbed up on the clock at Times Square and they were turning the clock back—I don't know for what reason—and needless to say, that whole group—they were arrested, as well.

So there we were in the cell together at the Manhattan Tombs, and they looked at me—'cause by that time I had a couple of lumps and bruises—and they said, "This guy can't be a cop. They wouldn't do this to one of their own." I was totally in, totally accepted. "He's no cop!"

We were in the can there, and we were just laughing, joking, and saying this is the length to which the establishment will go for freedom of expression. I was getting an absolute education.

Abbie, he was good. He was very open, very friendly, very informative.

From the Tombs we were taken (I don't know if I've got it in the right order) to the First Precinct. That's where I was held. And then when I was visited by someone from BOSSI—"You know, we really can't get you outta here." But wait a minute, I said, this wasn't part of the deal that I gotta spend the night in the can. I was fingerprinted and the whole bit.

We were represented by Arthur Turco. Arthur Turco subsequently got involved with the Panthers, and it just started to balloon—I just started to get more and more involved. I never saw Abbie again. Shortly after that, Abbie got into some really heavy stuff and he went deep under. Disappeared from the scene.

The only rallies a black Richmond, Virginia, high school kid went to in the mid fifties were pep rallies to spur the teams from the two fiercely competitive black high schools. Everybody was so caught up in the rivalry that nobody took time out to try and integrate the white schools. Softball, hardball, volleyball, you-name-it, were big in Richmond. Nobody ever heard of hitting the ball with a broom handle—except Ed Howlette, who spent summers up North with his mother's twin sister in Bedford-Stuyvesant, Brooklyn, where stickball is the game.

Howlette liked New York and looked forward to going back there to work and to continue his education when he got out of the Air Force. Little did he imagine that come 1965, he'd be a regular at anti-Vietnam War rallies in Washington Square, in South Jamaica, in Harlem, and all around the town. From a corner soapbox in Harlem, South Richmond seemed a world away—the orator's wild exhortations almost a foreign tongue.

Little did he think that within a couple of years, flyers head-lined "Enemy of the Black People," displaying his photo, would be circulated through the country.

The new undercover got involved in a community issue in Queens: the demeaning mural in the Jamaica Savings Bank that featured black "Banjo Billy" sitting on a log—replete with a big chunk of watermelon. Ed Lee joined the Black Brotherhood Improvement Association protests that sped the departure of Banjo Billy from the bank.

Why all the cloak-and-dagger stuff to insinuate yourself into such a benign cause? You never knew where it might lead, whom you'd run into. But the recruit from Richmond was still mostly going through the motions; his "awakening," he says, was yet to come.

He was staying with his aunt, as he had during those high school summers, and with his cousin. They puzzled over his nightly comings and goings, always wearing a black leather jacket—never a police uniform, even though they had seen his name listed in *The Chief* as having passed the test and they knew his pay came from the Police Department.

Not all the rallies were about murals. Some speakers "were

talking about how bad the police were, how to attack the police . . . 'Kiss 'em with a razor blade.' A lot of violence directed at the police."

Howlette had one other relative in the City, a teacher who lived in Jamaica. "He saw me at one of the rallies—worked in the area and he happened to see me there. Our eyes met, he looked—kind of a frown—and walked away. He contacted my aunt, and then we had my superior officers let him know why it was that I was participating in that kind of thing.

"All this militancy was very, very new to me. I hadn't even been exposed in the South to Malcolm X. I had just begun to hear about him and listen to his speeches when I came to New York." Never having had any problems himself with the police in the South, "that whole militant stance that was anti-police, I really didn't identify with."

He had heard a lot of stories about the way police treated minorities, but "while I was serving in an undercover capacity, I have to say, I really didn't see it going on. Maybe I was at different rallies."

Once, in lower Manhattan, the Mounted Unit was "trying to get the crowd to back up, and their horses went through quite a few people. I said to myself, somebody had to be hurt here—but I didn't really see anyone hurt, because I was too busy trying to get out of the way myself.

"I didn't see the kinds of abuse they were talking about and I couldn't understand why somebody would just want to direct a lot of violence at the police."

But soon, having been fully "awakened" to his role by Herman Ferguson and the Revolutionary Action Movement . . . by attending meetings of the Black Panthers and Malcolm's Organization of Afro-American Unity . . . Edward Lee was "taking Akido right along with the others in RAM. And this was all preparing us to deal with the cops out on the street. . . ."

### Detective Second Grade Edward Howlette:
### Terror Cell

I had been invited to a secret meeting at the home of a Herman Ferguson, who told me it was about the Revolutionary Action Movement. And it was like an awakening for me, because I hadn't known what it was going to involve. We had constant meetings after that, and I saw where we were going and what we were doing.

They were talking about revolution. I think they were using the climate of the country—the rioting in Watts, in New York; down in Bed-Stuy and up in Harlem, they had burned up a lot—and they felt that if this could be organized in some fashion, then they had what they would need for revolution.

RAM was an offshoot of a militant organization that I think really originated in the South with Robert Williams and a young lady named May Mallory. They kidnapped a white couple down there at the time they had the organization going, and then they fled the country. (Williams went to Cuba and Red China and after fifteen or twenty years eased back in. I don't know if he'd been working for the CIA or what during that time. . . .) The group I was in looked to him as though he was the leader.

Down the road we had classes on how to make Molotov cocktails, Molotov cocktail launchers. They organized a rifle club legitimately within the NRA, but the purpose was to get free guns and ammunition. You could get carbine rifles for a certain number of people. We got them and we got free ammunition.

I was very active. I was in charge of the Junior Rifle Club—high up in the organization. They didn't suspect me at all because I had just come out of the military.

We networked with another branch in Philadelphia. There seemed to be a connection with the ones in California, but I don't know that for a fact. I know there was a connection with the one in Philadelphia, because I met with the leader.

To avoid detection, we were meeting in the basement of a store where a compressor was going. We actually had a blackboard we were using to draw pictures of various things we were talking about doing. We had a map that was used to point out where the Fire Department control towers were and where we would locate stashes of things we would need, should we be successful in fomenting a revolution. I had to photograph this map with a Minox camera.

We printed leaflets down there, with the title *Total Resistance*, about what the community had to do in order to resist the police. When something happened—for instance if South Jamaica were to go—if somebody were to start some form of violence, then you would saturate the area with *How to Make Molotov Cocktails*, to keep the violence going. You would use young people to distribute; juveniles wouldn't be subject to criminal penalties.

They formed cells within the group so everybody knew what everybody else was doing. A terror cell was comprised of myself and Ferguson and Arthur Harris, who was tried and convicted, fled, and is still out of the country. We began to talk about doing something to make more moderate blacks understand what we were about and what the black power concept was about.

People like Whitney Young, James Farmer, and a number of others signed a manifesto against black power. This incensed the RAM because they felt that these people should be following the same doctrines. They said what we should do is assassinate a couple of them and leave evidence that it was done *by blacks* so that moderates would understand—either get on board or that's what's going to happen to them. We were given direction primarily by Ferguson to case Whitney Young's house.

Ferguson had another gentleman go down to Atlanta to get handguns. I had a .25; Harris would've had a .25; Ferguson had a .38. He kept the bigger caliber for himself. We practiced with the handguns in the New York State Armory, when we were supposed to be practicing as members of the rifle club.

We would get there early and go into another room and practice with the handguns before the other members arrived. This went on until we had cased the house to know which routes Whitney Young would be taking to and from.

Donald Duncan, an undercover who had gotten into the Panthers, came to a couple of meetings that we had. So did another undercover. It happened that all three of us were at the same meeting, and where Donald and I might have reported one thing, the other undercover reported something else.

Ferguson told me he knew this other guy was in fact a cop and that he was working for *them*. I reported this back; they checked into it, and he was eventually dismissed from the Police Department. Which is just as well, because Ferguson was talking about the fact that he might have to be killed.

When we were shooting in the armory, the others knew they were not to go into a particular room. Who burst in one time when Ferguson was practicing with his gun but that other undercover. So Ferguson had some questions as to whether he was working with us or against us. Which was good as far as I was concerned, because it took any attention away from what I was doing.

The cell decided that we wouldn't make a scheduled date for the assassination—so it wouldn't leak to the police. Ferguson would call us one day and say he's attending an affair at such and such, then we would know that's when we were supposed to go and do it. He probably would've called up Harris and me and told us we had to go do it. I think Ferguson would've removed himself from the scene, 'cause he was an assistant principal, he was our leader. He doesn't take the sword and run out with the troops, he gets carried on the troops' shoulders.

My wife became concerned as the plot thickened. When we got the handguns, she was concerned. "What are you gonna do if you wind up getting the call and you're not able to get your superior officers—?" Of course, they had told me if I got into a situation where I couldn't contact them and a deal was going down, I had to do everything I could to prevent it. Go, but prevent it. Fortunately it didn't happen.

She knew about the Minox and that there were times when I had to wear a Minifon recorder, which had a red light that went on when the tape ran out. One night when we were talking about this plot with several other people, I wore the Minifon. It was winter— I wore it under my sweater, and my coat, which I had to take off.

After the meetings, I would have to take a ride up three stops on the Jamaica el to meet the officer who took the Minifon off. This time he realized that there was a short tape in there and that light would have been on while I was in the meeting. Just fortunate nobody had seen it. After that, I used a device that the CIA had furnished—a little smaller than a cigarette pack. It transmitted up to five blocks away—I didn't have the slightest idea who was listening.

We were on the verge of doing the plan, but they were indicted before we could actually put it into operation. After we had gotten the guns, I testified before the grand jury. Twenty-two of them were picked up who were involved. The case went to trial in 1967. We introduced the tapes. . . . Ferguson and Harris were convicted of conspiracy to commit murder, as well as some other charges.

Then several years later when a couple of the others came up on misdemeanor charges, one went to trial. The defense was trying to say that what the RAM had been doing was holding ''lectures on current events,'' or something. But the tapes made it very clear that they weren't discussing current events. He was convicted, so then the others took pleas.

## Partners & Bosses

**Detective Leslie Hinds:** At each of these groups' meetings, they would always open it up, whoever was moderating the meeting, by saying, ''Okay, for all of you people who are FBI, CIA, military intelligence, whatever.'' And then we all just sort of looked at each other.

But a large percentage of those people attending were actually operatives. So what's funny was that if they were asked for contributions, it was the state police, the state, the city, and the federal government who were actually funding these activist groups.

Ralph White and I, we talked about that later. He says, ''I don't know if you made me or what,'' and I said, I don't know if you made me or what.

# 7

# SHOOTOUTS AND BAD SCARES

---

### Detective George Rivera:
### The Worst That'll Happen

"Hey, how you been, man?" This and that. *Blah, blah.* "Okay, so you want the hundred and twenty-five grams, right?" Well, I wanna talk about that. I've gotta first see what you got before I put that much money on the table. "No problem." So he says, "You're a cop, right?"

What?

He says, "You're a cop." I say, What are you, fucking stupid? You gonna talk like that I'm gettin' the fuck outta here and we'll come back another day. Or I'll send somebody else over here—you deal with this other guy that sent me down. He says, "No, no. Calm down. Don't worry about it. . . ."

George Rivera trained and got his shield in Narcotics, the largest training unit for New York City detectives. After nearly two years learning the job, he stayed on as a detective because drugs turned out to be the reason Rivera joined the police force in the first place: "I grew up in the South Bronx, and I saw stuff. I saw ninety-eight percent of the friends I grew up with die or ruin their lives because of drugs. As soon as I became a cop, I said, Well, this is what I'm gonna do."

For NYPD cops, the Narcotics Division of the Organized Crime

Control Bureau (OCCB) is a much-used stepping-stone—many times, a treacherous one. Your years on patrol and training in Narcotics units are likely to subject you to more danger than the rest of a career spent in the Detective Bureau. About ten percent of NYPD cops shot or wounded by bad guys in the last ten years have been Narcotics officers; three of six officers fatally shot in 1988 were narcs. Especially in Narcotics, the "career path" leading to the gold shield can be slippery with blood.

Two cops met their deaths on New York streets in 1991, and narrow escapes were rife; 430 other cops endured assaults, and 25 of them sustained wounds. Once through their training, detectives are less vulnerable to bad scares—except Narcotics detectives like George Rivera and Emma Principe, awarded the Combat Cross, the department's second highest honor, after their encounter with death in a drug spot.

The paradox of Narcotics undercover work is that though there's never any doubt you've got an appointment with some kind of desperado, there's just no foolproof way to prepare; risk management is at best a tricky business. The first dealer who searched Rivera—"tossed" is the New York City expression—taught the cop to approach undercover assignments unarmed.

I always did everything by myself, and I always did everything without a gun, 'cause I had a bad experience in the Lower East Side when I first started back in 1983. They had tossed me. They smacked me around—"Okay, get outta here." So I figured, if ever I got caught again, I'm not gonna get caught with anything that says police. This way, I could get out; the worst that'll happen, they'll probably kick my ass.

But one cool day, a leather jacket kind of day in November of 1987, at 190th Street between St. Nicholas and Wadsworth, Rivera went against his established habit.

This time they want someone else to go with me, a female. Now, I was always under the impression that a junky or dealer's never gonna take his girl. It's not a place where you take your girl for a date. But if I'm gonna go with somebody, I told them I'm gonna go with Emma. 'Cause I know what Emma's made of, and I thought she could handle herself in any type of situation that comes up. I'm not gonna do anything with anybody other than someone I'm comfortable with.

I tell her, You got a gun on you? "Yeah." I say I never carry a gun, but she says, "Well, I take my gun." Yeah, well, you're a female. Then I said, oh, let me take a gun. It's the first time I'm goin' someplace with somebody else. I'll just hide the gun in my jacket. I had a real heavy leather jacket. (By the time I got it back from the DA, it didn't fit me.) You wouldn't find a gun in it if you tried. Inside breast pocket.

You gotta picture this place. The door's down here, and it's a real long, narrow hallway. On the way down, we notice a guy getting a haircut, in a bathroom or something—two Dominicans, one guy cutting the other guy's hair. They're smiling like, Hi, how you doing?

In the living room back here, I'm sitting down and the guy's standing up, facing me. There's four people in the apartment at this time. There's a guy sitting over here to my right on the same sofa I'm sitting on; they're watching TV. *Eyewitness News* or something. Emma's sitting on the arm of a chair. She's just sitting there, like nothin'—

Guy says, "What kind of car you got?" I got a Chevy—plumb cherry, like a purple-colored car. "Yeah? Where is it?" In the front of the building. "Okay, wait right here a minute." So he goes into a back room, looks out the window, and he comes in with a smile. Right there, I already knew—we're fucked. He's got like this smirk on his face, this sinister smile.

Later on that night I told Emma, You know, when that motherfucker came out of the room, I knew something was gonna happen. She says, "You know, I was just gonna tell you the same thing—"

Anyway, he comes down, he says, "You're a fucking cop." Whaddaya mean, I'm a fucking cop? What's your fucking problem with "cops"? You want to talk to me? Talk to me. If you don't wanna fucking talk to me, we'll do it somewhere else. I'm not here for no bullshit. I got the fucking money. You got something—I'll give you the fucking money. Otherwise, we'll go. He says, "Calm down. Hold up a minute."

He goes to the back, comes back again. He says, "Yeah, come with me." Me and Emma get up. We're gonna get thrown out of the apartment. But he says to her, "No, you sit down. Stay there." So I get up; I go to the back. Get past the bathroom where I saw the guy getting the haircut—they're no longer there. I don't know where the fuck they're at. I got a bad taste in my mouth already. I don't know what the fuck's going on with this guy.

He's tellin' me, "Yeah, you got the one-twenty-five? I got it for you. No problem." This and that. He's trying to talk to me while I'm like trying to take the whole scene in at the same time.

I get into the room. He goes in before me, and as soon as I walk in the room, a guy grabs me by my neck and puts something on my back. And the guy in the front tells him, "Shoot him, he's a fucking cop." The guy in the back is doin' something. "Oh, shit"—

he's talking Spanish—"Shit, the fucking thing don't work. *It don't work, it don't work, it don't work.*"

The other guy tries to grab me from the front, so I push him like that, and I try to elbow the guy behind me, and I get to my gun. I got the gun on the guy in front of me, ready to fire away, and he grabs it, and it starts to be one of these things.

I remember from the Academy to hold your finger behind the trigger of the revolver and to try to hold the barrel as hard as you can. I'm trying, and I get cut up over here with it. I'm tryin' to hold it and tryin' to fight this guy. As soon as the guy grabs it, the other one says, "Shoot him, he's a cop."

I scream out, Emma! Emma! They're gonna kill me. (And I'm screaming so that if someone in the building—which is probably the stupidest thing. Nobody's gonna come down and help. But if somebody just calls the police or somethin'—) Screaming at the top of my lungs. I'm a cop! Emma, they're gonna shoot me! Get the fuck out!

All of a sudden I hear in the living room, *Boom, boom.* I'm thinking now, Oh, shit, they fuckin' shot her. 'Cause I know there's two guys in the room with me, there was one guy in there, and I know there was another guy in that apartment getting the haircut. And I'm saying, They fucking killed her. I don't hear her.

Now I'm screaming—Emma! just to see if she fucking answers me. I'm sayin' to myself, Oh, shit. The guy behind me is screamin' to the guy in front of me—they're brothers, which I don't find out till after the fact. And he's like, "It don't fuckin' work!" And the guy in front, "Grab him! Grab him! Hold him! He got a gun!" Back and forth.

Finally, all of a sudden, *BOOM.* I don't feel the guy in the back behind me no more. It's weird because this whole thing takes—it can't be more than twenty seconds.

He goes down. I fall back, but I get free. I tell the guy, Stop. Hold it right there, motherfucker. The guy keeps coming. I don't know why I didn't shoot this fuckin' guy at that point, but he don't have no gun, and I'm thinkin', if I shoot him, I'm gonna go to jail for this fuckin' scumbag.

The guy gets behind me, now he has the gun. At that point, he jumps me. I still have my gun. We're wrestling on the ground. Then I see Emma.

She's like screaming, "Get off him! Get off my brother!" Something like that. I'm fighting the guy. Finally, I turn around. I get him around. I think I did shoot him when we were going down. So now he's on the floor.

I said, Emma, go call 911. Why the hell I did that I don't know. I figured, it's better— call 911. *There's a shooting in there, with cops.* This way, if somebody did call, the cops come busting through that door, we don't get shot. We're in civilian clothes. I didn't look nothin' like a cop, and Emma, she don't look nothing like a cop.

She's walking out of the room. I'm not looking at her; I'm looking at the guy. The guy maneuvers himself on the ground. I'm telling him, Stay the fuck there. Don't move!

He's tryin' to reach the gun behind me. I thought he was shot. I didn't find out till later that he was never shot. But he's playing dead, facedown with his hands under his chest. And I'm looking at him, and I'm saying then, jeez, the fuckin' guy's shot, but then I don't see blood on the back, and I'm thinking TV—you get shot in the front, you gotta have blood in the back. But it's not necessarily so.

I'm keeping an eye on him and I'm trying to keep an eye on the first fuckin' guy. This guy's not moving at all, so he's gotta be fucking shot. Finally I see him trying to grab something. I tell him, Don't move! again. *BOOM.* I shoot him one more time.

This situation's out of control. Emma! Emma! Get the fuck out. I'm watching them 'cause the guy's still moving. I open the front door of the apartment. Run, run, run!

As soon as I open the door, there's this woman. She must have been a fuckin' ghost, because I never seen her again. This woman was in a blue housecoat or bathrobe or something. I opened the door so fast that she was still like trying to listen at the door. I don't know how the hell I didn't shoot that lady, but I guess that was my training. I don't even remember her getting out of the way, but I remember both of us going down, and the only other thing I remember was jumping the whole damn flight of stairs down. Getting downstairs and getting out of the building, and walking along the edge of the building because we knew that he had a window facing the front, because he went to look at the car.

Get to the corner. This is like five in the evening. Not a fucking cop to be found, like everybody always says. It's the truth. No radio cars. Maybe that was the best thing, because we woulda got killed. We both got guns in our hands; we're runnin' down the street. You're not realizing this. You just go through what happened in the apartment, you get to the street, you got your gun in your hand, you're looking for a pay phone that works. None of the phones work.

Guys are comin' up to you, "Hey, man, what's the matter with you?" Get the fuck away from me.

Found the backup team. Tell 'em, look—The shooting—He says, "What? What the fuck happened?" By the time we got to the building with the backup, we had the Emergency Service truck there, precinct guys, Mounted, just about everybody. That was real fast. It amazed me. We went maybe two blocks to the backup team, and as soon as we got back there, everybody was there already. The last thing I remember telling 'em, Look, man, they got guns.

When the guys went in, we went to the hospital. Had the nurse checking us out, that type of thing. Somebody had said, "You want a cup of coffee or something?" The nurse said, "What are you nuts? You give these guys coffee, they'll get a stroke." 'Cause the blood pressure was so high, and everything.

They found out from the brother, the guy that played dead, that they had new guns—

automatics. What saved us, they loaded them up okay, but they didn't know you had to chamber the round. They just put the clip in and they thought it was gonna work. Thank God they were that stupid.

They wind up sending the robot in to look for these guys. Sergeant Galligan was our sergeant; he goes next door. Like I thought: these guys had an apartment next door where the family lived, and this was their dealing apartment. There's a guy coming out with this jacket and this big bulge at the shoulder.

Sergeant Galligan grabbed the guy, and he was screaming with pain. What the hell is that? He opens the jacket, sees a towel with blood. Goes into the family apartment; in the back he finds the guy that was playing dead. They had one other guy that got out who they never identified. They found some guy in the park with a bullet hole in his head; they figure it might have been him.

Emma shot one in the shoulder; the other guy played dead. And then the fourth guy, who's the guy that they think died in the park, but nobody knows for sure—he's an unknown. Open case.

They only recovered the one gun that Emma brought out of the apartment, the gun they tried to use on her. They never got the other guns. But you had to take into consideration that when we left that apartment, and when they finally got back in, there was only one guy—the dead guy on the floor. So whatever guns were there went out the window with the other guys.

I told the DA, Look, man, when I pulled the gun, my jacket ripped on the pocket. He says, "Oh, yeah? Yeah? Let me see the jacket." I just happened to have the jacket that day, so I showed him. "Mind if we take the jacket for court and we'll give it right back to you?" From the struggle in the apartment, my arm was rubbing up against the wall; the jacket had some paint on the elbow from the wall there. I guess they wanted to match the paint and all this psychotic stuff. It took me almost four years to get the jacket back. I figured somebody in the property clerk's walking around with my jacket. I get it back, it didn't fit. What happened here, man? I outgrew it.

One guy copped to five, I think it was, or some retarded sentence like that. He probably did like two years, I don't know. The last guy—after about a year or something, they get to a plea bargain or some crap—he winds up doing two years and he's out. If the guy that got shot didn't die, what would he have gotten? Maybe another two years? Five years?

If I would've got killed, the fucking guys would've got away probably. Or they're gonna get a life sentence and do five years. They're gonna be out—I'm gonna be in the ground. You walk into this job with that knowledge and you can't complain about it. 'Cause when you go, how you gonna complain anyway? Can't lodge a complaint, right? You're gone. Out of the picture.

"I certainly think the fellas on patrol have a more dangerous job in the sense that they don't know what they are going to. Most of the time when we're going someplace—we know," says a detective from Manhattan's busy Midtown North Precinct. "So, mostly we are going somewhat prepared. But sometimes someone who you think is just gonna be a witness becomes very, very hostile. You just don't know the background of the person; that's where there is a potential for violence. Also, when we're riding around, we have a radio. Many times we will respond to a scene . . ."

*Reflexes.* You're a detective in a business suit and a trench coat, and now what you do is play head games with your perps and witnesses and write ironclad DD5s. Right, but what are all those detectives' business suits doing in gym lockers? You work out to maintain your strength and, hopefully, the speed of your street-patrol physical reflexes.

Detective Lieutenant Dan Kelly spent most of his thirty-eight-and-a-half-year NYPD career as a detective or detective supervisor. Though Kelly wore a uniform for only six-and-a-half years, he was the son of a patrol veteran who "put twenty-eight years on," the son says. Maybe Kelly was born with his dad's cop reflexes and never lost them. Meanwhile, he developed a detective's *mental* reflexes, the ability not merely to observe, but to zoom in, like a telephoto lens, on the essentials.

For Kelly, a detective lieutenant since 1968 and CO of the Queens Homicide Task Force since 1978, the year 1981 was a dramatic one. April was the cruelest month: on the sixteenth, Queens officers John Scarangella and Richard Rainey stopped a van they believed was connected to a burglary pattern—only to be trapped in a deadly firestorm by Black Liberation Army terrorists. Scarangella was mortally wounded, Rainey critically.

Kelly's Queens detectives and the Major Case Squad had tracked BLA soldier James Dixon York to South Carolina, where he was captured in the summer. York's partner, Anthony N. LaBorde, had also fled the City and the investigation was ongoing. Come fall, at a shopping mall in the northwestern suburb of Rockland County, New York, members of the BLA and the Weather Underground (the May 19 Coalition) killed again; this time a guard and two police officers in the course of an abortive $1.6 million Brink's armored truck holdup. The date was October 20.

Three days later at half past high noon, Queens Emergency Service officers John Russell and Alan Cochrane were eating lunch in their squad room. While they ate and chatted, only a few minutes and less than a mile from the day's shock climax, they monitored the police radio.

Both officers loved working the elite NYPD unit, famous for spectacular rescues as well as for what in other cities are called SWAT assignments. Little did they imagine that their days in Truck 10 were numbered. Suddenly the partners heard a Queens detective car radio for help: the detectives had reason to believe they were chasing suspects in that recent upstate armored car holdup. Russell and Cochrane had little idea as they ditched lunch and rushed to respond that this was the job that would land them in the Detective Bureau. (Cochrane would retire with second grade; Russell eventually became the boss of a Queens precinct squad.)

A number of the other best reflexes in Queens also sped toward the chase as messages went out on a second police radio band and a third. Transcribed in this account are excerpts from the actual NYPD 911 recording—including transmissions in which, in the excitement, a dispatcher doubled the number of suspects.

Suspect Samuel Smith, aka Mtajuri Sandiata, carried with him into the encounter a flattened .38 slug—souvenir of the holdup at Nanuet Mall—and he was wearing the bruised bulletproof vest that apparently saved him from a fatal chest wound in the Rockland melee. But as the chase ended with Smith taking aim at homicide detective Irwin ("Jake") Jacobson—Smith's body armor proved irrelevant. Jake's rounds caught Smith in the face and neck. He died at the scene. Reporters learned from the Police Department that Smith had been charged with attempted murder in another police shooting more than a decade earlier.

For Nathaniel Burns, aka Sekou Odinga, who was linked to the 1979 escape of convicted cop-killer Joanne Chesimard from a New Jersey prison, a brilliant career as an escape artist ended in the junkyard where Jacobson and Smith had faced off. Burns/Odinga, the professional fugitive, hid under a truck and might in fact have had the jump on the pursuing officers. But then came the telltale click. The world's most dreaded or most welcome sound, depending which side of the gun you're on. *Misfire.*

An indicted member of the celebrity Panther 21, Burns/Odinga fled their famous 1971 trial. During the early morning police dragnet for the defendants, according to *Briar Patch*, Murray Kempton's book about the Panther case, the black militant jumped thirty-five feet to the ground from his Brooklyn window—and escaped to Algeria.

The Kempton account downgrades Burns/Odinga's and Donald Weems's 1969 sniper actions against Bronx cops as inept efforts on a shoestring, whose criminality was blown out of proportion by a vindictive DA. Twelve years after the Panther 21 acquittals, though, the upstate Brink's job not only succeeded as a cop-killer operation but also must have been quite adequately financed—police found $2,446 and a trunkful of ammunition in the gray Chrysler that carried Burns/Odinga to the end of the line.

Then-Police-Commissioner Robert McGuire gave Burns/Odinga an ironic vote of confidence in remarks honoring the apprehension by Lieutenant Kelly et al. "But for the grace of God and a jammed gun—" *Newsday* quoted McGuire, "we may have been attending funerals instead of award ceremonies."

Testifying for the defense in the upstate Brink's trial (the second of the three in that case), Burns/Odinga said the BLA's assassination of the two Rockland officers and the Brink's guard were politically justified. But he proclaimed no motive but self-defense in the Queens cop shootings. At that trial, he argued his own case: "If I really wanted to kill anyone," the *Daily News* quoted his opening statement, "I had ample chance to . . ."

He was convicted in the final Brink's-related trial in Queens of six of eight counts of attempted murder of a police officer—sentences to be served concurrently after completion of the forty-year *federal* term for his part in the Brink's and other armored-car robberies. The Queens prosecutor called Sekou Odinga "the top criminal in the country," reported the *Post.*

### Detective Lieutenant Dan Kelly, Detective Sergeant John Russell: 911

**Lieutenant Kelly:** The Terrorist Task Force had so much to do two or three days after the Brink's robbery that they called over to ask us to check on a simple address—one of the females that was associated with the Brink's perps, a white girl who had a location over in Queens. They were overwhelmed with work in the task force—would you do us a favor? We did 'em a favor.

That day they had come up with some information about a maroon car with a license plate. We went over to that location (just happened to be right where we knew from the Scarangella and Rainey investigation LaBorde used to live). We stopped for a stop sign at Foch and about One-sixty—we're en route to this address that we were supposed to do the quick check on—and we spot a car with the license plate number they just gave us.

"Five-seven-three—" It's supposed to be on a maroon Ford; that's the way they put it out on the All Points we had earlier this morning. But it *wasn't* on a maroon car.

We had just moved the squad from the One-twelve Precinct to the One-eleven—I was just getting out of there because of all the confusion. Myself and two other detectives, Irwin Jacobson and George Alleyne, went on this mission. Now we stop for the sign— we see the car!

Our radio is out, wasn't working at the time. When I don't get my band, I call Major Case 'cause they're on the same frequency. Major Case was involved because they're part of the Terrorist Task Force, and I said to notify Central that we got a car under observation.

Bobby Louden, Lieutenant Louden, hears me on the radio. He becomes part and parcel to the communication now. He notifies Terrorist Task Force.

We start tailing. . . .

[The signal "K," used by New York police, indicates the end of a transmission, like "over." "Ten-five" means "repeat."]

CHANNEL 39, CHIEF OF DETECTIVES FREQUENCY

**Lt. Kelly, Queens Homicide Task Force:** Austin, Austin portable to—Madison base, K.

**Lt. Louden, Major Case Squad office:** Madison base, standin' by.

**Lt. Kelly:** Austin portable proceeding on Van Wyck Expressway northbound, havin'— '7-3 L-D-U occupied by two male negroes. Advise Terrorist Squad and Central.

**Lt. Louden:** Ten-five Austin portable, you're coming in broken.

**Lt. Kelly:** Subject auto just went onto the Van Wyck Expressway, northbound.

**Lt. Louden:** Description of the vehicle, K?

**Lt. Kelly:** It's a gray—looks like a Chrysler . . . LeBaron.

**Lt. Louden:** What is the plate number, Austin 5?

**Lt. Kelly:** Five-seven-three Louie David Union.

**Lt. Louden:** That's two male negroes proceeding northbound on the Van Wyck Expressway?

**Lt. Kelly:** It's Hillside Avenue . . . No—we're comin' up on Jamaica Avenue at this point.

**Lt. Louden:** Do you need assistance in stopping, K?

**Lt. Kelly:** Excuse me?

**Lt. Louden:** Do you require assistance in stopping?

**Lt. Kelly:** Yes—yes!

**Lt. Louden:** Stand by . . . Madison base to Central, K.

**Dispatcher:** Go ahead, Madison base.

**Lt. Louden:** We have a portable unit, Austin 5, northbound on the Wyck Expressway. They're in pursuit of a gray Chrysler LeBaron, plate number 5-7-3 Lincoln David Union, occupied by two male negroes. They are crossing Hillside Avenue. They require assistance in stopping, K.

**Dispatcher:** Ten-four.

**Lt. Kelly:** Subject vehicle movin' off on Main Street now. Hold on, hold loose now. Proceeding toward the Van Wyck Expressway. Hold it momentarily; we'll let you know—Okay, Van Wyck Expressway, Van Wyck Expressway, northbound—towards Jewel Avenue.

**Dispatcher:** They're now on the Van Wyck Expressway, crossing Jewel Avenue—as of last update.

**Detective unit:** Ten-four. What're they wanted for?

**Lt. Kelly:** I believe that's wanted upstate.

**Dispatcher:** Austin unit, can you advise—New York or New Jersey plate?

**Lt. Kelly:** New Jersey plates, blue plates.

**Dispatcher:** Unit, be advised, that plate is originally registered Chrysler. Operations advised . . . that is the plate we're lookin' for, that is the plate we're lookin' for from upstate, Nyack.

**Lt. Kelly:** Yeah . . . we know it.

**Lieutenant Kelly:** We keep following. They go to Van Wyck; they get off at Northern Boulevard going east. They're caught at the first light. Make a U-turn, jump the divider. Start to come back going west on Northern Boulevard, going over the bridge.

With that, they sent Emergency Service. . . .

**Sergeant Russell:** We were eating lunch. My partner heard Lieutenant Kelly calling for assistance. "Let's go give 'em a hand." One minute we were eatin' a sandwich; the next minute we were in a gun battle.

CHANNEL 37, SPECIAL OPERATIONS DIVISION (SOD), CITYWIDE FREQUENCY

**Queens Uniform Task Force Car 2926:** Two-nine-two-six is at Union Turnpike and the GCP [Grand Central Parkway].

**Dispatcher:** I don't know what they're wanted for at this time. We're gettin' it over a detective frequency . . . uh . . . They're chasing the car, believe it's a Chrysler . . . Van Wyck, northbound . . . just broke Hillside.

**Car 2926:** Ten-four . . . I'll respond to the GCP eastbound at Union Turnpike and cut 'em off.

**Dispatcher:** It's approaching the LIE [Long Island Expressway], northbound, the Van Wyck . . . approaching the LIE. . . . Again, it's a Chrysler LeBaron, gray in color . . . occupied by two male negroes . . . uh . . . just . . . uh . . . leaving the scene and resistin' apprehension.

**Car 2465:** Two-four-six-five to Central—this unit is at the base of the Whitestone. . . . We have the entrance to the bridge blocked off.

**Traffic unit:** Put the highrisers up!

**PO Joe Santore, Highway Car 308:** Detective car—

**Dispatcher:** Adam 10's out at the Whitestone, what's the location, please?

**PO Russell:** Adam 10's at the Whitestone and Linden. . . . Where are they, Central?

**Lt. Kelly:** Stand back a little bit . . . hold on now. . . . Wait one second, now. They took the cutoff where they're either goin' to Northern Boulevard— Northern Boulevard! Northern Boulevard!

**PO Russell:** Where are they, Central?

**Dispatcher:** Northern Boulevard, east. . . .

**Responding unit:** Somebody can stop them, possibly at the base of the bridge.

**PO Russell:** Adam 10's on Northern Boulevard, now, Central. . . .

**Sergeant Russell:** Lieutenant Kelly is following in an unmarked car, not being observed. Then when Highway 308 came up, Kelly told him, Don't go past, come behind us. Because they wanted to wait until they got enough reinforcements before they're gonna take the car. But I guess at some point Smith and Odinga looked in the rearview mirror, saw Kelly's car and saw a marked police car—and that's when they accelerated and started the chase.

As we approached the base of the bridge (we just called it the "Northern Boulevard" bridge) we observed a gray car coming down the crest of the hill followed by a car with a red dome light—the detectives.

Two-four-six-five had the base of the Bronx Whitestone blocked off, because if the Chrysler continued on the Van Wyck, that would be one of the ways that they could escape—the Whitestone Expressway Bridge.

The highrisers are on top of the Highway Patrol cars: the lights that come up straight so you can see them from a distance.

"Highway 308"—the first number corresponds to the district they're from—Queens is Highway Three. Joe Santore is probably telling the Highway dispatcher, "I just met up with the detective car."

**Lieutenant Kelly:** A Highway car picks it up, a Queens Task Force picks it up, and now we're back chasin' 'em again, going back west, toward the city.


CHANNEL 39, CHIEF OF DETECTIVES FREQUENCY

**Lt. Kelly:** Stay with us.

**Dispatcher:** Hey, Austin unit, what's your location now? Austin unit, what kind of car is it? Austin unit, what's your location?

**Lt. Kelly:** Chrysler LeBaron . . . you . . . [squealing tires] . . . going . . . going . . . hold it . . .

**Dispatcher:** Austin, you broke on me—10-5.

**Lt. Kelly:** Let's go . . . [sirens] . . . We got 'em . . . We got 'em. . . . Shake 'em loose.

**Responding unit:** What's the location—what location ya got?

**Lt. Kelly:** Get in there . . . in there [commotion, sirens] Go . . . go . . . go . . . go . . . goin' east . . . goin' east . . . goin' east . . . watch out!

**Dispatcher:** Emergency Service is right behind you . . . These guys are armed. . . .


**Sergeant Russell:** As we came into the intersection, Lieutenant Kelly motioned to us to ram them. And we had the momentum, we're comin' down Northern Boulevard, and we rammed the rear of the gray car against a retaining wall.

**Lieutenant Kelly:** *Boom! Boom!* Shots fired. Shots fired. That's *after* they hit our car—Jake pulled the car, tried to stop 'em; they hit our car—

**Sergeant Russell:** Lieutenant Kelly was behind us, 'cause we had the truck; we were like the protection. I think we had the Highway car behind us and also the Queens Task Force car.

After we rammed them, we pulled up alongside of them, and as we pulled up, the passenger in the car had a nine millimeter and he cocked it. The driver bent forward, and the passenger leaned out and started firing over the back of the driver's head at Lieutenant Kelly and myself as we were going over the bridge. Two shots come into our car door on my partner's side.

**Lieutenant Kelly:** Now we go up, following. They go along the Northern Boulevard, underneath the highway, and apparently they blow a tire when they go in the wrong lane. Going in an eastbound lane going westbound, they blow a tire.

**Sergeant Russell:** The perps mounted the median and that's when they tore out the bottom part of their car and it started to smoke. They jumped out of the car and let the car crash into a wall. When they did this, we were the next car behind them, but our truck had a high undercarriage—we mounted the median and we continued to pursue them.

CHANNEL 37, SOD, CITYWIDE RADIO

**Chief Richard Dillon, Car 39:** Car 39 to Central, K—

**Dispatcher:** Units stand by unless you have an emergency message.

**Chief Dillon:** . . . They're headed toward Main.

**PO Russell:** This unit's comin' down Northern on . . . ah . . . Northern and Main now, Central.

**Chief Dillon:** Central, is he off the Expressway?

**PO Russell:** We got 'em, Central. . . . Adam 10's goin'. They're down on Northern Boulevard now. . . .

**Dispatcher:** They're on Northern Boulevard now. Adam 10 is . . . ah . . . behind them, K.

**Car 2465:** Northern and what? Two-four-six-five to Central. Northern and what, K?

**PO Russell:** Emergency message: They're armed . . . be advised . . . they're armed.

**Dispatcher:** They are armed, units . . . They are armed . . . Use caution. . . . Where are you now, Adam 10?

**PO Russell:** Down on Northern Boulevard . . . Adam 10—Shots fired! Shots fired . . . shots fired.

**Chief Dillon:** Where are they, Central?

**PO Russell:** They're gonna run.

**Dispatcher:** They're on Northern Boulevard and Main Street . . . From there I can't get a location . . . It's too . . .

**Adam 10:** I'm shot! Ten-thirteen . . . 1-2-6 . . . 10-13 . . . 1-2-6 and Northern.

**Dispatcher:** One-two-six and Northern . . . 10-13 . . . They're on foot . . . 1-2-6 and Northern—

**Lt. Richie Young, ESU:** Eight-three-nine responding.

**PO Santore:** Three-o-eight to Central . . . shots being fired.

**Dispatcher:** That's 1-2-6 and Northern . . . assist patrolman.

**Car 276:** Two-seven-six . . . on the way.

**Adam 1:** Adam 1 also, Central.

**Lieutenant Kelly:** They pull up on 126th Street and then they go south; they run. Turn around, an Emergency Service truck is here. Right smack in the middle of the windshield is a bullet. John Russell was driving; bullet hole right smack—right between the two operators. So you knew they were playing for real.

**Sergeant Russell:** We were coming up on them. They got out of their car, turned around, and fired at us. The glass hit my face. I guess I was sweating—I felt my face and it was wet, and I thought I was shot in the face.

I stop, and I see them comin', and now I remember Scarangella and Rainey—that's how they were massacred. They pulled that van over, and the perps jumped out and fired fifty shots into their car before the cops could get out. I pushed my partner out—I didn't want to get trapped in the car.

My partner fired back—they realized we were gonna shoot and they fled. Dan Kelly and George Alleyne and Jacobson pulled up behind us; then they started the foot pursuit. That's where they split up; one went eastbound on Thirty-fourth Avenue and the other one went into an auto parts junkyard.

**Lieutenant Kelly:** With that, we chase 'em to a lot. Two of us get out of the car. Jake goes around with the squad car. This guy Smith starts to climb the fence—pulls out the gun.

*Bang, bang, bang.* DOA.


CHANNEL 39, CHIEF OF DETECTIVES FREQUENCY

**Lt. Kelly:** Shots fired! Shots fired!

**Dispatcher:** Northern and where? Northern and where?

**Lt. Kelly:** He's underneath the Van Wyck—Whitestone—Expressway . . . go back.

**Dispatcher:** What's your location, foot pursuit?

**Lt. Kelly:** Hold loose—he's gonna get away.

**Dispatcher:** One-two-six and Northern . . . One-two-six and Northern . . . 10-13 . . . One-two-six and Northern—a 13.

**Lt. Kelly:** By Shea Stadium.

**Det. Jacobson:** Thirty-fourth Avenue goin' eastbound. We're comin' up on it.

**PO Santore:** Okay, we have uniform and civilian; civilian-clothes people here.

**Responding unit:** By the Shea Stadium side, or the other side?

**Det. Jacobson:** We got one—we got one of 'em!

**Lt. Kelly:** What's the matter?

**Chief Dillon:** What's the location, please?

**Dispatcher:** Austin, 10-5 your location.

**Chief Dillon:** Central, would you give us a location on these perps, please?

**Dispatcher:** One-two-six and Northern by Three-four Avenue, by Shea Stadium—They have one perpetrator—They request an ambulance on location, also—And they're lookin' for more. . . .

**Responding unit:** Location?

**Dispatcher:** Austin, you're on the air, what's your location now?

**Responding unit:** What's your further information, Dispatcher?

**Dispatcher:** Last I got is one-two-seven, got a report of a police officer shot . . . We're lookin' for four male blacks. We've got a male black in a brown jacket—looking for a male black in a brown jacket.

**Chief Dillon:** One-two-seven and Thirty-fourth place. Bosses respond to those locations.

**Dispatcher:** Lookin' for a male black in a brown jacket.

**Chief Dillon:** What location on the shot?

**Dispatcher:** One-two-seven and Three-five Place. One-two-seven and Three-five Place.

**Responding unit:** One-two-six and Northern.

**Dispatcher:** One-two-seven Street and Thirty-fourth Avenue—Repeating, they got a perpetrator trapped. Lookin' for four male blacks, one with a brown jacket—

**Responding unit:** —Holdin' a couple of guys in the junkyard over here.

**Dispatcher:** That's in a junkyard, that location—in a junkyard—Three-four and One-two-seven.

**Det. Jacobson:** Austin 5 to Austin supervisor, K—just get down here.

**Dispatcher:** Units be advised—a helicopter unit is gonna be overhead momentarily.


CHANNEL 37, SOD CITYWIDE FREQUENCY

**Chief Dillon:** Car 39 to Central—we got one of the perps, we got one of the perps . . . Be careful, there's . . . All right . . . the other one went the other way—

**Crime Scene:** Fifty-one-hundred, a Crime Scene Unit responding.

**Responding unit:** Central, can you give us info? We're comin' down Northern.

**Chief Dillon:** One of the perps is dead . . . The other one has gone back—the other one went back . . . Any police officers shot at this time?


CHANNEL 38, CITYWIDE RADIO

**PO Joe Santore:** Three-o-eight to Central, K . . . Three-o-eight to Central, K—

**Dispatcher:** Go ahead, Unit.

**PO Santore:** Be advised, you've got Thirty-Fourth Avenue blocked off at 127th Street. That's where the other perpetrator is.

**Dispatcher:** All right, that's what we're relaying on the detective frequency, uh, One-two-seven and Thirty-fourth Avenue, in the rear yards—Aviation is approaching up there now, looking, K.

**PO Santore:** Central, that's a male black with a brown coat armed with an automatic weapon.

**Dispatcher:** Units, that's a male black with a brown coat . . . armed with an automatic weapon, so use caution—

**Highway CO:** You got the Highway CO and the S-O-D CO.

**Chief Dillon:** —set up some plan to cordon off the junkyard area.

**Highway CO:** It's the school-bus yard.

**Dispatcher:** What is that? The school-bus yard that you want Aviation to check, K?

**Highway CO:** School-bus yard, Three-four and One-two-seven—

**Dispatcher:** Aviation, the school-bus yard: One-two-seven and Thirty-fourth Avenue, K.

**Aviation 5:** Ten-four.

**Chief Dillon:** It looks like southeast corner. Ya can't miss it, 'cause it's all school buses in there.

**Dispatcher:** All right, southeast corner, Aviation, with the school buses.

**Aviation 5:** Ten-four . . . ETA about two minutes.

**Crime Scene:** Crime Scene Fifty-one-hundred to Central, K.

**Dispatcher:** Fifty-one-hundred—

**Crime Scene:** Is there a police officer shot at that location, K?

**Dispatcher:** It's unclear at this time. We have an ambulance goin' there just in case there is. I know the perpetrator is shot, but it was unclear on the police officer. Adam 10 was looking for his partner; he wasn't sure. Adam 10 on the air?

**Chief Dillon:** You've got one perp that's DOA. No member of the force at this time.

**Chorus:** Yay!!

**Dispatcher:** No members shot at this time, no member units.

CHANNEL 37, SOD CITYWIDE FREQUENCY

**PO Russell:** Adam 10 to Central . . . you . . . ah . . . Just got to get my partner . . . I'm just missin' my partner. A Team!

**Dispatcher:** Where is your partner, Adam 10?

**PO Russell:** He ran after the perpetrators—I'm tryin' to find him now.

**Dispatcher:** What direction did he run?

**PO Russell:** One-two-seventh Street—

**Sergeant Russell:** I'm yelling ''A Team''— Emergency Service had a team to rappel out of helicopters, the A Team. We kidded Al because he was one of the guys who was picked. That's what I always called him: A Team.

Al was with Queens Task Force POs Larry DiTusa and Ed Johnson in the back of the junkyard, looking for the second perp. As they came to the outer yard, glancing to the left, they saw a figure holding an automatic—which misfired as they came out. They grappled to the ground with Nat Burns and took him into custody.

CHANNEL 38, CITYWIDE RADIO

**PO Toumey:** Looks like they have a second perp, Central. Thirty-fourth Avenue—
**Dispatcher:** Looks like they got the second perp. All right, units—

**Sergeant Russell:** You just know shots are being fired, there's a car in pursuit, plate wanted in a homicide of police officer up in Nyack. We don't know the who, what, when, and where yet. But the press wants it. . . .

**911 Officer #1 answers phone:** Citywide, Officer Seward—
**Female reporter:** Hi. Channel 9 News calling—There's a report they have suspects in custody in the Brink's—
**Officer #1:** Uh, can you hold on. . . .
**Reporter:** —case? Yes.
    DIAL TONE.
**Officer #2:** Citywide, Officer Jordan.
**Reporter:** Hi, Channel 9 News—Any information . . .
**Officer #2:** Didn't you just call?
**Reporter:** Yeah, we were disconnected.
**Officer #2:** All we have is on 126 and Northern: one perpetrator possibly involved in that Nyack robbery in . . . uh . . . That's all we have right now.
**Reporter:** Why do you think they might be involved?
**Officer #2:** One-two-six and Northern—
**Reporter:** Yeah, why do you think they might be involved?
**Officer #2:** That's all we have. We're checking on the plate and the car; they're checking the car right now.
**Reporter:** What kind of car, gray . . . uh . . . gray . . . Chrysler . . . ?
**Officer #2:** That's all we have on it.
**Reporter:** Yeah—we have it comin' over that they have four suspects in custody . . .

**Officer #2:** Well, we're not there. . . .
**Reporter:** One-ten Precinct?
**Officer #2:** One-two-six and Northern Boulevard.
**Reporter:** Could I just get the precinct?
**Officer #2:** One-ten Precinct.

**Lieutenant Kelly:** It happened in the One-ten; we were under the jurisdiction of the One-ten—but I said, take everything back to the Borough. We bring 'em all back to the One-twelve. Now, we had just vacated that particular office; outside of a few chairs, there was nothing. But I knew it was the place to take 'em. It was home.

CHANNEL 39, CHIEF OF DETECTIVES FREQUENCY

**Det. Jacobson:** Queens Detective, Austin 5 to Queens Detective.
**Queens Detective Task Force:** This is Queens Detective.
**Det. Jacobson:** Order Forensics, Thirty-fourth Avenue and Willets Point Boulevard. Have the CO come down.
**Lt. Kelly:** Think there's another perp in custody, Central, hold on; Central, hold on—
**Dispatcher:** You've got a second perp in custody?
**Lt. Kelly:** We've got it all; we've got it all. Everybody else.
**Dispatcher:** Hey, unit on the scene, advise—Ya got all four, is that correct? Ya got all four of 'em?
**Lt. Kelly:** That's it. Goin' into the One-twelve. Austin to One-twelve.

**Lieutenant Kelly:** Everything was taken back to the Borough. Waited around.
The Bomb Squad came over to take a look at the car, 'cause they were afraid it was booby-trapped. We set things in motion there.

CHANNEL 38, CITYWIDE RADIO

**Bomb Squad CO, Lt. Charles Luisi calls 911:** This is Lieutenant Luisi, the Bomb Squad. On this incident out in Queens—please get it out there: they think it's connected with Nyack. Not to fool with the car or open the trunk . . . Might be explosives in the vehicle if it's connected with Nyack.
**Dispatcher:** I've got Lieutenant Luisi from the Bomb Squad—Who's got the car? Don't

want 'em messin' with the trunk or the car—any part of the car. Unit on the scene with that Chrysler—if there's any unit on the scene now, secure that car.

CHANNEL 39, CHIEF OF DETECTIVES FREQUENCY

**Lt. Kelly:** Austin leader, detectives and uniform are on it. It's being safeguarded.

**Lieutenant Kelly:** I relinquished my command at the scene, and I was sent to the Borough to answer on the events of that day. We were in good stead—made a tremendous observation. Ended up with somebody gettin' killed, but they had shot at us.

Everybody that was involved in it that wasn't a detective was made a detective. Everybody went up in grade except me, 'cause I already had it. Jake made first, George Alleyne made first. The papers played it well, and Chief Sullivan played it well because there was an observation—so great because the plate was on the wrong car. We saw the plate and we went after the plate; so happens that they'd changed plates from when the feds got the information that the car was being utilized.

And, the fact that nobody got hurt. The fact that they end up finding out that Nat Burns—he was using the heavy African name when we locked him up—was one of the Panther 21.

**Sergeant Russell:** This case brought me into the Detective Bureau, I was a detective three years—I worked at the One-ten Precinct, where this took place.

I studied, became a sergeant. The Seven-five, Bedford-Stuyvesant—one of the busiest detective squads in the city—that's where I was broken in as a detective supervisor, because there we average one hundred homicides a year. But you learn the job, and I learned it and nothing fazes me now in any investigation. *We had four people killed . . . He's holding two people hostage out in Long Island.* Okay, I'll be in to handle it.

Once Kelly "answered" in the NYPD internal investigation that comes after any and all police shootings, the months following the October 1981 shootout by the bridge on Northern Boulevard saw a return to just the normal homicide squad drill. For the time being, Anthony LaBorde, still wanted in the April 1981 ambush of officers Scarangella and Rainey, remained in the wind. But the following January, a lead shared by Lieutenant Kelly's task force with the FBI enabled the feds to pick up the fugitive in Philadelphia.

New York detectives rarely *fly* the ninety-four miles to Philly, but the NYPD ordered Lieutenant Kelly and Lieutenant Stan Carpenter to the City of Brotherly Love forthwith—by commuter jet. (Not for the first time or the last, New York cops on urgent company business laid out their own expense money and took off.) Kelly's mission, obviously, was to make sure LaBorde came before a Queens judge in connection with the ambush case—but of course, the feds wanted the fugitive in federal court. And the feds came first. A deputy U.S. marshal was assigned to transport him to New York.

Philadelphia cops favored Kelly and Carpenter with the "professional courtesy" of a radio car to take them around as they waited for LaBorde to get through the system. But Kelly had to keep New York informed: " 'What's happening? What's happening?' Don't worry, I got the marshal who's assigned to the move. He bought me lunch; I just bought him dinner. When he goes, I go."

Back to the Big Apple with LaBorde. "About eight cars in a caravan. Didn't take us long, from Philadelphia right to federal court over in Brooklyn. Escort the whole way. Say they're doing sixty or seventy, but the whole way. State troopers station to station to station. Our Motorcycle guys picked us up at the bridge here, and away we went to Brooklyn federal, then to supreme court in Queens. A tremendous end to a police homicide."

But in 1992, LaBorde, aka Abdul Majid, and York, aka Basheer Hameed, who were serving eight-and-a-third- to twenty-five-year sentences for the attempted murder of Officer Rainey, challenged their 1986 convictions in the murder of Officer Scarangella. Two previous trials on the Scarangella murder charge had ended in hung juries. The two defendants now contended that prosecutors in the 1986 trial had illegally rejected potential jurors on "racially discriminatory" grounds.

Supreme Court Judge Ralph Sherman heard testimony in late 1992 and decided in favor of the prosecution in November 1993. The case that had "taken on a life of its own," as the *New York Law Journal* commented in its page one report, was again in the hands of the appellate court. A decision was expected in the spring of 1994. Reversal of their 1986 convictions would entitle York/

Hameed and LaBorde/Majid to a retrial. If acquitted, they would be eligible for immediate parole.

———

All manner of politically inspired ferment, from "exile activities, antiwar protest, student unrest, terrorist bombings and revolution" to "urban guerrilla warfare," have fueled NYPD intelligence-gathering efforts ever since the succinctly named Radical Bureau of 1912.

Intelligence was always what it was all about, but the brass wrestled endlessly with how to organize and what to call the unit, depending not least on the political climate.

"I got there at the end of sixty-nine," says Detective James Ziede. "At that time, BOSSI had just changed its name; they used to change the name about every six months to protect the innocent. I think it was . . ."

Not even a detective could possibly keep track. Altogether, the name changed eleven times between 1912 and 1972, when somebody smartly came up with "Intelligence Division," but the 1946 handle "BOSSI" acquired a patina and continued in daily use for at least a generation after investigation was dropped from the unit's title. (Twenty-five years after the name change to Bureau, "Detective Division" also is still preferred by many "dinosaurs.")

Detectives of Intell, as the unit at last came to be informally known in the eighties, don't make arrests and never did. The intelligence they gather goes through channels to the particular NYPD squad or unit where, so to speak, it will do the most good.

Their access to information about politically inspired mayhem makers gives these detectives an edge when, as Jim Ziede soon began to do, they act as armed escorts for important politicians and visiting dignitaries (1972 name for this group: Liaison Section, Intelligence Division). Arguably, NYPD detective escorts hardly need that edge, because by any name, the intelligence unit has been highly effective. Even in the incendiary sixties, if you got the VIP treatment from the NYPD, you breezed through the City unharmed. Plots were foiled *before* push came to shove.

Detective Ziede had been in a Brooklyn precinct squad for several years. "The old squad work: you go in, you chase cases and 61s and different people. Got to a point where I wanted to open up my horizons." Good timing for the Arabic-speaking detective born in Brooklyn of Lebanese parents, who says that air hijackings in 1967 brought "the Palestinian question into focus" and made the NYPD begin to "start thinking of Arab groups."

He interviewed with the intelligence unit and was virtually assured he'd be called. "The glamour of BOSSI, everybody feels, is that you're escorting heads of state and all this nonsense. A street cop would say, Oh, boy, it's a nice job; suit-and-tie and all." Sure enough, he was called, and then: "I found out that most of this was not glamorous—escorting some beautiful princess, or a king or a president."

It was mostly "nitty gritty investigations. A boring accumulating job of getting information on people; dossiers, and God knows what else. Each country was broken down; everybody had to take a section and find out who's the pros and who's the cons. At demonstrations, who's the leaders? Are they bomb throwers—or just rhetoric?"

The glamour came later, starting in 1971, when Ziede guarded New York State governor Nelson Rockefeller for three and a half years, and still later, escorting everybody from the Middle East— Arafat to Peres—sometimes back to back. He says his "ego wall" has photos galore to prove it. Tall, dark, and fit-looking now, as then, Ziede currently is security consultant to the League of Arab States.

He was amazed back when he first interviewed for "BOSSI" that NYPD intelligence "didn't even have a Middle East desk that I knew of. They had nothing on the Arab world." Ziede was there to fill in that information gap—but he had to do some fancy dancing to avoid falling into a different hole in the coverage. Who the hell was this "WUFI" that had applied for a permit to demonstrate across from the Plaza Hotel on April 24, 1970? The acronym sounded about as dangerous as a stuffed toy puppy.

### Detective Jim Ziede:
### Beretta

It was maybe not even my second or third escort, 'cause the escorts were few and far between—the son of Chiang Kai-shek came to New York. It was a low-key escort.

Nobody really had the information on what was called WUFI, World United for Formosan Independence.

The Chinese community in New York, at that time and before, was a law-abiding community. Very few, very minor things; the biggest crime I think was gambling. (Now you have a lot of these Chinese gangs, a lot of southeast Asians coming in.)

So, okay—the son of Chiang Kai-shek? Great. We're going around to the airport. This was April 1970; I'd gotten into the squad the end of sixty-nine (I think it was November). I was a new kid on the block. It just worked out—I guess it was like a fluke that I got the escort, because the Far East wasn't my expertise. If you're a Russian expert, you get the Eastern Bloc, etc. So maybe they were short of manpower.

Anyway, we bring him in from LaGuardia. They just came up from seeing Nixon in D.C. It was raining. We have the film. Not that my memory's that great, but we played this over and over again when we went to trial on the case. At the airport there were a lot of people waving flags, welcoming; it was a friendly group.

And then we went to the Pierre Hotel. At the Pierre we had less than an hour, maybe, for him to go to a luncheon at the Plaza on 59th Street. It was just me and my partner, Hank Suarez, and State Department. State did all the escorts in conjunction with the New York City Police Department. (The only time the Secret Service was used, of course, was with the President.)

New York City security was myself and my partner, the two of us. On the moves, there would be at least four to five State Department guys—their team at that time consisted of about a dozen men and they rotated shifts. They used to stay in the hotel. They'd sleep over and we would share a room with them. (State Department used to pay for the room.) And we would stay around the clock. Of course, this was before they paid detectives overtime, so we were like the mules. They could work you that way because they didn't have to pay. That's changed since then—much changed.

So I was with my partner; I'm gonna go to the Plaza, which was only two blocks away. The rain had let up a little. I remember I walked over. Two guys from the State Department were there; we started bullshitting to each other. We had a half-hour wait or so before the subject came.

Usually the advance team takes a look at things. We found a demonstration point. This WUFI had applied for permits, so we knew that there was a group. That's one of the reasons I went over. We put them in the park right across the street; we had a uniform detail to take care of that. So the group was just forming—it was covered, police were there. And a member from our office was there to monitor the group, 'cause it's a new group. We never knew they existed.

Chiang Ching-kuo pulls up, and the rest is on film. A pool camera from ABC picked it up at the airport—waving the Nationalist Chinese flag, the arrival at the hotel, demonstration, the pros and cons, and the film of the struggle. The only thing they didn't get is the actual shot, because I think when the shot went off, the cameraman hit the ground and then he started filming when we were rolling down the stairs. But the guy was good, the cameraman—if *I* heard the shot, I would've run.

We're entering the hotel; here I'm thinking that we're going for a luncheon, wondering what's on the menu, and things along those lines. And there's this—*bam!*

There's a certain adrenaline that pumps in you when you're playing that role. Actually it is a role that you play: the idea that all your senses gotta be up on top. You hear a crowd shouting; you see people moving around you. . . . Somebody goes beyond a certain perimeter—you get a little nervous until you find out that he's one of yours, or he's a State Department guy or something. This is part of the training—a certain perimeter, a certain periphery of your eyes that you're supposed to cover. Look at hands, look at eyes, this type of thing.

As he got out of the car, the place was really shoutin' and yelling. And when a crowd shouts and yells, you sort of build yourself—gee, y'know, these people are really mad at him!

I stationed myself immediately behind the subject. There were State Department guys at either side. My partner was behind me, and we're going up the stairs of the Plaza. I don't remember this—I remember because I've *seen* it, played the film over so many times. My head turns several times as we're walking.

It turns out to be the assassin's brother-in-law who had broke from the crowd and was causing a ruckus to my right. Everybody's attention went to the right. Peter Huang was the shooter; he came running from my left. And it was just, I don't know—luck, instinct, whatever you want. Out of the corner of my eye (don't know how he got past everybody) the next thing I see is an arm comin' between me—and the subject, Chiang. And in that hand was a black automatic Beretta. This is all seconds—this is like, you're looking this way, you turn around, and all of a sudden, you see something coming at you.

I was fortunate enough to grab the hand and deflected the shot above the head of the subject—it went into the glass door of the Plaza Hotel.

Apparently what he was trying to do—after we analyzed it—he was trying to get to the same compartment in the revolving doors. We stopped using revolving doors after that. State Department was criticized for it. Now anytime you take a subject through the door, the doors are folded or you go to another entrance. You learn.

Anyway, the subject is pushed through the doors. At that time, all I know is I have the man by the hand, and I'm squeezing his hand so hard that he couldn't *release* the trigger. At the point that he turns the gun on me and it's sticking in my belly—You're goin', What the hell is happening? It's not *supposed* to happen. It wasn't meant to be.

I'm yelling, *"Nobody touch us!"* I'm yelling at my partner, *"Don't jump on!"* 'Cause there was a few motorcycle cops in the escort—these guys were real six-foot-something guys, linebackers—and I was afraid of somebody jolting me and jolting him and the shot would get off. Another shot.

We rolled down the stairs, until I finally broke the gun from his hand. Okay, I got it! And then it looked like a football pileup. We cuffed him, put him in a radio car, and got him out. Uniform takes him.

And, of course, I go up to the ballroom with Chiang Ching-kuo. We're at the ballroom. I notify the Command—assassination attempt. There was a lot of nonsense, but Chiang Ching-kuo stood there on his receiving line and greeted all these people like it never happened. Businessmen looking to invest in Taiwan, Far East/American Council of Foreign Affairs characters were there, politicians, and all that stuff.

He never even turned around and nodded or smiled in the course of things. I mean, it was weird. So I started saying, did this really happen? Maybe it didn't happen? And of course, I'm still hyped up. I get a relief now—they send somebody down from the office. First thing I did, of course, was call my wife and tell her I was all right, 'cause this was on the air. It got a lot of publicity.

It was really a media show there. And phones are ringin'. Big assassination attempt. Actually, it was. I don't think there's documentation, but where a shot is fired—a gun in hand—it was the first time in the City of New York. The boss was very happy and proud, and all that kinda stuff, that we did—we accomplished something. I got letters from all over, police departments, friends, people I thought weren't alive anymore.

Huang was charged with attempted murder of a diplomat, both him and his brother-in-law. His brother-in-law was charged at the scene, because he was acting in concert. We actually went to trial in 1971; they were both found guilty as charged. Attempted murder, weapons charge, and other minor things. They were facing something like thirty-two years each.

They were educated people—that's another story. We didn't have any indication—then we found out who in the hell is WUFI, and it turned out that they were no slouches; they weren't just a bunch of mutts. People that ran the organization were professors in universities throughout the United States.

I got the Medal of Honor, which is a very great honor. Most guys that get it aren't alive. In fact, the day I got it, I think out of six Medals of Honor, four were posthumous, one honoree was maimed, and I was the only guy that was actually on hand. I'm very fortunate.

The Medal of Honor to the dishonored badge. . . . An Internal Affairs detective's assignment is to catch cops who betray the job, other cops, and the public. "You do those kind of investigations the same way you do any other," says a detective lieutenant who once worked for the chief of detectives' Field Internal Affairs Unit. "The only difference is it's not fun—the other ones are fun. If you're successful, you don't have the privilege of celebration when it's over. It causes a sense of absence, a sense of void."

Another difference is that few true stories like the one that follows get into circulation. Rarely do you tell other cops what you did in Internal Affairs.

In ordinary squad work, you virtually always work with a partner. In Internal Affairs, it's not unusual to work alone. More often than in other squads, sergeants actively investigate instead of only supervising. The authority of their rank is an asset to this kind of probe. "In some ways, they're more difficult investigations, because the person you're investigating certainly knows the system. So to be successful it's arguably more difficult than in the general population."

Add to the isolation the sadness, the unwelcome weight of another cop's dirty secret—and sudden danger.

## No ID

This small unit that worked for the chief of detectives, in addition to the personnel matters, did any investigation the chief of D had a personal interest in. It was his little investigating group for whatever his concerns were, whether it was homicides that weren't being solved, or whatever.

I was following a person by myself, in a rented car. I was alone; it was about two o'clock in the morning. I had followed the person into Manhattan, and they were in a bar. I was crouched in the front seat of the car, and I was looking through the rearview mirror at the entrance to this bar. I was wearing a wool knit hat, pulled down.

I saw a shadow pass on my right side, and I heard a click. I had been leaning with my head against the window—and there was a cocked gun against my temple. It was a very—uneasy—few moments.

There had been a homicide in the location the previous night by a white guy in a rented car wearing a wool hat, and I matched the description of the guy. Knitted hat, rented car, I was a white guy. It was the same street corner where the homicide had been committed the night before. The precinct Anti-Crime unit thought they had a murderer. I had no identification on me.

I never carried any identification. Also, it wasn't in my best interest to admit what I was actually there for. So I had to explain that I was following someone I thought was sleeping with my wife. I wasn't a cop; just following . . . I had a reason to be there, a reason they could buy into: I thought "my wife was out with somebody else, and I was just waiting to see if—he'd come out. . . ."

NYPD detectives—all of them—were in jeopardy in the early 1970s. Not only was Police Commissioner Patrick V. Murphy overtly anti-detective, but the fiscal crisis and other circumstances combined to back up his efforts to bury the mystique.

It was during Murphy's tenure that the mayor convened the Commission to Investigate Alleged Police Corruption—the famous Knapp Commission—complete with televised hearings in 1971. The commission and its findings shook the City. Narcotics detectives, especially, were Knapp Commission targets—two were suicides. The Bureau reeled—and in 1973, the PC decided to cut it in half. Of three thousand detectives, half now reported to precinct captains—patrol types, mostly unfamiliar with detective work; some just as hostile to the shield as the PC.

Next came the budget cuts, hitting the police force in 1975 with 2,864 layoffs. If you had enough seniority to stay on the job during this period, you still had your cop's white shield—but nobody was about to hand you the gold. Detectives were a luxury the City couldn't afford. You worked hard over five, six, eight years and made a lot of quality street arrests, or risked your life undercover . . . You could even be catching detective cases in a precinct squad. . . . You still had neither a detective's cachet, nor the gold shield that symbolized it. Not to mention the raise.

John Skala, nine years out of uniform, finally got promoted in the spring of 1980—after he jumped into a dangerous situation he could have ignored with nobody the wiser.

### Detective John Skala:
### Line of Fire

I was a cop with a wife and two kids, moonlighting as a security guard. I was protecting a legitimate retail operation, but they were using that operation to conceal a drug business.

Having gotten to know me, they knew I had spent some years in Intelligence. They felt I must have been a rogue cop because I went back to uniform. And what am I doing in their place? Demeaning myself, working as a guard? I didn't find it demeaning, but that's their psychology. So they started hinting around about the possibility of bringing drugs into the country.

I ran right over to Brooklyn North Narcotics. I had some friends there, former colleagues. Bob Pugliese was an ex-partner of mine working for the sergeant, John McDonald, and Sal Blando. And they were go-getters, I mean, they were really a heavy team. They were doing a tremendous amount of work. So I sat down with John and he wanted to handle the case, but his lieutenant said, "Listen, this constitutes a bribe to a New York City police officer, this is an IAD thing. . . ."

Internal Affairs calls me in—Captain Hartman, fella they used to call The Undertaker because of his very solemn and sober demeanor. And after we laid out the story to him, Hartman says, "Well, we'd really like to wire you up and see what this is about, but you understand, we're going to have to give you a departmental complaint."

I said to the captain, I'm a big boy. I never was one of those who cried about IAD if you were wrong. (I was moonlighting without department sanction—you have to get authorization.) I'm wrong—I didn't put in the request for permission. Give me the complaint, I'll take it like a man, and you'll never hear me say an unkind word about you. But I'm not gonna go in there wired—you can't have it both ways. He said, "Yeah, you're right. Let's forgo the complaint."

I'm designated to go. I had experience doing intelligence with wires, and there were times where I wore a Kel device, but only on overt stuff, getting an organized crime guy's voice on tape, for example. I get wired, I have a Nagra. From guys who did some undercover work, I learned that the best place to put the Nagra is in the groin area, 'cause not many men are going to search you in that area. So I have the machine, which is flat, down in my groin area, and I have the microphone wire running up, taped to my chest. I had a sweatshirt on and a flannel shirt loosely over it. I had my off-duty gun in my dungarees waistband.

After we had closed up the store that night, I went into this room with two individuals. One was a fellow about my age—I was in my early thirties. His boss, who was running the whole operation, was sitting behind the desk. I was here, and the other fellow was here.

I said, So-and-so tells me there's something that I might be able to do for you. And he says, "Oh, yes, John, but before we talk—" and he's very polite. "Please excuse me," and he takes a .25 out of the drawer and he points it at me. And with this, the other fellow comes to search me. He starts to run his right hand across my chest—and I knew he was gonna come across the microphone wire.

I grabbed his wrist with my left hand, because all in one motion I could pull him in the line of fire—just pull him across, take my gun out, and hit him in the shoulder.

He can only fall back on the desk. So I had him over the desk, and I told the other guy, I'm saying, Throw that fucking gun across the room or I'll blow this motherfucker's head off right now. And I cocked the gun and I put it in his mouth. Tell me why I shouldn't blow this motherfucker away. Nobody touches my gun! You understand me? Nobody fuckin' goes for my gun! You want my gun? Here it is!

They bought it, and they apologized. And we had good rapport.

They wanted me to secure a customs agent who would allow drugs to come through Kennedy Airport—which I told them I could do. The Drug Enforcement Administration came into it, and they didn't want to use customs people, so they brought a DEA agent in from California posing as my contact. Transactions were worked through him. This investigation lasted about a year and a half.

The DEA was kind enough, along with the prosecutor's office, to request that I be promoted after this case. And that's how I got promoted. I got my shield.

## Detective George Rivera:
## It's Gonna Hurt for One Minute

It wasn't like, "I'm a hero, I ain't afraid to die." Everybody's afraid. But for that one minute, it's gonna hurt. It's like, when I was a kid I always said, if my father hits me—if I was punished—it's gonna hurt for one minute. And then you gotta weigh the issue. Is it gonna be that much fun? Or is the beating gonna be that painful?

I'm not afraid to die, 'cause when I'm gonna die, I'm gonna die. I'm not gonna feel nothin' when I'm dead. So it's kind of ridiculous—that you worry about dying. You want to live to see certain things, see your kids grow up and that type of stuff. I'm thirty-six now. I'm not a pessimist or anything like that. Don't get me wrong—I'm just sayin', you're born for one thing.

Let's go with the fun. It's gonna be a minute or whatever. Might be crazy, but my look at life is, enjoy what you got here while you're here and live life to the fullest. And try to be a good person. That's why I'm a cop.

## Partners & Bosses

**Detective George Rivera:** I think a lot of cops are good judges of character 'cause you gotta go out there, you gotta do the job. There's times you'll swear this guy is like the biggest fuckoff in the precinct, and it turns out like the guy's a hardworking guy. You don't know this guy from Adam, and right there on the spot, you gotta make a decision. That's the luck of the draw. So you learn from that.

They always had an attitude about the females. A lot of guys say, "Yeah, the females, they're full of shit. They ain't gonna do nothing." A lot of guys have that attitude: *I ain't goin' with no broad*.

From the very beginning, I always liked Emma. She was part of the team, and we confided in her more than in most guys.

Then it became the joke. We was ripping each other: "Oh, you're a punk, this and that. . . . No wonder Emma had to help you."

I said, Yeah? Well, I rather had been there with Emma than with you. I guess I got the upper hand on that argument. She's good people.

# MONEY, MURDER, AND THE MOB

---

The top mobsters of the top crime family of the top mob city in the entire U.S.A. hand over their bankrolls as they're booked by the feds in downtown Manhattan. Out of the pockets of John Gotti and Salvatore "Sammy Bull" Gravano comes a dollar total of four thousand four hundred and eight.

"Sammy—what are you doing with *singles*? You're embarrassing me. Remind me when we get outta here, I gotta give you a raise."

Not with a bang, with a punchline—that's how the tortuous four-year investigation of the "Big Paul" Castellano murder ends. To Detective Sergeant John Mullally, the byplay is like something out of an almost-top-banana Catskills comedy routine. The costumes, as we'll see in a moment, are good for a laugh too.

Playing opposite Gotti, Gravano, and Frankie LoCascio in this climactic collar are two Manhattan South Task Force detectives and Detective Sergeant Mullally, their supervisor, not to mention the FBI New York brass—and what looks to Mullally like thirty-five FBI agents.

Detectives Joe Brandefine and Jimmy Turnbull are the last of the NYPD team that kept going long after this definite contender for the all-time Most Professional Mob Rubout faded from view, this case of the *capo di tutti cappi* and his underboss Tommy

Bilotti taking the hit of the decade in front of an East Side steak house, splat in the middle of the evening rush hour.

In tandem with a couple of committed FBI agents and led by celebrated homicide boss, Detective Sergeant Jerry McQueen, city detectives had conducted the investigation. If McQueen had minimal organized crime (OC) background, he had plenty of experience with high-profile cases. To him, Castellano was just one of the more challenging homicides.

For starters, the team interviewed "everyone on Forty-sixth Street," says Manhattan assistant district attorney Patrick J. Dugan, "went through the buildings not once, not twice, but multiple times, looking for everybody who could have been near a window. Every waiter, every bartender at Sparks; every limo driver. Every shop owner on the street—and every patron of those businesses. They went through all the bills to see who was in the shops between five and six P.M. that day." Total witnesses interviewed came to something like two thousand. . . .

Now, here it is December 11, 1990. Christmas is around the corner and so is a long-sought collar; the local guys are having a good time. Gotti could go on the *Tonight* show if he weren't going to a cell at Metropolitan Correctional Center (MCC) in handcuffs.

Sergeant Mullally is a coolheaded observer—he's only been involved in this case for about a year, since he came to Manhattan South in 1989. Mullally, six feet three, blond, and streamlined, has a far better build for clothes than Gotti's and an excellent fashion sense: "You see this guy on TV and now here he is. He had a brown suit on, beautiful suit. His overcoat matched his suit. His shoes matched his suit. His socks matched his suit. I'm not talking the same color, I'm saying that everything matched. Matched perfect. Gotti's underboss, Frankie LoCascio—dressed to the nines. And there's poor Sammy Bull with his T-shirt on and his jeans, a short little leather jacket.

"Sammy's upset. Is he upset because he's been arrested for nineteen murders? Is he upset that he's going to go to prison for the rest of his life? No, there's two reasons why he's upset. The first one is, 'You arrested me and I'm gonna look like this on television?'

"The second thing which really annoyed him was that he had

just hired somebody to put Christmas lights on his house. Fifteen hundred dollars. 'Just drive by—' He didn't want a lawyer. The only thing he wanted was to see if the guy did a nice job putting his lights up."

Sammy must have been, for the moment, in denial.

"The FBI guys have them count their money out, and the agent gives them a voucher. John, twenty-three hundred dollars—no problem. Sammy Bull—twenty-one hundred, and eight singles. So Gotti's looking at him; he goes, 'Sammy—' "

Gotti's jocular dismay would eventually curdle, of course, into courtroom sneers and snarls as his once-trusted *consigliere*, Sammy Gravano, testified at the trial of Gotti and LoCascio. Sammy himself, suited up for the jury's sake, would see fit to pass up the last laugh. "I don't consider none of this a joke," he would assure LoCascio's lawyer from the witness stand. Throughout Gravano's testimony, the gallery is packed with press, and the FBI revels in the limelight—alone. Not one NYPD detective is called to the stand. The guilty verdict finally comes down in April 1992.

Traditional organized crime "responds to our police pressures; it changes and evolves—like Darwin," says one of those who map the opposition strategy. What began with street rackets and Prohibition, he explains, at the hands of such sophisticated mobsters as Castellano and crew, evolved into wholesale extortion of major industries. As a result, New Yorkers pay a "mob tax" on everything from concrete to coats and suits.

A Castellano relative, *capo* Tommy Gambino, also was arrested December 11, 1990, but stood trial (with brother Joe Gambino) in Manhattan on antitrust and extortion charges. The brothers copped expensive pleas—score another one for the good guys. New York detectives and prosecutors have chalked up some real victories over organized crime but still have their work cut out for them. By financial wiseguys, for instance, who commit everything from credit card larceny to stock manipulation, recruiting accomplices from the straight population in the bargain.

In the late eighties, a young blue-chip executive type from Wall Street dines with an old-time wiseguy at a posh restaurant. They are under surveillance by a detective at the next table. Mr. Blue

Chip's legitimate prospects may be reduced in this post-crash era—but there's still the mob route to millionaire-before-thirty.

"Let me tell ya something," warns Old Wiseguy, "when things go right, they go right. But when they don't—you wouldn't believe how fuckin' bad they can go." If Mr. Blue Chip's eyeballs had ended up on the tablecloth, the detective wouldn't have been surprised. "They think everything's cool, and before they know it, they're in over their heads."

The NYPD has attracted enough good guys from the same neighborhoods and background as the wiseguys, and with an instinctive feel for mafioso mentality. But what of "nontraditional" organized crime—the upstart immigrant racketeers invading the city's ethnic neighborhoods? True, the new international mobsters and the old mafiosi share a common brutal culture of blood and betrayal, and both dance to one drum—money—but the NYPD recruitment pool is no match for the influx of felonious mentalities, from Albanian to Vietnamese.

At least New York cops won't have to contend anytime soon with another matinee-idol thug like John Gotti. "The people aren't trying me," the boss ego told reporters attending his 1990 trial in New York State Supreme Court. "The people like me. . . . It's those four, those prosecutors."

Gotti did, in fact, beat the state charges of conspiracy and assault. No wonder his arrest ten months later for still more serious crimes struck him as little more than an excuse for a comedy bit. "I'm sure his lawyer told him, 'You're going to be indicted for murder and racketeering,' " says Sergeant Mullally. "—No sweat. No big deal. Let's face it, the world shuts down around the Christmas holidays. They probably thought everything was on hold."

Already frustrated by acquittals at two previous well-publicized Gotti trials, The Law was not about to wait. Here's how the beginning of the end unfolded for the man The New York Times called "the nation's most prominent crime boss."

### Detective Sergeant John Mullally: Locking Up Gotti

They decided they would arrest him on a Tuesday night, which is "tribute night"— the night he would hold court in the Ravenite and everybody would come in. The guy with concrete, the guy with asbestos, windows, everything else. They would all pay tribute to him. (We had gotten the information about a soldier, Louis DiBono, that he wasn't at tribute night the Tuesday night before he was found dead. Right away, you don't show up, there's a problem.) Everybody shows up; everybody *better* show up.

There was only four guys left working on the Castellano case when I got to Manhattan South [Homicide Task Force] in 1989—Al Licata, Phil Birde, Jimmy Turnbull, and Joe Brandefine; initially, I think there were ten or fifteen. They were all assigned to Homicide, but they worked out of the Seventeenth Precinct, which is where the hit happened. I was in charge of those four fellas, along with everybody else in the squad.

We were really kept in the dark until it was time to go to arrest him, because you had to have government secret-agent clearance to know the details of the case. It was joint: we were working the homicide aspect of it, the Eastern District was working some aspect, the Southern District was working some other aspect, and eventually it came to a point that they had to decide who was going to prosecute him. I guess the Eastern District won the game.

We knew it was coming down, but we thought maybe the feds might wait till after Christmas. All of a sudden we got a call. The only people left now were Turnbull and Brandefine; Licata and Birde are retired from the job. *Contact Brandefine and Turnbull forthwith, and have 'em report to 26 Federal Plaza.*

I made sure they were notified, and I was goin' home. Chief DeMartino sent somebody down to the garage. I was drivin' out—"The chief wants you to come back."

"John, I want you to go with them." Okay, Chief. No problem.

We all met with the FBI. They already had people surveilling the Ravenite. They were waitin' to go in and grab 'em. From 26 Federal Plaza to the Ravenite is maybe ten or fifteen blocks. It's all in this little cluster in lower Manhattan. Twenty-six Federal Plaza is in the beginning of the financial district, and the Ravenite is in Little Italy, which is to the north, just on the other side of Canal Street.

Myself and Joe and Jimmy went out to the set where they were. I think we were parked on 11th Street and the Bowery. (Right by Mordecai Levy's location, the Jewish Defense League boss. I was there when he was firing the shots a couple of years earlier, so I'm always a little nervous when I drive by that spot that he might be stickin' a gun out of one of those gun turrets and lettin' a couple of rounds go.)

The deal was gonna be two FBI agents and one detective to arrest Gotti, two FBI agents and a detective to arrest Frankie LoCascio, two FBI agents and myself were gonna grab Sammy Bull.

We waited. The mood was pretty upbeat; especially Joe and Jimmy, they were pretty pumped up. The FBI agents had been working these organized crime families for years. The fellows I was with—two guys who were just about ready to get out and they had been working Sammy Bull forever. This was like payoff time. Finally! A lot of police work is instantaneous. Something happens, you make an arrest, and it's over. Even a homicide investigation, maybe in a couple of days you make an arrest, or in a week or two. But we're talkin' years. Long-term investigation. They were feeling good, lookin' forward to lockin' 'em up.

At about eight-thirty P.M. or so, off we go. Joe Brandefine is in a car with two agents; I'm in a car with two agents; Jimmy Turnbull is in a car with two agents. The two guys that were in the car with Joe, I guess they were excited or whatever, but they went flyin' down there. We got caught at three or four lights. We didn't get there until two minutes after they did. They ran in by themselves.

The two FBI agents and Joe—there's about a hundred people in there. We get in and everybody's looking—"We're the police. *Nobody's leavin'.*" The way the Ravenite is laid out, when you come in there's a counter—a bar with an espresso machine, tables right near it, pastries and stuff like that. You walk straight through to an arched little alcove or doorway and here's a round table. Gotti was sitting in the middle, Frankie LoCascio on the right side, and Sammy Bull Gravano on the left. It struck me when I got in: just like television. You don't anticipate that it's going to be the actual way. We decided to leave the two FBI agents back there and get rid of the people in the front.

It almost looked like a little café. Very nice, clean. Gorgeous espresso machine. All the guys in the place were very cool. We told them we just wanted to get their names and information. Nobody gave us a hard time at all. Nobody. They weren't arrested. One other fella, Tommy Gambino, was arrested in Brooklyn. I think he was en route to the Ravenite.

We get all the stuff done, and we're bringing them out and putting them in the cars. Joe goes with the two agents that put Gotti in the car. I get in the car with Sammy Bull and the two FBI agents. "I'm never going to see those lights. Just drive by my house. Just let me see the lights."

No problem with Gotti or Sammy Bull. Very cooperative. LoCascio was like Mr. Hard-ass—"I'm not givin' you my name. Don't touch me." That type of thing. He thought he was a tough guy. The other two, very cooperative. Everybody was rear-cuffed. We bring them back to 26 Federal Plaza, and I'm telling you—there must have been thirty-five FBI agents. We bring them up to Processing. From our police department, there's just me and the two detectives.

Now the processing was done, and they are going to bring 'em over to Metropolitan Corrections Center. One of the bosses from the FBI says "Okay, two FBI agents and one detective walk Gotti out, two FBI agents and one detective walk out LoCascio, and two FBI agents and one detective walk out Sammy Bull." I guess these guys were so excited—the culmination of this whole investigation and they arrested John. . . . We're at the elevator banks—I think about this and I have to laugh—everybody got on the elevator with Gotti except me, Joe, Jimmy, and those two older FBI agents. We're still in the hallway with Sammy Bull and Frankie LoCascio. If the capacity was twenty, seventy-two people got into the elevator with John Gotti.

We just stood there and we all started laughin'. There's this herd around Gotti, and the rest of us walked out like, "Oh, yeah, just two other guys. I think they picked them up on the way down for drunk driving or something." It was just amazing. I guess he carries that charisma, and I guess the guys got kinda caught up in it. That was it. It was over. We didn't get caught up in it.

————

Even before John Gotti's last arrest, "tribute night" was a Gotti gift to the Mafia mavens in law enforcement, says Roland (Ronnie) Cadieux. Now a private investigator, Cadieux worked his first OC case in Brooklyn's Tenth Homicide in 1972, and ultimately became one of those NYPD detectives who know the silk socks set inside out. His is the sort of background preferred by LCN (La Cosa Nostra) defense lawyers, but Cadieux declines their cases.

If you were a Gambino family member during Gotti's six-year high-profile reign, Ron Cadieux explains, those mandatory weekly visits meant "you must go to him, bow down to him, and pay him his money. Literally dozens of unknown Mafia people had to surface because they had to come. So the FBI and the local police were able to zero in on a lot of people they never knew before."

Gotti successfully plotted Paul Castellano's demise, but did that mean he was a competent godfather? Not in Cadieux's view: "A guy like him is death to the Mafia." Gotti? A mobster "like a thousand others," many knowledgeable investigators agree. An egomaniac, Gotti gave good headlines and loved to dazzle his Queens neighbors with fancy July Fourth fireworks.

Big Paul, whose rise was a lot more gradual, became godfather in his sixties, kept a low profile—compared to John Gotti, at least—and ruled for nearly ten years. But in the Mafia, ruling hands come with sweaty palms. Big Paul's were soaking wet, reports Cadieux, when the Southern District Organized Crime Strike Force took him down on the last Friday in March 1984.

Castellano's arrest by strike force detectives Ken McCabe and Cadieux, FBI agent Art Ruffles, and supervisor Sergeant Joe Coffey was prearranged—low-key. It took place in defense attorney James

LaRossa's midtown office. McCabe and Cadieux clamped the cuffs on, and the investigators drove the godfather downtown for processing.

During his arraignment in the federal courtroom, Cadieux sat next to him. "He has a big foot, and I was looking at it—I was mesmerized by the size of Paul Castellano's foot. He turned and said to me, 'You know, I gotta thank you. You agents are not bad guys.'

"I said to him, Paul—we're New York City detectives. If we were agents, you'd still be on the street. He laughed—'No offense.' I said, No offense taken." Ten months later at dinnertime, the FBI knocked on the door of the *capo's* Staten Island mansion and staged a soap-opera style sequel to the strike force's businesslike arrest.

The clean-cut Cadieux might be mistaken for an FBI agent with a sense of humor. He somehow manages to look healthy even with a heavy cold. On the surface, at least, the most complicated thing about him is his French-Canadian name (usually mispronounced "c'doe" in New York). Even his hair is dead straight, with a touch of gray at the temples.

Cadieux *père* worked at Bethlehem Steel for many years as a machinist, and that was all Ron and the other sons knew till they were grown. But, "Back in Prohibition, he used to run liquor from Canada to Massachusetts. It all came out when I was married, already had children. . . . 'There's a roadblock,' my father warned his boss."

" 'Ah, these guys can't hit the side of a barn—' "

" 'I no sooner got done telling him,' " so the father's story went, " 'than a bullet went right through his eye. After I got through the roadblock, I pushed the body out and I got away. I went through backyards. I had clotheslines around the truck, fences up on top of the truck. I got away—but my boss was dead.' " The same detective who casually tells one mob murder shocker after another looks suddenly serious when he retells this long-ago story about his dad.

In New York mobsters say "pinch"; cops say "collar." Whatever you call it, the arrest of Castellano *and* much of his numerous mob family was an enviable coup. What's more, the godfather was only the pièce de résistance of the RICO (Racketeer Influenced and Corrupt Organizations) case directed by then-Assistant U.S. Attorney Walter Mack. ("We'd charge any machine-gun nest with him," says former-Marine Cadieux of former-Marine Mack.)

Mack's strike force roster read like a directory of law enforcement agencies. They linked up witnesses and amassed evidence against twenty coconspirators. Their indictment—citing twenty-five murders investigated by Cadieux and partner, Detective Frank Pergola—read like an encyclopedia of mob crime. The spark that started the case that became a seventeen-month trial was actually a stolen-car export racket with a Mideast connection. Cadieux describes it:

"They stole literally hundreds of Lincolns, Mercedes, BMWs; they all got shipped to Kuwait. We still laugh, looking at the Gulf War pictures, 'cause all those cars being stolen by the Iraqis we're sure were already stolen cars. Sometimes the wiseguys were stealing ten or fifteen a night out of Staten Island, Brooklyn, and Queens. Shipping 'em over at anywhere from nine to twelve to fifteen thousand dollars a car. This was Roy DeMeo's crew. He was one of the most feared hit men in any family.

"They had such a lucrative operation, they stopped doing hijackings, they stopped doing drugs. They were making so many millions of dollars and the risk was a lot less—'cause even if you got caught in a stolen car, who's gonna go to jail?

"Two of our NYPD Auto Crime guys, Harry Brady, a detective, and a sergeant, John O'Brien, went to Kuwait before the war to make the case. The government allowed them to take the VIN numbers off the cars—but wouldn't allow the State Department to seize the cars. Soldiers would take 'em around the country, grabbing these vehicle identification tags for the trial.

"DeMeo's crew was doing terrific. So good they started murdering competition—some of it legitimate. A resident of Kuwait was in a car lot business with a guy out in Nassau County, Long Island. The crew started to put the squeeze on this guy. He threatened to go to the police, so they killed him *and* his partner."

The money that mobsters live for has never proved bulletproof, not even for a godfather. Before Castellano could stand trial, he ended up a corpse in one of the City's tonier gutters. Several codefendants—including the hit man, Roy DeMeo—also fell victim to premature street justice before the jury could speak. But there were still enough targets to keep the trial going for nearly a year and a half, and, as Cadieux is fond of pointing out, "Everybody who lived and was tried, got life."

Having collared Castellano, the detective retired after twenty-three years—with enough tales of Mafia blood and betrayal to sustain an updated Scheherazade for a lot of nights.

### Detective Second Grade Roland F. Cadieux: A Rat in the Family

There was a Genovese boss by the name of Patillo here in Manhattan, who went to a prison to talk to a chauffeur that the FBI had in custody. I went to Jersey to interview the chauffeur. Patillo said to the chauffeur, "You know, I hope it's not true—we understand you're talking to the feds."

Well, once they think that's possible, you're dead, 'cause they're not gonna take the chance. So as soon as Patillo said that, the chauffeur must've got on the phone—called the FBI, "Come over, I want to talk to you." Not unusual—that's how we get a lot of witnesses. In many cases, the wiseguys actually do the work for us.

To get him to shut up, they might grab one of the guy's kids or they might get the wife. It's rare we don't get cooperation when they go kill a family member. If you were afraid for your life, but now they killed your kid, you might say, That's it—all bets off. I'm cooperating. I'm not gonna let them kill my children and not do anything about it! I'm not gonna worry now about what they're gonna do to me—they have to catch me. They already did my family.

Some of our best witnesses, the mob killed family members, and the witness immediately turns, comes over to us. A Gambino soldier by the name of Freddy DiNome was in MCC. The FBI was trying for a year to get him to cooperate. His brother, Richie DiNome, used to be the expert at forging VIN numbers for the stolen cars, and he would go along on hits and dump bodies. We never really got him for one of the murders.

I went with Ken McCabe and told Richie he was gonna be killed because of Freddy. He said, "If it happens, it happens." In other words, I don't believe you. "Ron, Ken—I appreciate your comin', but if it happens, it happens." He knew Kenny for years. Me, he met over that case.

A couple months later they shot him in Staten Island with a shotgun, but he survived.

Got hit with twenty-five out of thirty-something pellets. He walked out of the hospital. We went and told him, You're still gonna be killed. . . .

Unfortunately, they caught him with three young kids buying drugs off him, killed all of 'em at his house. We warned his brother, Freddy, they're gonna kill Richie. Says, "Nah—Richie? That's bullshit."

As soon as they killed Richie, we grabbed Freddy right away: They're gonna come here tell you *they had nothing to do with it, and they'll take care of you.* The very next day, three hit men went to MCC, signed in with their right names, and said to him, "Nino (Anthony Gaggi) told us to come over and say we had nothing to do with that. It was some drug dealers did that—we'll take care of it. You're gonna work for Nino when you come out." Exactly what we told him. "And we'll take care of you. Don't worry about anything."

They left. We were next door in the U.S. attorneys' office building. Right next door. Freddy DiNome went immediately into the witness protection program, and he was a great witness. In fact, his information was one of the keys in making a case against Paul Castellano.

---

Because electronic bugs were to the Gambino crime family social clubs as raisins to panettone, John Gotti conducted his business powwows on the Mulberry Street sidewalk outside the Ravenite. (Gotti's "walk-talks" also let him strut his fashion stuff for fellow mobsters and admiring neighbors.) Leave it to a band of inventive, very single-minded, and fairly madcap detectives assigned to the Manhattan DA's squad to try stringing bugs in the *air* in front of the Ravenite.

As far back as the summer of 1979, says Detective Joe Pepe, DA's squad detectives had overheard John Gotti giving vent to murderous resentment against Paul Castellano. The Gambino godfather, feeling the law's breath on his neck, had ordered the "family" to lie low for a time, Pepe explains—cramping members' style and flattening their wallets.

If it were up to the volatile, ambitious Gotti and other Young Turks, Castellano's restraint of trade, so to speak, would have been treated as a capital offense right then. But underboss Aniello Dellacroce, headquartered at the Ravenite, kept the rebels under control as long as humanly possible. The Castellano hit came just two weeks after Dellacroce's death from cancer.

The DA's detectives, hidden in an observation post directly opposite the club, usually could hear more and better with their own ears than they could harvest from the variety of listening and recording devices they jiggered with constantly. While they were at it, they also shot epic quantities of videotape.

Ravenite videos and bugs by the DA's squad produced a mosquitolike nuisance effect, resulting in court cases against eight wiseguys. Most of those who got stung by the caper pled guilty; one went to trial. Four heavyweights got a year for criminal contempt—refusing to tell what they knew about the assassination of Bonanno godfather Carmine Galante.

Temperamental though the squad's bugs were, they could and did produce malarialike recurrences. For years to come, recordings made by the Manhattan DA's detectives continued to get courtroom play at major Mafia trials. At the blockbuster 1987 federal "Commission" trial, for instance, the videotapes helped convict Anthony Bruno Indelicato on the Galante hit. He was sent to federal prison for forty years.

For Joe Pepe, the Ravenite effort—consuming and frustrating as it was then—is hilarious looking back. And certainly the highpoint of an eventful career. After all, who could forget the time the mobsters were overheard planning to firebomb what they were convinced was a hive of FBI agents?

### Detective Second Grade Joe Pepe:
### Bugging the Wiseguys

This was the case I worked the hardest on, the last big one up in the DA's squad. The two detectives who started it were new. They came in from Narcotics like I had a few years before. The two of them were cowboys—immediately made enemies with everyone. Everything had to be done Vic's way and nobody else knew the right ways to do it. I'm working with detectives that had been in the squad fifteen years, eighteen years, twenty-three years—these two kids come in. Vic smoked a big cigar, dressed like a mobster. Frankie would walk around with sunglasses all day. It was because of his eye problem—light hurt his eyes. Nobody would work with 'em.

They went and started an organized crime case on Castellano's underboss, Aniello Dellacroce, at the Ravenite on Mulberry Street. It was a big secret. *They didn't want* anybody from the DA's office to work with 'em. They got two detectives from Intelligence, John Gurnee, who's now deceased, and Jimmy Mullan, who's now—I don't really know where he is.

Frankie and Vic went out and worked on the case for about thirteen months. They had a tremendous amount of paperwork. Nobody knew what they were doing except Inspector Borrelli. (He's now the chief of detectives. One of the best bosses—this is a fun type of guy to work for.) One day, Vic Ruggiero hit the inspector with, like, two million hours of overtime. Borrelli went through the ceiling.

He called me in with Andy Rosenzweig, who was a sergeant then. "Listen, I got these two maniacs—I want to transfer both of them. I haven't seen them in months. I don't know where they are. Nobody knows what they're doing. They don't even tell me—I'm the inspector. They're hitting me with this overtime.

"Joe, I'm gonna put you in charge of this case. I need somebody I can control. Rosenzweig is gonna be the new boss on the case." (We had different units up in the DA's office; each unit had its own sergeant.) Listen, please, Inspector, Why me? "Because you have a good rapport with the Rackets Bureau, and if there's a case to be made, you're gonna help them make it. And that's an order. You're working on the case."

I could not get out of it. The fact was that these guys were *this close* to getting probable cause to write up a wiretap order and having a judge sign it. They just didn't know how to put it together for this one assistant, the chief of the Rackets Bureau, Austin Campriello. (I loved him. Little guy, like a little Napoleon.)

I told the inspector, These two guys and the two guys from Intelligence—they've been working and they've got it. He says, "When will I have a wiretap or a bug?"

About a month.

Actually in two weeks, we had the order signed. It was Frank's case and Ruggiero's case, and they made it—I just put the icing on the cake. They did all the rough work, the hard work.

The problem was, now we had to break into the club. They insisted they're gonna go outside the DA's office and have two wire men come, and a lock pick, to pick the lock on the club. They didn't trust anybody in the DA's office. They didn't want anybody to know where they were putting the bug. (By the way, that is not a bad philosophy to have.) We had our own lock men and we had our own wire men—this was a slap in the face. Borrelli insisted he was gonna keep harmony in the squad. "No, you're gonna get one guy from Intelligence, and I'm gonna give you somebody from our office, and we're gonna break in."

Well, by the time they got the lock picked, it was too late to go ahead. Sun was coming up.

Next try, they sent an army out. A production number. We had Rosenzweig on the corner in a Con Edison truck, four guys in the manhole, "working on the street," two lock picks dressed like bums, a couple of detectives pretending to be falling-down drunk—lookouts—and three in our observation post across the street. Plus two radio cars cruising with our detectives, in uniform. In case somebody reported a burglary on us, these cars would take the job. The reason nobody tried before to get in this door, it's on the street—just recessed a couple of feet.

The dog's name was Duke—he barked for hours, jumping against the old-fashioned wood-and-glass door. The lock pick would have almost all the tumblers up, the dog would jump, and they'd all fall down; have to start picking all over again.

A lady lived on the floor above. On the third floor was Mickey Cirelli, an old man that had a bookmaking operation with Gotti—he ran it out of the social club. Tough old son-of-a-bitch. She heard the noise and called him. When he came down, the "bums" took off. Cirelli walks over to the Con Ed truck—"Hey, Officer, arrest those guys—" He knew.

Later we heard Gotti say, "Should've shot the sons of bitches. We could've said we thought they were burglars."

Our observation post was an apartment, supposedly vacant, directly across the street from the Ravenite social club. (The club was 247 Mulberry, we were 244, something like that.) We would come in the place from Mott Street and go up over the roofs and come in through the roof, so nobody ever saw us go in and out.

We used to look out and watch 'em; we had video cameras. John Gurnee had a friend at CBS that made us one of these big shotgun-type microphones they have at football games. But part of the mike should have stuck out the window; we couldn't do that. We got a lot of hissing.

Dellacroce had an old wooden bench in front of the Ravenite, and we put a bug in there. We measured the two-by-four on the bench, walked by one day, chipped off the paint, matched it, and we painted a hollowed-out two-by-four. We stole the bench, replaced the two-by-four, and within six minutes, had the bench back in front of the club.

Buddy Dellacroce, Aniello Dellacroce's son, got to the club about nine-thirty the next morning, and an old woman called across the street. He crossed over, and from the observation post I can overhear her telling him that two guys took the bench. He comes back later; we see him pay her for her services.

They walked over, looked at the bench, turned it upside down; they found the bug. They unscrewed the two-by-four, set it on the side and they left it. Meanwhile, they're in there calling, telling everybody they found a bug.

We called up the office, a guy named Ray McCarthy. Ray was a ballsy type of a detective. He was an Irish-looking guy. Nobody in Little Italy paid too much attention to this guy with tattoos on his arms. Ray, we need a favor. There's a two-by-four leaning against the wall at the Ravenite. Want you to walk by and get it. We'll be watching you; I'll have two men on the street in case anybody comes after you. Ray walked by. I'm telling you, they were standing right there, and he just picked it up and kept walking.

John Gotti came with Dellacroce. They're running over to tell 'em that they found this bug. They went to get it—and it was gone. John was cursing. "You stupid bastards! You stupid fucking idiots! You mean to tell me you had it and somebody stole it from you?" They were afraid to touch it, to take it out.

We got our bug back. It happened to be a very expensive bug, like a thousand dollars. We didn't want to hear Borrelli on that.

Next to the Ravenite was a place called Ross Trucking. Next to Ross Trucking was a chicken market. John would walk up and down by the market. A detective named Pete Milo (electronic genius) made us six microphones that were about this big—a quarter of an inch. Less. We went up on the roof of Ross Trucking and hung a series of these microphones seven and a half feet off the ground. He made it run on one very, very thin wire. We could *hear* John telling Dellacroce that they wanted to kill Paulie Castellano. On the tape, we'd get chickens.

A little bug with a battery is a transmitter. You put it someplace and you walk away; it'll transmit to a receiver. A hard wire is like a telephone. You have a microphone with an actual wire that runs to someplace where you listen to it. Now, with a hard wire, you have to find a place to run it. You've gotta get into the club, hook up your wire, run the wire out to another location, where you hook it up to a tape recorder.

We got into the basement. The club floor was vinyl tile. Jack Gardiner, the wire man from Intell, drilled through till he got to the tile and put in a spike mike. On the other side of the Ravenite, on Lafayette Street, one of the assistant DAs had an apartment that we were gonna use to run the wire. But we decided that if they found out we were using her apartment, they may not know who she is and someone might try to kill her because she was cooperating with the police.

We ran the wire into the firehouse on Lafayette Street. Word in the fire department had it that a fire officer, unbeknownst to us, gambled—and he was a heavy drinker. His bookmaker was Mickey Cirelli (who was also a deacon of the neighborhood church). The fire officer went and told them, "The cops are up in the firehouse, there's a wire running out the window, and it comes right to your club."

We didn't know there was a pipe too near where we put the spike mike—all we got on the tape was running water noise. But as they go into the basement, we can hear *them* talking. The mike picks 'em up: "It's down here. The wire runs right into the building and it comes down here somewhere." They look up and they found it—"Right here." Then we hear, "Jesus Christ, who the hell could do work like this? It's gotta be the FBI. Let's follow it."

We cut the three wires, threw them out the window, packed our stuff up, and got out of there.

Borrelli went crazy. He thought there was definitely a leak in the office. Frank Imundi and Vic Ruggiero were screaming, I told you so. The DA went crazy. They had a big internal investigation. Everybody was suspect. Who sold the case out? We put more bugs in, and we found out it was the fire officer. (In fact, the wiseguys went back to him and asked him if he knew anything else.)

While we had the bug there, they killed Carmine Galante. July. Never forget it—right before Bastille Day. They came out and put a radio in front of the club early in the morning, and everybody was standing around. Hey, what the hell are they listening to on that radio? We can hear it on the bug that we had in the doorway, but we couldn't hear it real clear.

We finally got it; it was WCBS news radio and they kept flashing the bulletin. And each time—we have it on videotape—they're all hugging and kissing each other. They had the radio on way before Carmine was killed, and they were all standing around there, waiting.

Forty-five minutes after he was killed, the crew that killed him came to the club. Guy named Indelicato was the shooter. He had the gun in his waistband. There were witnesses that said as he ran to the car the shooter fell—and here he is limping; his pants were all dirty. And everybody's kissing him. There was no reason to kiss Indelicato at that point. Nobody kissed him before this. We had had him there a hundred times. No one ever kissed him. Today, everybody. That's how they got the conviction with our videotape. It was opportune that we were there.

In our observation post, we had about six hundred pounds of equipment. No lights ever went on. At night, we worked in the dark. One day, they thought there was somebody across the street and they were coming up. We hear them talking about it: gonna come up and burn the apartment out.

We disconnected all the bugs and the wiretaps, broke it all down, hid it in the closets and in the bathroom, and Jimmy and I hid in the closet.

Buddy Dellacroce and Norman Dupont took a ladder out of Ross's, put it up to the window, and they send a guy from Ross's up. He didn't see nothin'. Then Dupont. He could only get high enough that he can look in. We had a little screen, because the sun would hit it just right and you couldn't see into the apartment. He knocked it in and he looked.

"There's nobody up here." Buddy is saying, "C'mon, I got the gasoline; just throw it in there." The Molotov cocktail. "If he lights it, we shoot him off the ladder," Jimmy says. We both had our guns out.

The guy from Ross's says, "Listen, we can't burn the building down; there's people in here, Buddy." "I don't give a fuck—I'm telling you, the FBI's in there." "You're nuts! I'm looking in; there's nobody in here." They went down.

They came into the building with Mickey Cirelli, and now he's trying to pick the lock on *our* door. Jimmy and I are hiding. *They come in, we'll lock 'em up.* He couldn't pick it.

———

Gang warfare broke out in the Six-two Precinct in south Brooklyn in the late sixties—about the time ex-bus driver Bob Kohler went into the Bureau. Brooklyn Organized Crime needed extra men, and they borrowed a couple from the Youth squad—Kohler and another guy. Only one man could stay on permanently in OC. Kohler could hardly believe it, but the other guy preferred tracking down youthful offenders to investigating mobsters.

Older than average, thirty-three when he came on the job, Bob Kohler caught on fast. What's more, he says, he could learn from sharp OC detectives like Billy Burns.

If you wanted to interview a mobster, Detective Kohler discovered, you didn't even have to whistle. "All you had to do was put out the word, and they'd come in." *I don't remember* was about the most disrespectful phrase a mafioso would utter in your presence. Detectives and wiseguys fenced with one another in colorful Damon Runyonese—and threats to firebomb officers of the law were a specialty of political extremists, not goodfellas. That was then—the late sixties.

Kohler had several cops in the family. He'd quit driving a bus and signed on to the NYPD for job security, but he ended up with better working conditions too: in 1967 bus drivers could still expect more abuse from passengers than detectives got from gangsters.

Circa 1972, during the Colombos' internal wars, the Brooklyn Organized Crime group maintained a presence near the gang's President Street social club. Mob-cop relations were civil. Mob bosses sternly reprimanded underlings for disrespect to the law. President Street was an okay place for detectives to work. Come summertime, Kohler recalls, "the old man was hot stuff—Pop Gallo (Al Senior). He says, 'I'm-a-gonna-get a lemon ice. What flavor you want?' "

Kohler and his partner, Jimmy O'Brien, kept the terrain cool as lemon ice. Kohler says Al's son Joey Gallo should've stayed by the club. "We were with him on his birthday, the day before he died. That night he went out to Manhattan and got picked off at Umberto's Clam House."

Cut to September 1980; in connection with Detective Kohler's missing persons investigation of April Ernst, age nineteen, the detective phoned a John Gotti groupie—twenty-one-year-old Andrew Curro. The younger mob generation had by now dispensed with any quaint old respect for law enforcement.

"NO FUCKING WAY—" Curro informed the fatherly, gray-haired Kohler. "YOU'RE *NOT* HANGING THAT ON ME! I WON'T TALK TO YOU WITHOUT MY LAWYER." The following day, Curro, a Sylvester Stallone lookalike, refused to talk to Kohler in person at all. And as the squad canvassed Curro's associates, they ran into even more verbal abuse than a bus driver.

Kohler, the detective who locked up mobster Jimmy "The Gent" Burke for the 1979 execution of con man Richard Eaton, most certainly did hang on Andrew Curro the strangling and dismemberment of April Ernst. A young ADA named Eric Seidel proved the murder a perfect fit, but at the outset it was hardly a promising case. In the absence of a body, would a grand jury even indict? "Bob pushed me into it," concedes Seidel, "said he was gonna retire otherwise, and I pushed the Homicide Bureau to take it."

Mafia defense lawyers like to lecture juries on their clients' shining family values. At John Gotti's last trial, his attorney called him a "devoted" father and grandfather. The less said the better by even the most skillful counsel about Andrew Curro's family values; they left much to be desired, and he had cause to regret it.

Andrew, as it happens, put out a contract on his older brother Gerard's life, and it backfired. Gerard eagerly took the stand for the People during the 1985 April Ernst murder trial in Brooklyn and quoted Andrew on the postmortem of his jilted girlfriend: "The head was the most difficult to take off. The arms were easier and the intestines came out like big spaghetti."

Andrew Curro remains in prison, sentenced to twenty-five years to life state time—on top of federal time for two armored car stickups—(stickups with which Gotti also was charged, but acquitted). These were stickups that April knew were Andrew's doing and that, in the jealous outburst that led to her death, she threatened to finger him for.

The April Ernst case, a study in betrayal and blood thirstiness—literally—makes a classic example of killing as a way of Mafia life.

### Detective Robert F. Kohler:
### Spaghetti

"Do me a favor. Listen to these two girls—it's a missing person, but Detective So-and-so wouldn't take it." Two complainants were standing by when I walked in for the four-to-twelve; one was April Ernst's sister, Toby, and the other was Sharon, April's cousin. They said April had called her boyfriend last Sunday evening:

"Are we going out?" "No," Andrew Curro said, "I don't feel like doing anything tonight." So she went out on her own, left the house around eleven P.M. Cousin Sharon said she personally never liked this Andrew, he was weird. April was going to Scandal's on Flatbush near Clinton Road.

About five-thirty Monday morning, Sharon heard the house alarm. April apparently didn't push the right buttons when she come in 'cause she's in a little bit of a stupor. Then she corrects it. Sharon heard it go off for a second or two. Then about six o'clock, April leaves again. And that's the last they seen of her.

I was starting to say, Hey, she may be living someplace, and she'll be back. But the sister continues: The next day, around three in the afternoon, Sharon's younger brother—he's a student in grammar school—is riding his bike and he spots April Ernst's red Toyota in the middle of the roadway, right up against the island with a fender dented. Now, this car had laid there all day. Busy Queens street, cars come right off the Belt Parkway there. Still laying there at three in the afternoon—nobody checked it out.

Would I look into this case?

I said, Well, of course. It doesn't sound right at all—there's something wrong with all this.

We talked to a newspaper boy on the corner there. He sees a blond fitting her description leaving the car and walking in the direction of the house, which was 101st Street and Avenue M, I believe. She lived with her aunt—Sharon's mother—and Sharon.

She was a naive kid. She come up from Florida, and I think when she met this fellow, this was *exciting*. Boy, here's a guy carries a gun. They're into money—being taken to all these wiseguy joints. Much better than what she's been in down in Florida. "Real classy places," and everybody's "somebody."

Called him up: "I'm not talking to you. No, no!"

I said, Jeez, you're the boyfriend—just want to ask you something. What's the matter with you?

Zero.

Al Marini and I went over and talked to people at Scandal's. We could've stayed home. "Uh—yeah, we know 'em, but . . ." Nobody heard anything.

But we heard from a girlfriend of Sharon's about a conversation with another girl, Dana. Dana saw April's picture on the missing person poster at the Lindenwood Diner. She was at Scandal's that night too. She said April was following Andrew around, nagging him, trying to make him jealous, and he wasn't paying attention to her. April yells at him, *"I know you rip off armored cars and carry a gun,"* and things like that—and Andrew was getting pissed off.

He was getting scared. She would tell him, *I work for the DA.* He thought she was actually connected with the DA's office in Long Island, that she was gonna go to them with this information. Couldn't let that happen. We checked up and she no longer worked there. "Oh, she was out of here a year or so ago." She was nothing but a file clerk.

Sharon's friend asked Dana, "Do you think he did it?" "You know him as well as I do, and what he's capable of doing." Dana said April came around her that night too. "Get the fuck away from me!" Dana told her. She said April was high and Andrew probably had something to do with it. If he had something to do with her disappearance, Dana told Sharon's girlfriend, "he'd spread it out—like cut it up and put it different places so it would be hard to find."

The first thing I did with the information about the stickups and Curro carrying a gun, I had a friend from when I started going to Organized Crime instead of the Youth Squad, this fellow Bill Burns. We got to be very friendly, learned an awful lot from him. Great detective. He later went over from Brooklyn to Major Case. I called him: do you have any armored car stickups still open? I think I may have something for you.

We got together and I started tellin' him about this, lookin' at pictures. God, Curro fits the description of one of the stickup guys! Major Case was working jointly with the U.S. attorney's office down in Brooklyn on a RICO case. Every coconspirator they brought down and questioned, they would hit them with questions about April Ernst and Andrew Curro. Indicating that if you're gonna be helpful, we can be helpful to you.

I had Bill Burns sit down with Sharon's girlfriend, like he was in on the investigation of April Ernst. Sharon's friend knew about the stickups. Bill had questions that he would hit her with, and she knew what she was talking about.

Took time for them to build their RICO case because of all the intricacies. "We ask you, if you could just hold off on the Ernst homicide so we could complete our cases. And anything that refers to your case, we'll give you." It was a better shot for me if we could get something like that going, because this Curro's not gonna talk to me. We were almost positive that he's the guy, but the thing is, where's the body? How was it done? All these things. This armored car stickup stuff was a break—now we got the FBI and we got Major Case working right in conjunction.

Some of the powers-that-be said, "Ah, why don't you give that damn thing up? What are you gonna do with it?" Same with the Richard Eaton homicide. Honest to God! "Come on, how long you gonna stick with the case?" Gonna stick with it until it's finished.

It was a year after she disappeared. We hear from the One-o-six in Queens that they have Andrew Curro's brother; he would like to talk to the detectives on the April Ernst case.

One night about a year ago, he hears Andrew and his friend Johnny Ragano laughing, so he says, what's going on? Andrew starts bragging. He says, "I had to do April Ernst. She was shooting her mouth off; had to get rid of her."

She leaves Scandal's. Curro and others get in his Cadillac and they chase her. They're on the Belt Parkway, they get off at the Canarsie exit. Ran her off the road. She first hit the underpass, and then that collision caused the tire to go or jammed the wheel—she couldn't steer anymore.

They finally got her at her house, got her in their car—and he strangled her. There's a guy sitting next to Curro in the backseat with April, and Curro's strangling her as they're riding; she's grabbing this fellow's jacket lapel. (He wouldn't say anything to us. Wouldn't help us at all. "I don't know nothing, don't know nothing." I even tried to tell him, okay, You're going in; you're part of this. No good. He wouldn't bend. Scared to death of Curro.)

She's actually murdered in the car; then she's taken to an unknown Queens motel by Curro, Frankie Burke—son of Jimmy—and the other fellow. Curro has a machete that he bought down in Mexico. A souvenir. And he proceeds to hack her body up in the bathtub. Dismemberment is not an unusual thing for the mob, but it was unusual for this case because this guy Curro, he was a young kid.

Frankie Burke had the other guy drink a cup of her blood. And he's throwing up. He had to run into the bathroom.

They had a friend with one of these carting outfits. They put the body in the bag, the parts in, and "took them for a ride," he tells his brother. No one knows where.

We finally go to the grand jury—'85. (I had said that I was not gonna leave the job until I broke that case and the Eaton case.) We have father and mother, separately. Had to establish that if she were alive, "You would hear from her, right?" There's no way that wouldn't be—she was dependent on her family.

The father's attitude at the grand jury was, "If you get this guy, I'd like to have a little time with him." One of those things. Why didn't you have a little time with your daughter? Maybe this would not have happened. 'Cause Curro got her on drugs. She was nineteen years old. Pills. She was really naive, and this kid had her wrapped around his finger. So naive. Even after they chased her in the car—to have them come within fifteen minutes, *Oh, come on out, it's all forgotten*. She gets right in the car with them.

The mother was very interested, really concerned. And Toby—if it wasn't for her, we would have never known about it. She just *insisted*. Really great.

And then Andrew's brother in the grand jury. Seidel said, "I thought they were gonna throw up."

They had locked Andrew up at Lewisburg Federal Prison for the armored car stuff. We went and got him for trial. In the car, I don't say anything about the case. But he's mouthing off, "Hey, Kohler—you really think you're gonna get something here? Boy, are you gonna be surprised when April Ernst walks into that courtroom."

Surprised?! I says, You mean if they can ever put her back together and she shows up in the courtroom—we'll be surprised? Right. From then on, he wouldn't talk to me. When we convicted him, he told the DA, "I don't want that Kohler to drive me back." He couldn't face me because I "did this" to him.

———

"Tommy Karate." Martial arts expert, weapons collector, millionaire drug lord, nightclub owner, hit man. No one offers a more vivid example of the killing Mafia life than this bloody Bonanno soldier, Thomas "T.K." Pitera.

Surpassing most wiseguys in smarts and viciousness, this was a perp with a valid gun permit and no criminal record going in. According to a contemporary of Pitera's father, a detective who knew the family, "If you met Tommy, you'd think he was a perfectly nice guy." You'd never guess "he'd kill you in a minute." Assistant U.S. Attorney Elisa Liang of the prosecution team disagrees. "Until you look at the eyes," she says. Even to veteran Brooklyn OC detectives "Billy Jack" Tomasulo, Matty O'Brien, and George Terra, Pitera was different.

Pitera was the professional killer with a library of how-to murder books. Frank Gangi was his good-looking accomplice turned star witness. Then came the grisly finds in a bucolic site,

the likes of which old hands among New York City OC investigators had always heard about but never expected to see. In between
were a succession of gory crime scenes: put them all together, they
spell dream case—especially if you're an organized crime maven
like William Tomasulo. But Billy Jack was not simply lucky to
catch the case—he had prepared the ground.

*Reputation.* Huge and complex as the City is, it comprises a
number of small worlds where the paths of wiseguys and good
guys cross and recross. Someone like the chunky, flamboyantly
tattoo'd Tomasulo never knows when he'll meet one of his old
perps again, but he wants to be appropriately remembered if it
happens.

Tomasulo, a detective since 1980, had pursued murder suspect
Frank Gangi across the country without leaving Brooklyn. And
with the help of the LAPD, recaptured him. "He knew I was a
digger," the detective says. Gangi got off that time by foul means
(perjury successfully committed by his accomplice in the murder).
A jury may be had, but not Tomasulo. All business in court, larger-
than-life on the street, a jaunty yet unmistakable authority figure—
this is Detective Tough-But-Fair. Anybody he arrested knew that's
how you'd be treated by Billy Jack.

Five years after the original Gangi-Tomasulo skirmish, Gangi
was nearing the bottom of a downward spiral when he found
himself reentering the detective's orbit. Since their last encounter,
Gangi had hooked up with wiseguy Tommy Pitera and Pitera's
crew; now he reached out for the detective. On the stand at Pitera's
trial two years later, Gangi told the jury how it happened and why.
Assistant U.S. Attorney David W. Shapiro asked,

Q. What were you arrested for?
A. Reckless endangerment.
Q. And after you were taken to the precinct, what happened?
A. I was being arrested for reckless endangerment—or written a
   ticket—I don't know which one. [A desk appearance ticket.]
   And I seen a homicide detective that arrested me in 1985,
   named Billy Tomasulo.
Q. What happened then?
A. I—I asked to see Billy. And Billy called me in a room and I

discussed with him how I was feeling about how my life was
going and everything, and I—and I started talking to him.

Q. What did you talk to him about?

A. About cooperating. . . .

Q. And what did he say to you?

A. He said to—he said, Don't say nothing. He would call somebody [. . .] from the Brooklyn DA's office.

"Somebody" was George Terra, a former member of the Brooklyn DA's Detective Squad, who'd retired from the NYPD—and
come directly back to work with the DA's detective investigators,
a civilian unit.

"One of the wiseguy defense lawyers says I look more like a
wiseguy than a wiseguy." Terra got himself an undercover reputation to complement the look. "Why don't you call my friend
George," mobsters recommend when they want a witness killed.
Little do they know, phoning "George the hit man" is one of the
faster ways to get arrested in Brooklyn.

Tomasulo and Terra, both in their mid-forties, knew each other
since the start-up days of the NYPD Auto Crime Squad, where both
had worked when they were still "white shields," new in the
Bureau in the early 1970s. Tomasulo also knew if Gangi wanted to
talk to a prosecutor, Terra could get a prosecutor to listen. He
would get his boss, Deputy Organized Crime Bureau Chief Eric
Seidel.

Pitera had for several years been the subject of a federal drug
inquiry by the Drug Enforcement Administration. New York detectives now added Frank Gangi—whose information brought a lurid
new dimension to the case. The inquiry became a joint federal-
state effort, went into high gear, and climaxed a couple of months
later.

Within days of Pitera's June 4, 1990, indictment, investigators
in white antitick protective jumpsuits swarmed over the Staten
Island marshland where Gangi had guided them. "We went into
the woods, and we went back approximately about twenty yards,"
Gangi testified, "not as far as I thought Tommy would want me to
go. We dug about five feet deep, also not as far as, like, Tommy
wanted me to dig, which he tried to tell us to do."

The dig no one thought would ever happen lasted into mid-August and afforded the New York City media cops-vs.-mobbers photo ops galore. The *Staten Island Advance,* especially, had a field day and then some, chronicling the small army of forensic crime fighters as they foraged near the tranquil William T. Davis Wildlife Refuge. Detective Tomasulo "led a team," the *Advance* announced and, by photographing him regularly, let on to attentive readers that this prominent cop was a native son.

The quest for physical evidence in the Pitera case didn't end with forensic fireworks in the Staten Island woods. While cadaver-sniffing K-9s, backhoes, bulldozers, "void detector" gimmicks, and charismatic whatnot played to the media, vital minutiae went on behind the cameras. If you have dirt with potential as evidence, search the perp's universe for shovels—hopefully with dirt chemically like the suspect dirt. In making such a match, someone must safeguard Staten Island dirt to FBI test lab to court exhibit, for the jury's sake.

Matty O'Brien, a young-looking detective nearing the twenty-year mark and debating retirement, did what he had to do painstakingly, for months; then answered questions about dirt for an hour or so in the sterile, windowless federal courtroom. Witness number twenty-three of sixty-six—intelligent and credible as any prosecutor could desire. The court artists doodled on their oversize tablets. Not so much as a raised eyebrow from the defense team.

But Detective Billy Jack Tomasulo was grateful for those vital details—the shovels and the dirt. "That," he remarked, "was an important piece" of the case.

### Detective Second Grade William Tomasulo, DA's Detective Investigator George Terra, Detective Second Grade Matthew O'Brien: It's a Graveyard Out There

**Detective Tomasulo:** It's not every day that someone comes in and says, "Listen, I'll tell you where bodies are buried, and I'll tell you who did it." It happens once in a blue moon. It doesn't happen at all. We were listening to Frank Gangi—myself, Sergeant

Santimauro, and then George Terra came down. We were baffled. We thought maybe the guy flipped out or somethin'.

"There's bodies here—there's people in suitcases," he says. "They were Samson-ited."

They were Samsonited?

"There's people; they're packed in suitcases."

You gotta be kiddin' me.

"No, I'm not. I'm tellin' you the truth. Are you gonna believe me or what?"

I mean, we were stunned by it—And you know exactly where . . . ?

"Yes, I know exactly. Come on, I'll take you. . . ."

So we took him to the Brooklyn DA's office and they says, "*What* is he telling us?"

What I told you—there's bodies in suitcases buried out in Staten Island. It's a graveyard out there.

They started shakin' their heads too. This went on for quite a number of days. We told the chief of Brooklyn detectives at the time—Chief Ciccotelli. You have to inform the chief what's goin' on.

He says, "Yeah, what else you got?" He didn't want to hear it either. "I've got forty-some-odd years on this job, and I've been hearin' this for years—and no one ever turned up a mob burial ground in New York." I said, Well, I'm just informing you. He took it like a grain of salt, as did everyone.

At that point, we put Gangi up in a hotel under guard—the DA's office and the federal government. I think every federal agency you could name was workin' on Tommy Karate. They had wires up, and they had bugs up, and very much active—a lot of federal agents in this case. . . . And we come up with Frank Gangi!

So they agreed that we would put him up and he would be debriefed fully of all his crimes that he ever committed. We spent two months, at least. Once he talked about the homicides, I would check 'em out to see what we got to corroborate his story. I'd go back and pull the homicide-case folder—or the missing-persons folder, because most of these people were missin' persons. I had to open up like four or five homicide cases.

**Detective O'Brien:** I've dealt with organized crime, I would say, about eight or nine years. It just wouldn't shock you anymore what these guys do and what they're capable of. (I don't think I would have a problem even flippin' the switch.)

You talk to families of the deceased. For example, Marek Kucharsky's girlfriend— what a nice lady. She's single and Marek was living with her. How upset she was, visibly shaken when we spoke with her. Hadn't seen him in months. As far as she knew, he was missing. She made a missing persons report. He used her car that night, and they made a stolen-car alarm on it, looking for Marek.

He was just in the country a year or so. He was from Germany. Disappears. We interviewed her 'cause we needed to find his family. We had to go through Interpol to get dental records, fingerprint records, 'cause he was never arrested in New York or the United States. Interpol was excellent, and we got the prints.

The family of Phylliss Burdi—the girl that was buried, who was involved with drugs with Tommy—they really had no inkling. They knew she was into drugs, but it's just like anybody else in a family that you can't help. When you talk to those people, you really— He was an animal. He ruined these people's lives.

**Detective Tomasulo:** I'm used to it, but it was gory—the way the details came out about some of the homicides and how the victims were chopped up. Gangi had stated that when they were doin' Tal Siksik, the drug dealer, he was in the suitcase and he was zippered up to his neck. His head was sticking out. He was beggin' for his life and Pitera just shot him in the head. Right in the suitcase.

Tommy Karate is just a character, a dangerous kind of a character. There's no other way to describe him. I never ran into a person with his mentality—well versed on every aspect of criminal enterprise. Through his whole library of books, I didn't see anything there that was like, legitimate. Everything there was about killings and weapons and bombs and how to rip off drug dealers and how to break into safes and how to open up locks and how to sniper shoot. The guy was ready for war.

**DA's Investigator Terra:** I vouchered the books. I'd say there were two hundred. Not on shelves—a suitcase and a box full. He had law enforcement manuals too.

The knives we found in his place all had serrated edges.

**Detective O'Brien:** There must have been about twenty-two guns recovered in the raids. Pitera was known to fool around with the barrels, use silencers and stuff like that, to change the ballistic evidence. He had a tremendous amount of books—on surveillance, countersurveillance, intelligence, how to dismember . . . at least fifty books on how to cut up bodies different ways.

**Detective Tomasulo:** We arrested him on Atlantic. He had just dropped off his girlfriend at the Brooklyn House of Detention (her son was in jail at the time), and we took him two blocks away on Atlantic Avenue and around Third Avenue, I would say. We had followed him from the time he left his apartment.

We wanted to get him away from the area that he's known in which is the Sheepshead Bay, Bensonhurst section of Brooklyn, so no one would know that we had him—because we were contemplating doing other warrants. After he dropped off the girl, we figured it was prime time. Give him two blocks and then we'll take him.

It was all feds and NYPD following him. We had so many cars; I would put it like fifteen unmarked cars. Firebirds and T-Birds. You wouldn't make us bein' law enforcement. We had the whole Brooklyn/Queens Expressway filled up at that hour of the morning, eleven o'clock, twelve o'clock, like that. It was a Sunday and there wasn't too much traffic except for all of us, right behind him. We could have followed him all the way to Florida if we had to. He would have never made us.

There was a red light and a bus in front of him. All fifteen cars by this time, one behind the other. We blocked him in and overtook him. I think he thought he was gonna get shot or something. He didn't know who we were. The fellas had their shields hangin' around their necks, but all he seen was weapons. Shotguns, M-16s.

**DA's Investigator Terra:** When an informant first told me the name Tommy Karate, I didn't know who the hell he was. Just a name. I mentioned it to the bureau chief. "*Great target*," he said, "but you're not gonna get him!"

We stopped at the light, pulled up next to him. I hit the window with the butt of my gun, and he just dived across the seats.

**Detective Tomasulo:** That day was chosen as a doomday for him. The next couple of days, they had a target of about thirty-five people that they had to lock up, and they had warrants for 'em and search warrants. They wanted to do this as quick as possible because they had a lot of work ahead of them. The next big thing was gonna be the recovery of the bodies.

We conferred with other states where they had burial grounds from a mass murderer. At least we got a direction, how we were gonna go about this, an idea of what we were up against and what we'd need to find what we were lookin' for in this marshland. With all the agencies involved, I thought there would be a little bit of a power struggle. It couldn't've went any better—the cooperation from everybody.

A guy that charged the government two thousand dollars a day went runnin' around with a machine, a void detector, tryin' to find the bodies. Besides the K-9 dogs. And botanists to see if there was growth in the area which is not natural to the terrain—if a body could be in the spot. They activated a battalion of the National Guard, probing and searchin'. The dig went on for ninety days, strictly for one goal. To find these bodies and body parts.

The borough commander on Staten Island: "Lots of luck. Everybody's been diggin' out here for years and never found anything." So he was shocked—everybody was shocked—when we recovered the first body.

The first on the night of the fourteenth; the fifteenth, uncovered the first Samsonite suitcase: gray Hercules suitcase. We dug up two bodies that day, Tal Siksik and the boxer, Marek Kucharsky. Several days after, we dug up Stern and Leone and then the girl, Phylliss Burdi.

**Detective O'Brien:** After the arrests, the DEA got a lot of search warrants, and the police, FBI, ATF—we hit all Pitera's people. They recovered two shovels and a pick. I asked Crime Scene for soil samples, vouchered them. But the police department lab said the samples were contaminated. If they did the work, they couldn't testify to it. I couldn't take that chance.

So I got approval to take it to the FBI. Agent Bruce Hall (he's a chemist) told me to go in the grave and take samples from different levels, 'cause from the topsoil to the bottom soil of the grave, the color changes. I had twenty samples.

Through Bruce Hall's examination, we got hits on those two grave sites—matches with the soil on the shovels. Very important because the shovels were used in the two homicides from the time period where the government can ask for the death penalty.

A lot of behind-the-scenes work goes with a trial: chain of custody for the evidence—make sure there's no breaks in that chain. You have to document it—a lot of paper, time-consuming work. That's the other side of police work.

**Detective Tomasulo:** We got a "bonus" of one body that we didn't go out there for. Staten Island lieutenant was saying, "Listen, this is yours. It's a Brooklyn case." No, it's a Staten Island case. I came out here for five bodies; I had them all named.

It had no head, no hands; and I felt it was the same work as Tommy Karate. I was tryin' to see if I could do anything with the waist size, to see who it could be—but there's so many of 'em that it could possibly fit. We had a list of ninety-some-odd organized crime figures missing since 1972 in the State of New York.

**DA's Investigator Terra:** I first saw pictures of a mob victim in twelve pieces in Queens, 1973 or '74; I didn't understand who would cut up another human being. Thought it must be a foreigner from some obscure country where there's no morals.

Frank Gangi is very personable—then I find out he killed a few people and chopped 'em up to make himself look good to Tommy. They all look up to a made guy, and they'll kill anybody to impress him. Your daughter could meet a Frank Gangi somewhere. It's terrible and frightening. There's so many like that, waiting on line to get in. . . .

———

Detectives who work organized crime say that one of the missing blocks in John Gotti's power base was the Sicilians, nicknamed Zips for no reason that anyone has been able to identify. From the early seventies to the mid eighties, Mafia families imported a lot of Zips from Sicily—hundreds of them, by some estimates—to do hits.

The crime families wanted coldly effective enforcers who were unknown to police here, and the Zips were seen as the solution. Some would fulfill their contracts and zip right back to Sicily. Even if they immigrated for good, the Zips kept their Sicilian identity and loyalty, never owning any allegiance to the likes of Gotti.

Finding a Zip was a feat for a detective, but once you did, it was easier to cuff him than someone you once went to school with. A lot of detectives, especially Italian-American ones from south Brooklyn or Manhattan's Lower East Side, grew up hanging with wiseguys' kids. Tony Lotito comes from "the *low, low,* Lower East Side. Now it's 'SoHo,' 'south of the bridge' or 'east of Houston Street'? Ridiculous. It was the Lower East Side."

The streets of your boyhood might be poor in many ways, but they were rich with potential role models. "In my neighborhood," says Tony Lotito, "there was only two guys who wore good suits— detectives and bad guys. Detectives never went to jail, so I became a detective."

What signposts marked the beginning of the diverging paths taken by him and some of his friends? "Growing up with these young fellas, they were fairly compassionate, as I think back. They never disrespected schoolteachers, they never disrespected the police, never did any of these things that were blatant—that you would see a strong sign. Just the normal mischievous things. And then as they grew older, five or ten years later, you're reading about them in the precinct. You say, this can't be the same guy I grew up with."

Lotito doesn't think anybody can really explain why the paths diverge. "A cop I knew had the school crossing post on Catherine and Henry Street," he remembers. "Name was Billy Walker. Every morning I had a little conversation with him—he was the one who convinced me to go into the Police Athletic League and learn to box. We became good friends. But the bad guys had the same kind of contact when we were kids."

It would take more than a detective to solve the mystery of one Lower East Side family—a family, recalls Lotito, with five sons. "One become a research doctor. One guy got whacked right in the neighborhood; they blew him away. Another brother went to the can. Another brother became a pharmacist, and one became a priest. So how do you figure that? The same family, same peer pressure, same relatives, the same psychological— Growing up, they all had the same thoughts, and church and things like that. And look what happened."

One point at least seems clear: There was no stigma attached to the neighborhood because it was poor, violent, and redolent of the mob, nor to the kids who came from there. Just the opposite. Martin Scorcese made his name making *Mean Streets* about this very Lower East Side.

Lotito and many others say their ghetto backgrounds gave them a leg up as detectives. "I worked down in the Fulton Fish Market for the summer when I was sixteen years old. I'm a fight fan and I've seen some of the best fights of my life down there, that would last for fifteen or twenty minutes. People goin' by with their hand trucks would stop and watch. Some cops never see any kind of violence until they're confronted with it on the job.

"You can learn everything you can in the Police Academy, but if you're never confronted with that kind of an ideology, you don't know what a thief is really thinking. You get gut feelings about certain things. Your instincts start to become a little more acute. And that's what makes a better detective than another detective. It's not all just luck."

In the NYPD, if you looked down on anything, you looked down on the borough that was quiet, affluent, distant—and worst of all, unconnected to the rest. "In the *Rules and Procedures*, they would tell you there was a particular procedure or special order about something. And they would add at the bottom, *except Richmond,* because it really didn't apply to Richmond (the County of Richmond) or 'except Staten Island.' "

Eventually, the beautiful Verrazano-Narrows Bridge was built to connect the County of Richmond to King's County (Brooklyn), but "that stigma lasted forever. Nobody talks about poor Staten Island." A great place to live, but you wouldn't want to work there.

By the time Tony Lotito was twelve or thirteen years into a very active career, he had in fact moved his household to that island. One day one of the bosses did Tony "a favor"—transferred him to Richmond to simplify his traveling. Lotito had nothing against the trip, and he didn't have any kind of a hook whatsoever out there. But he went. And that, of all places, is where he encountered two guys from another island: Sicily.

### Detective Second Grade Anthony Lotito:
### Two Zips

If you did something wrong as a rookie cop or as a foot cop, a boss would say, We're gonna send this guy to Staten Island. Back then there was no transportation except the ferry. I spoke to old-time detectives out there. They used to go to work in their pajamas at night. "A case come in—when that phone used to ring," they said, "we would jump off our seat and start dancin'." They were like the Maytag commercial; Maytag guys, I called them. Nobody calls.

If you were a Staten Island detective, you had to have just a little more skin on your back. Because everyplace you go, the guy'd say, Where you from? Staten Island? Catch any birds or anything out there lately? How many cows did you have?

Tommy Scotto, my partner, was in the Staten Island Robbery Squad before I was. He was number one when I came in, and we were working on competing teams. I'd have forty collars, he'd have forty-one—stuff like that. Finally, Sergeant McCarthy put us together, and it was good for the robbery squad.

Our office was in the One-two-o, but as detectives under specialization we weren't confined to one precinct—we responded to a robbery wherever it was. The One-two-two Precinct is bigger than Manhattan—it's larger in square miles than the whole island of Manhattan. Sometimes we could've gotten to Manhattan quicker than to the robbery.

But I'll tell you how good Staten Island was. Our informants—if a guy urinated in the street in Tottenville, thirty minutes later, I would know about it twenty miles away. We had a network of informants that would constantly keep you going. And good strong cooperation from the DA's office, if we needed a little bail for somebody, and things like that.

Then, in the late seventies, Tom and I were assigned to the homicide squad (which, in Staten Island, only, is officially called Crimes Against Persons), but we would often go on a "steal" to the Property Squad. This particular time, they had a rash of severe drug-related burglaries, maybe twenty, where people were at home—daytime shots, where people were injured—and they wanted two guys who had Narcotics background. So Tom and I went down. Our old boss, Sergeant McCarthy, asked for us.

In this "sleepy little borough" (which it probably still is), you had some of the most exciting cases you could possibly have, and some of the most difficult to solve. And there was competitiveness in the squads, but there was a pride and a dignity; everybody really worked very, very well together. Very, very strong.

In 1976 we had the largest indictment in the history of the City of New York: two-hundred-and-fifty-count robbery indictment. In Staten Island! We worked on them for four months, day and night, sitting on locations, freezing in cars and vans.

The perps were five black guys and two Sicilian guys—what we call Zips. Guys who were imported for discipline purposes when the families couldn't control their crews. The Zips were supposed to be cold, objective. They'd come over here in the late sixties, early seventies to do whacks that other people were reluctant to do. We thought the two Zips in this case had been working for the Brooklyn Gambinos.

But that discipline system didn't last, so the Zips were at loose ends. Now, these two out-of-work Zips went into stickups. They recruited five black guys—but they would only use three on a job, so the descriptions didn't match and it was confusing. It would be the same MO, but not the same crew. They'd stick up a whole restaurant, fifty people; everybody'd line up and put everything they had in the center of the floor; the team would scoop it up and run. They used to go in with shotguns—once they fired a shell in the ceiling of a place.

The same MO showed up in Brooklyn. They did factories in Brooklyn and Staten Island and a beer distributorship in Manhattan. The result was we ended up with a lot of complainants that were willing to come forward.

We knew the perps were from Staten Island because the jobs started in Staten Island, but we had nothing on 'em. We hooked up with some strong guys with good informants—Joe Guido and Al Hooker—and a good paper man, who since passed away, a detective with a clerical forte to help us with the 5s, 'cause you could have fifteen to twenty 5s a day with something like this.

We had a meeting with the sergeant, and we hit the street. Pretty soon we got information about a certain area, Mariners' Harbor, and we came up with a black guy with a street name, something like Jaz. We decided to sit on Jaz. It was the coldest time of the year—warmest it got was seven degrees. We had four cans of Sterno to keep our hands warm.

A white guy shows up and goes in; we run the plate and his name is Vitale. Tailing him, we eventually get to the other Zip—Tritta.

One of the restaurant owners remembered that before the robbery, a nicely dressed Italian guy was sitting at the bar, talking to the bartender in broken English. He wasn't particularly noticed because it was an Italian place. After he left, the black guys came and did the stickup. The nicely dressed guy fit the description of Vitale. . . . Then we had an incident at a Staten Island factory. We find out Vitale's wife works there and she always used to admire the owner's wife's diamond ring. Before they left—one of the perps took the ring off the wife's finger.

We finally pop one of the black guys—he had a bad record, worked for the Mafia. And the black guys all started rollin' over on each other. The Zips had to make do—couldn't find people who'd be loyal to them!

We executed a search warrant on Tritta's house, but we didn't come up with too much. Nothing special. Now we were worried that Vitale's gonna flee before we can search his house. Tommy and I went and staked it out about nine o'clock one winter's night. A one-family in a nice area of Staten Island, near Clove Lakes.

The sergeant and detectives Guido and Hooker are at Judge Gabarino's house getting the warrant signed, and we're sitting on Vitale's. Vitale shows up with his wife and goes in; the lights go on. At a certain point, he comes out again with a box, a tricycle box, I remember. Puts it in the backyard someplace. I said to Tommy, We gotta get that box included in the warrant. He watched the house and I went to call the judge. Had to ask a lady down the block to let me use her phone, and at first she was suspicious.

I got back; Vitale was leaving! Decision—wait for the warrant or jump him? We thought he must be gonna flee. Tommy's driving our van. We get him stopped behind a truck, but he wasn't really pinned. Tommy runs around the front; I jump out the passenger side.

Vitale opens the car window. *He's gonna try and flee.* Tommy's on the other side— but that door is locked.

I thought I was gonna have to shoot this guy. I put the pistol in. He looked at me.

*Vitale, one move, I'm gonna splatter your brains all over this car.* And I cocked it. I said to myself, I hope I don't have to shoot this guy like this, because it's terrible. But if I had to, I was gonna shoot him. He really was cold, beady-eyed. A killer. He was sitting on a loaded gun, tucked under his thigh. We pulled him out of the car and put him in the van.

Our guys showed up with the warrant in ten, fifteen minutes. We found the shotgun in that box—and handguns, the diamond ring, and a lot of other identifiable property from the stickups.

The DA's main man, his chief assistant, Bill Murphy, tried this case himself—now *he*'s the DA. In the middle of the trial, they stopped, gave the other Zip, Tritta, ten years—he took a plea in the middle.

When they were putting them away, they passed me. Vitale said, "You're dead." He said, "I'll get the two of you. You're dead. Ten years, twenty years, fifty years. You're dead." Tritta never said that, but he looked as mean as Vitale. They were both very disgruntled that they even got caught. Vitale threatened his lawyer. One of the assistant district attorneys got a threatening letter. It was really wild.

About eight years went by and I had to renew my driver's license. I'm in the Motor Vehicle Bureau, and a woman comes up to me. At first I didn't recognize her. She says, "Aren't you Detective Lotito? Tony Lotito?" I knew I knew her from someplace. Oh. Andrew Tritta's wife. "It's good to see you," she says. "Boy, you look great. You know, my husband's here, and he wanted to come over and say hello." She said, "Would you mind that?"

I carry my pistol eighty-five percent of the time, just for that reason, aside from my work now as a private investigator. I carry my pistol most of the time, when I'm thinking about it. That day I didn't have my pistol with me, didn't have my shield with me. I didn't have anything. I said to myself, This could very well be the moment of truth in my life.

I see him standing in the corner, and I eyeballed him and I looked at his hips. It was a fairly warm summer day; I had a suit on. He had a little light jacket on—a guy who wears a jacket's carrying a gun. There was a lot of people on the line; I figured, let me walk to this guy.

Now, after Tritta was arrested, they confiscated his car—it was used in crimes. His wife had two children, and I felt sorry that she was paying for something that he did. Eventually, they would have released it. I talked the DA into giving her the car back sooner. She called to thank me, but I never accepted the call. I don't like conversations with wives whose husbands end up goin' to the can. They want to call you up and thank you—we have that all the time. It could lead to bad things.

When I went over to him, he said, "Lotito, my wife told me how kind you were. I never forgot that. By the way," he said, "I'm in my own business. I'm still on parole." He had his own company now. The guy was a talented mason and he was doing very very well.

That's when I found out Vitale was deported after he served the time, went back to Italy, and got blown away in Palermo. Tritta told me, "Oh, he was bad. I made a bad mistake; I was young."

I think originally these two guys were friends in Italy. One was really not a bad guy, and one was. They see a way to make some easy money. One friend didn't have the ability to say no.

# 9

# UNDERCOVER

*You know, we have no problem with police dogs in Thailand,* the grower of opium poppies told the dinner party of ten. The group around the table is approximately half drug traffickers, half undercovers from the NYPD and the FBI. "Mind you," notes Robert Chung, "*where* the grower is telling the story: we took him to Tavern on the Green—all these fancy people around us eating dinner."

Around the table with NYPD undercover Chung, "Yellow Bird, his bodyguard Jack Ma, and a couple of other bad guys. And this whole entourage of undercover officers: myself, Dave Huang, a Cuban-born FBI agent who looks like he got off the set of *Miami Vice*, and Damon Taylor, the FBI supervisor, who's supposed to be a casino guy from Las Vegas. Very WASPy-looking fellow. A female FBI agent is his 'wife'; we got the rented hundred-thousand-dollar Rolls-Royce outside. People are looking. *Who are these people? Doesn't make sense.*"

The "United Bamboo" undercover drug operation has progressed to the point where, to impress their New York contacts the bad guys have imported the first link in the drug supply chain, direct from the Golden Triangle. "Interesting character, the grower," mused Detective Chung, fascinated to be face to face with The Source. "It would be like talking to a Bolivian grower of coca leaves. 'Unlimited amount—' the grower says. 'You got the money; I can get it to you. Just a matter of working out where you're gonna pick it up.'

"He's very proud of this tattoo on the inside of his lip. He goes like this—in the middle of dinner. And we're going, That's *very* interesting. But I thought what he said made a lot of sense: 'There's no problem with police dogs in Thailand because they get the tiger shit, and they rub it on the heroin package.' He says, 'And the only thing that dog knows when the package is near is that there's a tiger nearby. The dog does *not* operate.' " Chung made a mental note to run that by the customs people.

"On the set" in a city of world-famous backdrops, undercover conditions for NYPD detectives can range from tricky to hair-trigger dangerous—sometimes in the course of a single case. If you're in Narcotics (a division of the Organized Crime Control Bureau, OCCB), undercover can mean a couple of "happy hours" watching for white-collar drug deals in a Wall Street bar. A few high-tension minutes making a buy on a ghetto street or in an inside drug "spot"—the decaying remnants of a room in an abandoned tenement, or an illicit apartment in the midst of law-abiding neighbors.

"When you're doing basic buy-and-bust on the street," says Detective Tiffany Collins, Manhattan South Narcotics, "the undercover goes out first, buys the drugs, tells the investigator what to look for. An undercover has probably the hardest job out there, 'cause you're going up against the unknown. You're getting the descriptions of the persons, where they are, who they're working with, if they have any weapons, where the drugs are. Then you're walking back to wherever you came from, remembering all this, watching your back, and then informing the backup team of what they have to look out for."

"There's a lot of pressure on Narcotics guys. They make the majority of arrests in this city." Manhattan North sergeant Brian Patton talks about sending his undercovers—"uncles"—Lorraine and José, into a situation where typically "nothing goes the way you want it—you just have to ad lib." The supervisor, you're off the set; even a block away is uncomfortably far. "This office lost an undercover in 1988," Patton says, "so we know the pain of losing an undercover."

You've built your team over three years. Black and Latino narcs who fit neatly into the street scene, dressing hipper than the white kids from Jersey and Long Island who come to buy in northern Manhattan's cocaine crossroads, Washington Heights, on West 160th Street between Amsterdam and Broadway.

Wall-to-wall trafficking, indoors and out. "At its peak, probably the worst narcotics block" in the five boroughs. "You couldn't walk down that block without being propositioned over drugs," says the blond sergeant with the sturdy baseball catcher's build. You need Patton's kind of tensile strength to supervise young detectives on this drug turf.

One evening in April 1991, you're sitting in a van with the backups—"ghosts." Lorraine goes with José to a drug apartment, they knock. You follow the action coming over the concealed transmitter. . . .

Nobody home.

### Detective Sergeant Brian Patton:
### Uncles

When they were leaving the building, the uncles were approached by a group of male Hispanics in the hallway. I heard Lorraine in conversation with them. The apartment we were interested in was on the second floor, and they brought her into a first-floor apartment. She looked around, she saw some drugs, but she decided she wanted to buy off this specific person that I had asked her to buy off of, to further the case. She left them and she left the building. She transmits descriptions of the three guys.

Lorraine was always in a happy, giddy mood, and I hear her singin' along. Everything is going perfect except that the buy didn't go down. A lot of times, undercovers—they try too hard and they feel upset if something doesn't go correctly. But that's the name of the game. You just can't make everything happen. You try not to force anything; you try to let it go natural. Now I had three other possible subjects for another apartment.

Lorraine is walking east on One-six-o toward her undercover car. It had New Jersey plates. As she gets close, she observes a male black sitting on her car. She tells me over this device that something doesn't feel right. *I feel weird about this; there's somebody sitting on the car; I don't like the way he looks. I'm gonna walk across the street and have a cigarette or something.*

I transmit that to the rest of the backup team, another undercover car that was keeping an eyeball on the uncles. At that point, I sent three other guys out, black guys— they're dressed to look drug-oriented to mix in with the block. Two of them, Garry Ferguson and Kirk Burkhalter, walk past the undercovers; if they see these three that were in the other apartment, they're gonna frisk them, question them, and go further with it.

When the third backup, Detective Waithe, got out of the car, I told him to walk like twenty feet behind. I wanted the first two to walk on the set, past the group of male Hispanics; then when Cecil was coming up, he would let me know on the radio. We'd roll in and we'd have them pretty much where we wanted them—in the middle.

Cecil Waithe—he's got the braids, he looks like a Rasta—comes up the block. He's in the backup team now, but from years of being an undercover and working with Detective José, he feels that something isn't right. He approaches this male black on the car and gets him in a drug conversation. José and Lorraine walk over to the car.

I've been out of this conversation for a while, but when the uncles go by Cecil, I hear the car door open. I hear the bells going off in the car. Lorraine had sensed her chance to get in; her radio was under the seat; she wanted to get down the block to bring me up.

As she opens the door, I hear a yell, "Hey, Bob!" One case where the Kel transmitter worked—as many times as it doesn't. And then I hear shots. What the fuck—the guy never said, "Give me money," or anything. We couldn't put it together. I hear Lorraine screaming. I hear, *Man down!*

The worst feeling in the world . . . all you could think of was one of your guys hurt. The van we're in doesn't have any red lights or emergency equipment, and the cars are double-parked. We're pushing through traffic lights.

The guy ran around the car as Lorraine was trying to pull out—he just opened up and shot out the windows of the car. The two backup guys up ahead heard the shots, they saw a male black running, and they grabbed him. He was the accomplice, we found out.

The guy must have seen them pull up, two people, Jersey car. He said, *These are my next victims.* He saw his opportunity slippin' past when his partner yelled, "Hey, Bob!"

Lorraine rode down the block about thirty feet. In the height of something like this, you get nervous, but she gets out of the car with her gun and goes back to help her partner, not knowing what was going down. Detective Waithe and José opened up on this guy, and thank God they killed him. Thank God all my people were all right. I don't know what would've happened. . . .

———

To a member of the Drug Enforcement Task Force (NYDETF) or a DA's squad detective on a heavy case, *undercover* can mean weeks or months spent cultivating the trust of a dealer big enough to sell "weight" and making the buys, weeks or months posing as a felon the *real you* would lock up before breakfast.

Back in the glory days of the Public Morals Division, before AIDS and crack made prostitution unprofitable, you could go undercover as a pimp "in the life" and rip away the illusion of glamour to dislodge a mess of murderers, rapists, robbers, and kidnappers too slippery to yield to ordinary overt police action.

Since the political turmoil of the Special Squad 3 era, nothing has elicited *deep cover* performances like those of the Bureau of Special Services recruits (Chapter 6). The ultracovert political intelligence effort by BOSS was a ground breaker in the late 1960s and early 1970s.

When City police detected a new wrinkle called "Mafia activity," the NYPD formed a Criminal Investigation Bureau (CIB) in 1955, two years before the famed Appalachin meeting of Mafia minds, and began pioneering intelligence. Even as J. Edgar Hoover denied that there was any such thing as the Mafia, La Cosa Nostra families and their members were first being identified by CIB detectives who operated more or less overtly. Their unit was officially renamed the Organized Crime Section, OCS, in about 1971, but they went right on calling it CIB. Much to the discomfort of incompatible types in the two units, BOSS and OCS were merged in 1972, to become the Intelligence Division—"Intell."

Even though CIB detectives did overt surveillance, they had to be discreet. Bad guys (and everyone else) knew the NYPD of those days required cops to be at least five feet eight inches tall—so on the theory that short guys wouldn't be "made," CIB targeted the shortest applicants and proceeded to literally stretch the height requirement. The doctors would measure you on the table, so the story goes, and were adept at finding as much as an inch that would hold for a few minutes after you stood up again. Thanks to such medical creativity, a legend-to-be named Jimmy Mullan, in reality five feet seven, went to work for CIB and became a one-man mob encyclopedia, a first grader in a mere six years.

As did CIB/OCS detectives, Intell now assists NYPD operational units by taking surveillance photographs at mob weddings and funerals and just going where you gotta go to collect "the latest gossip on who's hanging out with who," explains Robert Chung. So when Detective Chung got involved in a case that called for heavy-duty undercover work, the bosses moved him out of Intell to a new FBI-NYPD joint task force—powered with FBI resources and clout.

In CIB you might be called upon to pose as, say, a regular in bars such as the ones around Kennedy Airport, where mobsters huddled. In Intell, you don't make arrests. If you should overhear an actual heist being planned, as Detective Mullan once did, you give the case to the appropriate squad. You might be assigned to check out reports, as Mullan also did, that the Mafia had designs on Bachelors III—Joe Namath's celebrity watering hole in the early seventies. The reports proved unfounded; but it wasn't a boring assignment.

Wherever you operate undercover, whatever your squad, success demands more than smarts. You need nerve—"*chutzpah*," says Sergeant Bill Brereton, who's been handling business-as-usual-type undercovers since 1972, but never before or since has he supervised anything of the undercover depth of United Bamboo.

Along with chutzpah, you need good judgment and moral muscle tone. You better be a good psychologist and a fair bluffer, if not a natural actor. No matter how complex or deceptively simple the undercover script, more often than not, you're auditioning for an audience that boos with deadly weapons. Your safety depends on the quality of your act. When an undercover is promoted to detective, there's no ceremony or applause; your family watches you get your shield from the PC and that's it. You are one actor who never wants your picture in the paper.

Undercovers who haven't so much as walked on stage in a high school production, let alone studied with a famous acting teacher, have been the rule in the NYPD. The exception, Robert Chung, happens to have been a pro going in.

"Detective work is all acting anyway," contends the Korean-born first grader. Of course, you don't have to be undercover to play a role or put on an act in the course of any given tour. A handful of NYPD detectives have recycled acting skills for stints in film and TV—but they first rehearsed those skills as *detectives*, and not in any such undercover saga as Chung got caught up in.

While taking college courses in the seventies, Chung also attended Stella Adler's acting classes, and he acted and directed off-off-Broadway. The field wasn't overcrowded with Asian-American actors and he got parts—among them, that of a Chinese gang kid in a script based on real incidents. But, "One day I just woke up and I said, Gosh, I don't think I want to do this when I'm fifty. Waiting on tables, driving a cab, waiting for the next show. Maybe I'll try the other thing I always wanted to do."

A couple of years into the fast eighties, he landed in Intell as a white-shield investigator—and before too long, teamed up with detectives Bobby Lum and Albert Chan to monitor Chinese and emerging Korean nontraditional organized crime. He'd left the theater behind—but as Detective Robert Chung, undercover, he became the featured player in the drama of United Bamboo, a Taiwanese gang that was as deadly as it was real. It was almost as if the Chinese-gang-kid stage role came to life. "Funny how it all comes around," he reflects.

From basic intelligence-gathering, United Bamboo quickly escalated to the status of a case—a case that sprawled far beyond the confines of New York City. The FBI wanted it, and they wanted Detective Robert Chung and Sergeant Bill Brereton, Chung's boss on the Intell Asian desk, to help them work it. United Bamboo started out local and became a spectacularly successful FBI/NYPD collaboration. Dave Huang got his shield out of it, ultimately Robert Chung got second grade (with more promotions to follow). But the drama might never have unfolded had not a little boy from Seoul suffered an ice-skating accident years before in a New York City skating rink.

"The ice was turning red. My mother, who's a doctor, just totally panicked." Enter the cavalry—a cop in winter "dress blouse," all brass buttons and high choker, armed with a grin that let you know, "Everything's gonna be fine. And he leaves and comes back with a candy bar. So I had a good impression of cops. Jeez, maybe that's one of the things I'd like to do when I grow up."

To the bad guys, Chung was a star, and his performance won

him the underworld Oscar—the gift of a gun from the subject of his investigation. "Getting over is not my intent," he stresses. "But it shows you that when you do undercover on a long-term basis or on a very intensive basis, you're really taking people. Dangerous people, but they may be great people to have a drink with too. I think you have a double responsibility to give them an opportunity to step away. Whereas, perhaps when you're just making a buy-and-bust on the street, you don't know him from Adam, he don't know you—boom, he sells it to you; he's gone."

As part of their act, Chung says, the undercovers exploited the intimidating killer image of Chinatown Asian gangs. "We could look the part, play the part—so they didn't expect us to act too hungry." In a later incarnation, the "traditional squad detective" he'd always dreamed of becoming, Chung had an almost professorial air. But undercover, he looked like "the stereotypical sinister Chinaman," says his old partner. "Long hair, dark clothes, and black leather gloves with the fingertips cut out."

"We could actually afford to come across as careful," Chung explains. " 'D'you really want to do this?' we'd ask. 'What about the cops? What about the FBI?' If you're willing to be bold, if you're willing to take calculated chances—you can do things that people will say can't be done."

In a milestone for organized crime law enforcement, Detective Chung and his partner, Detective Dave Huang, were formally inducted into United Bamboo—bona fide "made members." But in perhaps the most dramatic tribute to the undercover work in this case, when the world's second largest gang decided to move on New York City—NYPD detectives and their FBI backup successfully barred the way.

### Detective First Grade Robert Chung, Detective Dave Huang, Detective Sergeant Bill Brereton: United Bamboo

**Detective Chung:** This is the new gang on the scene. United Bamboo, a Mandarin gang from Taiwan; different from the Chinatown gangs—the Ghost Shadows, the Flying Dragons—which were Cantonese, up to that point. In Taiwan they're extremely big;

Bamboo membership runs into the thousands. They had just established themselves in LA, getting involved in all kinds of naughty things. Their stronghold was basically Los Angeles, a little bit in San Francisco, little bit Houston.

Most gangs are strictly money. This group was very involved in politics. It made them more dangerous, in a way: their ideology gave them some sort of legitimacy in their own mind. But at the same time, they have no problem importing heroin or profiting from it. When you're dealing with Chinese gangsters or organized crime, their view of heroin is—this wasn't started by them. It was the British, the Caucasians, if you go back to the history of it, who exploited heroin and opium. Opium was used by the colonial powers then, the last century. It was not the Chinese who were trying to sell to the rest of the world.

**Detective Huang:** A lot of Bamboo members were children of well-established politicians, military types, business people, that had money.

**Detective Chung:** Henry Liu, a writer, gets killed in the early part of 1985 in a suburb of San Francisco, Daly City—becomes apparent to everybody that this Bamboo group was behind it. They do this murder with some sort of cooperation or agreement with the head of the Taiwan government intelligence apparatus. An admiral ultimately is arrested and charged and is under house arrest, I think, even to today. He would be like the head of our CIA. He admitted to his government, Yeah, we ordered this because this writer's writing these horrible things about the grandchild of Chang Kai-shek, who's the president. You can't have that!

Pressure was being brought on the Bamboo hierarchy out there, so they decide that they might be interested in coming over to New York. We had a confidential source who met this crew in LA: Steven Wong posed as some sort of a wiseguy from New York, showing off—and they called him on it, expecting to be taken care of as a matter of etiquette among gangs. He talked himself into a situation and didn't know how to talk himself out of it.

**Detective Huang:** Steven Wong grew up with this Asian detective. How he came to work with us—he met the detective one day in Chinatown, so he said, "Hey listen, you know that *60 Minutes* thing—I know these people."

**Detective Chung:** The detective came to us in the Intelligence Division because we had worked with him in the past. We quickly find out what we could from the LAPD, and we realized these are very serious people. Let's see what their plans are.

We used Steven Wong to introduce the Chinatown detective to the gang as a wiseguy colleague—and me as a fresh-off-the-boat Korean, who's his bodyguard. We meet this guy named White Wolf, who was gonna head the group in New York. Everybody in this gang takes an animal name. If you're a wolf, that tells you what year you were inducted; if you're a dragon—Very organized.

It turns out the person who orchestrated the Liu hit was actually the head guy from Taiwan in San Francisco—he orchestrated it, used a few people, and they went back to Taiwan. Supposedly, when it became apparent that this gang was involved and possibly the Taiwan government, they got a lot of pressure from the American government. White Wolf sees that the Taiwanese are turning on his group—"Look, it was just them and that was it." The Taiwanese decide to go after the Bamboo gang. One guy flees to South America. The other guy—the leader of the whole group in Taiwan—is arrested in Taiwan.

Meet White Wolf and he says they plan to bring their operation over to New York. He has some contacts here already—some members that have been inactive but are ready to be, once again, involved—and he wanted to import a lot of people from the West Coast. If the gangs in Chinatown have any problem with it, there's gonna be some serious bloodshed. So we said, oh, we better really get involved in this.

About this time there was a big shooting in Chinatown where a couple of people got killed on East Broadway. Police Commissioner Ward decides he's gonna deal with the Chinese gangs.

**Detective Huang:** "These Chinese gangsters, they can never shoot straight. Every time they wind up in a shootout, an innocent bystander somehow gets shot." Big uproar. They realize we don't have a task force in the NYPD to combat Chinese organized crime. Let's interview some Asian officers.

This is 1984, 1985. I've been in the States since I was six years old. My Chinese is limited to what a six-year-old can speak. Conversationally, I do very well, but talk about science or finance, you lost me. I don't have the vocabulary. I was a police officer, a patrolman in the Twentieth Precinct, I went for my interview for the task force. When I came back from vacation, I was told I was transferred. Because I know I'll be working with the FBI, I went out and got a really short haircut.

**Sergeant Brereton:** We almost turned him down.

**Detective Huang:** I didn't know they wanted me to work undercover. What would I know about detective work?—I was a patrolman. So I had this nice Marine-type haircut, a nice suit. The agents took me out to Queens to meet the CI, Steven Wong. He shook his head, "Oh, my God, this guy's too clean."

**Sergeant Brereton:** Robert said the same thing.

**Detective Huang:** "Could we dirty him up?" So then, somehow I got accepted. I said, I can be dirty! I was twenty-five, finished with college. I really had no direction in my life at the time, except being a police officer. I was single, looking for some excitement.

**Detective Chung:** There's a joint task force created with the FBI and the NYPD, under Inspector Lavin (now Chief Lavin). We decide let's give these people this case. This is perfect! It's interstate; it involves gangs. Some serious potential—we had also learned this gang could move some serious drugs. The Liu murder took place in California—a perfect case for a predicate because under RICO, the predicate crime could happen anywhere within the United States.

**Sergeant Brereton:** The lieutenant calls Damon Taylor at the FBI. "We have this fabulous case, but they want us to go to Houston and San Francisco. It would be something to start the task force. . . ."

**Detective Chung:** We're trying to give 'em the case, but we wanted to work with them—we would do the undercover. They like the case, and they feel that my sergeant and I should work directly at the task force. He had many, many years in Intelligence; at that point I had about four years. Before you know it, we're transferred.

We said, Well, let's make the best of it. The task force was headed by FBI Supervising Special Agent Damon Taylor. He had the imagination and, really, guts to push this. This kind of stuff is a relatively new thing for the FBI. They stayed away from organized crime for a long time—and drugs and nontraditional organized crime, that's even a more recent thing for them to be involved in.

**Detective Huang:** The first day, they had me watch a *60 Minutes* segment; Diane Sawyer did a profile on Henry Liu, how they believed that the tentacles of the Taiwanese government had sent these assassins over here to the U.S. to kill this writer. I said, Wow, this is amazing. White Wolf by this time had come to New York for a press conference, to talk about the *60 Minutes* tape and defend himself. Robert, Bobby Lum, and Albert Chan attended the press conference, wired for sound.

So then the sergeant sent us out—just hang out with Steven Wong, go hang out. Steven is tutoring me in different words of the criminal world, like the term for being extorted. You pick up the mannerisms, you know the role you gotta play. You gotta be subservient to him—he's supposed to be your boss in the gang. We had a rapport going, started working good together.

We found out White Wolf got arrested in LA for a kidnapping. What do we do? Gotta show some respect, 'cause we were his brothers here in New York. So now you got me; I'm just green. We're going to LA? Oh, baby!

Anyway, we went there. We found out who the new boss that we had to contact was—Yellow Bird, in Houston. So happens, when we came back to New York, Yellow Bird was up here raising funds for White Wolf's defense.

**Detective Chung:** Yellow Bird, it turns out, helped the killers of Henry Liu get out of the country. He wants to get back at Taiwan for doing this horrible thing to his brethren. But at the same time, they wanted a source of income for the gang—the drugs.

**Detective Huang:** Now, with him was Jack Ma, the karate expert. Looked like Odd Job from the James Bond movies, the guy who threw the hat. He was Yellow Bird's bodyguard. He had these big hands, like hooks. The quiet killer type. He was always with us. Supposedly, he trained the Jordanian secret service in martial arts. He spoke Arabic.

**Detective Chung:** I'm pretty much accepted because they can speak Chinese when I'm around and they know that I can't understand it. They and the informant are having all these conversations about what they're gonna do, all these drug deals.

The trick is, as an undercover officer, you have to provide security for the informant who's posing as the leader of this little crew in New York. I gotta provide security for him—I also have to make sure that the Nagra's working. Sometimes the informant is wearing it, sometimes I am, sometimes Dave is. It lasts only two hours, so every two hours you've got to change it or at least make an effort to change it. New batteries. New tape. Sometimes, you just can't. They're very intricate little machines and to do that under pressure is very stressful.

**Detective Huang:** A lot of things Yellow Bird had to say in English because he liked Robert. He told Steven Wong, "Oh, you're smart having your second guy as a Korean. He does everything you tell him, I notice that, but if you have deep conversations with people, he wouldn't understand what you were doin'."

**Detective Chung:** He took a liking to me. My job was to light cigarettes, open doors—and I think, like anybody does, they like that kind of attention. He was looking at my undercover pistol, "That gun you're carrying is too big." Next time he came, he actually bought a pistol for me, a Colt .380. At the time, I was carrying a Beretta. In that world, that is probably about as righteous a thing as a man could do for another man. Undercover, you're seeing the human side of the bad guys.

The culmination was, Yellow Bird invited us down to Houston. "Well, we're gonna do some business with the coke, but I'd like for you guys to be inducted."

**Sergeant Brereton:** It's such a big group, the second biggest group in the world. The Yakuza, the Japanese, is the largest.

**Detective Huang:** Originally, he wanted to induct us in their farmhouse. We understood it was like sixty miles out of town. How are we gonna have the backups tail us? The FBI was gonna give me a "firefly." It emits a beam, straight up in the air, and a plane could follow it. It was ridiculous.

**Sergeant Brereton:** They were very free with our undercovers.

**Detective Huang:** And the bosses fought it, thank God, and we ended up in the hotel. The sergeant was next door listening with Agnes Chan, who was translating. Fantastic. First female Asian detective, first female Asian cop. Very capable woman.

When Yellow Bird came to the room, his beeper went off. On the bureau we had a wire for the video. (They drill a little hole in the bottom, and they were shootin' straight up, to photograph the induction.) When his beeper went off, we thought some surveillance equipment malfunctioned. We got scared.

"This is the contact," he said. "I gotta go pick up the stuff." The contact for the drug buy. So he wrote down the number that had beeped him, made a phone call, and he left.

We give the phone number to the backups to check; the backup gives it to the agents.

**Detective Chung:** The FBI agent actually calls the number, which was the drug location: "I'm the duty agent from the FBI. I'm trying to get a hold of so-and-so." When he was supposed to just *check* the number. So then we see Yellow Bird not coming back to the hotel but going someplace else. We felt it was all over.

**Sergeant Brereton:** We sent tail teams to pick him up. He was stoppin' at different locations—we thought he was gathering his troops to come up and hit the hotel.

All the FBI agents were over in another hotel. We're in a second hotel, and I'm next door with Agnes Chan. Damon Taylor calls, "I'm alerting the Houston FBI. We're movin' 'em out in a motorcade. We have to get 'em out immediately; start closing the room down, get all the equipment out." So I go in and we started discussing it. Robert said, "No, we're staying."

**Detective Huang:** We had to start flooding the hotel with our guys, the cops and the agents. Hiding them in the closets on the floor, with shotguns. And what we were afraid of is one of the maids'd come over and see one of these guys standin' in the closet with shotguns. So when Yellow Bird comes back, we're gonna be on top of him. I think it was Steven Wong on the left, Robert Chung on the right, and I had the couch—he was sittin' in the middle. We were all leaning forward, in case he was doin' something. Steven Wong was holding an ashtray or somethin'. I had my gun here and Robert had his hand on his gun.

**Sergeant Brereton:** Agnes and I are in the next room. Agnes had a baby at home, six months old or something. I'm looking at her like, My God, I have this young female with a baby—It was getting tenser and tenser and tenser.

So a knock comes at the door. I told Agnes, Stay back here and listen on the thing. I'm going in behind him. And I turn around and she's standin' behind me with her gun. Tough girl.

**Detective Chung:** He comes into the room, and he's very tense. He goes into his ankle. We thought he was goin' for the gun. We didn't realize he was tense because he was trying to impress us with the drugs at the time. Turns out he was goin' for the cocaine.

**Detective Huang:** We're sittin' on the edge of our seats, and he pulled out the *samples*. It's a home run!

**Detective Chung:** Things like that—your heart doesn't recover from things like that.

**Detective Huang:** He gives us the samples, and then he proceeded to induct us into the United Bamboo. I ordered the wine for these ceremonies. Pouilly-Fuissé. I just had that with my girlfriend right before I left. At the time I was constantly traveling, I was never home; we both had crazy hours. I had just had that wine and I liked it, so I ordered it for the induction.

Steven Wong opened his big mouth, "Oh, I've got a knife—" I said, No, these hotels come with these sewing kits—

**Detective Chung:** They did it in English on my behalf. But there was this elaborate ritual with candles, a bowl of rice and incense, a portrait of Guan Di, which is, ironically, the historical person of loyalty. Yellow Bird pricked our fingers and we put some blood in the glass of wine and we all shared it. Dave's name was White Dragon and mine was Black Dragon.

It's foolish, but to a young teen who's probably very alienated in this country and feels totally out of place—*boom,* he's part of this historical thing that goes back thousands of years—the secret brotherhood, all these rituals. Probably does have some real impact on someone young.

That was the first time that law enforcement officers, as far as we know, actually joined the Triad, and it was even videotaped. The ritual—these are things I had read about, and here Dave and I were actually being inducted into it. This was going to the mouth of the tiger. This is what we've been chasing; it really does exist.

**Sergeant Brereton:** Yellow Bird, he's gettin' bombed. He has a wooden leg. I'm calling into the room, Get him the hell out! The end of the night comes—about three o'clock in the morning. We have to catch a plane at seven. We haven't slept; we can't shower. We have to pack all this equipment, a ton of equipment.

Up to this point, we don't know they've gotten the drugs, and we wanted a drug collar as part of the RICO. We thought that was a complete bust. The camera we had didn't show his boot!

Now we finally get 'em out. Everybody rushes over to congratulate them on what a great job. And Damon keeps saying, "Look, even though you didn't get any drugs, this was fantastic." He's huggin' everybody. Robert is sayin', "No, no—" and nobody'll let him talk. So finally he pulls us in the bedroom, lifts up the mattress—he's got it under the mattress. Now we're ecstatic; we got heroin, marijuana, and coke. He gave us a little bit of each.

**Detective Huang:** They said, We're taking down the case. We didn't have enough people. I was at a wedding or wherever I was—home. They called me in.

**Detective Chung:** We had made all these arrangements to get tons of heroin over. They're downtown at the Vista Hilton; they're sitting around watching TV after we had left them. I think it was the girlfriend of one of the guys who was playing with the dial. Dial falls off. They look into the TV and they see a camera looking at them.

It was over. We had the predicates for RICO. We really would have liked to have gotten the heroin, because that would have eventually come over here. We just tried to grab everybody as quickly as possible.

**Sergeant Brereton:** So, they're going out to the airport to see Yellow Bird off. We have three cars, four cars tailing. We don't realize it's been blown.

**Detective Huang:** On the plane ride to the airport, Yellow Bird was telling Steven Wong, "You know we found this camera in the room. By the way," they said, "where's Dave?" They blamed me right away 'cause I hadn't been around.

**Sergeant Brereton:** Damon is in the lead. FBI radios are notorious—you go around the building, you can't hear anything. Halfway over, Damon said, "Anybody hear that? I just heard somethin' about a camera in the TV—" Then he picks it up again; they're questioning Robert and Steven on how this camera got in there. And the transmission keeps cutting out. And with that we lose the car. We don't know where the hell it is.

So now we start riding all over the airport. We can't find them. I'm figuring they killed Robert and Steve.

The three cars stay in the Newark airport looking around for this long stretch limo. I spot it in the dark area behind the Marriott Hotel—but I can't get in. I can't find a way to get in with the car. It took me about three minutes of riding around, I keep seeing the limo. I finally get in, it's gone. I keep looking; now I can't even talk to the office. Finally I get a signal: a 10-1, the radio operator says, "Get in the office quick, we have problems." I figure they found the bodies.

I get back in—they were calling everybody in, they were taking the case down.

The PC finally said, "I will never, never allow an operation like this again. They went too deep. It's scary." Because they were telling him all the stories.

**Detective Huang:** I felt like John Dillinger's lady in red—the bait. They sent me to get the killer, Jack Ma. I said, Why me, why me? They sent me to call him up from his room. He stayed behind because he was with the guy from Thailand. Translating—he was the only guy who could speak whatever it was they spoke. It's like the drug language.

So, I call him up, *I'm downstairs, I'm waiting for you.* Now, I have the limo; the agents are in the backseat of the limo. Just wanted to get him outside and we jump him. The sergeant was there too. I call him out, he comes out. I have my FBI jacket on. I have my gun out, *Jack, get up against the wall, FBI!*

He thought I was joking. He comes over to shake my hand. I said, Get up against the wall; you're under arrest. FBI. When the sergeant came running out, the other agents come running out, he realized.

**Sergeant Brereton:** He was ready to stand us off. It was like, incredible. He finally put his hands up. But it took like ten seconds.

**Detective Huang:** When he realized he was under arrest—boy, he had this expression on his face, I could never describe it. Rage, betrayal, panic—everything together. It was like, he was gonna kill somebody.

**Sergeant Brereton:** The people we're gonna lock up—we have three or four of them in pocket. We have the guys that are going to sell us the three hundred kilos of heroin from Thailand.

**Detective Huang:** The guy with the tattoos.

**Sergeant Brereton:** The others, they're spread out all over the country, the hierarchy—Vegas; they're on the Coast,

**Detective Chung:** Some of them were in Houston. One of the triggermen was in Brazil—got him extradited. Dry Duck, the overall leader from Taiwan—he was arrested in Taiwan. I don't know if they even tried to extradite him, but he got convicted over there.

United Bamboo felt they were betrayed by Taiwan after having done something patriotic. Certainly, I think they expected a certain kind of arrangement with their government for having done that. And Mr. Henry Liu was an interesting person. There were allegations that he himself was a spy of some sort.

And who knows? I'm just a local police officer.

---

You never saw a more temperate "radical firebrand" than Sam Skeete. Tall, with a benign look on his face, and bedroom-voiced, Skeete wore an "afro out to there" but didn't try to distort his personality to "playact at being militant or aggressive" during his six years as a political undercover. Late in his career, when his undercover skills came into play at the Queen's DA's Squad, the one-time "revolutionary" with no narcotics investigation background whatever, asked himself—*If I were a drug dealer, who would I be?* And he walked right into the thick of the mid-1980s cocaine scene.

Skeete, a black Latino, grew up in a small town in Panama and broadened his horizons while stationed in Europe with the U.S. Army. His plan, to work steady midnight tours in the NYPD while getting a college education by day, went out the window when he was picked up right off the police list in 1969 by the Bureau of Special Services (BOSS). He became *Minister of Education*—in the Black Panthers, one of various danger-ridden roles he played with aplomb during his lengthy deep-cover stint. (He managed college too, jigsawing classes into a complicated lifestyle.)

He had never so much as donned a blue uniform when, less

than two years after being recruited to the ultrasecret Special Squad 3, he was awarded his gold shield. A hypothetical-seeming honor, since the last thing he could do was wear it.

It was another four years or so till he finally surfaced, ten years older than most of his Police Academy classmates. They remember being surprised to find the celebrated undercover so quiet. Sam Skeete, violently opposed, as it were, to blowing up buildings and people in the interest of changing society, had been living an ideological lie in his Panther identity. To live the lie convincingly, he integrated it with his true personality: "My way was to mediate problems." And no one was a more passionate procrastinator: "Let's do it—later." If and when "later" finally came, so did the authorities who had been warned in time.

Sam Skeete says his undercover MO is like Eddie Murphy, "playing himself in all the movie roles." The lure of undercover work always was being able to "walk right in and become part of somebody else's picture." Being bilingual without appearing to be so couldn't hurt your chances of success either.

After decompressing from deep cover and after graduating the Academy, first he was one of seven detectives in the elite citywide Auto Squad, then he worked hijacking cases in Safe, Loft and Truck, and finally joined the DA's Squad in Queens.

A common scenario in New York City prosecutors' squads is this: An informant becomes the detective's entrée to someone else's illicit reality. Detective Skeete's partners knew he was a tourist first and foremost; they made sure to hook him up with a colorful snitch.

### Detective Second Grade Sam Skeete:
### Teach Me the Business

Drug dealers from all along the East Coast came to Norman Johnson's after-hours joint in Jamaica to hang out; they also transacted business there. Johnson was a kind of a godfather figure, in the sense of *respected*. Distinguished-looking black guy; very thin, wiry.

He happened to have a friend that had been in Vietnam and kinda flaked out; the guy always wore fatigues, just as if he was still over there. He was constantly getting in trouble and he would always give somebody up to get out of it. He had become sort of a professional informant. Always doing some petty thing—he was kinda harmless.

This time, the guy was accused of impersonating an officer, and then, considering that he may have been on parole, he could have gotten in more trouble. In order to work it off, he contacted two guys in the DA's Squad, John Cestare and Jack Holder, partners a long time, who had used him before in various things. So they took on the case, and we're gonna have him introduce me to this guy Johnson.

After we worked it out and got permission from the boss, I went to the after-hours place. It was right in this residential neighborhood. You could tell the plain storefront was a bar, but there was no name on it. Once you got in past the double doors, you were in the club and it was like—transformed. If you walked in there at high noon, once they closed the doors, you would think it was a Saturday night. Not that fancy. Nice mood to it, though—blue lights and things like that. Plenty of people there. Music. Dancing. You couldn't even tell it was daylight outside. Drug dealers and their hangers-on don't have any time frame. Doin' their own thing.

For backup, I had Jack and John—but these were two white guys in a predominantly black area of Queens. They had to stay at least six blocks away. Not that initially I needed backup—my main concern wasn't so much being found out, because I felt I had them convinced. It's that drug dealers get hit sometimes. You don't want to be standing next to them.

The guy in the fatigues took me into the club and he introduced me to Norman as his "main man from Vietnam": we'd been in Nam together, we did a lot of things, and we were tight. In other words, he trusted me. From the first time I went to the club, I wore a thing they call a kufi (mine was black). It's a knit hat that most Muslims wear, has sort of a militant connotation. I wanted a different mystique from the other dealers.

So Norman says, "Well, what do you want to do?"

I'm interested in getting into cocaine. Strictly a business. I want to find out what's happening and get involved. As a businessman, I said. (I really didn't know too much about drugs myself. Your undercovers in Narcotics, they know the slang words and whatnot.) Teach me the business.

"How much you want to start with?"

I had five hundred dollars in buy money. I said, I want five hundred worth of cocaine. "All right, no problem. Give me the five hundred."

Wait a minute—you have the drugs?

"No. Give me the five hundred and come back later. I'll have the stuff for you."

Well, I don't do business like that.

"Who do you think you are?" He took this indignant attitude. "C'mere, lemme talk to you." He told the informant, "You wait here." He pulled me in a small room, he says,

"Look, lemme tell you something—" He takes out a wad of hundred dollar bills about two inches thick. Real hundred dollar bills. "You think I need your five hundred?" It was really like being in a movie.

I can understand you don't need my money, I said—but business is business. You wouldn't give me the drugs and have me come back tomorrow and pay you, right?

"I'm beginning to like you."

Well, you know—maybe we can work it out. Laid back.

He put his arm around me. "I think we can do something."

I went out into the club—Look, I wanna deal with you one-on-one. (You want to get the informant out of the picture, so when the arrest comes down, he never got too involved.) Norman says, "Fine. Come back tomorrow."

Went back to the office. I could always do the work, but the paperwork, for some reason—But Jack and John were very good. So they kept up with it.

I think I went back the next day in broad daylight. I didn't have my weapon with me because they searched you—a guy would pat you down when you were going in. So I figured, okay. I went in there and this guy said, "Whatever you want, it's on the house." I had a Heineken. In drug deals, there doesn't seem to be any hurry—never any hurry. Time doesn't mean anything.

I sat there and I talked to different guys; found out guys had come in from Philadelphia, Hartford, Boston. Big group of people from all over. It wasn't these teenagers; mostly older guys, thirties and forties. Business people in a business that's completely illegal—and every once in a while, somebody gets killed.

The girls were there, trying to be friendly. I kinda kept them at arm's length. Norman noticed that I didn't really pay too much attention to the women. He said, "I like that. I know these guys are just here for sex, partying. But you're serious." His office was, like, adjacent to the bar. Once he closed that door, it was almost soundproof. He was in the process of remodeling, so there was a look of sawdust; he was gettin' it together.

He took out the coke, "Well—how many times you gonna step on it?" I figured what it meant, but I said, I don't know. What do you think I should do? "Step on it a couple a times—" He showed me how to mix it. "I'll do it for you." And he mixed it and everything. I gave him the five hundred. He said, "Why don't you take a taste?"

I told you from the beginning, this is strictly business with me. I don't use drugs. I don't party with drugs. I'm just here to make money. He hugged me and said, "My kind of guy! I *like* that. Other guys, like I said—they're here foolin' around. Stick with me, you'll get rich."

I took the package. You have to do vouchers, go to the precinct, get a supervisor there with you, and seal it. I waited maybe a week, showed up again. . . . Norman, it was good. My customers are *impressed*. I wanna get five hundred more.

You couldn't get it when you wanted it. It was always, "Come back later. Tomorrow. Sometime." I kept coming back, and I'd sit drinking Heinekens at the bar.

The women there *were* friendly. Seemed as if everybody in there had big money. Nice, relaxed atmosphere, not a rowdy scene. It was quiet. So I was sitting there one evening and Norman said, "Take a ride with me." He had one of those Broncos, little Jeep type things. Fancy. We got in it. He always wore one of these leather Marlboro Man hats. Very impressive-looking guy. We got into the Jeep, and of course, that threw the backup team into a panic. But they kind of stuck with it, and we went to his house.

He introduced me to Maria, his girlfriend—nineteen-year-old kid. He was forty-nine. "Maria, get the stuff—" And he took me to a bedroom, so I'm like really *in*. He gets his scale—some precision scale. "Don't use the cheap stuff. Get the best. Whatever you do, get the best." And he told me the brand name of scale to get. He had a large piece of glass that he poured it out on, cut it and showed me how. We discussed how many times to step on it, what kind of customers you might have, and so forth. Fine. I want to work my way up fast in this thing, I said, because I think we can do good.

"Stick with me and we'll get rich."

That tied the house into the drug case—for search warrants, things like this. Shows he was dealing drugs out of his house. And, of course, it tied the girlfriend into it. She went to get the drugs that he cut for me; she brought the scale. She was in.

This went on for a couple of months. I made a thousand-dollar buy, but I spent a lot of time hanging out in the bar. Went there several times where nothing happened. We had a female black police officer in the squad, Alicia Parker; now we're gonna have her go with me as my girlfriend, be good for my image and we'd have another cop there. She's very impressive—used to be a model. Really tall, like six feet two. She didn't drink, so I think she had orange juice; I had my Heineken. And I introduced 'em and everything; it just killed time. I went there with her a couple of times—I think on the thousand-dollar buy.

I said to Norman—No problem, I can move this; my customers are happy. After I got the thousand-dollar buy out of the way and went back a couple of times, I started to take my weapon. One day I knock on the door. Norman comes, and his guy wants to pat me down. I said, I'm with Norman. I'll tell you—I'm packing, but everything is cool. He looked at Norman. Norman goes, "Yeah, I know him." Now, I established that I can go in with a gun. I said to him after that, Look, I want to go a little bigger; I want twenty thousand—can you do that?

"We can do anything you want. Twenty thousand, fifty thousand, anything." I asked him how much I could get for twenty thousand. (I forget what it was; it's always changing.) "I'll have to make some connections," he said, "but we'll get it. No problem."

I went back a few times, and it was always, "Well, I'm working on it." In the office we had a room with a phone for undercover officers so you could give somebody a number. They call, it comes through the office. So I get a call and Norman says, "I got the stuff."

So I show up. I didn't have twenty thousand dollars; I had a sealed envelope stuffed with paper. And I had Alicia with me. I had the envelope in the trunk, and the idea is, when I lift up the trunk, the backup team (now probably about six or eight people including a sergeant, you always have a sergeant on something like that)—everybody would know it was a go, I had seen the drugs. I would go to the club door with Alicia; she would stumble and drop her purse so the door would stay open long enough for the backup team to come crashing through.

As usual, Norman said, "My man's not here." Everybody's poised outside waiting to strike and there's nothing happening. I said, Well, look, I'll be back. The door opens and I circle around the block: No fellas, nothing. He doesn't have it.

I went back in. I had a beer, but the time was going and nobody's showing up. Finally, a black guy comes, but he's Colombian—speaks hardly any English. So he came in and Norman called me and showed me the stuff. I said, the money's right outside in the car. I'll get it out.

Now we know the drugs are there—we're ready to go.

I go open the trunk, take out the envelope, and now Alicia is coming in with me. She stumbles at the door; the guys come crashing through and make the arrest. But they arrest me too. Cuff me and I'm on the floor; the Colombian is on the floor. They're shouting, This guy's got twenty thousand dollars! Asking me, Where'd you get twenty thousand dollars? *No hablo Ingles.*

I'm saying to the Colombian in Spanish, *No:* Don't talk, you don't have to tell the cops anything, shut up, keep quiet. There's nothing they can do to you; you don't know anything. Norman is hearing about this twenty thousand dollars, this guy's got twenty thousand dollars. Then Alicia presents herself as a police officer; she takes her shield out, and it's supposed to be, like, she betrayed me.

So we had them all confused. I'm rear cuffed. Talking Spanish. Even Norman is shocked. I'm saying to the cops, I don't know what you're saying, I don't speak English. The Colombian guy's talking to me, "This is my first delivery! I never did this before. I needed the money—I don't know how I got into this." Things that are incriminating him.

Alicia comes by—she's eyeballing us; we're laying on the floor. And of course, you have a full bar and everybody's in confusion; the cops are searching the customers for weapons. I said to Alicia, in English—*You're dead.* She hears, Norman hears. She made detective off this case. *Post* story calls her "the teetotaling detective."

They're starting to question him. "What's the story? Whose are the drugs?" Norman says, "The Muslim guy, he's the main guy. He's the connection." He's putting it all off

on me—and he says, "He speaks English! Don't pay him no mind, he speaks English."
The whole thing, he's giving me up.

They arrest his girlfriend, search the house—take 'em all down. But a week later, the
club was open—you know the same things were going on in there. Norman pled to seven
to fifteen years; with what we had on him, he wasn't gonna go to trial. I'm sure his
lawyer told him who I was.

———

*It's amazing how you can convince people of who you're not
and who you are.* Yet nobody could be more cop than this Long
Island–bred Narcotics undercover, whose cop father had made a
career of patrolling one sector of downtown Manhattan. When the
patrolman became a father, he handed out cigars but kept the box.

Twenty years later, the recently retired father put his brass
collar numerals, his nametag, and his shield in the cigar box and
handed them to newly appointed police officer Tiffany Collins.
"My father was the one who inspired me in the first place. When I
was sixteen, he asked me to take the test—so I did, just as a goof.
Just to try it. And that's the test I got hired off of. For my twentieth
birthday, I got sworn in as a police officer." Still in the Academy,
she vowed, "I'm gonna be promoted before I'm twenty-five."

Officer Collins delightedly succeeded her dad in a radio car in
the Thirteenth Precinct; "mundane" was hardly the word she'd
have chosen for patrol. Soon, though, the five foot eight-and-a-half
rookie with the creamy Irish complexion and the farm-fresh Long
Island air caught the eye of a talent scout. He was from Public
Morals (PMD), which, like Narcotics, is a division of the Organized
Crime Control Bureau (OCCB), not the Detective Bureau. As Plainclothes once did, PMD investigates liquor authority, gambling, and
prostitution complaints from the public.

"PMD wanted me to go into the schools—do the underage
drinking; act like a runaway and a prostitute." Opportunity city!
PMD, like other divisions of OCCB such as Narcotics and Auto
Crime, is a step in the direction of the gold shield. Narcotics
numbers about a thousand, PMD only a quarter of that size.

"I turned them down," Collins admits. "All the stories you
hear about undercovers getting hurt—I said, it's too dangerous. I

don't want to jeopardize my life for my job. I'm happy where I am and I want to learn patrol."

She didn't lose sight of the gold shield, however. "I wanted to look into different details and a career path. . . . I went to Pressure Point One, working mostly on the Lower East Side. They have a hot line set up for the community: any drug complaint, Pressure Point would respond. . . . I kinda wanted to learn more about Narcotics, got interested in it."

Now it was the people she met from Narcotics who talked up undercover work. "It did sound dangerous; I *was* leery of it. But it also sounded exciting—I figured I'd give it a shot. So I tried it out, and there was no going back. I liked Narcotics right from the beginning."

Undercover first commandment: *Blend in*. They put her to work in a white-collar ghetto. "What amazed me on Wall Street was how people could make such great money and have such a good life, and they would just go out and buy drugs. Hang out in the bars.

"I liked telling these people that I worked in the area—I was a secretary. And they believed me. It was fun—just to make up the stories. You could live any role you want to live at any given moment. And the people go for it. That's what makes it so exciting—to walk away from it and say, Wow, I was pretty convincing.

"I remember one night going out after work with my friends, my whole team from Wall Street. We're sitting in this bar and we met a group of people. These two girls liked two of the guys I worked with. One of them turns around and she's looking for some coke.

"I said, Well, I don't think they have any coke on them. Just as a goof, I said, Y'know, you can go to this bar down the block, McCann's—they're always selling in there. She goes, 'Oh, no! They raided it a couple of nights ago.' I just wanted to see what she'd say: 'That place is hot; you don't go in there. They're onto it.' Meanwhile, we were the team that busted the bar.

"A lot of people lived in Brooklyn, but they came down to Wall Street to sell in the bars. Marijuana is big there, and crack. Whenever you think of crack, you think of lowlifes and junkies. It's affecting middle-class, upper-class, lower classes—the whole economy. And it's probably the saddest drug around, 'cause it takes you down the fastest.

"Everyone thinks it's cheap, but you spend so much more money on crack than you would most other drugs 'cause the high doesn't last as long—and you just want to feel that high. So people are known to throw their whole paycheck to crack in one day and sell anything that's of value to them or their family; they'll get rid of it just to get high. It's a very sad drug."

When people hit on the undercover in the Wall Street bars, offering her drugs for free, "I would tell them I was with some guy that I worked with in the office and he liked me—he gave me the money. I would buy the cocaine, saying we were gonna go home and do it together.

"I was really fortunate. I was asked to do drugs, but it wasn't life threatening. They'll throw a gun right to someone's head and cock it: 'If you're not a cop, and you wanna get high, get high.' In that circumstance—and also wondering how your body would react to the narcotic . . . Just the idea of it. I was never put in the situation, but there was a lot of nights I thought about it."

Collins went from Wall Street to Hell's Kitchen on the west side of midtown—an ethnically diverse neighborhood where she dealt with much more street-smart types. She used the name Tara. "People in the street use short names. I had an ID that said Patricia Sullivan, but I used Tara 'cause I felt more comfortable with it."

Just as they had in the Wall Street bars, sellers on Ninth and Tenth avenues offered "Tara" free drugs. "One time this guy—I bought basic marijuana from him. I think I bought a dime bag. He wanted to give it to me, and I wanted him to take the money. The serial numbers are recorded. The purpose the money serves is additional evidence in court, so you want to spend it. You hope they don't get rid of it real quick. A lot of times they're onto you, and they'll give someone else the money—they'll say, I owed it to him. Or they'll spend it in the store."

Collins ditched that "guy from the office." Now the script went, "My old man gave me the money—I can't go home with it. If he finds the money on me, he'll beat me up. I don't want to fight with him. Just take the money. 'Well, only if you go out with me.' All right, I said. He's working tonight; I can get out of the house for a while. What do you want to do?

" 'We'll go for dinner.' It was in the Village—he goes, 'We'll go here for dinner.' Okay, I promise. Just take the money so I don't get a beating. I think you're really cute; I'd love to go out with you. I just don't want to get in trouble with the old man.

"So he took my money. I left with his phone number and plans for dinner; my backup team came and arrested him. He pleaded with the team to come back tomorrow and arrest him 'cause he had a date. They were busting my chops: 'Oh, Tara, you goin' for dinner, huh?' ''

Blending in was a more complicated challenge in Hell's Kitchen. "You have the Westies up there. There's Irish, so am I. Maybe that works to my advantage in the Westies area, maybe it doesn't. But also, I'm dealing with Spanish people, mostly Spanish and black. I don't speak Spanish." If Tara had mixed feelings about being able to blend into the ethnically-diverse scene, she was sure of one thing: being female worked to her best advantage. Usually.

"I hated buying from females because it was the hardest thing. 'Get off my territory. Who are you? Where you come from? You're not gonna take over my block.' They're more vicious. You play on a male's ego, it's a lot easier. To go up to a woman and say I was gonna buy heroin, they'll say, 'Lemme see your tracks.' Sometimes I painted fake tracks to make it look good. You use eyeliner, lipliner. You use pen. If you get good enough at it, you can make it look so real. You just better hope it doesn't rain that day.

"Or you tell them it's in your private area. I say, I'm not pulling down my pants for you. She goes, 'Go in the hallway and pull 'em down.' I say, Yo, I don't know what gets you off, but I know you're not gonna get me off. A guy would say, 'Okay, okay, that's cool. Whaddaya want?' She's like, 'Get outta here.' ''

It went better with a Ninth Avenue prostitute and a cocaine score. "She thought I looked good. She asked me where I was from. Lon-*Guyland*, I said. She goes, 'Oh, you come from the big bucks. You played with this for a while?' Yeah. 'Are you addicted to this? Do you need it?' So I said, I don't think so. I just like to get high, but my family thinks I'm addicted. They want to send me to rehabs and everything. She went for it, so I played with it. Told her

I can get money whenever. My father cut me off, he won't give me any more money, but I can still get it 'cause I know where he keeps it. He doesn't even notice it's missing."

Like Sam Skeete, Collins instinctively understood the nuances of identity scamming. "You can't make up who you are. Like I have the accent, so I have to say that I'm from Long Island. I can play the role from just growing up in Long Island better than I'd ever be able to play the role of growing up in the city—I would probably put my foot in my mouth."

Collins fulfilled her vow—a few months before she turned twenty-five, she was promoted to detective. Now she was an investigator in Narcotics. After two-and-a-half years of undercover buys, though, she had it down—and still enjoyed it too much to stop altogether. One of her buys developed into a case—"Batman," Collins calls it—that spread from Manhattan to the Caribbean and Colombia, netting her team what Narcotics always aims for: bigger "fish" than you deal with at the street level.

### Detective Tiffany Collins:
### Batman & Co.

It started from my buy on Ninth Avenue. This male white that was a heroin dealer up on Ninth Avenue, he knew most of the undercovers because he sat back and watched the way we worked and familiarized himself with it. Which is a pretty good drug dealer.

He didn't make me as a cop. I went down the block and I went right up to him. I didn't say heroin—I went with the brand name. I said, Yo, Batman. He goes, "How many?" I go, Two. And he handed me two Batmans. Didn't even look at me, and he was arrested. And man, did he talk. He gave up everyone and his brother. So now we had a lot of people involved in this one case.

It was coming in from Colombia, Cuba, and being distributed through Florida up to New York. And we had wires on the phones. Pretty intense. It's like working for Manufacturer's Hanover, that's how organized it is. Like they have the manager of the company, the vice president, the president, the little distributors, the secretaries, the bookkeepers, the warehouses. It's run just like a regular company. That's what amazes you.

I switched over to being an investigator, and that's when the case started taking off. From this guy talking. And you have to do a lot of research before you can just take someone's word on something. We had a couple of wires up, two wires in Spanish, two wires in English. I usually worked with an English one. You research it. You do the wires. As you're doing the wires, you have undercovers making buys, making friends, building confidence, building trust, learning more, finding out more on the street levels, finding out more through the management.

You make buys from people that they say you can buy from. Then you talk to those people. If my friend told me her deepest secret, that's her secret—this is like a big secret to these people. If there's twenty people involved, ten were talking. "Oh, I'll take you for a slice a pizza." Over a slice of pizza they'll tell you everything you want to know. You just have to talk to them right. You have to get the right information.

They are under arrest, which makes it more intimidating. You tell them, "You can talk to me—or you're gonna go away for a long, long, long time." And you play with that. The way the system works, they might not be going away for a long, long, long time, but you're gonna make sure that they think they're goin' to the death chair.

Probably one of the best cases I worked, 'cause just from buying on Ninth Avenue for so long, all these people that I was buying from, a lot of them were involved. So you look back at your reports, or you look at the faces, and you say, my God, it's a small world.

We closed up warehouses. Apartments all over the West Side—Ninth Avenue, the Westies area. And uptown in Harlem down to the Lower East Side of Manhattan. That's how far it went. It's one big company, and they distributed it from the warehouses to their office buildings. And then it's like, their salesmen go out in the streets.

———

Hell's Kitchen theatrical teamster, bartender, racketeer, and murderer—your typical Westie mobster—Billie Beattie became a pawn in Detective Steve Mshar's offensive against the lawless West Side Irish mob. Mshar picked up Beattie in the park in Hell's Kitchen after dark so that other Westies would not be tipped to the arrest. The detective launched the offensive not long after his 1983 arrival in Manhattan South.

Investigation is like a chess game, he suggests. "You can teach anybody how to play, but you can't teach them to have a feel for it." You absorb that feel, growing up in the right kind of neighborhood. Mshar's was "Alphabet City" in downtown Manhattan—so far east that they ran out of numbers (and imagination) and the bleak avenues are lettered.

Westie turf was up in midtown, west of the city's glittering

Broadway theater district—almost as far west as you can go before you hit the Hudson River. It still happened that one of the Irish crew had gone to Manhattan Vocational High School with Mshar. No one else in his Russian family had even considered a police career, but he felt at home in all these war zones. "This would be a profession I would do well at," Steve Mshar decided.

The detective had enough to grab Billy Beattie, who was perfect for an "undercover" role that Mshar and his partner, Detective Patrick Barry, had in mind. "Billy Beattie is one of the guys who killed Ruby Stein, the big loan shark—" Paddy Barry relates. "They found Stein's torso floating in Jamaica Bay. They killed him up in McCoy's Bar—Forty-third and Tenth. Butchered his body in the bathroom, cut his head off, put it in a hatbox, and then they dumped his body in the bay. The torso surfaced and he was identified from a scar."

Beattie "was a bit of a tough nut: 'I'm not gonna be a stool pigeon—,' so we said to him, Well, what about you work for us? And he didn't see that as being a stool pigeon." Well, Mshar clarifies, "he definitely didn't want to go to jail."

The Westies' murderous world was predictably drug-ridden, and Mshar had spent half a career in Narcotics before coming to the task force. "If witnesses to the Westies' homicides were in-volved in narcotics activity, my way of talking to them was to arrest them on drug cases and get them to 'turn' on the homicides."

In Narcotics, the blue-eyed, graying blond cop had made a few small undercover buys (he passed for *northern Italian*). His forte, though, was big-time Manhattan drug deals: twenty or thirty pounds of heroin at a time. He had earned his gold shield the hard way, and now he was Detective Mshar in the Homicide Task Force in the *Bureau*. The Bureau brass nixed his drug-case strategy for solving Westies homicides. " 'If you have a narcotics case,' they said, 'give it to the Narcotics people.' "

Mshar maintained that the Homicide Task Force needed control of an investigation that was sprouting new offshoots every which way. "Plus, I have the Narcotics background—and I would like to do it." The Bureau saw his point after all. He used Billy Beattie as a middleman in making drug cases against Westies. The task force and Sergeant John Donohue's Narcotics team collaborated—and nobody regretted it except the Westies, who are paying with centuries of jail time for decades of bloodying Hell's Kitchen.

After the blockbuster Westies case, what next? Keep it simple, maybe—one-on-one. A game of psychological "chicken" with an educated, middle-class bad guy, Allan Stern, who believed he could get away with million-dollar fraud *and* contract murder.

When Stern's two indictments—one for murder and another on a hundred-and-thirty-three counts that included fraud and grand larceny—hit the papers, a photo showed the wealthy land-lord laughing off the charges. Murder? "Bull." The rest—"outra-geous," quoted *Daily News* reporters Patrick Clark and Stuart Marques. Well, no wonder. Free on six-and-a-half million dollars bail, Stern could afford to laugh.

Mshar got considerable satisfaction out of using his Alphabet City skills to outmaneuver an adversary from easy street. To engage Stern, who was armed and at least six feet to Mshar's five feet ten, Mshar went undercover as a hit man too confident to pack a piece.

### Detective Second Grade Steve Mshar:
### Package Deal

Arthur Katz was found under the West Side Highway in 1980, shot and killed for no apparent reason. It didn't look like a robbery and nobody knew why he was killed. Augie Sanchez, a detective in the task force, had worked on this homicide with the First Precinct when it first started. There were no real leads. After a period of time the case was dormant, nothing really being done.

One day in 1988, there came a call to the task force from this fellow DaSilva, who said he worked for Arthur Katz's brother-in-law, Allan Stern. DaSilva is a super in several of Stern's buildings, he says, on the West Side, 99th Street, did a lot of handyman work for him. He said he had some information regarding the Katz homicide. Augie Sanchez met with him.

Katz was also involved in the family real estate business. There were other family members involved in it, as well. Katz had a falling out with Stern that ended with Stern telling DaSilva, *Get somebody to kill this guy for me.* DaSilva went and brought the hit man, and Stern hired him to go out and kill his brother-in-law. Now DaSilva was afraid that Stern was getting out of hand—talking about killing two of his tenants that were forming rent strikes against him in his buildings. He already told DaSilva to go get the same guy, the same hit man. *I want to talk to him about having these two people killed.*

He was also looking to burn out his neighbor up in Westchester—Greenburgh, New York—because the neighbor, to sell his house, showed it to minorities on a few occasions. Stern said he wanted a "message" sent, by having all the shrubs burned around the neighbor's house.

The reason DaSilva came to us: he could implicate Stern, and Stern is the type of individual who may want him bumped off. So to save his own hide, DaSilva was gonna come forward on the Katz hit. And he was giving other information to the DA's office about how Stern is stealing power from Con Edison and stealing gas, by having DaSilva get into the lines. At the same time, Stern was charging his own dummy corporation for fuel oil, which they were not using because they were stealing fuel from Con Edison!

DaSilva goes back to him, tells him he couldn't get ahold of the same guy, but there's somebody else that he could get—which is me. During the summer months, May or June of 1988, I meet with Allan Stern. We first discussed his problem with his neighbor, he wanted his neighbor's bushes burned. I told him that wasn't really my cup of tea, I didn't mess around with small stuff like that, but if I needed to do it, I would—to get the job of killing his two tenants.

I went to his office without a gun. He was checking me out, and I let him know that I didn't normally carry a gun. If I wasn't gonna do a hit, there was no reason to. He showed me that he did have a gun on him—he wore an ankle holster. (We checked and found out he had a pistol permit, legally.)

When he showed me the gun, I indicated that it didn't bother me. Had we had a disagreement, he would never be able to get to his gun fast enough. He seemed a little concerned about that.

My normal fee was like fifteen thousand per person, I told him, but I was gonna give him a package deal. I asked him how he would like this done. I explained to him, on the last job, the person definitely wanted the intended victim to know where it was coming from. I looked him right in the eye: Before I killed the guy, I shoved the gun in his mouth and said, This is from Joe Mazzerats! and then I blew his brains out.

Stern said, "No, no, I don't want it done like that. I don't want him to know." Not even in death? "No." Not even in death, he didn't want him to know.

He started to say, "Well, I'm not really accustomed to doing things like this. I never got involved in something like this before, and I'm not—" Which he had. I was wearing a wire. I said to myself, this is not gonna look good. I felt I had nothing to lose at this point, no choice but to bring up what he did in the past.

This guy—Crazy Joe in Brooklyn, I said—I've done work with him before. We've done hits together, and he told me he *did* work for you. He did your brother-in-law for you—weren't you happy with his work?

He said he was.

Well, I'm sure you're gonna be happy with mine, 'cause I'm gonna give you a better price and I'm willing to do whatever needs to be done. For me to get this job, I'm willing to burn the bushes, or I'll get somebody else to do it. He left it at, "I'm not ready to go forward just this minute, but I'll contact you." He wanted my beeper, I gave him my beeper number.

After my dealings with Stern, John Moscow, the DA, just wanted to get a reaction from him. Augie Sanchez went back and interviewed him regarding the Katz homicide— his brother-in-law's homicide. After the detective left, Stern had a conversation with DaSilva, who was wired. Stern was now very concerned that this guy Steve that he met—that he was gonna hire to do the hit—was talking to the police.

But he felt I was a bad guy and maybe it wouldn't be all that much of a problem. The cops probably caught me doing something, so I was giving him up. But he would be able to take care of me on the stand, because I probably had a lengthy record—so it wasn't that big a concern to him.

When I went to him, I had background. From being out on the street, from wiretaps— you pick it up, you know how they'd act. And from interviewing hit men in the past, I knew what to say. I'd been involved in an investigation on a hit man from Local 3, so I wore one of their jackets.

Stern was arrested and charged with these other counts of stealing from Con Edison, beating other people out of money—it was like a state racketeering case. Meanwhile he had also been charged with the homicide of his brother-in-law. He eventually went to trial. I testified and the tape was introduced as evidence. Stern was convicted of murder and sentenced to twenty-five to life. On the other indictment, he took a plea, he got two to six years concurrent—and was fined two-hundred-and-five thousand dollars.

---

No pain, no gain. If you grow up in Manhattan's Alphabet City or in Brooklyn's Bedford-Stuyvesant, and you make it to enlistment age, you've probably been pounded into shape for Vietnam combat. And after Southeast Asia, says Marine Vietnam combat vet James R. (Ronnie) Waddell, the NYPD had to be a piece of cake. Having served in the Marines and worked as a phone company lineman, what Waddell wanted in 1969 was not so much to be a cop as to confront a Challenge. It took him a good seven years to come up against the first serious challenges of his career. That's when he went undercover playing the pimp role "Ronnie Love."

Waddell called the Academy "a breeze." He then patrolled a Brooklyn precinct close to home, part of Bedford-Stuyvesant. "A lot of the people I was policing I knew, and they were glad to have one of their own in the black community as an officer." The cop felt he wasn't getting enough exercise.

Plainclothes? "When the plainclothesmen came into the precinct, everybody gave them respect. It was a prestigious position— below detective, above police officer. Getting promoted to detective was a long, drawn-out procedure unless you knew someone highly placed or you did something extremely spectacular." Waddell was assigned to Thirteenth Division Plainclothes, staying on after it was revamped as Brooklyn North Public Morals in the wake of the 1971 Knapp Commission purge.

Before the Knapp purge, a system of essentially corrupt cop-criminal relationships allowed some criminals to earn a living at assorted rackets and the cops to know exactly who the bad guys were and what they were up to. Order was maintained—a corrupt order, no question, yet the streets were calm. "Earning a living" could be winked at, but not harming innocent victims.

Cops controlled the streets. Plainclothes controlled Known Gamblers—and your "KG" collars were second in glamour only to homicide arrests. That's what gave you the prestige, that and the privilege of working in civilian clothes. The gambling and loan-sharking investigations that offered clout also offered rich spoils to bad cops. Nevertheless, Waddell stayed as fit morally as physically, and he had other Plainclothes cops for company. Temptation didn't affect him as he charted his police career.

Crime incidents involving harm to innocent victims brought dire economic consequences for racketeers—one form of New York street justice. The "system" derailed and "everybody came down on the bad guy. The 'rules' were out. Until he was caught, everything was shut down. Shut *totally* down. You had the ability to go to a *capo* and say, 'Hey! We believe one of your guys did this. Now we're *tellin'* you this is what's gonna happen—' " Then it didn't matter who you were—explains Ron Waddell, you couldn't earn that criminal living. But, "Now who can go to *anybody*? The department saw to it that 'the old-timers,' of which I was one of the last, weren't able to pass that ability on to the younger officers."

During the mid-1970s fiscal crisis, Officer Waddell worked in and out of uniform at the department's whim—on patrol in Harlem at one point, under light cover with black plainclotheswoman partner Mollie Gustine at another. "We would go in and bet, place policy bets and get in places that were selling illegal alcohol, selling guns. Whatever came under the umbrella of Public Morals, we engaged in it if it was in the black communities. We would go from place to place, and at the time I was very skinny and didn't look anything like a cop. I looked like somebody's kid."

Personality kid, you could say—altogether engaging. "I don't know why, but I never got that demeanor you can identify right away, that look that cops take on that spells *police officer*. And I could relate to a lot of people because I didn't have that." *Relating*—a survival skill when Waddell went undercover, a mainstay when he worked as a detective—was still nothing you could really call a stretch for him.

Meanwhile, the financially strapped city, hurting for cops, needed them worse than ever. The crime rate soared, the public screamed in outrage—and the brass devised ways to get more enforcement from the manpower they had. Waddell got wind that "something new was going on in Manhattan South."

The Public Morals Division's Pimp Squad proved both effective and splashy. "Raiding pimp hangouts, we would lock up fifty to a couple hundred players wanted for various felony crimes, not only pimping. Homicide, bank robberies, confidence games . . ."

Before slipping into "the life," Waddell had to learn all its lore and intricacies from the bottom down. Demanding as that was, it was only a script. Going deep undercover as "Ronnie Love" required more than just good acting.

"You have to assume an identity, rather than play a role—because if your role's flawed, you can very well be dead. It's just that simple. You can assume a role easily, but you may easily be preoccupied with something outside it too.

"Just breakin' up their operations, we were costing 'em a lot of money. And when somebody's running from a kidnap or homicide rap, and they find out you're 'the man'. . . . When you get to a certain level, criminals are very adept at their game."

Assume an identity, but watch out for more pitfalls: "You got to maintain who you are, as well." A tougher moral challenge, a test of your concepts of trust, loyalty, friendship. "I had some problems in the beginning. The whole thing about being a black cop working on blacks is difficult because you're labeled as a traitor. And once you're dealing with people, even a criminal element, you begin to develop some camaraderie with them.

"Goldie was a pimp from Brooklyn, congenial type, had a nice personality—he wasn't gonna go very far in the business. But he was trying. (The nice guys are not gonna go very far. Only the real hard-core guys.) They're all tellin' me their secrets—you have to document everything. You're looking at this Goldie guy—thinkin', *You're in the wrong arena,* and feeling like a fink. 'What the hell am I doin'?' "

### Detective Second Grade James R. Waddell:<br>"Ronnie Love"

Sergeant Trapp was running the Pimp Squad, and the guys there, Vinny Sciacca, Richie Confers, were knowledgeable about prostitution and pimps, but they just couldn't get into pimp locations, break through to the real culture. They picked me up and brought me down—this was 1976 or the beginning of seventy-seven. I knew very little about that underworld.

They gave me some time to familiarize myself. I read some of the cases. I sat in on interviews with prostitutes who were comin' in with complaints and being interviewed about their pimps. I learned the trade so I could sit down and discuss it with another pimp and not be tripped up. If he threw something out that was unusual, I would know whether he was testing or legitimate.

The first night I went out, I went to a club on Eighth Avenue, called the Sans Souci Bar and Grill. At that time it was a notorious pimp hangout and organized crime hangout. I was lucky—I met a guy I knew from my old neighborhood who didn't know I was a cop. He thought I had been out of town all this time. He was younger than I was, his name was Prince Jettison. We knew him as a kid as "Jet."

He asked me how deep I was in the City, and that meant, how many whores do you have? I told him, Well, I'm only one deep; I'm new at this. "No problem," he says, and he begins to show me the ropes—who to watch out for, what the different terminologies are, how the game is played.

I'd say there were at least ten to fifteen places operating specifically for drug dealers and pimps on a large scale back then; pimps from different regions would group together. After four or five in the morning, the whores would come in and they would drop off the receipts to the pimps.

You have the street whore, you have the inside whores, and you have the call girls. Usually the call girls work for organized crime. The inside girls are usually a better type of pross and usually they're white, and then you have the street girls. And none of them get to keep their money.

Convincing a whore to bring the money to the pimp requires programming: intense punishment for the slightest indiscretion, and a de-escalating reward. In other words, if she does something good, she'll be rewarded less and less. She's required to bring a certain amount of receipts every night; if she obtains a thousand dollars more than that, she may be rewarded or she may not be, but she's going to do everything she can to get those rewards.

It's in these locations you'll find your felons, because they feel safe in there. You cannot get in, period, unless you're known. I'm known from the circuit, the fast track, which is Eighth Avenue. I'm Ronnie Love, a "mack man"—a player—out of Washington. (That's an old terminology for pimps, dating back to the twenties.) I have girls that work in the whole stroll.

When I go to the door, I'm given a certain amount of respect. I'm able to bring in other cops—which I did, because they'd testify for the warrant and in whatever legal action we take. This would leave me clear to continue on, working undercover. Ultimately, I was able to go anyplace in Manhattan where drug dealers and pimps frequented.

Karen Krizan, a white shield who came in from patrol, was one of my girls. When I had to bring my entourage with me, I'd also use another policewoman, Betty Katzr, but that wasn't necessary all the time, because pimps don't travel with their whores all the time. The whores are supposed to be working. I had Dawn and a girl named Maureen, regular prostitutes who had reported their pimps. Now they were informants for the police and they thought I was too, because we couldn't trust them, even though they were working with us. I was their pimp on the street—contrary to what people believe, no pross can work the street without protection. If they ran into a problem with another pimp, he would have to contact me and deal with them through me. They kept their earnings. And for that arrangement, *when we need you, you'll do certain things for us.*

They were like my eyes and ears. If I had to work on any particular person and couldn't pay attention to background things, they never let anybody stab me in the back. They'd be ready to go to war. (I don't know what they had in their bag.) They were loyal, very loyal.

Pimps usually seek out young girls who are "fast"—flirtatious. They say, "The whore was always a whore; we didn't make her into one." If a girl has some reluctance in getting into the game, they use a process known as stripping from society. They'll learn everything there is to learn about her family, her friends, her likes, and her dislikes. Then they'll start degrading her and breaking down her moral character. It's a process that goes on over several days. They'll have all types of sexual acts perpetrated on her.

Then they'll place her with a "bottom lady," who's like a lieutenant in the stables, a hard-core whore. She runs the show; she'll get her her first trick and cultivate her on the street. The pimp will be the enforcer to keep the fear at its optimum, make sure she does what she's told.

Some people have the perception that prostitution and pimps is a glamorous lifestyle. It's ugly. Not because of the volume of sex, because of the enslavement. A bar that used to be on Twenty-fifth and Lex—Leo's Lounge—a whore disrespected a pimp in there, and him and another pimp threw her on the bar and sewed up her vagina with a needle and thread.

Sergeant Trapp and my partners Karen Krizan and Vinnie Sciacca had gotten a call: A woman who was just turning seventeen at the time went with a pimp named Squeaky Byrd to a social club in Brooklyn. She was instructed not to speak with any other men (pross are never permitted to speak with black men other than their own pimp). A karate instructor for the pimp spoke to her. She put her head down, but he spoke to her anyway. She was brought home and thrown into a hot bathtub, snatched out of the bathtub, tied to a bed, and burned extensively with a steam iron.

Karen and Vinnie were able to talk the pross into calling Byrd, and they recorded the phone conversation. She was in the hospital now, and he didn't have any control over her. He did acknowledge on the phone that he was trying to kill her. Based on the burns—the evidence of assault—plus his own admission, they had probable cause to lock him up. But the next step was to find him.

Byrd was out in Brooklyn, and they felt that maybe I could get into some places and we could catch him. I started looking, but I didn't find him right away. She got better, got out of the hospital, and he was still on the loose. One day, she was downtown buying some clothes with her little sister. He walked up behind her and told the little sister to go home.

He took the woman with him to a lawyer and made her tell the lawyer that a trick had done it—it wasn't him, she had lied to the police. Between him and the lawyer, they had concocted that defense. He would turn himself in after she made enough money for him to bail him out.

He put her back on the street, and during the day, he would tie her around her neck like a dog while he got some sleep. But she was able to get loose and break away, and that's when we finally caught him.

They were staying in the Penn Terminal Hotel at 215 West 34th Street. It was February and she ran out not wearing much. A cab picked her up—she told the driver to go to Brooklyn, told him her story. He would only take her to the nearest precinct, which was Midtown South, where we had our office; the desk sent her upstairs. She told us he had a .25 under his pillow. He woke up when we went in, he was reaching for it, but he changed his mind.

Got ten years and did the full time. He's back out on the street.

I was beginning to get known quite a bit, and there was a contract placed out on me by a guy from uptown, Doc Something. He didn't think I was a cop: he thought I was an informant. (Now they would kill a cop—then they'd just really mess you up, but they would kill an informant.) The DEA or the FBI had picked it up on a wiretap that they were going to do a hit on me. So on the last raid they did, they got me on TV and made sure everybody knew I was a cop.

After that, they sent me to the beach—Rockaway, in Queens—and I more or less stayed in Rockaway for a couple of months working as a white shield detective with the squad. Because life was so slow there, I requested out, and I went to Jamaica—the infamous One-o-three squad. That's where I got promoted, out of the One-o-three.

## Partners & Bosses

**Detective Maureen Ayling:** Paul Gibbons, he would get mugged sometimes five or six times a night. The bad guys prey on people who are vulnerable. He would dress sloppy and act like he was a little bit drunk, and that made him so vulnerable. And they were definitely gonna rob somebody, so they zeroed right in on him. His partner, Abe Walton, would dress just like a real bad guy, and he would be right next to him.

Abe Walton, he was an excellent detective. He got killed off-duty, in a social club in Queens. They executed him. He went to help the owner, they hit him. He was one of the best cops I've ever worked with. Excellent cop. Bilodeau was in my squad also; both of them were. They both got killed in the same year, 1980.

The night Bilodeau got his throat slashed, I was doing decoys. I was on 41st Street, and he was on Eighth Avenue. Right after it happened, we all went over to the hospital. He was very lucky he survived that.

When he got shot, he got shot by a person that Abe Walton had locked up a year before on the same block, for a gun collar. True story. He was goin' for his gun and Abe tackled him. I often think, had they shot him that day when he was goin' for his gun anyway, Bilodeau wouldn't have gotten killed by that perp. The same one that Abe locked up a year before killed Bobby Bilodeau. On the same block in the Two-eight precinct.

You have to play it by ear. You have to do what you feel you have to do. You can't say how things will work out.

# 10

## PERPS AND COLLARS

---

When Patrolman Tommy Sullivan got off work, he'd go upstairs to the squad and watch. Before the Marine Corps Vietnam combat vet knew it, he was a detective buff. "They were sharp, suave. It was like meetin' a Green Beret; they just carried themselves well. People treated them differently than cops. And they just got things done." Arrests, among other things. Collars.

Grab 'em, bag 'em, pick 'em up, take 'em down, nail 'em. You can say it a lot of ways, but how do detectives get the cuffs on perps, anyway? "Confrontational mind games," declares Detective Sullivan, Manhattan North Homicide second grader. Games cops on patrol almost never play. In the next breath, he compares investigation to "body and fender work. You fix things."

Sullivan is slim and trim, close shaven and bandbox neat, whether kilted up for a bagpipe gig with the NYPD Emerald Society Pipe Band or sharply tailored to confront a suspect. He looks like a businessman but chooses, often, to sound like a mechanic. Just as often, his patter mesmerizes, his faster-than-the-eye-can-follow style dizzies; you think he's some kind of magician.

And you're persuaded that he was born with that image; it's not easy to picture Sullivan in the blue uniform. During the three years he wore it, his passion to be a detective deepened, reinforced by "a thousand epiphanies"—but he calls this particular collar "one of my main confirmations."

### Detective Second Grade Tom Sullivan:
### Ambushed

Me and Eddie Mahoney, we were radio car cops. We get the call: Everybody out! Meet the detectives—119th Street and Madison, Spanish Harlem. All the radio cars go. We're standin' there, about five cars, angled. They got everything way up to the corner blocked off. And the cops are all out on the street. A couple are up on the fire escape, just hangin'.

Here come these two detectives—cigars, gray hair, long overcoats that make 'em look bigger than they are: "Get Emergency Service over there." They come over. "Put the lights on." The lights go on. The detectives are lookin' for a guy that shot somebody, and they think he's in the second-floor apartment.

I was twenty-two, just out of Vietnam: I know how to set up an ambush. And these guys are makin' all kinds of noise, radios are squawkin' back and forth. I say to my partner, who the fuck are they gonna catch?

So the detectives go, "All right, Sarge? Everybody ready? Ready—let's go!" And we walk in, of course knock on the door.

Girl opens the door. "C'n I help you?"

"Are the Martinez brothers here?"

"Ohhhh, no—we haven't seen them in years."

"Yeah? They're in a lot of trouble."

"Ohhh!"

"You be sure to call us if you see 'em?"

"Oh, *yes*, Detective—gimme your card." He gives 'em the card.

"Okay—" he says to us, "thanks, fellas."

I'm goin', Look at these idiots! These guys—these are detectives?

What happened? We got in our cars. We all closed the doors. Put the stuff back in the Emergency Service truck. The lights were off. Everybody took off. The detectives went and had a cold beer.

They went back half an hour later, the two of them; they knocked on the door.

They open up—and there's the Martinez brothers, sittin' there. They figured, "Oh, they'll never come back. They hit the joint—that's it."

Amazing! I said, I wanna do that.

In uniform, Sullivan "collared up" and swiftly moved on to plainclothes—in this case, a brand-new, wave-of-the-future squad, Citywide Anti-Crime (CWACS), turning out of Randall's Island in the murky waters off Harlem to patrol the five boroughs in "soft" clothes and unmarked cars. CWACS evolved into Street Crime (SCU)—predecessor of today's effective catch-'em-in-the-act Anti-Crime precinct units.

Awarded the gold "detective specialist" shield, Sullivan was a decoy in Street Crime. He spent some of New York City's most financially desolate years roaming the potholed streets, picking up garbage.

Then in 1980, as light began to glimmer at the end of the municipal budgetary tunnel, Police Commissioner McGuire started a pilot program to target Manhattan's worst bad guys. Sullivan was among fifty top Street Crime cops chosen for the new Career Criminal Apprehension Unit (CCAU). Precinct detectives would identify the targets, CCAU would chase them for as long as it took to make the collar.

The program was a winner, and after about a year, CCAU's companion investigation unit went citywide. A few months later, CCAU itself followed, moving its office across the river from Randall's Island to the Two-five in Harlem—and, into the Detective Bureau. By this time, Sullivan had hooked up with partner Joe Sofia.

The classic New York Irish–Italian cop team jeered at each other's tastes in food, tracked and collared a slew of bad guys. But in their five-plus years together, the perp they most wanted to nail was a devious rapist, Richie Esposito, armed with a "signature" secret weapon: the veterinary drug, Kedamine. A *20/20* report on the case that detailed the drug's arrival on the street, its bizarre effects on people, and the detectives' mission, landed Sullivan and Sofia on national TV.

"*Master*" detectives, anchorman Hugh Downs innocently called the partners on the air—and of course, the squad never let the pair forget it. On a day-to-day basis, mastering their craft, doing a job, kept them going. But in this case, they were beyond driven—they were jet-propelled by their commitment to the victims, past and potential, of Esposito's assaults. Fourteen women that they actually knew about; how many more—they shuddered to imagine.

If Sullivan and Sofia could ensure that the only bars this perp would frequent for the rest of his life would be the ones in prison, everybody's sisters could breathe a lot easier—and not only in New York. Response to the *20/20* segment made it all too clear that this guy left a long, lurid trail.

### Detective Second Grade Tom Sullivan and Detective Joe Sofia: Close to Home

**Detective Joe Sofia:** Right from the beginning, the case was a good case that would intrigue any detective. Any investigator would want to go out and try to lock these rapists up. The girls were brutalized—like one of them was dumped, just dumped, rolled out of the car, left for dead in front of her house. Her mother was looking out the window when this happened.

Plus the fact—I'm not saying we would have worked the case any less—but these girls lived in my old neighborhood in Queens. I didn't know them, but it hit home. Ironically, we got the paperwork on this and I looked at it, and the one girl lived right around the corner from my mother in Astoria. The other girl lived up the block.

Tommy Sullivan is originally from Jackson Heights, which is the adjoining neighborhood. As we grew up, we hung out in the same areas, drank in the same bars. We probably stood next to each other many a night, back when we were eighteen, nineteen, twenty years old, at Donovan's, local bars in Jackson Heights. Never knew each other until the Police Department.

**Detective Sullivan:** I have five sisters. I drank in bars, and my sisters went out and bounced around—Well, I was annoyed. Here's a fuckin' guy that could slip somethin' in their drink and get them to a state of—not unconsciousness—a state of muscular immobility. Out on the Coast, this drug was called "Special K"—'cause it brings them up, like cocaine, but then it relaxes 'em on the way down.

**Detective Sofia:** In CCAU, we got cases from different detective units throughout the city. Once a perp was identified in any of these crimes, they would send it to us, 'cause we had the time and all the resources to go out and look for these guys—where the precinct detective, every three or four hours, another case is thrown on his desk.

**Detective Sullivan:** This incident started at the Sheraton Hotel at LaGuardia Airport. Randy Jacobson, detective in the One-fifteen, went over to Valentine's disco in the hotel.

"Got a little problem," he said. "Some girls said they were raped; drugged or somethin'."

The cocktail waitress goes, "Sonofabitch—Richie!" And Randy caught that—"What are you talkin' about?" She didn't want to cooperate, but he leaned on her, and she said, "Yeah, there's a guy I know named Richie Esposito."

What was goin' on in the bar in this disco: he would use bad credit cards, she'd take the card knowing it was bad and run it through, and he would throw a heavy tip on her. He'd give her fifty, a hundred dollars. *Bing.* So she knew Richie, but she didn't like him. Randy Jacobson put in a Wanted card for him.

**Detective Sullivan:** When we first called to interview the girls, I made a blunder. I said, Detective Sullivan, Career Criminal Apprehension Unit. I have your case. Can we meet with you? "Well, I don't know—Who are you?" Lady, I'm a policeman. "Okay, you can come and meet us." We want to come to where you are. What's convenient by where you live? Why don't we meet in that bar—Suspenders?

"What?"

Joe gets on the phone. "Whoa, whoa. My name's Joe Sofia. You live on such-and-such? My mother lives four doors away." So we went to his mother's. Tremendously excellent move.

**Detective Sofia:** She was deathly afraid, so she came down the block and met me in front of my mother's. We did the initial interview at my mother's dining room table. My sister was older, but Tommy's sisters, the youngest one was about the same age as the victims. Early twenties.

The girls told us they had met this guy Richie and that there were two other guys, Neil and Angelo. They remembered these names from the disco prior to being drugged. Richie put something in the girls' drinks, they started to get dizzy and sick.

**Detective Sullivan:** It was like—nervous. Men talking to women. I'm not a rape investigation expert. I don't know how to talk to 'em and ask whether it was vaginal or anal. . . . I had to get those pertinent questions asked and answered, but not in a leering manner. Rape victims, they don't want to be reraped. They don't want to have to say, "Well, then they made me do this . . . ."

**Detective Sofia:** The guys helped both girls out to the car and then put this stuff into a Bic pen that was hollowed out and blew it up their nose, and that's what really made them go.

This drug resembles coke. They meet these guys. "Listen, I've got a gram with me. You want to do a couple of lines?" She doesn't have a hundred-and-twenty-five dollars a gram, so of course, the average girl that uses coke is gonna say, "Hey, why not? A free hit."

Of course, how could they possibly tell their parents they've been raped? What are they gonna say? They thought they were doing coke and it turned out to be something else?

**Detective Sullivan:** They went to the hospital; they weren't treated well. "Yeah, yeah, two little cokies." Like a drug thing.

**Detective Sofia:** We both dropped our cases and we worked on this as a team. It was Tommy's case, Tommy did most of the DD5s; we basically did everything else together.

**Detective Sullivan:** They put one of the girls, call her Bobbie, in the car outside the Sheraton, driving away in two cars. She went to get out. Every time she went to the lock, the guy would go *Zzzt* from the front—close it automatically—and laugh. She said, "I tried to get out." She grabbed the button; it'd go *Zzzt*. She remembers she was raped in the car. She was later dumped on the lawn of her mother's house.

Arlene was taken to a motel somewhere and raped. All she remembered about the location was seein' an exit sign on the highway. She remembered somebody paid by credit card. She said the other guy who raped her—"Neil or Angelo"—described him as looking Italian or maybe Irish. They took her home, threw her on the bed, then they looted the house.

The mother comes. "What are you doin'? Who are you?" And they ran. She called the police.

**Detective Sofia:** Richie Esposito gets stopped; he's speed-trapped by a Yonkers cop. There's a gun in the car; he gets locked up for the gun. There's also some white powder and they run it; it's not coke, it's not heroin.

**Detective Sullivan:** The Wanted card pops. We went up to Yonkers and talked to the cop who locked Esposito up, always a good thing to do. There was no drug charge against him. We got a sample of the unidentified drug, took it down to our lab, and they came up with Kedamine—animal tranquilizer.

**Detective Sofia:** We find out Esposito had this drug on him! We went up and took him out of Valhalla County Jail, put him in a lineup for these two girls. We knew that there were three perps involved—they all met in the disco.

**Detective Sullivan:** We went to the disco, introduced ourselves; we ask the bartender for the charge card receipts. They don't wanna give 'em to us, and they don't have to give 'em to us.

We're not looking to hurt you, I told them, we're looking to find the guy who did it. The quicker we find him, the more you cooperated. Sounds good. You don't cooperate? Hey, look, you're breakin' my balls. If you break my balls, I'm gonna break *your* balls, and I'll have the fuckin' *New York Post* in here.

*Bing.* We got the slips. We find like sixteen individual accounts, looked at the bills to see what they had. Bobbie said she was drinking screwdrivers, and there was screwdrivers on the bill. Looked good. Then we saw "Michael Maietta." There was a few other possible names. Joey Alonzo, things like that. Wait a minute, let's look at these. Richie was using the name Richard DeLellos.

We ran a simple criminal-records check downtown, found out there was a warrant on a guy named Michael Maietta.

We took Richie outta jail. We drove slow to the City—for the first half an hour we didn't say nothin'. You could take the parkway; it'd be a lot faster. Bullshit about the Yankees, or something. We made him initiate the conversation. "Ah, can I ask youse a question?"

Yeah, what's up? Make it quick.

"What am I supposedly charged with?"

Rape.

"Rape? Get the fuck outta here!"

Rape, robbery, the whole thing.

Not another word from any of us for another seven miles. Then he says, "I don't know how you guys can do this. I didn't do nothin'. I don't know what this is about."

Lemme tell you something, Richie. You raped these girls. He says, "C'mon, c'mon. Who was I supposed to rape? Like, if I *did* rape somebody."

I told him, Two girls, you burglarized the house. "Yeah? Was I alone?" No, you were with two other guys. "Yeah? Look, you got the other two guys?"

I don't give a fuck who the other two guys were. That only fucks up my case, I said. If you get on the witness stand and you say, "Me and Santa Clause did this"—How am I gonna find Santa Clause? If, on the other hand, I lock up the guys that were with you and you're all on trial, you say—"I didn't; this guy did it." The jury looks at the other two—y'know, maybe there *is* a doubt. Right now, I got *you*. You're on the stand, you're lookin' at the jury. You're dead.

He says, "Y'know, maybe I could help you."

I'm tellin' you—I don't give a fuck. Tell you another thing, I'm lazy. This case is closed, in my mind.

**Detective Sofia:** So we put Richie in a lineup, and he gets ID'd by both girls—guy that they met in the disco, the guy that wanted to buy them a drink. . . . We know at least we got the right guy as far as the meeting, the acquaintance.

Goin' back to jail—the old story, good-guy–bad-guy team. Believe it or not, Tommy Sullivan was the good guy. Funny. This guy was Italian, as I am. Every time Tommy would say something and say, "What do you think, Joe?" I'd say, I don't want to talk to him. He's a fucking swamp guinea. He embarrasses me. I'm ashamed I'm Italian; he's a fucking scumbag. That's the way we went along.

**Detective Sullivan:** He wants to know, "Where we goin'? We're goin' back?"

Yeah, we're goin' back up.

"You know, my mother's dyin' of cancer."

Yeah?

"Think I could stop by the house to see her?"

Hey, do me a favor. Don't start breakin' my heart, awright?

"No, I'm just sayin', I'm not gonna see her."

Little cruel. It was a little cruel: Why should I do this for you?

He says, "You do this for me, I could like—help you." I look at Joe. I don't know now, really. If he gets away, we're fuckin' dead.

We go over to his mother's house. "Hey look, I don't want my mother to see me in handcuffs."

Yeah? Tell you what I'll do, I'll put a coat over your arms, you'll walk in. That's the way it's gonna be, Champ. We go in the house; she comes out. She is dyin' of cancer and since has died.

Once we're in the house, we look around. There's nobody else. His mother's makin' Eggplant Parmesan. My partner Joe goes absolutely crazy 'cause he loves eggplant. The mother starts to give it to us.

Richie needs a knife, he says.

I go, Oh, man.

**Detective Sofia:** Richie's a hustler. One victim he robbed, he left her naked out by the Hamptons—a professional woman. Took fifty-thousand dollars' worth of jewelry off her. He was a punk. He used to run errands, from what we understand, go get coffee for the biggies. Forty years old, he never amounted to anything. His mother said, "My son always takes the rap for everybody else." Typical cop-out for a flunky.

**Detective Sullivan:** "Ma, I didn't do this, I know who did, but I didn't do it."

Joe forgot where he was. He thought he was down on Mulberry Street, Little Italy, eatin' fried eggplant. The other guy's eatin' it, cuttin' it with a knife. I'm countin' the silverware. Make sure all the knives are on the table when we're done. We stayed for about an hour, put Richie back in the car.

"You guys were nice to me. You were decent. I'm gonna tell you something: The kid's name is Mike you're looking for." Yeah? Mike who?

"I don't even know his last name. Mayo maybe?" We already know from the credit cards. *Boom. Boom.* He tells us Mike's built, he works in a gym. . . .

**Detective Sofia:** One of the biggest breaks we ever got in this case was looking for this particular exit that Arlene remembered in her stupor. "Chester Avenue exit."

There is no Chester Avenue, but this is what she remembers; getting off at this exit, going around this circle, and possibly an underpass or overpass—and that's where the motel was.

She felt she was up in The Bronx. First she went over a large bridge. This all started at a hotel at LaGuardia, so it's one of two bridges, the Whitestone or the Triborough. We knew Richie was from The Bronx . . . from the LaGuardia area, the Whitestone would be the cross.

I worked up in The Bronx as a rookie in uniform. It's a big borough, maybe there is a Chester Avenue (to this day, I don't know). Let's just give it a shot. Let's take a look.

Anyway, we went over the Whitestone Bridge and up the Bruckner Expressway towards the New England Thruway. We're riding along and I look—Tommy, stop the car. I see this sign. Westchester Avenue, but "West" was spray-painted out, graffiti'd out. All you see is *chester Avenue.* Holy shit.

We get out, and we're taking some pictures of this big exit sign. While we're taking the pictures, one of us looks over and on the other side of the expressway—there's the Andrea Motel. Interesting. She said, "I remember this Chester Avenue exit—and the next thing I know, I'm in a motel."

Arlene remembered somebody paid by credit card. She said the guy who raped her, name was Neil or Angelo.

**Detective Sullivan:** Running Michael's record, we also find out he was arrested before with a guy named Patsy Ciocia and another kid: stolen car. We got Michael's picture, Patsy's picture, put 'em in an array—the girls picked 'em out. "That's him. Neil—the guy that raped me in the back of the car."

**Detective Sofia:** So now we go over to the motel and talk to the kid on the counter. He was like so-so. The owner came down—very cooperative. Tommy and I said we want to look at your register and any kind of receipts.

What happened was, the perps took Bobbie's pocketbook—took her ID and everything out of it. We start looking through receipts for the dates that this happened, and believe it or not, there's an AmEx receipt with Bobbie's name on it.

Kid was like half a moron that worked the desk there; he just thought Bobbie was a man's name. So one of the three guys actually used her card to pay for the room. And there it was in black and white. Now we had the location where Arlene was raped and sodomized; we had Bobbie's card number right there on the receipt.

These two young guys that were arrested also—they claim that Richie was doing this for ten years, using this drug. Ten years. So if he's been doing it for ten years, how many other victims are out there? A hundred, two hundred? Are there a thousand? I mean, if he did it two or three times a weekend for ten years, you have a couple of hundred victims right there. So you don't know. They're saying ten years. Who knows?

**Detective Sullivan:** We convicted them. We were sittin' behind the women, the two girls and the mother.

"How do you see count one?" "Guilty." "Count two?" "Guilty . . ."

We did it. We won. We walked out of there—they were cryin'; I had a lump in my throat. We went to the DA's office. I picked up the phone and called my lieutenant. Jack Gallagher, great fuckin' man. He'd told us, "You run with this case. You got carte blanche."

Called him at home. "Tommy, what's up?" I says, Guilty, all thirteen counts. He says, "Lemme tell you something, and I mean it"—he's a veteran detective commander—he says, "You and Joe, you did a great fuckin' job." I said, Well, boss—he says, "You were the two right people for this."

This is a guy that's always a knock-around guy. He'd come out of the office, "Hey, you're not doing much here. Go down and—" Salty, Marine Corps type guy. Made me feel good.

The girls threw a party, invited us. We got the cop from Yonkers; we all went to the house.

And Esposito got sentenced to more time than Son of Sam. Sixty-eight and a half to a hundred and thirty-seven years.

**Detective Sofia:** We were getting calls from other states because of *20/20*. They showed his picture, and now other police departments are saying, "I've got cases. I've got a case where a girl was drugged and raped, and that's the guy." It was like a positive ID. One detective from Connecticut called me: "This girl saw it—she said, this is the same thing, and that is the guy! That's the guy she met"—in a bar or wherever— "Definitely the guy." Almost like *America's Most Wanted*.

————

Your perp is not a punk pervert but an educated political extremist whose well-planned bombings dramatize a nationalist cause, Puerto Rican independence. "I'm Puerto Rican, but I don't sympathize," says the homicide detective who looks like a tough teddy bear, " 'cause I think we'd starve."

Danny Rodriguez, son of a merchant seaman who liked cops, was a "white shield" investigator in 1975 when the bosses plucked him from Harlem's Sixth District Homicide Squad and sent him downtown to 1 Police Plaza. Six years into a promising police career, he was one of a group of Latinos assembled to identify the perpetrator or perpetrators of the terrorist bombing of Fraunces Tavern near Wall Street, by the deadly FALN—the Fuerzas Armadas de Liberación Nacional Puertorriqueña. Rodriguez and the other Latinos were assigned to the Arson-Explosion Squad and a special joint task force with FBI agents.

In the mid seventies, the terrorists loosed death and destruction on New York, among other mainland U.S. cities. The Fraunces Tavern explosion left four dead in January 1975 and more than forty injured. A string of bank bombings followed that fall. If Rodriguez had no use whatever for the FALN independence goal, he had even less for their terrorist tactics.

And yet, an encounter between FALN bomb-maker Willie Morales and Detective Danny Rodriguez didn't turn out quite as either man would have predicted.

## Detective First Grade Danny Rodriguez: Escape Risk

A lot of people began referring to this task force as the Rice and Beans Squad, there were so many Hispanics involved. They took a bunch of Hispanics to work on the Fraunces Tavern case because most of the organizations that we believed the FALN members were coming from were of Puerto Rican ancestry.

In the seventies, like seventy-six, we started following a lot of people we suspected of being sympathizers of the independence movement for Puerto Rico. Twenty-four-hour surveillance; we installed beepers in their cars. It turns out we followed the right people.

I was out in Brooklyn on one of the suspected terrorists, one of the bigwigs in the Puerto Rican Socialist Party. About three in the morning, I went and placed the beeper on his car. While I was doing it, he came out to walk his dog. So he thought I was trying to steal his car. Now he's chasing me with the dog. I'm running and he's yelling, Police! Police! Running down Sixth Avenue in Brooklyn. I get away from him. Those were my younger days; I weighed about thirty-five pounds less than I weigh now.

One day we're following him and he pulls into a gas station, probably for an oil change. He goes in the garage, they put the car up on the lift, and three guys are looking and they see this little box with a long wire, 'cause that's what we used as a beeper in those days. They're all looking at it, and the next thing you know, the two mechanics and him were runnin' out of the garage. They think it's a bomb, so they run out.

Of course, there's always one guy who's gonna be more macho. He goes back and he looks at it, and now he decides to take it apart. It's a little box and it beeps. They call it a Wackenhut. If you stay far behind the car and it keeps beeping, you still have him within range. The beeper gets louder the closer you get. Today they have ones that tell you left or right—we don't have the money for those. Now you can't use 'em without a court order. Before you could. They took the box off the car. They must've known it was a transmitter of some kind.

We followed him around for a while.

He led us to some other people, one of which was Willie Morales. He was the bomb maker for the FALN. The bomb placers were a woman and a guy; Torres was the couple's name. Everybody involved in that cell knew each other. In other words, they wouldn't take anybody from the outside.

These people all went to school together, like in the University of Puerto Rico, and they wouldn't take any outsiders. We tried to infiltrate, but it was impossible. We got to the fringes, people who supported them, but we could never get into where they would allow us to make bombs with them or anything like that. We were always at the fringes— political action, raising funds and stuff.

We had had a surveillance on Morales, and there was a lull in the bombings. It had been a while since we'd got some bombings. The powers-that-be decided we're spendin' a lot of time on this guy.

We decided, let's bring him in and talk to him. The guy was working for TWA at the time. We brought him in, and of course he said, "I'm all in favor of independence for Puerto Rico, yes. I support this, but I'm not a bomber. I work for TWA." The sergeant who used to run the squad was a Puerto Rican guy, very, very sharp. Streetwise. Sergeant Valentín. "Well, you say you're not a bomber; we're telling you you are a bomber. Sooner or later you're gonna get caught, or one day we're gonna show up in an apartment and you're gonna be blown to bits."

Shortly thereafter, we get a call on an explosion in a Queens apartment. We go out there, and there he is. Willie Morales, the bomber. I guarded him in Elmhurst Hospital.

He lost his hands. He also had some problem with his breathing: he must have seared his lungs from the fire and the intensity. When the firemen who were the first to respond got into the apartment where he blew himself up, they found him—in the condition he was in—trying to flush some codes down the toilet. He was a fanatic. There was blood all over the place. We did get some stuff like that out of the toilet bowl.

So I guarded him for a while, and he kind of got a little friendly with me, although I don't sympathize with his cause. We became like friends. He had trouble breathing. One night I'm guarding him, and all the bells go off. Apparently his tube had come out of his throat, I realized. I went over. I didn't want to leave him alone, because I didn't know if it was a ploy or not, but I'm yellin' for the nurse and nobody's comin'.

So I look down and I stick the tube back in, and he starts breathing. Now he takes his little stumps and he motions for me to come over, closer to him. I come over closer, and he takes his stumps, and he hits me in the face, like, "Thank you." I guarded him till he got well and we moved him out of there to Bellevue Hospital. He was always tryin' to talk me into his cause. I never paid much attention to that.

To show you what kind of a fanatic this guy was—first of all, he wouldn't take any pain medication at all in the hospital. He wouldn't accept anything. He thought they were trying to dope him so he would give up the other people who were involved in the cell with him. He wouldn't take any pain medication. Every time the nurse came, it was a fight. "What is that?" he would ask. If it was an antibiotic, he'd take it. If it was a needle for the pain, he wouldn't. And he'd just, like, meditate so the pain would go away. He was a fanatic.

We took him to Bellevue, and we went to trial with him. It was the briefest trial ever, because he wanted to be tried as a prisoner of war, a revolutionary. Military tribunal.

I got up on the stand; they asked me my name, who you are, where do you work? What I knew about the case. Then, the next thing, the defense attorney'd get up and say, No questions for the detective, and that was it. There was no cross-examination, because he wanted to be treated as a prisoner of war. He wanted the Geneva Accords to be implemented in his case.

We brought him back over to Bellevue. He didn't want to be there. He was in the ward because they were looking to fix him up with some artificial limbs. We had told the people at Bellevue that this guy was an escape risk—because while we were guardin' him, even though he was sick, he was still exercising. This guy's a fanatic.

We took him back. We told the correction officers there, Look, this guy's an escape risk, and they laughed. They laughed at us. "He ain't got no hands!" Well, Willie Morales escaped from Bellevue Hospital—he went out the window, nobody knows exactly how he did it, and he fled the United States, went to Mexico.

Somehow the FBI traced him to Mexico City, I think, and he was at a phone booth and they knew that he was at that phone booth. They had an informant. They went over there and they got into a shootout with the Mexican police. One of the Mexican cops was killed, but they grabbed Morales.

He claimed the same thing there, that he was a political prisoner. Being that he didn't do the shooting, 'cause he had no hands, I think he got maybe seven or eight years. When he'd served his time in Mexico, they sent him to Cuba, because he claimed he was a political prisoner of the United States.

They didn't return him here, but he had been sentenced to ninety-nine years for the Fraunces Tavern and the other bombs. They charged him under an old statute. Charged him with sedition—trying to break up the Union. It's an old federal charge somebody dug up. It was probably used during the Civil War.

Right now, he's in Cuba. We know for a fact he went to Cuba.

———

No one sold heroin in the streets of Olga Ford's 1950s Brooklyn girlhood. No black extremists spread "off-the-pigs" propaganda.

On "dish night" at the movies, women walked to the theater unescorted through the remote neighborhood on the outer edge of East New York. The City's harsh realities, such as they were, didn't affect Olga.

Grown up, she already held a perfectly good insurance job when her mother, a government payroll supervisor who had lived through the Depression, clipped an item from *The Chief*. The civil service weekly announced the test for policewoman. "Take it—" she advised Olga. "Twenty years and you can retire."

With no particular yearning for police work, the daughter complied. "Little did I know I would get swept away." She was appointed to the old Women's Bureau in 1958. Pert, with deep-brown skin, Ford says she started out naive. "I grew up in the Police Department, came into my own."

Her squad in the Women's Bureau investigated illegal abortion mills, interviewed victims, and took the cases to the Manhattan DA for prosecution. ADA John Keenan handled a lot of them. In 1963, thanks to Ford's boss, her work and her partner's were recognized with gold shields—the first, she says, for the women's unit. When the Women's Bureau closed, Detective Ford did stints in the Criminal Investigation Bureau and in Narcotics, where she worked major violators in the elite Special Investigating Unit.

Cut to 1971, the year black extremists' bullets would assault and kill or maim ten New York City patrolmen. Following the first incident—the crippling assault on Thomas Curry and Nicholas Binetti as they guarded the Manhattan District Attorney's residence—prosecutor John Keenan mobilized Detective Ford and other black women officers to interview female friends of the black revolutionaries. Ford's interviews helped identify the shooters.

That same springtime week in Harlem, the extremists assassinated patrolmen Joseph Piagentini and Waverly Jones. Months later, in the aftermath of the attempted drive-by murder of a police sergeant in San Francisco, authorities there locked up one of the shooters in the Harlem double slaying. But leads to the second perp fizzled, leaving the NYPD detectives distraught.

"Guys brag to the women," Ford reminded them. They had detained three female associates of the perps. Questioning each in turn, Ford came on as if she knew a lot more than she did. The women unwittingly gave up links in the chain that led to the identification of one Herman Bell, aka Samuel Pennegard, among other aliases. In *Badge of the Assassin*, an account of these events, former New York prosecutor Robert K. Tanenbaum says Ford accomplished her mission by dint of "motherliness"—surprising those who knew her only as "one of the toughest cops in Harlem, male or female." Olga Ford got second grade. Bell would be scooped up in a dramatic but bloodless joint maneuver in New Orleans in 1973 by New York City detectives, New Orleans detectives and FBI agents, and San Francisco detectives.

"It was a high point," Ford says. "Women never got into those heavy cases then. If I hadn't worked on the abortion cases—and now they needed to have females who could do interrogation . . . I was like, wow, you worked on a case where other cops were killed, the only woman on it."

But the only woman was overlooked when the patrolmen's union honored "the men who broke this case." "One of the toughest cops in Harlem" was devastated. She had to fight for the same plaque the men received. She won, but too late to be included in the honor festivities—a slight she never really got over.

When Detective Ford went back to Narcotics SIU, the name she heard over and over in the streets of Harlem was Leroy "Nicky" Barnes. A few years later, Barnes would go before a federal judge, and in a *New York Times Magazine* cover story—"Mister Untouchable"—reporter Fred Ferretti wrote, "his name itself inspires awe."

Barnes was infamous before Ford even came on the scene, yet nobody was going after the bad guy. " 'You'll never catch a black guy with a key,' " Ford heard somebody say. "In other words, you're not gonna make headlines with guys like that, this kinda stuff. And I'm saying—we got this discrimination in who we're gonna go after?"

Other theories also occurred to her. "Maybe the NYPD didn't realize yet that blacks were major heroin dealers, because the stereotype was definitely that the big guy is Italian. If it wasn't an Italian name, forget about it. Black guy, no way."

Ford wasn't the only person Barnes would fascinate. Larry Gerhold, later a detective, was only a patrolman in 1971. But an ambitious one inspired by the career of his older brother Mike—a detective whom he idolized. Larry Gerhold would gather intelligence for the federal drug conspiracy cases that finally crashed the black heroin business. When he started out in Harlem, though, the sidewalks could have been fourteen karat.

"It was the day of the fedora, the sharp clothes, the gold chains, the cars," Gerhold says. "Everybody had a brand-new car. This guy Cisco was *limo*'d around—he had a driver. Incredible, what this kid was doin'. I wanted to know about him, and the more I learned about him, the more I learned about other people. Nicky's name came about, and that was it—it was like a love affair. This guy's gotta go to jail.

"You want to get promoted, you want recognition—and if you're going to come to work and spend that eight hours a day, it should be fun. You want to take the car away from 'em, take the jewelry away from 'em, you want to kick 'em in the ass, and you want 'em to go to jail. That's what it's all about.

"But how do you get Nicky Barnes? He was like an untouchable already, because the way law enforcement was set up you worked on targets of convenience. You made cases to go up the ladder, make the bigger and better case all the time. So cases were made, until they hit that level where they couldn't go any further. He remained Mr. Untouchable."

### Detective First Grade Olga Ford:
### Nicky Barnes

A new sergeant, Larry Mullins, must've decided Barnes was worth getting. That's when I started working on this case and got to know more about Barnes. We were up in Washington Heights, where he lived on Haven Avenue with his common-law wife, Thelma Grant. We were surveilling them. We did a lot of surveillance, a lot of tails.

My function was to sit in the window of an observation point directly across the street from this huge building, to photograph whoever I thought was suspicious—people were coming and going, I didn't know where—and of course, to try to get pictures of Barnes, who would come out every now and then in a vehicle. But it was almost impossible to get pictures of him.

When I first went into SIU, we went out one night on a guy named Roosevelt Bentley up in The Bronx, and we took him. He had adjoining houses. He'd knocked the wall through and made one house. It was dark and gaudy and red velvet and black velvet. Just cheap, as far as I was concerned. I'm still a rookie in Narcotics; I said, Why has he got all these typewriters in every room in the house, including the bathroom? IBM Selectric typewriters. The guys are laughin' at me. Stolen property.

For a while, I went to the Major Investigations Section, working on the Italians on Pleasant Avenue. The Drug Enforcement Administration had shot all these yards of videotape, but they couldn't ID anyone. Finally, they got an informant, Delores, who grew up right there. I turned her and she was able to sit down and identify all the people in the tape. We locked up about eighty mafiosi in seventy-three, including Carmine Trumanti, the Lucchese don.

But SIU kept going back to Barnes, and now I really got involved. We'd go up to make small heroin buys on 116th Street—the press was calling 116th Street and Eighth Avenue the marketplace. It *was*. I'd never seen anything like that in my life—they were hawking it. We sent an undercover in to make a buy, and he was wearing a Kel transmitter. We could overhear, "I got the Blue Tape!" "I got the Gold Tape!" "I got 007!" "I got Blue Magic!" I couldn't believe what I was hearing.

They were hawking glassine envelopes marked with tape. If you wanted to get killed, take somebody else's color tape and put it on your product. They would find you, you'd be dead. It turned out that that operation on the corner involved Barnes, his source, a guy named Frank Lucas, and others. It used to blow my mind that they all operated so peacefully on that corner, but there was room for everybody.

Barnes was on the street a lot; I used to see him on 116th Street. Matter of fact, I testified to that. I got a phone call—by now I was becomin' the Barnes expert. "In your observations of Barnes, did you happen to see him around this time?" I had seen him the next day, going into the Tiger Lounge, on 116th Street. He was clean-shaven—but the day before, he had a beard. It turns out he had stuck some guy with an ice pick, that was the charge. The guy died.

I went on to testify that I saw him on 116th Street stepping out of his blue Mercedes-Benz. His lawyer went crazy. I couldn't say that; it was inflammatory. It suggests money. They didn't convict him.

A garage on 145th Street was known at the time as Harlem River Motors. My partner, Jimmy Copeland, and I, we tailed somebody up there, a kid named Cisco. We start sittin' up there. And one night we see Nick come out. Oh, ho, what is this?

So now we get an observation point across from the garage. I photographed that garage for the longest time. We're taking license plates. We're ID'ing people, and they're gamblers and they're druggers. Almost every car that came out of there was registered to a leasing corporation called Hoby Darling Car Leasing in Pennsylvania. Turns out Hoby Darling is kind of a shady character, and he also was showing up at this garage. They were transferring the stuff in there. Large amounts of drugs. Cars used to go in, cars used to come out. And Barnes was constantly in there.

Myself and Jimmy, we go back and we show all this to our bosses, and they go—"Oh, yeah, something must be goin' on up there."

I had to go back up to Haven Avenue eventually. They're gonna take Nicky Barnes this night. They called me back. I knew the cast of characters. I'm now again sitting watchin' the window to see when he's gonna come out. And we did take him, early in the morning.

They got shotguns and all this stuff, and Barnes comes in in this green Chevy and goes down in the garage. And they all go and they pounce on him. Somebody who was down there told me that Nick gets up and he's brushin' off his shirt, and he's saying, "Fellas! I'm known as a *gentleman* in the street." I said, I love it.

But the thing that really increased my fascination with this Nicky Barnes guy—I remember Roosevelt Bentley and the red velvet: my concept of what a major drug violator—how he lives. Now we get into Nick's apartment. I can't believe this! Excellent taste. White rug on the floor that *was* white. In my house it wouldn't have been white. And he's got a library. Black history. I don't believe this guy. Incredible. I'm sitting holding his baby, trying to find out if the set of car keys we found in the place went to his Citroën. He had five cars, we thought the Citroën was hot. He said the keys were to a Jaguar, but I knew they weren't.

Kinda anticlimactic. He had some pot or whatever in the apartment, very little stuff. We didn't convict him on that case, either.

He went from nobody to the guy Jimmy Carter said to get. They pulled together a task force of city, state, and federal people. I wasn't in it; I was working on somebody else in Queens. At that point in his career Nick really should have insulated himself from the street, but he came from the street and he couldn't stay away from the action. They got an informant, one of Nick's guys that *we* wanted to get on our Queens case—who also turned out to be a part of their case.

They locked him up and some of his guys, on a violation of the RICO statute. So now Barnes is convicted of a continuing criminal enterprise. And he's gone.

I went out with this bunch of us, all black, and we set up another observation point across the street from a Barnes associate, a guy named Frank James who had the Oasis Sandwich Shop. We said, How many sandwiches do you think he's selling in there, right? So we set up an OP. We tailed this gang, videotaped them together; we made very clear, precise notes.

All of our reports were very detailed, because when I worked up on Pleasant Avenue, the DEA had a lot of videotape and notes—which worked out good when they got an informant. So now I'm saying, let's do the same thing. In a historical statement, after you take the statement from the informant, you have to now document as much as you possibly can. Let's videotape them and make this thing solid. Let's make detailed notes so we've got all the backup. Who knows when we're gonna get an informant?

Never in my wildest dreams could I imagine that the informant would be Nicky Barnes.

Somebody tells me, "Hey, they got Thelma Grant on a direct sale!" In order for his wife to deal drugs to somebody, the informant had to be really high placed—this is what we're figuring. Turns out it was Nicky. I answered the phone one time in the U.S. attorney's office—said my name, Detective Ford.

"This is Nick, I hear you're retiring—" This conversation—he felt compelled to tell me why he set up Thelma. Why tell me this? I'm the cop that's been chasing you for a long time. He said she took up with this guy, Tito Johnson. The one guy he said to her, I don't want you to have nothin' to do with—this guy answered the phone at the apartment one day. He said to me, "I hadda send a little heat her way."

Then he gets mad at the rest of the gang because they're not doing the right thing by him, as far as he's concerned. So he becomes an informant. Of course, we had already documented his statement because we followed his gang all over the place.

When I retired, my last request was to talk to Nicky Barnes. I was fascinated to know what makes him tick. The DEA guy says, "If he'll talk to you." I said, Well, ask him. He agreed to talk to me.

So I go downstairs from the U.S. attorney's office to MCC, Metropolitan Correctional. He comes out, and I almost didn't recognize him 'cause he had lost a lot of weight. He pumps iron. And I guess in jail you're not eating all this great food. So he came out. Like rock—muscles, all that stuff.

We sat and we chatted for a half an hour or more, and I didn't want to talk about, "Remember that day I saw you at such and such a place and we lost the tail and you went so and so? What was in that bag?"

I'm leaving now. It doesn't matter to me.

He's talking about the castration of the black male. I'm saying, Yeah, but you sold drugs. I don't get it. He said, "Well, if I didn't do it, somebody else would have." And I couldn't figure that out for the longest time. Why would he say that?

At least the way I'm putting it together, he's born uptown around the area of 116th Street in 1932. It's the Depression, the whole country is in it, so you can imagine what was happening to black families. I understand he came from a fairly nice family, went to school. But he gets hooked on heroin.

Now, I've read many books, and I think one of the first Mafia informants said the organized crime figures didn't want to touch drugs—but they agreed to bring it in and sell it in the black communities. I think that's what Barnes was kind of gettin' at, because he got hooked by these Italians who decided to sell to blacks. He eventually went to Lexington, he kicked it and never went back on, as far as I know.

Most of them are just hoods; he's not totally hood. He's got an amazing brain. He was running a business. Selling a product. I understand that since he's been in jail, he's gotten his degree. Bright, bright guy—but what a waste.

———

In the real world, bad guys sometimes get away. Well, not if Detective Lieutenant Timothy Patrick Byrnes has anything to say about it. Don't let the good looks and Irish charm distract you—he's uncompromising.

At the scene of a bowling alley murder, then-Sergeant Byrnes of Crime Scene made sure his detectives found a way to dust the *holes* in a bowling ball for fingerprints. They did lift a print—and the game was over for the perp.

When Lieutenant Byrnes was CO of the Crime Stoppers Squad, any callers' anonymous tips were always followed up. One tip about a body in a vacant lot in Bushwick, Brooklyn, didn't languish on a desk just because the caller didn't know *which* vacant lot. Byrnes and Crime Stoppers Detective George Kennedy pinpointed the lot—only to find it spick-and-span.

Eager to sift mountains of landfill to locate the body, Byrnes and Kennedy were disappointed when Sanitation said no way. Disappointed but not discouraged, they painstakingly built a case that did the impossible—satisfied the DA *without* a body. Meanwhile, they openly kept tabs on their suspect.

"We got to his family, and we told them we were looking for him about a missing girl. Basically we haunted the guy. We haunted him in Bermuda. He came back to the West Coast; we haunted him on the West Coast. He was in Virginia; Virginia authorities worked with us and haunted him in Virginia. He went back to Bermuda, back to the West Coast—over a period of almost a year.

"Finally, he called his girlfriend and told her he wanted to surrender because we weren't leaving him in peace. We were haunting him no matter where he went. He came in, not knowing we didn't have the body, and made a full confession to the homicide. We indicted him, he took a plea to manslaughter—and we still had no body.''

If you can't psych your perp into giving himself up, put his picture on TV—on a Crime Stoppers local news segment—and somebody *else* may be persuaded to give him up. Crime Stoppers, nicknamed Tips, pays cash rewards for good tips, given anonymously, and the program pays tipsters by assigned code numbers. If it's a cop killer you're looking for, park the Cop Shot promotion bus in the area where the murder happened.

In the Crime Stoppers Squad, if you get a good tip, reach out to wherever the suspect skipped to. Your counterparts will definitely be there for a New York detective. They'll make the collar—hey, they'll even starch it. You'd do the same for them.

### Lieutenant Timothy Byrnes:
### Long-Distance Collar

Somebody called our Tips hot line from Florida. "I understand there was a policeman shot up there . . ." The detective said yes, and the caller said, "Well, I want to speak to your supervisor." The detective tried to get the information, but it wasn't forthcoming. So finally I got on the phone.

"I understand you have a policeman shot and you're looking for a particular individual." Yes. "And there's a reward being offered?" Ten thousand dollars, yes. "Well, how does it work?" I go through the whole litany: We don't want to know your name. We give you a number and you're forever known to us by that number. Calls are not recorded; you can't be subpoenaed or voiceprinted or anything like that. You give us the information, we check on it, and if it leads to his arrest and conviction, you're eligible for ten thousand dollars reward.

"Well, are you looking for this particular individual?" We knew who the shooter was; we had passed out photos. We had the Cop Shot bus out on the street, and my guys were there with the microphones, appealing for tips. But somehow the caller had heard *in Florida*. "I know where he will be in two hours." In the same breath, he said, "But I ain't coming back to New York."

We'll make arrangements to have the money shipped to you. You don't have to come here. We have Crime Stoppers units throughout the country; we can pay you very easily.

"All right—" he said, "he will be arriving on a flight from New York to Florida. [This] is the flight number. He's in the air right now; he'll be arriving at [this time]." I asked him to hold on. I said, Can somebody call up—flight number so-and-so, see if this guy is listed on the manifest.

The caller said one of two people will be meeting him. "Either [this person], his cousin, or [this person], who's his uncle, will meet him at the airport. They'll be going to the cousin's house on [this street], or the uncle's house, which is on [this street]."

We were unable to verify the fact that he was on the plane, but we called Metro-Dade and we told them the situation—that it was a cop killer coming down there. As we were talking, they were dispatching people to the airport. I mean, it was that quick. They said, This is a cop shooting. We faxed them a copy of the arrest warrant and his photo, and they dispatched a SWAT team.

I told the tipster to call us back if he heard anything more, or if not, call us back right after the flight had landed.

We were on the phone with Metro-Dade as he called us, and the supervisor had a field dispatch—he could hear what was going on. The caller is saying, "He's landed and [this] is the guy who's gonna be meeting him, the cousin, and they're gonna go to [this address]." You could hear it coming over the radio: "We have him in sight. We got a positive ID on him. This is the guy. He's being met by the person they described, the cousin."

The caller said, "They're going to [this address]," and the SWAT team was following him. They were outside the house, formulated an attack plan—who was going in front, who was going in back—and they hit the place. Within five minutes, we were back on the radio, and I heard him saying, "We got the guy in custody. Tell New York we got him. No casualties, no nothing."

They nearly missed him. They went through the house, knew he went in, but couldn't find him. When they went inside, he jumped into the dryer—he was in a front-load dryer. And finally, they looked down and they saw him.

They couldn't get him out the opening. Once he was in, they couldn't extricate him—they had to take the top off, take the side off, and yank him out.

A little synopsis of the case goes with the reward record: we put that he was apprehended inside the dryer. And the question was asked but never answered, Did you turn the dryer on before you took him out?

———

Take a New York City desperado out of his element and stash him in a middle-American family appliance—he's gonna get stuck. Everything's upside down in that picture. More predictable, in a crazy way, to a young detective working one of his first ghetto homicides, is the discovery in an abandoned crack house of human skeletal remains crammed into an old icebox.

Mike Burke at age twenty-six, a bit gangly, like a kid who shot up too fast, had the attention span of someone a lot older, and he had learned about all there was to know about the exploding street drug scene in New York in the early and mid 1980s. By the summer of 1986, when the "Refrigerator Case" fell to him, he was assigned as a "white shield" to a squad in a notorious Harlem precinct, the Two-eight. But he'd started in an area as bad or worse, and bigger: the South Bronx.

Instead of staying on uniformed patrol there, he'd hooked up with Joe Blanck and another new guy in the Four-four, Luis Bauza, working narcotics "conditions" in plainclothes. "I didn't know anything at all—Joe was showing me everything. He'd jump right into the fire. Every day we were making arrests, like thirty a month. He was really superaggressive. Got his shield in six months.

"One sergeant, an old-timer, came up to me and said, 'Don't work with that guy yet. You should be learning other things.' But you learned a lot from him. You didn't really get to deal with decent people at all. You got mostly the worst—drug dealers and drug addicts, guys robbing. They'd come and hang out; buy their drugs and hang out in the shooting galleries." After Blanck was promoted, Burke and Bauza worked with him in the precinct RIP (Robbery Identification Program). "We were like one, the three of us."

Burke, who had only one relative in the department until he married a cop, really got into what he was doing. "I come from just a simple kinda family, like really workin' people. I was brought up since I was a young kid: just work. Do the best you can at it. Joe Blanck came from the same mold. If I never worked with him, I probably wouldn't be aggressive or into the job as much as I am. We'd always see things through."

What amounted to a four-year course in street people, with Joe Blanck as instructor, paid off for Mike Burke when it came to unlocking the secrets of the old refrigerator. And when the murder case dating from 1983 or 1984 unfolded in Judge Leslie Crocker Snyder's courtroom late in 1991, decent people could only sit horrified in the jury box.

Foreman David Newton, an advertising writer, saw Detective

Burke as "lean and tough; correct and thorough"—made human on the stand by a mild case of stage fright. The defendant, known on the street as Tom Slick, never testified, but the tape made by Burke's informant conveyed the evil of his deed. During the jurors' three-and-a-half-hour deliberations, according to Newton, "there was never anyone who voted not guilty."

Handing down a sentence of thirty years to life, Judge Snyder said a thousand years would be more appropriate. This perpetrator, she insisted, must "never be paroled to walk the streets of this earth."

### Sergeant Michael Burke:
### The Savannah, Georgia, Crew

All we knew from the medical examiner's office: just an unidentified female. Totally skeleton, with a little bit of leathery skin. Willie White got this case the day the body was found. I remember, I was in the office. It was a hot day, July of eighty-six.

Guy was going through abandoned brownstones looking for old refrigerator parts, that's what he said. Found this refrigerator in a closet and pulled it out. There was a foul odor. Finally, he got it open, and all this stuff kind of fell out on him. A sweater was found on the body; I don't know if they threw it in or if it was on the bones. But it really stunk. The fumes must have really hit him. I interviewed him later on; the guy was a dusthead, zombie'd out. Finding this probably snapped what was left of his mind.

Willie got transferred in September. A couple days later, I was given the case. September 24 the medical examiner said it was a homicide by strangulation. Something like this was kinda unique, usually you get a person shot or stabbed.

I went down to the ME's office—you try to learn everything right. Dr. Fernando explained that the ligature around the neck was like a tourniquet. Set up like an old torture technique, the way he described it—from the early Civil War, I think he said. They'd tighten the tourniquet, apply pressure to get more information out of a person. He thinks that's what happened. The scrub brush, or whatever, was twisted, causing the wire to tighten up. Cut off the circulation.

After talking to Fernando, Joe Rendine and I went up to interview the guy who found the body. Same story: going through the building, found this. There was a girl (who's since died) in his apartment, name was Linda. She told me and Joe, there's been a girl missing around here for a while. Linda didn't have any more information. I didn't know if this could have anything to do with it.

Peggy Caldwell was the consultant for the ME's office, forensic anthropologist.

Fernando recommended, speak to her. After her examination, Peggy was able to tell me that it was a female black, approximately five feet five, thin build, dead approximately two to three years. She was in the refrigerator, but the building where she was found had a hole in the ceiling—top floor. The cold air and the hot sun could cause a rapid deterioration. That's why they couldn't pinpoint the exact time of death, but she was found July '86—so you figure two years would be eighty-four, maybe eighty-three.

We started going around in that area, talking to different people. The bosses in the Two-eight were really good, Dolan and Flanagan. Whatever you needed done, they were always willing to help you, encourage you. They looked out for their workers, which means a lot.

Does anybody know about a missing girl? I described her: black, age I think was twenty-one, thin build. After a while, probably weeks, somebody who didn't want to get involved said the name Phyllis. Go see Phyllis at the Regent Hotel down on 104th Street. Pretty big building. They said go see her.

I found a girl named Phyllis, and she said to me there was a guy named Cory from the neighborhood who was going with a girl named Pam—who had a sister that'd been missing. Phyllis was able to get back to me with a phone number of Pam's mother, Jean King.

Mrs. King came into the precinct, didn't really want to have anything to do with me, didn't want to believe anything. Kind of pissed off. Pam was with her, and they gave me some information on the daughter: Veorah Turner. She'd been missing about two years. Went to buy Pampers for her babies, two young babies, a boy and a girl, who the grandmother's been raising.

Jean King tells me people told her that they seen her daughter standing on a Welfare line. We checked to make sure she wasn't getting Welfare or any kind of Social Security or anything like that. All those things were negative. Somebody else said she went out to California.

From that day, I kept talking to Mrs. King, trying to let her know what was going on. From the get-go, I told her, I don't know if this is your daughter, but I'm gonna try to find out. I'n not tryin' to pin some dead body on your family and say this is your daughter. I basically told her we'd found a female, badly decomposed, and she had been strangled, been dead about two years.

When Peggy Caldwell heard we had this female who was missing, she was really excited too. Asked me to get dental records, medical records, hair samples from the house, whatever. So we went runnin' around to all her schools and everything from when she was a kid. Nobody could find any records. I must have asked about ten times goin' back and forth. Kinda had the determination—you're not really getting anywhere and all of a sudden you get a leap.

The medical records I got weren't really of any value. Thought maybe she might have had an X-ray or a broken bone that they could match up. But nothing. No dental records at all that we could locate. The mother didn't have any hair samples. Peggy said we could try this new procedure called superimposition—if we can get a photograph, try to match it up with the skull.

I got the photo of Veorah Turner and I had it blown up in the Photo Unit. Peggy liked it—she was talking about the way the nose fit.

We had to wait because the body had been buried in Potter's Field, had to wait for months. This all takes time. And one of the teeth fell out of the mouth, one of her front teeth, from handling, I guess. But we still had one tooth; Peggy said it was good enough. You take one video camera and you put it on the skull, take another video camera and you put it on the enlarged photograph; they have a mixer and they superimpose one over the other.

We made a copy of the videotape up in the Academy somewhere. Peggy showed it to the doctors at the ME's office, and they were all ecstatic. She called me up and told me that it was definitely a positive ID. That was June '87. Almost a year after we got the case, we knew who she was.

But the hardest thing I find on this job—trying to tell people that a family member is dead. By the time Peggy Caldwell made a positive ID and I had to tell Jean King, we were good friends. She accepted it. I became pretty good friends with Pam too. We got the sweater from the homicide clothing room. As soon as Pam seen it, she started cryin'.

July. A lot of people were on vacation. It was kind of quiet. I remember one day I was working by myself. I walked into the precinct a couple of minutes before eight, there was a girl sitting in the lobby, and her nose was broken. Young girl from Philadelphia, kind of heavyset. She had been beat up. She'd gone to the bathroom on herself, she stunk. It was hot. Couple of people were complaining. A uniform guy was taking a 61 for assault. Guy named Kool Aid, she called him Porky, assaulted her.

I had to interview her, brought her up to the squad. She had no money. She wanted to go back to Philadelphia. I never try to sluff anybody off. I kind of felt sorry for her, went across the street and I bought her some cookies and orange juice. She was sitting there eatin' and talkin' to me. The police administrative aide came in at nine. The place stunk. "Open these windows, Burke!"

Anyway, it was just about an hour she was there. I was saying, How you goin' to get back, Alfreda? She didn't have a dime, so I was thinking of giving her a couple of bucks or tryin' to do somethin' for her. She wanted this guy arrested, but she was scared to death of him. She told me the whole story of the assault. I didn't know if she was gonna be around to press charges on this guy. He was a pimp. He tried to put her out on the street and she really didn't want to do it. I think she did do it and she wasn't making any money, so he beat the hell out of her.

If something had happened—a homicide—and I had let her go in about ten or twenty minutes, it wouldn't have worked out. She looked at pictures, she looked at the photo books, trying to find a picture of him for me. She was hangin' out and she says, "Y'know what he said to me?" What? She goes, "He said to me he was gonna kill me and put me in a refrigerator like his friend done to a girl."

The area where she was assaulted was 127th Street and Lenox Avenue—Veorah was found right there, 127th between Lenox and Fifth. I was like, jumping up and down. Inside. I don't want her to go back and say— Things were going through my mind, was he the guy that done it? But this is too much of a coincidence. One-two-seven and Lenox is a Savannah, Georgia, crew. They had a whole crew of guys, all southerners.

I must have asked her that question about ten times, tell me what he said again? I wanted to keep hearing it, see if she could remember anything else. So she was there about another hour. She left me some information about him. She had his name too, Gregory Capers.

I found him in a Jersey jail, Bergen County, like ten days later, from assaulting his common-law wife. They had two kids in foster, and none of the kids looked like him, but he says he's the father. She was a prostitute, he was a pimp. She was his main girl, and he was having a fight with her—that's why he was trying to get Alfreda out there. His lifelong dream is to make it in the big city, to be a pimp. Real character.

I was telling John Maxwell all this, and he was really ecstatic, 'cause he went to the scene originally—he had worked a little bit on it with Willie White. Asked the boss if I could go out to Jersey and talk to this guy.

But first we found the common-law wife—living in a hotel in Jersey. Asked her if she knew about the murder. One night, a couple years ago, Gregory came home, she says, he started talking about his friend. The friend killed some girl from the neighborhood and put her in a refrigerator, told Gregory about it. Gregory was kind of a boastful character—came home and told the wife. She said the friend is in jail in Savannah, Georgia, right now.

Ridgefield Police Department. Gregory Capers was just going to be sentenced to sixty days in jail. I went out there with John Maxwell, and we sat down and talked with him. I was kind of like a stern guy. John was being a good guy.

John brought up a homicide of a white female in that area, 127th and Lenox—she went up there to buy drugs, a bunch of guys took her in the lot, they all raped her, and then they killed her. So John was saying, "You weren't a part of that, were you?" Maybe Capers was gettin' a little bit nervous.

What helped us—he's a buff. We found out he helped out detectives in Georgia. He was from Savannah, helped out detectives with the murder of an old man. This gang was doing robberies, and they did a murder in the commission of one of their robberies. Capers was able to help the detectives.

After a while we told him, We're homicide detectives, maybe you can help us. He talked about a couple different homicides, little bits and pieces. Then he jumped out, "Oh, yeah! A guy I know who did a homicide, he killed a girl and put her in a refrigerator and told me about it." Oh, yeah? What's the guy's name? "Tom 'Slick.' " Street name. He was able to give us a little more information. He gave me a written statement that day on it, said the guy's name was Tom Crawford, he was in jail in Savannah.

So I give Capers my card. Like you're excited on one hand, but on the other hand, you're let down a little. The guy's a couple states away. Gregory said he was doing twenty years for another murder. You feel like you reach a dead end. You think, maybe you can get an exceptional clearance if he's really gonna do twenty years? Your wheels are turning—how are you gonna prove it? But we were really happy, more so than anything else. Excited we found this guy.

When Gregory Capers got out, the first thing he did was he came to the Two-eight. I put him in the room and left him. Guess he was wondering about me. We had a bunch of phone books there. Come back in. He had the phone books open. He's goin' down the name "Burke." I'm kind of leery about it. This guy's trying to find out about me. I found out about him. I verified that he helped out in a homicide investigation.

By that time I'd found out who Tom Crawford was—he used the name Tony Williams. I had a picture of him with a turban on, all bandaged up. He was arrested with a gun and he must have resisted. He did eight months in Rikers and we never even knew.

Show the picture to Capers. "That's him." It was like August 3. We were trying to think of ways to do something. We took him down to ADA Bill Hoyt's office. I met Hoyt through Jack Donovan—Hoyt was really on top of the Two-eight cases. Gregory was a hundred percent cooperative. He says that when this happened, he felt real bad about it, even though him and Crawford were childhood buddies in Savannah. He was really upset. He knew that Crawford had killed a guy in Georgia. Then supposedly he told Gregory he killed a girl in Virginia on the way up here. Went to Baltimore, and from Baltimore he came to New York.

He hung around Times Square and then he hung around 127th and Lenox. There's a drug dealer, Big Dave from Savannah, Georgia, who's still out there—we don't have anything, just word on the street about him. Crawford was supposedly starting to do muscle work for him. Taking care of people that owe Dave money and working the door in crack spots so he wouldn't get stuck up. Crawford always wanted to be a gangster, Capers was telling me, always wanted to be a hero on the street. He was doing real wild, crazy shit up there. There was a warrant for him in Georgia, and no one here knew he was wanted.

After Crawford told Capers that he'd done this murder, Capers was really upset. Started calling 911, anonymous calls, telling the police there was a body in the building. Had a girl call too. He knew her from the neighborhood; he was telling her to call and say there's a body in the building. The cops would go there, but they'd never find anything.

It was hard to get up in. I got in through a ladder from around the corner—Sylvia's Restaurant. Joel Potter was holding a shaky ladder; me and Tony Krassas were climbing up it. (I didn't go to the crime scene originally, but later on I went, looking for more clothing.) So maybe the cops didn't want to go three stories up. Maybe he wasn't specific where the body was, what floor.

Crawford got caught on his warrant finally, went back to Georgia, and was sentenced to twenty years. I figured out maybe Capers could make a phone call to him, we'd get him on tape and maybe verify his information. Nobody can just go and see you in the corrections facility; the rules there are pretty strict.

The day we were down in Hoyt's office, we had Gregory make a taped call to Crawford's family. Gregory hadn't heard anything in a couple of years. So he started renewing acquaintances through the mother—he remembered the phone number. He didn't ask too much about the son the first time. We had given him some instruction, but he was willing, he was the one who wanted to call.

He says, "Tell Tom I was asking for him." He was a bright guy, real likable guy, colorful guy. Really articulate. I really liked him. He had a problem one time in a hotel that was closing, throwing him out of the room; I go down and get him. Another time, there was trouble in Jersey; I run over there. Got to know him—he'd tell me his dreams were to be the Iceberg Slim of New York. He wanted to be a great pimp.

We already knew about the strict rules in the Georgia prison system. The mother went to Tom and told him that Gregory was asking about him. Then Gregory called back a couple weeks later, asked the mother if she visited her son. Tom was excited that Gregory was asking about him. Gregory put the seed in the mother's mind to tell Tom that he was coming down to visit, I forget exactly when, maybe for Christmas.

After a couple more phone calls with the mother, Gregory got the address and started writing to Tom. He wasn't getting the letters, 'cause he got jammed up for assaulting another inmate and he was transferred to another prison. He was in the bing, the hole. Then after a while, Gregory would send a new letter. We didn't want to raise him up; we wanted to be really careful.

Finally Crawford answered. Then Gregory would write and tell him, "I'm coming down. I'd like to come see you, but I understand I can't unless I'm a family member."

Crawford wrote back that you're now on the visiting list. I thought, what if we wire Capers and see if he could get a statement from Crawford about the homicide.

I talked to Bill Hoyt about it. He said it's a great idea, but he didn't know if it could be done. He went to the law library for me for a couple hours, and he said, "Mike, I can't find anything that says Don't. There's no case law, so you might as well go and do it."

We talked to the legal bureau in the Police Department and they let us go, Lieutenant Martin, who was the boss down there. They said it was okay to go, so me and Maxwell went down with Capers. Two tape recorders, in case one failed.

We took off out of Kennedy, June of '88 on a Friday. Capers was sitting between us, and the plane started lifting off. He grabbed the lady's head in front of him, and he started screaming. Then after he settled down, I was teasing him. He was still nervous, but he was quiet. Gregory, put your hand in mine, I said, now's the time to tell me if you ever did anything wrong. Any murders or anything. Maxwell was rolling all over the place, laughing.

Capers hadn't been down there in years. It was his hometown. Big-time New York guy, came down with all his clothes in a green garbage bag. We made sure he had nothing in it that would get us in trouble with the airline, 'cause he was a street guy. Just a pile of dirty laundry all messed up. Got him his own room in the hotel. Hanging out with him for a while.

Saturday morning, around eight or so. James Horn was coming at nine to pick us up and take us to the prison, couple hours' drive from the Savannah area to Reedsville Correction Facility. We were knocking and Gregory wasn't answering. We get the maid to open the door, and the TV's on. He took all the duds out of the green garbage bag, and he put them on a rack. And my man's gone. Before we left New York, somebody tightened him up. I don't know if it was me or one of the DAs; I think I gave him a couple bucks. He just was gone.

Me and Maxwell were pacin' up and down in the motel. James Horn is there. We're like, Sorry. I'm sweatin' and my stomach's upset. Maxwell put everything in the bag, the clothes, "Fuck this guy! Mikey, he's staying with me tonight." Maxwell put it in his room.

And all of a sudden, Look, John! I see him struttin' like a real king. He's coming down the walkway, walking with his bebop, real serious strut. He's got like five, six guys wide-eyed behind him, lookin', saying, oh, shit! So we start hidin' in, like, a little garden around there, behind pillars. He's braggin' to guys about how he's a big-time pimp. He musta been tellin' them all night long. He was fired up. I don't know if he was real stoned, but he'd been partying.

He's bringing these guys to show them his New York wardrobe that he had laid out. He took out his key, opened the door, and his face dropped. All these guys, country guys, had been all psyched up—Yeah, Gregory made it big in New York! And the room was empty. Me and Maxwell, we were dyin'. We were holdin' our stomachs. We were just so happy to see him too.

He was saying some shit like, "Maid musta took my stuff." He had nothing to show these people. He had all these silk suits, these hats all balled in this one green bag.

We let him know we were there. I guess he saw we weren't too happy. So he told the boys to split. Drivin' out there, he was falling asleep in the car. He'd been up all night. I was like, oh, no.

When we got to the prison, Capers says, "Don't worry, Burke, don't worry." He knew me pretty good by then. "I'll be all right. I'll do what I gotta do." Put the wire on and everything. Went in and it was the wrong guy. He went back in and was in there for about an hour with Crawford. Came out, he's all excited. Me and Maxwell were excited. I took the evidence, put it in my black shoulder bag. I wasn't letting those tapes out of my sight at all.

I played the microcassette in the car for about two minutes to make sure. I could hear two voices on there—both very thick southern accents. I couldn't hear exactly, but it was something about a girl. He says, "He's talking about it on there! He's talking!" Capers yelling in the car. Me and Maxwell, we were real happy. Horn said, "If you get anything about prison breaks, anything that can help us, let us know." He drove us all the way back to our hotel.

Back to New York. Everywhere I went till Monday, that black bag was tied to me. Wherever I went, bathroom, sleep, everything. Right next to me.

When we started on the transcripts, Ellen Corcella worked hard on it, the prosecutor. She had a lot of other cases. Really a hard worker. Capers would come down and help us with the southern accents.

## TRANSCRIPT

**Crawford:** Goddamn. What—what is happening in New York, man?

**Capers:** What?

**Crawford:** I'd have write the man—the motherfuckin' letter come back, man.

**Capers:** When you write me, that bitch must have sent the motherfucker back, dirty motherfucker.

**Crawford:** Goddamn sure was writing you. I was looking at that address this morning. Letters, send them back. Damn, boy.

**Capers:** Damn, man.

**Crawford:** Hey. [laughter] U.S.A. on his finger, a nigger got a Rolex. That ain't no slum is it?

**Capers:** No, that's real here, jack. Goddamn, Tom. [laughter]

**Crawford:** Hey, did they find out about that girl yet?

**Capers:** Huh?

**Crawford:** You know who I talking about. Nose's girl. Do you know if they find out about that whore? I croaked the shit out of that whore.

**Capers:** Huh?

**Crawford:** Nigger croaked the shit out of that whore.

**Capers:** [laughs]

**Crawford:** I left her right in that motherfuckin' house.

**Capers:** Who is that?

**Crawford:** That base house. I left that bitch right in the motherfucker before they were closing that motherfucker up, man, before I got locked up, man. They were cinderblocking that motherfucker up.

**Capers:** Uh huh.

**Crawford:** The Japs still open?

**Capers:** Yep! Sylvia done bought the whole damn block.

   [. . .]

**Crawford:** How many base houses Dave got now?

**Capers:** Plenty of them.

**Crawford:** He got a lot of them? Who up here from Savannah now? Same niggers?

**Capers:** Yup. A bunch of his younger dudes up there hanging out. You weren't down when I had to fire up a nigger.

**Crawford:** Huh?

**Capers:** You weren't down when I had to fire up a nigger.

**Crawford:** You fired a nigger up?

**Capers:** Yeah, man. He chasing me with a knife.

**Crawford:** New York nigger.

**Capers:** Yeah.

   [. . .]

**Crawford:** [unintelligible]

**Capers:** Huh. Nose, Nose and all them boys, man. Nose got twenty-five to life.

**Crawford:** Twenty-five to life. I'm glad too.

**Capers:** Huh?

**Crawford:** I'm glad he did got that.

**Capers:** Why?

**Crawford:** 'Cause I killed that nigger's bitch.

**Capers:** Huh?

**Crawford:** I killed that nigger's bitch, man.

**Capers:** Damn.

**Crawford:** Bitch crossed a nigger, man, out of nigger's scratch, man. You know that old saying, our little homeboy. What that little nigger's name who had those golf clubs, remember Dave? You know that little nigger—man used to talk all that shit. Used to live somewhere right on the same side where you had lived at.

**Capers:** Uh huh.

**Crawford:** What that little dude's name there from Savannah who been in New York for a while?

[. . .]

**Capers:** Barry.

**Crawford:** He had a little girl. That nigger Barry.

**Capers:** Barry got killed, man.

**Crawford:** Yeah.

**Capers:** You ain't know that?

**Crawford:** No.

**Capers:** Man, Barry dead, man.

**Crawford:** A nigger killed him, eh?

**Capers:** Yeah, an old nigger kill him. A landlord killed him.

[. . .]

**Crawford:** Damn, everything goddamn came out straight. That nigger's killed. Nose is fucked up. That nigger with the bitch, man.

**Capers:** Who's that—Barry?

**Crawford:** He was with her when I say I want to see her. He was sitting at the goddamn table with the bitch.

[. . .]

**Capers:** What bitch?

**Crawford:** Nose's bitch. Man, you know, Nose's bitch—that old black-ass, skinny-ass girl, man. Used to be with black girl. You know that old skinny-ass motherfucking bitch, man—Nose's bitch. That bitch who used to live over there in the St. Nicholas goddamn projects. Dark, skinny old ugly-ass whore. You don't know 'bout her?

**Capers:** I'm trying to remember, maybe?

**Crawford:** You remember when I goddamned told you I had done croaked that whore. Man, I killed that bitch in the base house, and you say, Man, you a bad motherfucker, boy, you working up in there. And the bitch still in there. [laugh]

**Capers:** I think I remember you telling me something like that.

[. . .]

**Crawford:** Man, I choked that whore out.

**Capers:** What the bitch did to you?

**Crawford:** The bitch crossed a nigger out of his money, man. Me and her smoking, man, had Big Dave's goddamn money.

**Capers:** [laughter]

**Crawford:** Shit. [unintelligible] Ain't nobody know but me and you. I ain't told none of them other niggers.

**Capers:** You ain't told nobody—

**Crawford:** Nobody. Not my momma, daddy. Nobody know about it—

**Capers:** Yeah, man.

**Crawford:** but you.

**Capers:** The body still up there then?

**Crawford:** I believe the bitch still up there. I put it in the icebox.

**Capers:** Huh?

**Crawford:** I put the bitch in the icebox. I put her in a plastic bag. I had to crunch, crunch that whore all up together like this, man.

**Capers:** Oooh, shit.

**Crawford:** [unintelligible] Put it in that closet. Got some goddamn putty, putty'ed the door all the way around.

**Capers:** [laughter]

**Crawford:** Boy, for all I know that bitch still in that motherfucker. I sure want to get back to New York, and I ain't bullshitting. The nigger want to get back to that motherfucker there. I don't believe I'm going around Big Dave and them no damn more.

**Capers:** How much of Big Dave's money did the bitch take?

**Crawford:** Three-hundred.

**Capers:** Three-hundred?

**Crawford:** Yeah.

[. . .]

**Capers:** That's how much that bitch stole from you?

**Crawford:** Mmmmhmm.

**Capers:** How'd she stole that?

**Crawford:** Out of that closet—Me and Dempsey, you know me and Dempsey staying together.

**Capers:** Uh, huh.

**Crawford:** The bitch took it out of the closet. I was all high and paranoid and shit. I kept taking the money back and out, back and forth out of the goddamn closet, all paranoid. That bitch had done peeked it, right? Goddamn, I went in the bathroom. The bitch went in there and got the motherfucker, right?

**Capers:** Uh, huh.

**Crawford:** I ended up seeing the bitch about two weeks later. I saw her that day at Dave's and then base house, across from the State Building.

**Capers:** Huh. That's where you got her, in the State Building?

[. . .]

**Crawford:** No. She was in that base house by the State Building. Remember that base house Dave and them had, at 126th Street.

**Capers:** Yeah. Yeah.

**Crawford:** [unintelligible] Right there.

**Capers:** That's where you kill her. That's where you knock the bitch off at?

**Crawford:** I knocked her off at the goddamn base house on 128th.

**Capers:** 128th? Huh?

**Crawford:** I mean 127th. That's what I thought, man. I should have kept hanging around that goddamn Mayfair instead of slumming that motherfuckin' dude.

**Capers:** Man, Cabbie and them, right?

**Crawford:** Man, I don't know where that nigger is. Somebody told me he back in Savannah.

**Capers:** Oh, I think I know who you're talking about now.

**Crawford:** [unintelligible]

**Capers:** Nose's girlfriend.

**Crawford:** Yeah.

**Capers:** Yeah, that bitch ain't dead, man.

**Crawford:** Shit, man. That whore dead.

**Capers:** Huh?

**Crawford:** Man, I choked that motherfuckin' whore out. Man, I got a goddamn hanger and turned that motherfucker. The bitch started grunting and shitting, every goddamn way. Man, that whore dead as a motherfuck.

**Capers:** New York don't know you did that one, boy. Man, you'd be in some shit then, jack.

**Crawford:** I know that. I would have been sure enough fucked up. I'd be fucked up. That's one they'll never prove. That bitch done turned to goddamn dust now.

**Capers:** Huh?

**Crawford:** That bitch done turned to goddamn dust now.

**Capers:** How you feeling? It don't scare you or nothing?

**Crawford:** Shit, no. I don't even think about it.

**Capers:** You ain't got no [unintelligible]. You don't have no nightmares, nothing?

**Crawford:** No. Not for that bitch there. That bitch wasn't nothing but a old whore. Junkie-ass motherfuckin' whore, that whore wasn't shit. That's why a nigger croaked that motherfucker. [unintelligible]

**Capers:** That bitch got a sister named, ah, Pam. That's who you talking about.

**Crawford:** Pam. Sound like, I believe that bitch name is Pam. Might be [unintelligible] she had a little, short, dark skinned sister.

**Capers:** Yeah, Pam. I seen that nigger walking around here looking all bug and shit. She smoking crack. She has a sister named Veorah.

**Crawford:** That's her.

**Capers:** Huh?

**Crawford:** Veorah, that's her.

**Capers:** Huh? That's her. Yeah, Veorah. Nose's girl. Nose would be a mad motherfucker, boy.

**Crawford:** Yeah, he is. I'm glad that dude got twenty-five to life.

[. . .]

**Capers:** You fuck the bitch?

[. . .]

**Crawford:** I fuck around and jump hard one time.

**Capers:** That bitch body still up there. Bag of bones by now.

**Crawford:** Yeah.

**Capers:** Huh?

**Crawford:** That bitch ain't nothing but dust. I know that be damn near two years. The [unintelligible] still up in that motherfucker.

**Capers:** You don't be thinking about that?

**Crawford:** That shit don't bother me. Now and then I think about that shit.

**Capers:** You do? [unintelligible]

**Crawford:** Well, I think about the shit because when I be thinking about my kids. Some old shit [unintelligible]. Damn, I killed that whore there. The bitch had about three or four kids.

[. . .]

**Capers:** Who's that? Nose's girl? Damn.

**Crawford:** I feel sorry for the bitch kids. I don't feel sorry for her. [unintelligible]

**Capers:** Uh, huh.

**Crawford:** I feel sorry for the bitch-ass kids. Had to leave the kids behind.

**Capers:** [unintelligible] Damn, man [unintelligible].

**Crawford:** Told you, man, that crack had a nigger fucked up, man. If I wasn't high off that crack, I probably wouldn't have croaked her, probably would have whooped her ass. Nigger had that old killer attitude then, fuck that shit. I choked that whore ass, the whore ass fell.

**Capers:** What did you do?

**Crawford:** I got a coat hanger. I choked the shit out of that whore.

   [. . .]

**Capers:** What the clothes hanger for?

**Crawford:** To finish that whore ass off with.

**Capers:** You choked her?

**Crawford:** Mmmmhmmm.

**Capers:** With a clothes hanger?

**Crawford:** Yeah.

**Capers:** How?

**Crawford:** Put that motherfucker around her neck, tighten that shit up. I say, whore, hold that motherfucker. I say hold it. I hold that motherfucker for about five minutes and sure. The whore farting and shit. That bitch gone.

**Capers:** Huh.

**Crawford:** I say I better have to get rid of this body. Base-house niggers were downstairs in the den, about fifteen to twenty motherfuckers in the downstairs den.

**Capers:** In the base house?

**Crawford:** Yeah.

**Capers:** How you all got upstairs?

**Crawford:** I went up there with her. I tricked the bitch—I trick her that I have some crack. Come on, woman, I've got some crack. The bitch followed me on upstairs. She forgot all about the goddamn money she done took from a nigger.

**Capers:** Yeah.

**Crawford:** I croaked [unintelligible]. "No, Tom, I pay you." "No, bitch, you think nigger a chump." That whore ass fell on the goddamn floor. I'm going to have to kill this bitch because Nose might get out of the penitentiary. And that nigger Barry had done seen me take the whore around there. After I choked the whore out, Barry come back to the base house, ask me where that girl at. I say, that bitch gone, nigger. But the bitch was upstairs—she ain't walk back in. I went back up where I choked the whore out. I wanted—I wanted to just goddamn throw the bitch out the window, but that nigger named Mohammed—

**Capers:** Yeah.

**Crawford:** I was going to throw that bitch out. Sitting on the stoop downstairs—I know that nigger sitting by the backdoor and shit, right?

**Capers:** [laughter]

**Crawford:** I had to go through the base house because they might see the bitch dropping from the second floor. So I said, fuck that shit. I come around and grab that whore. Man, I had to ball her up because the bitch wouldn't fit in the plastic bag. I had to ball the bitch up, then tuck that bitch up, and put her in a plastic bag then. I had to drag the bitch in there all alone.

**Capers:** [laughter]

**Crawford:** Tuck that whore all up, put her in a goddamn bag and tie it up, because I knew the shit would be smelling. And it still be smelling, nigger could have smelled that shit anywhere. Smelling strong like a son of a bitch.

**Capers:** Yeah.

**Crawford:** Somebody had went in the goddamn closet. When I came back kicking the shit, right, the door was goddamn open. During that time, they were closing that base house up. They were cinderblocking and cementing that shit up, all them windows and doors. I say fuck that shit. Dave had them over in that other base house. Nigger, the nigger out of Brooklyn.

[. . .]

**Capers:** I want to go by there and check it, to see if thing still up there. See if it's still up there.

[. . .]

**Crawford:** I don't believe it still there. People was cleaning up, cleaning out them house.

**Capers:** Ain't never find it.

**Crawford:** Nigger [unintelligible]. The smell was strong as hell. Strong as shit! There were a bunch of flies flying all around that motherfucker. A whole gang of goddamn flies.

**Capers:** Umm. God. That shit don't bother—that shit don't bother you?

**Crawford:** Hell, no. She ain't nothing to me, man. That shit don't worry me. I ain't lost a near drop of sleep over that shit there.

**Capers:** Goddamn. How you feel?

**Crawford:** I feel nothing. Bitch dead, that's all.

**Capers:** [laughter]

[. . .]

**Crawford:** Where you living at, man?

**Capers:** Hundred, uh, thirtieth street.

**Crawford:** Thirtieth?

**Capers:** Yeah.

**Crawford:** Why you have thirty-seven on the motherfucking address?

**Capers:** Huh?

**Crawford:** It says thirty-seven on the address.

**Capers:** Yeah. One thirty-seven West 137th.

[. . .]

**Capers:** I got one of your letters, man.

**Crawford:** That's the one that didn't come back. Because I wrote in your girl's name.

[. . .]

**Capers:** You should have had that whore Veorah. You should have kept that whore.

**Crawford:** Shit, damn, that whore was a crackhead. You can't pimp no crackhead.

**Capers:** Shit, that's bullshit.

**Crawford:** You can't pimp no crackhead whore.

**Capers:** I'd have made that bitch got my three-hundred dollars back, man.

**Crawford:** That whore ain't had shit. The bitch ain't want to do no hustling.

**Capers:** I don't believe the bitch dead, though, man.

**Crawford:** You'll see.

**Capers:** Huh?

**Crawford:** You go all over Harlem and look for that whore. [laughter] I bet you won't find that whore. All you got to do is ask Stephanie where that bitch is? Ask her sister where she at?

**Capers:** Damn.

**Crawford:** Walking around looking for that bitch right afterwards, looking for her sister, man.

**Capers:** Nose probably don't even know where she is. She probably don't even visit Nose.

**Crawford:** The bitch can't visit Nose. Unless spirit going to goddamn go where that nigger at. [laughter]

Crawford was returned to New York in March 1990. Me and Tony Krassas went and got him. We went in there—he was fightin' three COs, he was rollin' around with them. Tony says, "Hey, Mike, this guy ain't gonna be a happy camper. Thought this was just gonna be a regular extradition." We had to talk to him. Told him we don't wanna play no games with him, this and that. There was no problem bringin' him back.

Two months later, Capers gets whacked. What could've happened, but we had no proof, is that Crawford could have got the word out to someone to get back to Lenox Avenue, have somebody come visit him. Could have been a girl or anything. Said that Capers is talkin' to the detectives. We had played the tape of Crawford braggin' about the homicide to Capers, to try to get him to confess.

It's always in the back of my mind that these guys have done several murders up there, some of them unsolved. All Crawford had to do was tell them, "Yeah, he was talkin' about you and you and about you, and they have pictures and it all came from Capers.'' They could pay someone to take care of him, which probably did happen. Let's hope someday somebody will enlighten me.

Continuously working on the case; a lot of highs on it. Finally we got this guy—when we got him, that was probably the best. Until he was convicted. Working on other cases, I've been runnin' with them, so it really didn't sink in. There's still some days when I have a little time, I stop and think about it.

———

"Red was a tough piece of work, well known in the neighborhood. Anything to make a buck. He was good at pinball; he was good at pool and 'mushroom' pool. Any kinda hustle," Terry Quinn says, "he could do. He taught me how to survive in the streets." In the sixties, in the gang-ridden streets of Williamsburg, Brooklyn, where the Quinn boys came from, a kid's idea of a hero was not a cop but a guy like Red—Terry's big brother.

At the time, cops were "just not something you wanted to go around bragging about becoming." In fact, Terry just plain didn't like cops and never really intended to be one. At a certain point, though, he did begin to like the idea of economic stability—and what was someone to do who was not "an office type of guy" but was pretty good in the street? "I took the test and passed, and I said—Y'know, this looks like something I can do."

But would he get the chance, after all?

The Police Department's background investigator, convinced that Red Quinn's ultimate hustle was big-time numbers—a Known Gambler, no less—didn't feature Red's kid brother in the ranks of New York's Finest. Only by insisting that teachers at their good Catholic school, Power Memorial, could tell one brother from the other and would vouch for the attendance record and general integrity of Terrance Quinn—did Terry finally get the job.

His Williamsburg street credentials did come in handy. Like the night in 1969 when Quinn and his radio car partner caught sight of a burglar in a big commercial bakery in an industrial section of Queens, Long Island City. Quinn's sturdy figure hurtles out of the car, scrambles over a chain-link fence, and dashes across the wide asphalt factory yard. The partner blocks the escape route with the car, in case the burglar slips past Quinn.

But no—before the suspect knows what hit him, the cop jumps him, grabs his .45. Only one more challenge: landing badly on the asphalt, Quinn fractures his leg. In serious pain, he manages to cuff the burglar, and—holding the .45 under his prisoner's chin— rides him piggyback out to the radio car.

Well into his late thirties, as a sergeant supervising homicide detectives, Quinn is reliably reported to have relished a good tangle with a perp—bit off a chunk of a guy's ear, if you really want to know. Just like the good old days in Williamsburg, before your garden-variety turf dispute was an excuse for a nine-milli-meter firefight. But as a detective boss, of course, Quinn's street thinking evolved beyond one-on-one into an operation pitting his troops against a single bad guy, or a whole gang.

Since the early nineties, as a supervising rackets investigator for Manhattan DA Robert Morgenthau, Quinn has been with joint task forces taking down the homicidal Jamaican drug posses and Dominican cocaine gangs that terrorize the city's ghettos. But probably the most feared and infamous *lone* perp ever collared by Quinn, then a detective sergeant, was one who robbed and raped his way through Manhattan's fanciest high-rent districts.

During the "Silver Gun Bandit" investigation in 1985 and 1986, police passed out more than a thousand photos, sketches and posters of the perp's innocent-looking face. The bosses put a task force of about twenty detectives on this brazen career criminal's case—with backup, at one time or another, from a dozen different squads and patrol units. They put Quinn in charge of street strategy.

### Detective Sergeant Terry Quinn:
### The Silver Gun Bandit

His agility was really striking. The guy was doing tremendous-type things. He scaled huge water towers. He was seen walking around on the edges of high buildings, no fear of height, nothing. Leaped huge spaces to go from one building to another.

I'd say he's about five foot nine, but he was very muscular, very solid. There was no kinda meat on this guy other than muscle. Very limber. He was in excellent shape, which gave him the ability to do what he did.

In the beginning, they had some problems in the Nineteenth Precinct—posh, plush Upper East Side places where he had scaled straight up a wall. There was some indentations in the concrete ornamentation of the building—he just went right up it, like a ladder. And that's where he raped and robbed a pretty elegant lady. Really in the domain of the Robbery Squad and Sex Crimes, but the bosses were afraid he was gonna start killing people at the same time.

The chief of Manhattan detectives, Chief Voelker, and John Carroll, the lieutenant that was put in charge of the special task force—they sent for me because of the operations side in the street, my background in homicide and street robbery, street activity.

It was probably a nine- ten-month period that most of his activity was taking place. Before I even got into the case, he was all over different precincts. There was a pattern, and we were made aware of it through the borough command.

Detectives from the Robbery Squad, some Sex Crimes detectives worked this, then some Homicide detectives. And the precinct gave us some Anti-Crime and uniform personnel who worked in a plainclothes capacity with us. We assigned 'em to observation posts, street posts, roving patrol. We had two precincts covered at the same time. One sergeant had the North—the Nineteenth. One sergeant had the South—Soho, the First precinct.

We were hitting everything—any kind of prowlers, anything in progress, we were hitting it hard. And we had recovered some property up on a roof, but we could never really find what apartment it came out of. We felt he was still up there, but we searched and searched. He escaped. All of a sudden, the North just got real quiet. He'd hit the South. He seemed to keep coming back into SoHo—that he had an easy mark there. The lieutenant decided to send me to the South.

In a lot of the places, we had recovered some partial prints. We had a very rich woman on West Broadway who was burglarized, robbed, tied up. He didn't rape her, but all the earmarks of the Silver Gun Bandit were there. Rape seemed to be more or less an afterthought with him. All of a sudden he appeared by her bedroom door. She was French, quite an accent—kind of hard to get the guys to continue to work. She explained to me, she didn't believe he came from down, up—she believed he came from up, down.

Well, from where?

"I have a foyer up here." I went up, and I saw some smudges and things. I told Forensics, Get up here with a ladder and do this. I believe this is the same guy that we've been hearing about. This was in fact him. He tied up her boyfriend and her kids, had them in another bedroom.

He was known to use backyards, come up the fire escapes in back of these renovated factories made into luxurious apartments—he could actually be seen across the roofs. I took a high point on the north end of the First Precinct, a big building on Houston Street, put an observation post up there. On the south end, we used a window at the telephone company, facing north.

When I was a kid in Brooklyn, if we were going to do bad things, we'd go through yards, through roofs. If you're watching the roofs, you're gonna see stuff. Gotta know your enemy in order to capture him. You gotta think the way he thinks. You gotta go through the same things he would go through. Take the same mental path.

I took a look at places he hit, and I determined that he came into these different places through adjacent parking lots, jumped the fences, and made his way through alleyways and up fire escapes. Some of these parking lots had old booths in them; I put people inside the booths. If they caught a guy startin' to jump fences, we might have him that way.

We also had roving patrols, two-man teams in each unmarked car. From different past crimes he committed, cops on post felt he would come out through this one, go through this way. We had grids—four-block squares, whatever. I tried to concentrate the roving patrols on the places he would come into or leave from. One was Houston Street and Wooster, right off of Houston.

It was a street where we had robberies, burglaries, that we felt he did. Maybe four or five. He had a fetish for that street. Two or three different parking lots for access. Nice, lucrative apartments. They worked for him, so I felt now he was gonna come back again. Why not? In and out like a song.

I never realized how many people in SoHo have picnics on their roofs. But every so often my guy would spot the light: *There's an open skylight on such-and-such*—and we'd respond. We took the building from the bottom up—halls, elevators, everything. We raised people up quite a bit, but they never really gave us any kind of problem. They realized we were tryin' as best we could. We interrupted a lot of barbecues, to say the least.

Just off Houston, there was an old building with iron metal shutters and a huge open space, probably twenty feet, up about nine stories or better. The apartment he wanted to get to was across this huge space. A lady was actually in the house—he came flying right through the window. He told us he went from iron shutter to iron shutter, just let his weight drop, then the momentum put him into the window. Takes an awful lot of moxie to do that.

He had the silver gun, but I always felt it wasn't a real gun, because on many occasions he had picked up a stick, a pipe, a knife. Why the extra weapon if you got a real gun?

We were continuing to investigate telephone leads. We had a hot line. They were going through the past records of any recidivist rapist, robberies, guys who had this kind of pattern. And of course we had all the cops in the precinct alerted: You might have a burglary in progress, you might have a prowler, a trespasser; he may be tryin' to get into an apartment, somebody may stop him—it could turn into an assault. It could come over in any form and wind up being this guy.

He told a girl on the West Side— He came through her window another day—big iron gates, fourteen- fifteen-foot gates, he scaled that, no problem—right through the window. The girl was panicking. He told her, "Don't worry about it. I'm a professional; I'm the guy you been readin' about in the papers."

Even though we had looked on the Upper East Side and SoHo, we had a feeling this was him again. All the motions, a lot of the same verbiage that he was using. Did the same kind of things. Tied 'em with telephone cord or electric cord, cut it with the silver knife—he always carried a silver pocketknife. He did that in that apartment too.

From the descriptions of various people, he had sort of slanty, Chinese eyes. They all said that. And very neat all the time, no matter what he was wearing. They say even if he had dungarees on, he had creases in the dungarees. A meticulous guy does that. A black three-quarter-length wool overcoat he wore a lot. With a scarf. He was climbing fences, dressed for a tuxedo ball. He'd be a hard guy to challenge, because he looked like a SoHo yuppie-type individual. SoHo had minorities, all different people, artists, writers. He was dressed like he belonged there.

He used to grab a lot of VCRs, things he could just off. And whatever cash he could get. VCRs, he was getting a hundred bucks a shot—he knew he had a market and that was a priority of his to take.

One day we were riding, and I saw him come past with a big suitcase. It was hot, a lot of people. I thought about him for a mutt that day. Detective Ronnie Olivero was driving. I said, Turn around—that guy reminds me of the sketch. That's the way I feel his eyes would be. He never flinched. He just kept going, into a subway and he was gone. I only saw him for a second.

We never knew how he was leaving, if he had cars, an accomplice? How could anybody carry that much stuff without a partner? But he was strong. And he did take public transportation. That's how he made his way out most of the time.

We said, well, if he's comin' from the Houston Street subway, he would come in through here. So I used to patrol that way a lot. And I knew his clothing. When I saw him coming down Houston Street and later turn into Wooster, I said to Ronnie—That's him.

"Sarge, how can you say that's him?"

'Cause I've been waitin' for him for nine months. He's got that arrogant walk to him. Look at the way his eyes slant. He's got on the exact coat he's worn many times. He's comin' right from Houston, goin' right into Wooster. I said, He's gone. This is him.

I started immediately calling the other units in, to cut him off. I knew this was gonna be a trial and tribulation. He was strong, he's fast, and he's young. He knows the area and he's got a lot of ways to go. So I wanted to try and bring in as many people as I could, in case he started to run and I couldn't hold on to him. Guy was in excellent shape.

They started to move in. He was goin' down—he realized we were following him. First thing he's gonna do, he's gonna get arrogant—that's the way the pattern goes. He's gonna back it up and go. It didn't pay to try to play games. I told Ronnie, all right, tell him—

"Police—"

"What are you messin' with me, pal? Because I'm black? I live here. I don't have to stop. I don't have to talk to you." With that, he started to move quickly.

Ronnie, go up ahead of him— I rolled out of the car. There was a van or a truck. As the guy came past the truck, Ronnie jumped the sidewalk with the car.

He had stopped and turned, and I was already standin' there. He tried to come up with his hands. I just grabbed him in the shoulders and threw him back to the car, then Ronnie grabbed him. We searched him. He had on a gray dungaree jacket, which he had worn on other occasions. Neatly pressed. I knew that jacket too. I opened up the jacket and he had the silver knife on him.

I had my guys pullin' up. One of these cops had been in a parking lot booth when he had left the scene of a robbery; he looked at him. "That's the guy I saw—that's him!"

Put him in the car and I got in the back with him. Didn't cuff him at that point 'cause I wanted to keep him talkin' to me. I never let his hands go anywhere; his hands are on the seat. We had the knife already, and I was confident that he didn't have anything, because two of my best guys searched him.

They did a good toss, but they missed the gun! He had a jacket and a coat, and he had his arm flexed—he had it right in here between his bicep and his pec. All they felt was muscle. It's a small gun.

What's your name? "Michael Dirton." Where do you come from? What are you doing here? I wanna hear his alibi. Oh, is that what you're here for? Okay. Just keep your hands up on the seat. I didn't want to alienate him by getting tough. I felt the ego would prevail and he would start comin' around. That's the way to get these guys talkin'.

We brought him upstairs: This is him.

"Yeah? This is him?"

Lieutenant Carroll came, Inspector Plansker came. "Terry, why—? You say you don't have the gun!" Well, we searched him. . . . "You searched the car again?" I said, Not really. I'm gonna go down and check it. Just in case.

He had let it slide down through his coat, and it dropped between the seat and the door. *Sonofabitch*—here it is. But he had painted it black. Just scrape the paint, you could see the silver. He painted it because of all the stories in the papers. It was a .22 starter's pistol. Imitation.

Meantime, we had taken his prints, and we sent 'em to Latent to be compared with the ones from West Broadway. We had a print technician on call for this case. I said to John Carroll, Look, we stopped hundreds of people, I never said it was the guy, did I?

"No—"

*This* is him. I feel this fucker in my chest. In here: *this is him.*

The inspector was saying, "Terry, I got a lot of respect for you, but—" He wasn't gonna let us make something fit.

I'm tellin' you, I'd eat my hat if this ain't him.

They were talkin' to him in the room, so I went in with the gun. He's bullshitting. I was like the bad guy now. Showed the pistol to 'em. I said, Yo! What the fuck d'you thinka this?

We got the confirmation that the prints hit. We had him. We told him, We got the gun, your clothing, y'know—everything's the same.

He knew the shit was up.

We flattered him about his great ability for leaping buildings. We said, You know, well—some of these places, we're not too sure . . . how could a human being really have done this? "Oh, I'll show you." We took him in the car, he showed us. Went through a whole routine.

He told me he saw me that day he got into the subway real quick. And he said, "I knew you were coming back because of the way you looked at me."

Everybody said it was two people—the press was trying to do that to us right off the bat: "How do you know you got the right guy? How do you know it was the same guy?" It's the same guy. I'm telling you that this is him. "Well, maybe it's two different guys." It ain't two different guys. It's one guy. It's him. He told me he did it!

By that time, we also did ten lineups from north and south—and west. They ID'd him like that. *Bang, bang, bang.* "You were right," Voelker said.

So we had him. Took us out of a bad spot. The SoHo people—absolutely relieved. This guy was petrifyin' everybody.

The day of his arrest, he wanted to look good for the camera. He wanted to change clothes. No problem, we said, you can have your clothes brought. He dressed himself up in a suit and tie. He was so impressed with himself that he thought he was a star.

———

Even veteran members of the famed Detective Bureau, elite and envied, often look back a little wistfully on their days as lowly cops: plainclothes precinct Anti-Crime cops. They treasure those glory days—and nights—when they made the street collars that opened the exalted Bureau door. Days when results came fast and gratifying, when handcuffs were the name of the game, not paper. Anytime they stuck a piece of paper in the typewriter, it was an arrest report, thank you. Next customer!

Detective Patrick Brosnan, thirty-two years old, never looks back. His shield gleams gold. He's in the Bureau. *And* he's still out there wearing his favorite sneakers and "soft clothes"—jeans, sweatshirt, bulletproof vest—jumping bad guys, taking machine pistols and sawed-off shotguns off the street. Aware that most of the perps he meets up with have already done jail time and done most of it on the bench press, he's at Gold's Gym five days a week. He's a walking ad for the benefits.

A member of a South Bronx squad, the Four-six RIP (Robbery Identification Program), that regularly takes honors as the annual arrest leader for the whole city, Brosnan himself kicked off the nineties with a total of thirty armed gunmen collared in a year. He got two of them on the night when astounded members of a camera crew from *America's Most Wanted* were filming him for a feature, "New York City, City Under the Gun." New York governor Mario Cuomo named him the state's 1990 Police Officer of the Year, calling him a "one-man war on crime."

Yes, but can he write a respectable DD5? (For each important step in an investigation, the detective writes a Detective Division follow-up report, known as a "Five," and adds it to the case file.) Well, Brosnan can handle a typewriter okay for an English major, which he was. But aren't his cases so open-and-shut that he's really just a glorified Anti-Crime guy? "There's a lot of jumps that are straightforward," he allows. "You're robbed—BOOM!—That's the guy. There's no real investigation.

"But there are a lot of two and three Fivers. And there's also good cases where you get a plate number and you're running summons checks; you're doing canvasses, you're doing histories, you're doing family connections, schools, stakeouts. So they might be ten or fifteen Fivers. But you're doing it part of the day, a little bit of the day. And you're still running around making the quick collars."

Precisely because Paddy Brosnan is so well known for chasing perps through the streets of the Four-six, Detective Ricky Fogarty, of the Five-o Squad to the north, hoped Paddy might run across two of the most-wanted felons in Bronx County. Heroin dealers Thomas "Black Tom" Cross and Felipe "Afro" Concepción were being sought for kidnapping before they did the triple homicide that Fogarty caught in February 1989. In March, Fogarty gave Brosnan their photos.

Tom Cross and Felipe Concepción didn't just rest on their laurels. One or both racked up additional murder, extortion, and weapons possession charges in the months between the triple homicide and the night of July 4. That was the night Brosnan had been waiting for: when the pair ripped off a guy in *his* precinct. Fireworks. Brosnan turned up the heat. With Brosnan, Fogarty, and Homicide detectives Johnny Tierney and Jimmy Finnegan all in pursuit, things got so hot in The Bronx for Cross and Concepción that the two bad guys just went in the wind.

### Detective Patrick Brosnan:
### Valentine

Black Tom and Felipe laid the three victims on the floor, put pillows over their heads, and executed all three. The miracle on Strong Street: one survived. The bullet circumnavigated her crown.

If you do a triple, you gotta kill 'em. That's where they rued the day, 'cause she was able to identify them. She wears bangs now, testified at the trial.

These guys invaded an apartment and it turned out to be the wrong one. It was supposed to be a drug-related apartment—girlfriends and wives and a lot of money, a lot of drugs. It was actually a bank manager—a forty-five-year-old career woman, her daughter, and a girlfriend. The women had good jobs and no records. Legit, nice street. Bad news, really bad mistake. I remember reading about it, and I generally don't catch stuff like that. I remember saying, that seems really odd. I think they hit the wrong place.

Ricky Fogarty just happened to be in the RIP one day. "These guys are known to hang around the Four-six. Their mother lives over on a Hundred Eighty-first and University. They were living in a single-room-occupancy hotel." He says, "Your kinda guys."

I took an immediate great interest in 'em, but I had nothing to hang my hat on—I had no robberies for them. I kept their photos and I was just looking to grab them with a pistol. I would see Ricky and he would update me. They kinda dropped out of sight.

July 4, sure enough, I catch a robbery—it's them. Perfect. I said, this is like a gift. Now I can really fasten on to it. The black guy who was robbed knew their nicknames: Black Tom and Afro. I started to work it, and gradually it evolved where I tied them in to four robberies over the period of time—I only needed one.

I don't work homicides, but there was the two in the Five-o. During the course of the investigation, Black Tom also shot and killed a guy on Buchanan Place and Davidson Avenue, which was a Four-six caper. That even fueled it more: now it was a Four-six homicide case, in addition to being a Five-o homicide case.

Johnny Tierney and Jimmy Finnegan from the Bronx Homicide Task Force were looking for 'em since February, with Fogarty. They were hot, hot on his trail and the whole time, because he was a prime suspect in the homicides and a kidnapping of a seven-year-old on the Grand Concourse. A variety of different shootings. A lotta stuff. A *lot*ta stuff.

With Johnny and Jimmy, we shared a lot of information. It was an unofficial task force. A lot of nights we'd stake out together. We knew a tremendous amount about them. They were Attica cellmates. *Really* bad. Both wore vests, they carried two guns each. Felipe had served seven years in New Jersey for killing a businessman in cold blood, a father of three.

I was still making my robbery collars and gun collars, but Ricky had other homicides. Johnny Tierney and Jimmy Finnegan were total pit bulls, really fastened on to it, but they also had other guys they had their tentacles out for. I was able to focus—undivided attention. Which is really a prize. It's rare. I just lucked out.

Tom had been in several shootouts, been shot anywhere from three to five times, and he had a bad limp as a result. He'd had multiple felony arrests. He was a big-time playboy, five or six girlfriends. They all have sisters. It seems like a trifling matter, but the amount of misinformation they generate—it's unbelievable. They all throw you red herrings all the time. They lived all over the precinct, and even though they knew that he was sleeping with other girls, or *an*other girl—they didn't know about all of 'em—they still stood behind him. None of 'em cracked until the end—the toughest one. The other ones I thought I had a prayer with, and I didn't.

Tom had a green Jaguar, but he got away from that because the heat was really heavy, and the close calls spooked him big-time. Changed vehicles every day. Nightmarish. Every vehicle they had, I would run downtown and get a summons history, hoping they got a summons somewhere, and check the address where they got it. But there were so many vehicles. And the plates! It was just a hodgepodge; it was impossible. A lot of rentals too, and it was always different rentals. They wouldn't stay at one agency or one car. They were sharp.

I was using my custom van, which was very unlike a police van—it had all dark-tinted, etched-glass windows, "tattooed" like a biker van. Mag wheels. We were using it a lot as a surveillance van. They never made it.

We had an informant called Crazy and his girl, a junky. He hated Tom because Tom shot him while he was sitting on his porch. Drug-dealing stuff. Pulled up and opened fire on him. He lived in the Five-two, off of Fordham Road and Loring Place South on the first floor of a three-family house, one of the last houses like that in the area.

Crazy went to the hospital, and he was imploring the cops to give him protection: "He's gonna come back! He's gonna come back!" He didn't get any protection. The fact is, everybody says that. And it's so incredibly rare that they come back. Crazy was superterrified of Tom all along, knew Tom was after him for other drug stuff, 'cause they were big-time heroin dealers. Drugs were an understood feature.

Crazy was sitting on his porch—with his bulletproof vest on now. He would always have a nine. (I would pull up, he'd run into the house and play it off, hide the gun, and come out with the vest on. Like I was born last night, or the night before.) Anyhow, Tom came by a second time, three days after, and opened fire again on him.

So Crazy was on *my* team, big-time. Not that he had any affinity for the police. He just wanted Tom to go away for a long time. He wanted to be on the porch dealing; he didn't need the gigantic thorn.

He was in the van with me every night, with his girl. We're canvassing endlessly. Without him, I wouldn't have known all the little, hidden secrets. He knew their idiosyncrasies, a lot of the hangouts in Harlem, other girlfriends, the ex-girlfriends, ex-friends, likely places that he could be holing up. 'Cause they were holing up. But there were still enough infrequent sightings, we knew they were out there. Maddening. I could accept if they had just blasted off to Atlanta. Outta sight, outta mind—maybe they'll come back. But they were around. They just weren't around *me*.

"Tom used to be really tight with this guy who's in jail," Crazy says—a real long shot. "His girlfriend's cute; she's a pretty hot little number. Maybe he's doin' her." Which would be perfectly acceptable: the old man's in the joint, maybe he's accommodating her. I said, that sounds like perfectly up his alley. "Well, she lives like in the vicinity of Bronx River projects in the Four-three."

We go over there—and this probably took ten to fifteen years off my life, that night. The worst. Johnny Tierney and Jimmy Finnegan were with us, and Eddie Murphy and Chris Baldassarri from the RIP.

I get out of the van a block away. I'm not dressed at all like a cop. I'm sure I had the vest on, 'cause I always wear it, but I probably had a big jacket on. The girl was supposed to live on the first floor. I said to Crazy, I hope that's not her hanging out the window.

It *was* her hanging out the window.

She immediately alerted him. I had no more time. I tried to play it off so nonchalant, not even going near the apartment. I go in the *other* buildings, just talk to one or two people and flash the photo quick. And I didn't even know until much later that they went out the window.

I went up to a bunch of black kids, like, twenty-year-olds, playing hoop on the other side of the projects. I showed the photo. "That motherfucker! He pulled a pistol on me the other night because he thought that I had knocked down one of the girl's kids, and he came out with a big gun." He says, "They come in every night." They'd both come in with pistols. Tom would go in first, with the gun out, look up and down the hallway. "In fact, he just went in twenty minutes ago," the kid says. "That skinny-ass guy with the limp."

His big thing was pulling up in a cab, laying real low in the back of the cab. There was a lot of sightings like that.

I knew it was him. I also knew it was too late—'cause she was in the window, and she went in *out* of the window when I went in. Their antennas were up so high. They believed in No Mistakes. The first-floor apartment was his ex-buddy's girl. Whether or not he was with her, I don't know. But they were holing up there infrequently. Crazy was right.

If there's even the remotest chance that that's the Man—out the window they go. We did cover the windows a minute later, but we were five, ten minutes too late. Just simply vanished, both of them. We still stake the place out endlessly, just on the outside chance they'll return. But it became a joke almost, 'cause she was so hip, the girl who was out the window all the time. Ridiculous, but you just still had to do it.

There was a girl on Loring Place who was deeply into Tom. She had a little Tom, and I knew I didn't have a prayer with her after I noticed his name in a tattoo on her leg. She was busy trying to convince me that they were no longer an item, and then I see a freshly scabbed tattoo with his name in it. It was the summer, she had shorts on. She was superarrogant and superradical. Tough. I couldn't get nothin' out of her. She stood by him the whole time.

Crazy, toward the end, got busted for a burglary in Connecticut and had to do five years. So that didn't help, but I also had a super on Loring Place, who was even better. The super was like Tom's personal trainer. They built a gym in his basement with leg eguipment. He was a handy guy and was into working out. He had helped to rehabilitate Tom after Tom got shot.

I think the super was probably low-level dealing. They were friends, but Tom ultimately turned on him too, and then the super came on my team. He was a family man, and he was in mortal terror. And he was a great asset.

I kept asking him where they might've went. You keep going over it, maybe they'll remember stuff. He says, "Well, two summers ago, he was hangin' out in Queens—" This was new! "He gave me an emergency number, and I wrote it on the wall in the basement." Meantime, they painted. But somehow, he found the number—they missed the spot, or something. It was unlisted, but we were able to ascertain the address with a court order. It was a girlfriend's number—Yvonne, a name that kept coming up. I knew that was where he was. Now it was crystal clear.

A week or so after the fiasco at the Bronx River projects, twelve of us hustled out to this quiet residential street in Queens. Nobody home in the apartment but a couple of pit bulls. Two guys spoke to the landlord. He knew Tom. We tried to play down why we were looking for him—just a burglary. The super picked up on all the vans—he knew it was bad and he was real nervous about the police presence, got paranoid.

We're setting up a stakeout for the next morning and the super calls the precinct, the One-eleven Squad. "Somebody's home!" He heard the shower. He runs out with his kid. We go in—complete chaos—dogs get shot, *nobody there*. Yvonne gets back and goes ballistic. That really put Tom on warp drive. He was gone. No more sightings.

I was able to break down one girlfriend of Felipe's. She gave me some letters that showed he was communicating from Interlaken, Florida, and his concern for the heat in New York. She was pregnant, and we staked out the hospital while she delivered. We were hoping his machismo would make him show up just to see the baby—we were praying it was a boy. It was; we were there, like, a solid week, and he never showed up.

When he was in Florida, we got information that he was in a brother-in-law's duplex or something. We were corresponding with the police. We had them crash through there. Gone.

They had a really highly tuned sense of survival. And they were always a step ahead. Or two steps ahead. They had inordinate luck too. Like the window was tremendous luck. They weren't just blundering fools who did a few stickups. They were out there on the run a long time. A big crew of guys who were serious about gettin' 'em and who knew all about them weren't able to put a hand on 'em. Tom thought he was a folk hero.

A lot of little mini subplots along with this. I locked up six of their associates for a variety of different things. Just killing some time. Picked up three loaded guns from three different people. I had a tip that Tom and Afro were in an abandoned apartment on Creston Avenue. Went in through the fire escape and we got Santos Cruz with a pistol.

Took him in and Santos offered me fifty-one thousand dollars in a bribe to let him go—and to protect their "Legend" heroin operation against Narcotics units. I was *living* in that area looking for these guys, and I was basically bad for business. So part of their new overhead should be that they would put me on the payroll and I would keep the narcs away. "Hey, back off on the Creston spot," which was where Tom and Afro were employed in the beginning as drug hit men. By having me on board, they would proceed with business as usual.

There was a Spanish girl who lived on 132nd on the West Side who I was pestering. I was taking it personal that she wasn't giving me any information, 'cause she was spotted with Felipe in Sears on Fordham Road. I had two independent sources, so I knew she was lyin'. I was pestering her and her family on a bi-daily basis. I remember her kid had balloons; it was his birthday. I had no idea she knew Santos Cruz.

So Santos says, "I'll get my girl here to give you a weekly payoff," which came out to fifty-one thousand dollars. Really nice collar. And I got it all on tape and I drew up affidavits. They signed everything. If the drugstore was open, would have had it notarized, but it was late.

And who do you think comes strolling in? The Spanish girl was his girlfriend! She came with the money! And she didn't even catch on. She thought I completely turned around and became a bad guy. The kid went to the Bureau of Child Welfare, mother went to Rikers. No mercy for them. No way. It was just great. They always think anything can be bought with drug money and that's why it's so sweet when you bust them on the bribe.

We get a lot of that. I've had ten bribery arrests. This was the ninth or the tenth time. Maybe it's the way I dress or something. They think I need some clothes or sneakers. I don't know. It's a riot. I really get a kick out of it.

The other six associates I arrested—they all were in fear of Black Tom and Afro, so each of them generated misinformation, which led me in a number of wrong directions. They were in such *fear* of them that even in exchange for time, they'd give me wrong information. Made it even tougher.

I found out that, as a result of a near-capture in Florida, they ultimately split up. Later we heard Cross went to Tennessee and went on unemployment somehow, I don't know how. Then he went to Detroit, where he was staying at his aunt's. Concepción went up to Boston, then swung back down to New Haven.

With the investigation at a temporary standstill, Ricky Fogarty and I flew down to Washington—on my thirty-second birthday, incidentally, February 25, 1991. We appeared on *America's Most Wanted* and appealed to sixteen million viewers for assistance. Finally, just had to get it out there. Had to kinda spook 'em.

Normally the DA Squad would go down, in case there's an extradition out of there. But I knew a lot, I had so much detail. I think I had ninety, a hundred DD5s—it's comin' out in hardcover. So they felt I would be in a very leveraged position to volley the questions that were comin' and to sort through the wheat and the chaff. Which made great sense. Because I was, and so was Ricky. So we went together.

I was working the phone for about five or six hours. Tom's aunt called and one of the operators switched the call to me. "Listen," the aunt says, "I didn't know he was wanted, this and that—he was just here in the house in Detroit."

We received five hundred tips, maybe seven hundred tips altogether, because the girls down there would keep overnighting to me all the additional tips. They did a sheet on each one. Time, Date, Caller's Name, Return Phone Number, Location, Description, pedigree information. For instance, "I just saw Black Tom. He's walking a pink poodle on Hollywood Boulevard." "I seen him in a nightclub in Detroit." Some were just patently out of the question. "He's been a male nurse for ten years in a hospital," that kind of stuff.

One tip on Felipe was from a heroin user in New Haven. "I shot dope with him just the other day, and I know exactly where he is. For five Gs, I'll tell you." So we put him in touch with the New Haven FBI, he got his money, and he led them to an attic apartment in New Haven. And sure enough, he was up there.

They stormed the building and they got Felipe on the roof. At the end, he was screaming like a typical punk, "Don't kill me. Don't kill me." He wanted to live—just like his victims did. He's a tough guy all along, but in the end, he was a little baby. "Please, please, don't shoot!"

But Black Tom was the best. He was livin' with his mother's sister and the young Cross crew and workin' in construction. They were gathered around the telly, watching *America's Most Wanted*. What are the odds of that? And lo and behold, on the screen pops Tom's face. She said, "Everybody in the place jumped through the ceiling"—except Tom, who leaped up, grabbed his coat, and shot out into the night. *Boom,* out the door. They all went crazy, screaming. She called the program.

We didn't know it yet, but he took a taxi cab from Detroit, Michigan—pretty smart, must've had some big bucks on him—all the way to Toledo, Ohio. To a downtrodden area in Toledo, and secreted himself in a small, out-of-the-way, ramshackle type of motel, the Garden Inn.

In the meantime, I coordinated with the FBI, the state police, and the city police—from Washington, which was like a nightmare. They went to the aunt's house. Helicopter, dogs, and had 'em all laid out on the lawn. It was snowing, I think. I said to her, "Oh, yeah, no problem. You won't be involved." On the other line I have nine thousand guys on the way over with dogs and helicopters. "Just relax, take it easy." They took 'em all out of the house; they searched. "Relax. It'll be okay."

I said, we gotta get the buses. We got the timetables. The state police pulled over

Greyhound buses that had left within that time frame on the interstates, pulled them over and searched them. It was dynamite. We got the train timetables. The trains, they were checking at the stops. Couldn't do a train stop. But the buses were smart; you cut 'em off with a state police car, you pull 'em over and search everybody. You figure the chump would jump a bus, right? If the show came on at eight, any bus that would leave from eight to nine or nine-thirty, from any direction. They shut down any buses goin' out of Detroit. They froze everything. But he still escaped, jumped in a cab.

The real great thing—the Detroit FBI found in his room letters from his girlfriend Yvonne. She had been writing to Tom and, according to the letters, had been sending him money. Now I'd been to visit her maybe twenty or thirty times down in the garment center, where she worked as a secretary. I had put her on notice, 'cause I had put everybody on notice. "I'm letting you know, he's wanted for a felony. If you harbor him in any way or provide him with any money, any sustenance, any shelter—you're harboring a fugitive: an E felony." I checked with the district attorney, because it's not frequently used.

I was hopin' that I could just collar more. I always try to disassemble the family unit, disassemble the friend network, by making 'em drop out of sight into jail, and that pisses them off. And sometimes they'll turn and give you information. Especially when they start going in alarming numbers. So I put her on notice.

And the FBI forwarded overnight to me all kinds of letters, lovey-dovey nonsense, but a few key things like, "Tom, I hope the seventy-five dollars I sent you helped." Money! It was all over for her. She'd sent him a Valentine's Day card that was like, nine feet. It was great. She was engaged to someone else, to boot. So I crushed that end of it too, informed the fiancé—a basketball player, about six foot ten.

I go to visit her. She's at the reception desk. I come up with my partner. I have a long coat on, but I have the card underneath the coat, underneath a jacket, taped to my vest—it's about the size of the bulletproof vest in the front. Big, giant heart on the front of the card. I had to get her 'cause she was torturin' me. She wouldn't give me no information, and I knew she knew all about him.

She's on the phone. She says, "Oh, it's that *Brosnan* again," and hangs up, like, "I'll take care of him." I come in, and she's going wild, really arrogant, going crazy. "I told you—I got nothing to tell you. I never see him. I hate him, and I'm engaged—"

As we're talking, I go to use her boss's office. (I spoke to him—couldn't *wait* to talk to him.) I took her in the office, and I said, Gee, you never see him? Never write to him? "Nothin'! Never!"

I'm unzipping my jacket. She doesn't see it until my jacket's off, just standin' there with the card taped to the vest. She went absolutely insane, actually tried to claw at me. "You motherfucker! Where'd you get that card!" On the floor, in cuffs, I drag her outta the building. She gets fired. We go uptown. On the way up, I'm reading her that lovey-dovey stuff in the car. So sweet.

I get a district attorney. I round up her whole family. They all come in, big crew. We're threatening her with jail—the DA was there for that. I had a multiangle attack. The fiancé on one side—he was still standing by her, even though she was sweet on this guy. Him workin' her on one side, her mother, me, the district attorney. Finally, her armor began to chip a bit. Like, ten hours. She said, "He's in—Toledo. I spoke to him . . ." that day or the day before.

Then it became like a nightmare. I got right on the phone to the FBI. They had a bowling match going on or something. I was calling bowling alleys. They "patch you through"; patchin' me all around Toledo. I was trying to be calm, 'cause I knew he wasn't going to stay there for long—he moved all the time. And finally we got it goin'. It just became real luck from there.

The FBI were all set. They knew how bad he was—wanted for multiple homicides, on the run, *America's Most Wanted*. They were really superhyped. They got a task force together—they were gonna go to the hotel, knew the name of the hotel. I had everything. They were gonna try to smoke him out, and if he didn't come out, they were gonna go in and kill him. That's how it was put. They weren't takin' any chances with him. He was like a crazed animal.

They sent two advance scouts—like a confirmatory thing, maybe to warn the desk people that there's gonna be a problem or— At that exact time, he pulled up in a cab across the street. This is really strange—I'm tryin' to think how he could have known this. He had somehow gotten a message that his squeeze was busted by me. The family knew where he was—they called.

He went to the Dunkin Donuts across the street, to the phone. But first he threw his nine millimeter in the shrubs, he told us later, 'cause it was lit across the street. That's why he didn't have the gun. He was a predatory animal—he knew where the light was. He had to dump the weapons: he was a wanted felon, a fugitive.

He called into the Four-six Squad, "This is Tom Cross, I wanna talk to Paddy Brosnan." They switched the call into me, and he says, "Is this Paddy?" And as we were talking, just as I was sayin', Yeah, Tom, this is Pat, he was saying somethin' like, "Let *her* go—"

Next thing I heard, they moved in on him right from across the street—*ZOOM!* He dropped the phone; an FBI agent picked it up and said, "We got him." That's exactly how it went. Just like that. Nobody hurt. It was perfect, except that the gun wasn't recovered. I felt kinda like I was there—and then they got him, which is the best part. For being a thousand miles away, it was the way to get him 'cause I was still talkin' to him. I was almost in on the pinch.

I suspect what he had in mind was just strokin' me—"Let her go, and I'll give myself up." If he was to *assure* me, I'd just, *Why certainly, Thomas, I'll release her right this moment—and we'll see you in the* A.M.? They really think that kinda stuff. Ricky and I flew down the next day and brought him back. We were looking forward to putting him away.

While he was awaiting trial, he tried to reach out and touch me from Rikers—put ten thousand dollars on my head. A street person overheard something about it in the Four-four, and she came up to the squad to tell me. We also got it from a registered informant. The department treated it seriously.

He and Concepción both got fifty-eight to life: We thought that was adequate. Proper.

## Partners & Bosses

**Detective Evrard Williams:** Lieutenant Doyle was always thinking. He knew exactly what he was doing. He made McCrossan the Dominican expert. He made me the Chinese expert. You'd think it was the other way around—I'm half Dominican. He made me the Chinese expert when we started getting this extortion—twenty or thirty cases—with Chinese restaurants in the Two-four.

This Puerto Rican guy would call up the restaurants and say, "This is the Mafia—" He had been raised with Italians. "Take seven hundred dollars, put it in the phone booth right outside the place, and then walk away. Or else I'll blow your place up." They would do it—and the thing is that he would come back a second time. This guy was slick.

They would always call us too late, after the guy left. "What are you going to do about it?"

Why don't you call us before? Did you ever think of that?

This happened in the late seventies, early eighties. They were coming in left and right. Guy was getting rich. Well, it was my case—they were all my cases. What the hell am I going to do with this? So I started checking records, MO, to see if there was anything similar to that in the past.

Sure enough! A detective from Chinatown had had a similar case, and they had locked this guy up for that. I started looking for him. Do you know what this guy would do? He would call me up. "Williams, you looking for me?"

Yeah, I left messages all over the place. Why don't you come on in, and we'll talk about this.

"No, uh uh. I'm not coming in. I just called to say hello. You've been out looking for me so much. Everywhere I go, you've been there."

You are presenting a problem here. All of these Chinese restaurants . . .

He says, "Well, I won't be in that area no more." And he stopped. He did. He got out of the Two-four, went up into The Bronx. Some months later, the Bronx DA's Squad came looking for me about this guy because he did seventy extortions in The Bronx. I don't know if they ever got him.

If Doyle put me in charge of the Chinese, he could always use me for the Dominicans anyhow. I had a sort of reputation. There was no way to lose on that. You got two for one. He knew that I was going to give him a fair shake. Doyle's always thinking.

# 11

# TRUE CONFESSIONS

―――――――

"Six Murders in Six Weeks!" the media raved. For the half-dozen best-publicized New York City murders of 1981, David "Nicky" Bullock is currently serving his hundred-and-fifty-year sentence. But when he first unburdened himself to detectives Jimmy Varian and Bob Doyle, New York City's original serial killer admitted to a total of *ten* attempted or successful homicides. Among several crimes that had not previously been reported to police, probably most notable was the murder of the killer's partner in crime, his roommate and lover, Michael "Mink" Winley.

The People of the State of New York were satisfied to indict Bullock for six murders. In state supreme court, Manhattan, Judge Burton Roberts accepted Bullock's guilty plea—but first the judge insisted the defendant repeat for the third time his shot-by-shot confession. Never faltering, Bullock recited the string of Yuletide shootings that made headlines well before "serial killer" became a household term. But in open court, the male prostitute and murderer took pains to watch his language—as, indeed, he also had in the second go-round, when ADA Patrick Dugan videotaped the formal Q & A excerpted below, transcribed from the original video.

Only to detectives Varian and Doyle in the privacy of the squad' room did Bullock repeat, unexpurgated, his single most original line. Bullock's farewell to an unsuspecting hundred-dollar trick he knew only as Victor: "Merry Christmas, *motherfucker.*" Victor toppled under the Christmas tree, one bullet from a Colt .38 in his head.

### David Bullock to Assistant District Attorney Patrick Dugan: A Pretty Black Gun

Q. . . . Now, would you tell me a little bit about yourself? What your full name is? Where you live? How old you are?

A. My name is Charles, David Charles Fine Bullock. I live in 1937 Madison Avenue. I'm twenty-one years of age.

Q. Okay. Are you born and raised in New York City?

A. Yes.

Q. Does your family—You have a family here in New York City?

A. Yes.

Q. Okay. What do you do for a living, Mr. Bullock?

A. Nothing. I just hustle.

Q. Okay. When you say hustle, what do you mean?

A. Male prostitute.

Q. Okay. How long have you been doing that?

A. Since I was ten years old.

[. . .]

Q. Sir, I'm investigating a murder that occurred back on December fifth of last year, 1981, in Central Park, in the northern portion of the park. A gentleman by the name of James Weber was the victim of a shooting incident. Would you tell me what, if anything, you know about that?

A. I shot him.

[. . .]

Q. Okay. What did you shoot him with?

A. A thirty-eight.

Q. Where did you get this thirty-eight from?

A. A friend named Michael.

Q. Michael who?

A. Wunyeah (phonetic).

Q. Okay. Did, does Michael have a nickname?

A. Yeah.

Q. What's his nickname, or his street name?

A. Mink. *M-I-N-K*.

Q. Okay. Tell me a little bit about how it was that it came to pass that Michael gave you this gun? Did he give it to you, first of all?

A. On my birthday.

Q. When was that?

A. November thirteenth.

Q. Okay.

A. Which was on a Friday.

Q. What's your relationship with—with Michael?

A. With Michael, we were supposed to have been lovers.

Q. Um hum.

A. And partners, and anything that goes together like that.

Q. Okay. How long had—had you known Michael for?

A. For about five years.

Q. How long have you been lovers?

A. Not really that long. I wasn't in—I don't know. I wasn't into him.

Q. Um hum.

A. I was just into getting the money.

Q. Well, when you say you were into getting the money, what do you mean?

A. Whatever he can make. When he was boosting, whatever he brings home or whatever he be doing, trying to get the money.

Q. Um hum.

A. And go out, enjoy myself.

Q. Okay. When you say boosting, you mean?

A. He would—he would go down to the stores. He would steal some items, clothes, whatever, merchandise. Sell it on the street and get the money.

Q. Okay. Do you know where Michael got this gun from?

A. He said he stole it from the girl who live in the projects.

Q. And where did Michael keep this gun?

A. Under the bed.

Q. And you said you took it back on your birthday?

A. The gun . . . I took it from him on my birthday.

Q. Okay. When was that again? What day was that?

A. November thirteenth. On a Friday.

Q. Okay. Did you keep it on your person? I mean, was it your practice to carry this gun?

A. Right.

Q. Okay. Why did you carry the gun?

A. Well, because I was on the streets.

Q. Um hum.

A. And I been in—I'm into some dangerous streets. It's a dangerous area where I was at.

Q. And a dangerous occupation that you're in?

A. Right.

[. . .]

Q. All right. Where did you shoot him?

A. On his head.

Q. Do you recall what portion of the head?

A. It went into his nose.

Q. It went into his nose?

A. Right. Right here, this side.

Q. Yeah?

A. It went in and I think it came out the other end.

Q. Well, what do you mean, "you think"? Did it? Or didn't it?

A. Because when he hit the ground, the blood was just covering the ground.

Q. Afterwards, did you—did you tell Michael what you had done?

A. Right.

Q. Okay. Did you tell anybody else?

A. Right.

Q. About this?

A. I had to tell somebody. I had, you know—I was—I was scared, like I said.

Q. Um hum.

A. Because I had never done nothing like that before.

Q. Um hum.

A. And I was nervous.

Q. Who—who did you tell besides Michael?

A. I told my girl. . . . I said, yo . . . I'm a hired killer. I kill niggers for a living. And she laughed in my face.

Q. You told her that you were a hired killer?

A. Yeah.

Q. What did you tell her that for?

A. Because we was getting high on the spot.

Q. Yeah?

A. And I was running around big telling people, so I just act—figure, you know, I say something like that. Keep, you know, keep their mouths shut.

Q. Well, did you tell her anything about the fact that you had offed this guy in—in Central Park?

A. Not to the detail. No. I just told her I had offed a few fellows.

Q. Yeah.

A. You know, bumped somebody off.

    [. . .]

Q. The shooting of this person that you called a whore, when did that occur in relationship to the first one? About how much time elapsed?

A. I don't even know. I just know it just happened. One right after another.

Q. Okay. How did it come to pass that on this particular day or night of this shooting, you met her and went to her apartment?

A. She, you know—I seen—like I said, we was out there on Park Avenue.

Q. Um hum.

A. And then we had a few words. We stopped. Went to a coffee shop. Like I said, we was talking about doing something that night, which we did not get into.

Q. Um hum.

A. And then she said let's go to my house.

Q. Um hum.

A. Which we did. You know, and on the way there I was thinking that she, like I said, she may get kind of queasy and start talking.

Q. Um hum.

A. So I said before anything gets off or happens or she speak to anybody, I have to eliminate her.

Q. Okay. This happened during the day? The night?

A. It happened during the night.

Q. About what time? Before midnight? After midnight?

A. After midnight.

Q. Okay. And was there anybody in the apartment while you two were there?

A. No. It was just us two.

    [. . .]

Q. Okay. When you went from this coffee shop to her apartment, what did you do at her apartment?

A. We had sex.

Q. Before you shot?

A. We had sex. We smoked reefer, had some sex.

Q. Okay. What kind of sex did you have?

A. Straight up sex. Oral sex. Straight sex.

Q. Okay. Now, you were carrying a gun?

A. Right.

Q. A . . .

A. A thirty-eight.

Q. The same thirty-eight?

A. Right.

Q. And was anybody in the apartment?

A. Uh uh.

Q. Okay. Now, after you had sex with this girl?

A. Right.

Q. What happened next?

A. She went to sleep.

Q. Um hum.

A. I got up. Took the pillow, put it over her face. Made a little sound. I said *pst, pst, pst, pst*. So she—you know, wake her up.

Q. Um hum.

A. And then plugged her. I shot, I fired one.

Q. Okay. Just out of curiosity, why was it that you had—you saw fit to go *pst, pst, pst, pst*?

A. That's to get the attention.

Q. Why?

A. So they could see it coming.

Q. But is that something that interests you?

A. Yeah.

Q. What is it that interests you about that?

A. What? They know, they know they gotta get it.

Q. Does that make you feel good?

A. What do you mean feel good?

Q. Well, does it make you feel good when you know?

A. Well, I don't like—I don't like nobody—I don't want to shoot nobody in the back or shoot nobody when their back is turned.

Q. I see.

A. I like them to look up.

Q. Okay.

A. And let them know it's coming.

Q. Okay. How many times did you shoot her?

A. Once, in the head.

Q. All right. Why the pillow?

A. Why?

Q. Yeah?

A. That's the way the Mafia do it. That's the way I've always seen it done.

Q. Um hum.

A. If somebody's in the bed, you throw the pillow over their face.

Q. Um hum.

A. Because after you shoot somebody, and they has the ugly look—they have a ugly look on their face.

Q. Yeah?

A. And plus the blood was just gushing out all over the place.

Q. Um hum.

A. So I just, you know.

Q. Did she cry out or scream?

A. No.

Q. When you—when you woke her up?

A. No.

Q. Where did the shooting occur?

A. In her—in the bedroom.

Q. After you shot her, what did you do?

A. Put on my clothes and left.

Q. Okay. Did you do anything else inside the apartment?

A. Yeah. I set it afire.

   [. . .]

Q. What about this Spanish fellow? Where—What did you know about him?

A. I just knew he was quiet.

Q. Do you have a name for him?

A. He told me his name was Victor.

Q. Victor?

A. Right.

Q. Did he have any other name that he used?

A. No. Not that he told me.

Q. Did you know anything about his life? Anything about . . .

A. He was quiet.

Q. . . . what he did for a living?

A. No.

Q. Where did he live?

A. He lived uptown. One Hundred Seventy-ninth Street [and] [H]aven.

Q. Um hum. Okay. That night—Was it at night?

A. Right.

Q. That you shot him?

A. Right.

Q. Are you sure?

A. Positive.

Q. Tell me about that night? What did you do with that fellow that night?

A. Okay. We go back to his apartment. I told him I had to go to the bathroom because I was drinking a lot of liquor.

Q. Yeah?

A. Because I had to move my pistol to the other side. Took it out of my jacket and moved it to the other side so I can use my left hand.

Q. Yeah?

A. Then I come out the room. He fix a drink for me. I sit the drink down. As soon as he get up, I shoot him in his head, and he falls under the Christmas tree and I tell him, Merry Christmas.

Q. You said Merry Christmas to him?

A. Right.

Q. After you shot him?

A. Right. Because he fell under the Christmas tree.

Q. I see.

A. And then from there, I like went over to the Christmas presents, opened the presents up to see what he—you know, what was in there. If, you know, anybody send him money or anything . . .

[. . .]

A. Oh, after I had ransacked the apartment, I just lit up.

Q. Um hum.

A. Just lit up.

Q. How did you light it?

A. With a Bic lighter.

Q. With a Bic lighter.

A. Yeah.

Q. Did you use any kind of fluid or anything?

A. Yeah. The cologne I had threw around the room. It was thrown on me. I had, you know, Christmas—He had Christmas cologne.

Q. Yeah?

A. And I was throwing some on me and I said this shit don't smell good. I just shook it all around the place. Wasted it.

Q. Where was Victor when you set fire?

A. Under the Christmas tree.

Q. Did you enjoy shooting Victor?

A. Yeah.

Q. Did you—Did it give you a good feeling?

A. Yeah.

Q. What kind of feeling? How would you describe it?

A. Christmas spirit.

Q. Christmas spirit? Okay. There was—Was there anything that prevented you from shooting this man?

A. Yeah.

Q. What?

A. Took too long to get up.

Q. Yeah. But I—What I'm saying is may—Maybe I asked you the wrong way. Was there anything causing you to shoot him?

A. Cause me to shoot him?

Q. Yeah. Other than the fact that you enjoyed it?

A. It was right on time. That's all.

Q. Okay. You didn't have to shoot him?

A. Not really.

Q. You could have walked out of the apartment?

A. Yeah.

Q. You could have walked out of the apartment of the lady that you call the whore too, right?

A. Right.

Q. And you could have walked out of the apartment of this businessman?

A. Yeah.

Q. You like shooting people apparently?

A. Yeah.

Q. Does it make you feel good?

A. You could say so. Yeah.

[. . .]

Q. What gun did you use when you shot this fellow called Victor?

A. The thirty-eight.

[. . .]

Q. All right. Well, what does a thirty-eight look like? What does this one look like?

A. Oh, this particular one?

Q. Yeah?

A. It was black. Black all the way.

Q. Um hum.

A. It had a horse engraved on it, a unicorn.

Q. Um hum.

A. A pretty black handle. It's a pretty black gun. That's all I can tell you.

[. . .]

Q. How many people, all told, have you shot?

A. Well, Michael. I did Michael too.

Q. You did Michael?

A. Yeah. He knew too much.

[. . .]

Q. When—when did you shoot him?

A. Before Christmas.

[. . .]

Q. As best as you can recall, tell me about how that happened?

A. He had stole some money from me, cut out.

Q. Um hum.

A. I had, you know, combed the streets a couple of days. And I didn't say too much to, you know, too many people. Then he came home. So, you know, I figured he got the best of me. So I just said I'm gonna get him.

Q. How did you do it?

[. . .]

A. I was standing on a, um, chair, and Mike was laying on the bed. So I just said, *pst, pst, boo.* Fired another one.

Q. Where did you shoot him?

[. . .]

A. In his head.

Q. How many times?

A. Once.

[. . .]

Q. When you shot Michael, was it daytime? Nighttime? Or what?

A. It was daytime.

Q. Do you remember what day of the week it was or what date it was?

A. No. It was—it was the twenty-third.

Q. How do you know that?

A. It was before Christmas.

Q. Well, the twenty-first and twenty-second are also before Christmas? I mean, what makes you say it's the twenty-third?

A. That's the—That's it. The twenty-third. Because I know I had to see my P[arole] O[fficer] on a Thursday.

Q. Yeah?

A. And I had to go see my family Friday.

Q. Did you go see your PO on a Thursday?

A. Right.

Q. And did you go see your family on Friday?

A. Right.

Q. Did Michael say anything to you before you shot him?

A. No.

Q. Did you tell him that you were gonna do it?

A. Uh uh.

Q. Okay. What did you do after you shot him?

A. I had to get rid of the body. It was in the way.

Q. And how did you do that?

A. I left first to go get high. And then I came back. I had made some money, you know, to eat some dinner.

Q. Um hum.

A. Came back. I had some rope in the house. I tied him up. You know, put him in a certain position because he was too—He was a tall person. Tied him up. Excuse me. And I put him in a box, right?

Q. Um hum.

A. Then I went and got a shopping cart. Put him in a shopping cart. And I went and got—got a dope fiend to go help me take him and put him in the river.

Q. Okay. You—you had who?

A. A dope fiend.

Q. A dope fiend?

A. Right.

Q. What was the dope fiend's name?

A. "D."

Q. "D." Do you know his real name?

A. No. "Dope Fiend D."

Q. Okay. What—what do you know about "Dope Fiend D"? What does he look like?

A. A dope fiend. He's bowlegged. I'm gonna tell you: He's got—His hands are puffy.

Q. Um hum.

A. Glassy eyes.

Q. Why did you get him to help you?

A. Why? Because people like him don't talk.

Q. Um hum.

A. And he needed a fix that day . . .

[. . .]

Q. Where did you see him that particular time that you went and asked him for help?

A. I came around the corner of Madison Avenue and a Hundred Thirty-fifth Street.

Q. Okay. Did you tell this guy what it was that you needed for him to help you with?

A. To move a package.

Q. The package?

A. Yeah.

Q. Did you tell him what was inside the package?

A. Uh uh.

   [. . .]

Q. . . . How—What did you do with Michael after you had shot him?

   [. . .]

A. Took him. Wrapped him up in a sheet. Put his head in some plastic.

Q. Um hum.

A. So the blood won't get all over the place, which it did anyway.

Q. Yeah?

A. Put him in a box on the floor. Cleaned the room up. Lit up some incense. Smoked some more reefer in the house.

Q. Put him in a box, did you say?

A. Yeah.

Q. What kind of box?

A. It was a, you know, like a large Pamper box.

Q. And where did you get it from?

A. Off the street, from the garbage. You know, put all garbage and shit in there.

Q. Okay. And how did you move him out of there? How did you get him out of the apartment?

A. Yeah. I tell you I got a shopping cart.

Q. Like in a grocery store?

A. Yeah. But it was—The shopping cart was chained up outside.

Q. Yeah?

A. Busted the chain. Brought the cart back.

Q. What did you do with the shopping cart eventually?

A. It's in the river with Michael.

Q. Okay. And you mean to tell me that this fellow "D" didn't realize that there was a body in that shopping cart?

A. He wasn't interested about that, Man. He wanted the fix.

   [. . .]

Q. Okay. Did you meet anybody on the way to the river with the shopping cart?

A. I—I seen people that I knew. What's up, how [unintelligible]?

Q. What about people who live there in that building? Did you see any of them?

A. Did I see them when I came out?

Q. Yeah?

A. No.

Q. Weren't you concerned that they were gonna hear that gunshot when you shot Michael?

A. No.

Q. Why not? Why weren't you concerned about that?

A. Farthest thing from my mind.

Q. What?

A. I wasn't thinking about them. They would have got it too, if they would have heard it.

Q. You would have shot them also.

A. Yeah.

　　[. . .]

Q. What happened to this gun . . . the thirty-eight caliber Colt?

A. I had a—When we was in the poolroom, the police raided the spot. I had put it down.

Q. Yeah?

A. And you know, get rid of it because it was dirty.

Q. Why—Where was this?

A. What? The—the poolroom?

Q. Yeah?

A. A Hundred Twenty-seventh and Lenox.

Q. Well, did anybody—When was this? Do you remember?

A. The second.

Q. The second?

　　[. . .]

A. Right. A Saturday night.

　　[. . .]

Q. Okay. And who was in the poolroom when this was?

A. It was packed with locals and regulars.

Q. Well, how come the police didn't arrest you . . . for the gun?

A. Because they didn't find it on me.

Q. Did they find it on anybody else?

A. No. I was—I put it down.

Q. Yeah?

A. I put it next to somebody. This—I, like, put it right here.

Q. Yeah?

A. And when the police said, Everybody catch the wall, I was way on the other side of the room.

Q. Okay. Anybody get arrested for that?

A. Yeah. A dude named Reggie.

Q. Did you know this guy, Reggie?

A. Yeah.

Q. He got arrested for possessing your gun?

A. Yeah.

   [. . .]

Q. Okay. Listen, let me see if I can get this clear in my own head. When you shot these people, was it your intention to kill them? To murder them?

A. Yeah. That's the purpose of shooting them.

Q. Okay. And—

A. Why do you think I did it in the head? [Witness made guttural sound.] No other place. If I wanted to hurt them—I would have shot them in their kneecap or in their shoulder. The purpose to kill them. Eliminate them. Make room for somebody else.

Q. Sir, I have no further questions. I appreciate—Thank you very much.


A Harlem pastor, who was also David Bullock's landlord, told Varian it must surely have been the roommate who'd led David astray. Bullock never exactly struck the detective as pious, even if he did keep a Bible in his room, underline passages in it, and could actually quote from them. When they took him into custody, the detectives naturally confiscated a shotgun found under his mattress—and they scooped up his Bible, as well.

If not for this last inspiration, Varian and Doyle might well have ended up with little to show for their legwork but fizzled leads and a shotgun minus its serial number.

New York detectives going after a confession have ways of letting a perp know whose side God is on. They play the religious angle as readily as other oldies but goodies—good-guy–bad-guy, we-know-more-about-you-than-your-wife-does, and we-got-your-prints-at-the-scene. When Jimmy Varian dropped David's roommate's street name, Mink, he scored some "we-know . . ." points. But not enough; Varian says, "we were at a dead end."

The Bible sat where the detectives had first left it, on the table in the interview room. Varian didn't feel that this suspect was gonna sit still for a lot of God stuff, so the detective made a simple prop out of the Good Book, letting David cite favorite texts. David came up with "Do not covet your neighbor's wife." Varian pounced, *"Do you also know the one,* Don't lie to the police?"

These two detectives know a lot . . . They knew David was lying. . . . The truth was gonna come out. . . . Might as well tell . . .

Detective Varian, right across the table, was suddenly larger-than-life and paying close attention to David Bullock too—something that God, wherever He was, didn't seem to have enough respect to be doing.

The detectives may have made more of an impression than God this time, but this time was the exception. When you bring God in on a case, you usually find that He can get a confession where you have tried and failed. You and your perp usually have religion in common: homicide detectives from Catholic backgrounds tend to put God to work on murder suspects, often young ones, who were brought up in the Church too. That's where the similarity generally ends, though.

The detective is older, more experienced and sophisticated: unfair to a suspect from a disadvantaged background? Especially since a more equal suspect might be slower to believe the detective's version of God? Well, God doesn't get calls on hijackings, only tragedy and carnage. Yes, probably in the ghetto or the Barrio—with ghetto or Barrio *victims.* It would be unfair to them, wouldn't it, not to try to avert further tragedy and carnage.

———

Detective Jack Healy talks about Sister Mary Agony, at whose knee years ago you had no choice but to learn right from wrong. Thus firmly grounded, all that remains now is to become an adroit improviser, scavenging with all five senses for the smallest useful cue, any dust mote or thunder clap, that might help lure the bad guy over to the side of the angels—for at least as long as it takes to confess.

Faced with a babysitter in big trouble, homicide detective Tommy Sullivan played good guy—with Mother Nature for backup. Sullivan, a Manhattan North second grader with nearly a score of years in the Bureau, was a divorcé with no kids. For this assignment, though, he reinvented himself as the strong but forgiving father: the I'll-stand-up-for-you-buddy kind of dad so many cops cherish—and so many ghetto kids never had.

Throughout the lengthy interview, a young detective sat in with the subject and Sullivan, absorbing even the slightest shading in Sullivan's voice. Detective Louis DelCastello's gold shield was exactly a year and a month old.

### Detective Second Grade Tom Sullivan:
### Limbo

I got up to Metropolitan Hospital to look at the body. Two-year-old little girl. This kid looked like Diana Ross, good-lookin' little kid. Fuckin' shame. Facial bruises, bruises here. I mean big. Not obviously all over, but a couple of lumps that would indicate a punch or a shot or a kick.

Louis DelCastello's got the babysitter, who was a nephew, in the squad. Nineteen-year-old guy. A bit of a psycho, everybody felt. "I did nothing wrong. I didn't do it." And he believed it.

So we walked in there, me and Louis. Then Lieutenant Doyle and Bill Kelly were there. And nothin'. "No, no." And the guy was so rational and so eloquent, so logical, that you almost wanted to believe him. He says, "Look, I know why I'm here. It's obvious. I was the last one to be with the baby. And I watch her. You think I did somethin'. I have no hard feelings, I don't. But I didn't."

Tell us again what happened.

"She was runnin' around. And she says, 'I wanna go lay down,' and I picked her up, I put her in the bed, and then she just never woke up. When she wouldn't wake up, I picked her up and rushed her to the hospital."

The mother came home, says, "Where is Monae? Where's the baby?" "Upstairs." And the mother knew that was not right, 'cause the baby's always runnin' around. "What did you do to my baby?" 'Cause the mother said, "He did it. I know he did it!"

So I'm talkin' to him. Say, what do you do for a living? "Well, well, I used to work for the Department of Social Services. I don't anymore." He just watched the baby and he's like a yuppie. Why not? "Well, well, you know, I worked in an office full of women. Oh, I don't know. Y'know. I guess women have their days and stuff, and I was—" He used the word "interloper." He said, "and I was an interloper, you know."

I'm looking at him, and I'm gettin' like—a profile of him. He had one arrest for assaulting his mother, hit her over the head with a hammer. You wouldn't know it to look at him. Neat, clean.

You don't get along with women, do you?

"Oh, I s'pose you could say that. According to my arrest record. Not really—I like women. They just— You know how they are."

I said, Yeah, I know how they are. I got five sisters. Listen, what'd you do with Monae?

"No, I didn't do nothin'."

What were you doin' that day? You had to babysit, huh?

"Yeah."

You babysit a lot?

"Well, yeah, you know, the mother works."

But she stays out late sometimes at night, right?

"Yeah."

I say, Beautiful woman, right?

"Well, I guess you could say she's attractive, yeah, I . . . guess."

She was out dancin' every night?

"Yeah."

But you have to mop up and clean up and watch the baby, right?

"Yeah."

Now, get back to the date. Baby was running around and you were mopping up?

He says, "Yeah, I got cross. I got cross with her because you know how you sweep dust, and she's runnin' back and forth in it, and it's blowin' up, and . . ."

Yeah, that gets to be a pain in the neck. So did you yell at her?

"Well, yeah, I told her, 'Monae, honey, *please* stop that.' And she did."

I says, What was on TV? He tells me. He just wouldn't give it up.

Now, it's late at night. We're in the office, me, Louis, and him. And it's windy and rainy out. And there's this wind howlin'.

Listen, Herman, there's only two people who know what happened to that little girl. And one of 'em's dead. He looked at me, and then, just like that, *WHOOOOSH*—the wind! I couldn't have asked for a better Hollywood effect, and I said, Are you Catholic? And he says, "Yes, I am." I said, You know what limbo is?

"Limbo?"

That's where the souls go that aren't baptized—where the babies' souls go. Where do you think Monae is now? You think she's up there howling and crying for the suffering?

"Well, I didn't *do* anything."

She's got *past* broken legs—right across, not from a fall. Like, hit with— I said, That baby's out there howling and suffering.

The wind's howlin', and he looked out the window. And *Louis* is lookin' out. I said, That's her out there. I thought, well, what the hell, this is my last—

And then the guy looks at me, he went. He's tearful. "I pushed her."

You pushed her?

"Yeah."

Against what?

"She hit her head against the—the television."

It was an accident, wasn't it?

"Yeah, I'm sweepin' up—" he says, "and she's goin' on. And all them women—and all they think I am is some houseboy . . ." You could see it was somebody who hated women.

What else?

"That's all. I swear that's all." He gave up the whole thing, right?

I go out and I tell Jack Doyle. Doyle's goin', Good, good, *good*. But then the morgue calls, and they got, like, a ruptured spleen, lacerated liver—I had to go back in.

Listen, remember I told you if you were good to me and you cleared your conscience, I'd stand with you? I'd help you— Because lemme tell you, y'know who's gonna try you? A woman! Who did you kill? A woman. Again, you're in the hands of women. Look, we gotta stick together. . . .

You wanted to go in there, take off your coat—C'mon, you little mutt, you like to beat up babies?! But what's our object? Our objective is to get a case against him, make it go to court; make it withstand grand jury scrutiny, get him indicted, get him convicted, and get him *in jail.* You give him a punch, stick his head in the toilet—your case is in jeopardy. You gotta turn off all of your likes and dislikes and just: *How* you doin'? *You know how kids are. I give 'em a shot or two once in a while.* . . .

But he went! He went with that Catholic routine about the soul of the departed. Holy shit.

And Louis! He says, "God, you had me goin'." The wind—I said, "Hear that? That's Monae!" And the bad guy looked out. *Louie*'s lookin'—Catholic guilt.

---

"Every time we went out looking for somebody," says Detective Bob Snyder, "we grabbed the person." Snyder and Detective Ann Martucciello partnered up to work on special cases with the blessing of their supervisor in the Bronx Sex Crimes Squad (renamed "Special Victims" in the nineties).

Martucciello is dark-haired, Snyder gray-blond. Both are on the chunky side. They look comfortable together, like Mom 'n' Pop detectives (he's married, she's single). They are kindly, understanding toward the women and child victims they work with, and for.

But they are detectives—they can tell the real rape victim from the one who's trying to get a guy in trouble, the real abused child from the one who doesn't like her mom's new boyfriend. Rapists and child abusers also confide in Mom or Pop. Mom once spent a year and a half in a convent.

"We are fortunate—" Snyder says. "We get a lot of statements from people. They just like talkin' to us."

*Martucciello:* We play the good-guy–bad-guy sometimes.

*Snyder:* I'm always the good guy.

*Martucciello:* And from our religious background, we also play the priest-and-nun-type situation.

*Snyder:* I've been called a priest.

*Martucciello:* With certain perpetrators, different things work. Sometimes you have to use, "Don't give me that bull! You know you did it." Or you go the other way, "Well, it may not be proven that you did these things, but someday you're gonna have to answer to a higher authority." And sometimes it works. Sometimes it doesn't.

*Snyder:* A lot of people still don't realize there's no hot lights and rubber hoses. It's amazing how many of these criminals are willing to talk to you—you don't even have to say much to them.

Most rewarding, says Detective Snyder, "is when you can get the confidence of the sex crimes victim, whether it be an adult or a child, that will come out and tell you something that's difficult to admit to *themselves*, much less to a complete stranger. They actually feel enough confidence in you to let you know what happened to them."

Snyder and Martucciello caught the bizarre case of Herman McMillan, who dominated and abused his wife and nine children, ranging from age fourteen to less than a year old.

On the night in August 1989 when Four-four Precinct patrol officers and the Bureau of Child Welfare (BCW) took McMillan's children from his care, Snyder says the apartment in the Highbridge section of The Bronx was without lights, strewn throughout with garbage and clothing. A "House of Horrors," reporters called the scene. The children "moved in unison. Like little mice, they went from one corner to another," officers told the detectives, "in complete fear and never said anything. No eye contact. The only time they would respond is at the father's command. Including the wife. McMillan was totally in charge."

### Detective Ann Martucciello and Detective Bob Snyder:
### Dad

**Detective Snyder:** They removed the children to the hospital to be examined, standard procedure, and that's when they found that the eldest girl was sexually abused.

Unfortunately, our office wasn't informed of the case until a month or two later. Everybody in the bureaucracy thinks they're doing the right thing. But when I saw photos of them in the hospital, I couldn't believe that this just went by them at BCW. It was just amazing the way these kids looked. Talking to the children was eye-opening. It was unbelievable.

**Detective Martucciello:** Child Welfare, their thing was, get the kids out of the house and put 'em in foster care and, you know, that was the "answer." We were there to investigate how the kids came to this point.

**Detective Snyder:** When you work with a partner—If I know I'm not getting anywhere, I don't have a problem stepping back. And Annie's the same way. So only one of us is driving the interview; the other one sits. You catch the moment when you hit the stone wall. You have to know how to maybe just glance over, and Annie will know, she'll start asking questions, and I step back. You can't have two people asking questions. Sometimes the kids will react to both of you, then it doesn't make any difference. But you have to watch.

We are looking into the criminal aspects of the case, whereas the Child Welfare social worker is asking them to vent. Their form of questions could be a lot different than ours, a lot of times it might be suggestive. We have to be careful of: are the kids giving a response that we're gonna be happy about rather than give us the truth? We have to weigh what they're saying, what's factual and what's the part they think they want us to hear. I think that's the hardest part of the interviews with children. Especially when they've been questioned previously by other agencies.

Our main concern in talking to the McMillan children is the three babies that died—in childbirth? due to lack of nutrition? or were they killed? The father wouldn't tell the children what he did with the dead babies, because he felt that if the children were ever questioned by the police, they couldn't give up the location where they were buried.

He delivered the babies—he was the doctor, the dentist, he was the teacher.

We did develop a rapport; he did talk to me. And he, like, one minute he loved me, next minute, he didn't like me. But his statements to me more or less knocked out the fact that he was crazy. He described how he went to Social Security. "I went during the summertime. I put a load of sweaters on, put an old black hat on, pulled it over my head, went down there, acted stupid, and they gave me Social Security."

**Detective Martucciello:** When we gained entry into the apartment, I couldn't believe my eyes, and I'd been on the job, what, eighteen years. Bob's been in twenty-some-odd years. I don't think he has come into an apartment like this. Their refrigeration consisted of a box out the window with rancid food in it. McMillan felt the kids were getting undernourished; he had to change their diet!

**Detective Snyder:** While he was in jail, he was writing letters to his wife, and in the letters, he says, "Detective Bob is okay, but still don't talk to him about them babies because they'll bring up manslaughter charges on us." So he was well aware of what was going on. But I honestly don't believe that the babies were killed on purpose.

**Detective Martucciello:** "I'm going to tell you the truth now. I buried them on a hillside next to the Forty-fourth Precinct." And we got in the body-sniffing dogs, dug half the hillside away. Then he would say, "Well, I buried them in the park." And again, we would go there and dig up spots, and no babies. He was not going to tell us where these bodies were.

**Detective Snyder:** One, I believe, was a miscarriage. The other two—One was stillborn. There was one, though, that was born and lived for a couple of weeks. How it died, I don't know. It sounds strange saying I don't think he was that cruel—meaning that he wouldn't *kill* 'em on purpose. I think it was a matter of lack of nutrition, and whatever. Also the way he was describing the baby, it was deformed.

If there was extra food, the kids would try to grab it. That's when they got punished—tied up, beatings. In statements McMillan made to us, he actually said he realized the beatings he was giving them was starting to scar them. So he had to change his method, and he started placing them under water until they couldn't breathe and then pulling them out. That didn't leave scars—physical scars.

The oldest boy would do anything his father said because he was afraid. He was brutalized pretty bad. And, in fact, the father would take him out, because he was priming him as the future leader of the group.

**Detective Martucciello:** He was too embarrassed to admit the fact that his father was sodomizing him, tried to recant it a couple of times.

He stated that he was forced to have sex with his sister. The father wanted to teach him how to have sex. Eventually, he would be the head of the family.

**Detective Snyder:** I think the boy might have had something to do with it, but it was on the father's direction. McMillan didn't really deny about the girl. But the boys, he denied. He was trying to blame everything on the oldest boy. "He's the evil one. He's the one that does everything bad."

It came to a point where he actually wasn't hiding too much from the kids. When he had sex with the older daughter, he had it right in bed with his wife layin' there. Then sometimes he'd do something with his daughter, then he'd go to his wife.

The oldest girl was thirteen. She was the one that started realizing something was wrong here, and she started demanding a few things. And that's why he started becoming more aggressive with them.

**Detective Martucciello:** You'll find with most kids, not only these particular kids, no matter how brutalized they are, or sexually abused or physically abused, they still love their parent.

Up to the day of the trial, the older boy was talking about when his father gets out, how he was gonna hook up with his father and they were gonna go all over the country. You could still see, no matter what these kids went through, they still had that relationship with their parent. They do not want you to lock this parent up.

**Detective Snyder:** These kids become very wise. They're aware somethin' wrong was done to them, but they say, They *are* my parents and I still love them. And you sit there and wonder, How can you? But you just agree with them.

McMillan felt that his children would never testify against him because of his control and dominance over them. But after the third child testified, he called his lawyer aside and said, "I think I was crazy when I did those things." They switched to insanity. But the jury didn't buy it. He was found guilty of numerous counts of sexual assault and assault with no sex involved.

**Detective Martucciello:** Unfortunately, not only in this case but in many cases, the children don't realize what has been done to them. We try not to build up a barrier towards their parents, but to have them realize that Daddy or Mommy did something bad. Mommy and Daddy should know better. They seem to understand that part of it.

Our basic question—at least mine is—years from now, will these kids dislike men; will they also brutalize their own children?

**Detective Snyder:** A lot of the offenders we arrest—not only parents—that do these things to kids, yes, they were victims.

———

If suspects "give it up" when someone like Bob Snyder merely walks into the interview room and sits down, it's thanks to the New York City detective *mystique.*

Part of the complex mystique is a reputation for knowing what you need to know when you need to know it. That's reality based—if you're experienced, there *are* certain things you can intuit on sight. "You deal with people," Tommy Sullivan says. "You know 'em like a bartender does. A guy can come in here and order a beer, the bartender'll look at him and say—guy's gonna be a problem around *eleven o'clock.*"

*Intuition.* Could Detective Sullivan be practicing that supposedly feminine specialty? Just goes to show you. And patience. Both are practiced by good detectives, male and female, and by anyone whose work depends on reading people.

You might not know diddly, and people just assume you know plenty. That's the mystique working for you. "The vast majority of the public," claims Detective John Monahan, "think a detective is higher than a sergeant. And they don't want to talk to a captain." Success, says Tommy Sullivan, is "forty percent hard work, fifty percent a little bit of luck and a little perseverance, and then this ten percent mystique."

"You can see when a guy's just about to give it up," Monahan says. "You know when you have him right on the edge." Sullivan warns, "Don't ask one question too many. I've seen it. Just as the guy was gonna say somethin', the young detective says, 'What's your mother's maiden name?' And he threw the whole thing off. The whole thing is ruined."

Everybody plays good-guy–bad-guy. Try and find a Catholic detective in New York who hasn't used the religious angle. Why don't the perps wise up? Because successful NYPD detectives don't succeed by dint of IQ or advanced degrees in criminal justice—though some hold them—but by endless creativity in their approach to people. By patience, and sensitivity.

*Creativity.* No two hotshot New York detectives' renditions of a standard ploy are the same. You reuse what works, always improvising, tailoring your approach anew for each subject. . . . Queens Homicide lieutenant Phil Panzarella swears by stage props, such as the pair of huge mariachi sombreros displayed on his office wall. "Sundance" Panzarella says the unlikely decorative accent counters his unapproachable double-breasted image—suggests that maybe a young male killer or homicide witness can talk to him after all.

Reputed to carry a dagger in addition to his regulation weapons, the madcap lieutenant's arsenal also includes the lineup of jock photos on his office windowsill. Clapping a Raiders hat on his head, he'll barge into the interrogation room: "D'you have Bo's picture? *I* do."

Any kind of show biz to "soften 'em up."

Manhattan South Homicide detective Joe Brandefine and Sergeant Kenny Bowen were on surveillance late one night during the 1988 "Pizza Connection" federal Mafia trial, when they were paged. FBI calling. Agents were holding a suspect in the botched hit on a Pizza Connection defendant who was free on bail. For ten or twelve hours, the agents talked, Brandefine recalls, but the kid still had little to say. In more ways than one, the hour was late. Soon the feds would have to let the kid go.

Two agents actually sat behind the partition and listened to the New York detectives do a special adaptation of good-guy–bad-guy based on uncommon sense.

### Detective Second Grade Joe Brandefine:
### State Prison

We kind of explained to this white kid that if he didn't tell the FBI, we were gonna arrest him and put him in state prison, and that his option was much nicer to talk to the feds and confess to them, as opposed to us bringin' him back to New York and puttin' him in a cell with some guy from Harlem. You always say that to white guys, but it's ninety-nine percent true. We told him what could happen to a kid like him goin' to a New York prison—not a funny thing.

We explained he wouldn't have these problems in federal prison, and he could probably play tennis and eat good food. In about fifteen minutes he gave up the whole story. These FBI guys were amazed. Me and Kenny Bowen were like, why didn't they think of this?

———

Since 1966, when the Supreme Court decided *Miranda* v. *Arizona*, your suspect must be given the Miranda warning about his right to counsel. Omit the warning and you'll surely lose the case. The creative challenge is to read him his rights and get the statement anyhow.

Romolo Imundi, aka the "Roman Gladiator," knew the glory days of Manhattan West Homicide before *Miranda*. Detective Imundi had the case of a Puerto Rican victim kicked to death by a hood named Jimmy Carr. Variations on the ethnic appeal that Imundi used decades ago are still called upon today—the gut appeal of hatred strong enough to outweigh Miranda. The lowest-common-denominator can be the most creative solution. . . . The trick is knowing when.

### Detective First Grade Romolo Imundi:
### Hate

Say you were Croatian—of course, my mother was Croatian, and I understand about the Serbians fighting the Croatians. The individual I'm talking to thinks the fact that we are from the same background will give him an edge. I'm using that as part of the mystique. You're gonna go for it, because you're looking for help, you're in danger. You're gonna get locked up, so you'll grab for any straw.

Jimmy Carr—tough Irishman, the West Side was loaded with Irish in those days. He kicked the teeth out, kicked his face out, broke his cheekbone, kicked his ribs out.

I picked Carr up. It became my-gray-matter against your-gray-matter. You may be smarter, but you're not sharper. There's a difference. Naturally, I played with him. I told him my name was Ronny Collins, I came from County Mayo and County Sligo. And I can understand why you kicked that fuckin' spic to death, but why did you rob him?

I got him now. I understand, I'm sympathetic, I'm Irish. Same background, same feeling, same hate. Just like Terry Anderson was saying: Take me physically, but don't get my mind, 'cause once you get my mind, I'm *gone*. I'm accusing Carr of being less than a man—robbing a dead guy.

He said to me, "I never, never, never robbed him. I kicked that sonofabitch and he deserved to die, but I never robbed him."

Now the question becomes, is it admissible? In those days, all I had to do is outsmart you. Don't have to beat you up—I can out-con you.

He goes for it. And then later on he found out my name was Romolo Giuseppe Imundi. He got beat at his own game. That's part of the mystique—you have to play it. And you have to get the feel of it.

———

Getting the feel of it sometimes takes all night, or longer.

*Patience.* Queens Homicide detective Katy Stanton's legendary CO, Lieutenant Dan Kelly, says the athletic-looking brunette's forte was interviewing—and in Kelly's view, patience is an interviewer's bread and butter. Detective Stanton was in demand.

But an on-duty injury forced Stanton to retire from Queens Homicide at age thirty-one. "I don't think I'll ever find anything in my life again that I love doing more than being a detective," she says. "If I could've stayed on the job, and you said to me, I'll make you the chief—you're gonna get extra money, and you can be the chief—or you want to be a detective? I would say, I want to be a detective."

In the Homicide task force, Stanton had worked for Kelly and Sergeant Phil "Sundance" Panzarella, and worked with detectives she admired to a point just short of worship. Ronnie Waddell, Steve Weiner, Bob McKnight. . . . She'd started in the Bureau in Queens Sex Crimes and excelled at talking to abused kids. A world-class talker, she could listen too.

Patience was Stanton's great virtue, but don't slight her intuition or her creativity, either. When others' patience ran out, or when someone *had* to get a statement from a female, probably a scared female, they'd get Katy. One time, it was the infamous and gruesome "baby case" to end all baby cases.


## Detective Katy Stanton:
## Bad Dream

Jason Radke came to Queens from Nebraska in 1990 with his nineteen-year-old common-law wife, Linda Boyce. At a kennel in Ridgewood, Jason was learning how to train German shepherds to be attack dogs. Linda had a job at the kennel, but she was pregnant and quit when the baby was born. Jason had a Shepherd dog they kept in the apartment.

Six days after the birth of Linda and Jason's baby, detectives in the One-o-four were called to the apartment. Homicide. They took a statement from Jason in which he said he had killed the infant and panicked. He didn't know what to do with the body. He figured if he fed it to the dog, there wouldn't be any evidence.

I tried interviewing Linda several times. She kept saying she had slept through everything and didn't know anything about what happened. Then we decided to take her for a polygraph exam. We went down to do the test, I'm talkin' to her all the way.

Linda failed Detective Maria Silva's key polygraph questions—Did you have any knowledge of who killed your baby? Did you have anything to do with the death? Detective Silva felt that Linda didn't kill the baby, but she was holding back information.

The two of us were sittin' on a bench in the hall—waitin' for the elevator, I think—and it just popped into my head. I said to her, Linda, do you think maybe you were dreamin' and you don't want to remember? D'you think you had a bad dream, and maybe the dream was the truth?

That thought came to me from dealing with abused children who couldn't outright say what happened, so first you get them to accept it as a dream—dissociating themselves from the event. I said somethin' to that effect to Linda and it clicked. She said something bad did happen, and she started remembering more and more. She told me she saw him feed part of the baby to the German shepherd. I took part of her statement right there on the bench and then took another one when we went back to the precinct.

Not everyone agreed with me, but I believe that she was so traumatized by what she saw, she couldn't recall it. Somethin' clicked when I said *bad dream*. That finally got her going, because after that, she gave a full statement. Maybe the polygraph interview had helped jog her memory too.

People said, Why didn't she do something? I think she was so overwhelmed. She knew what happened, but she just couldn't believe what she saw. And she was so frightened that she couldn't move outta that bed. She was like, paralyzed. Can you imagine waking up to that sight?

———

*Empathy*. Special victims, as the NYPD now calls sexually abused women and children, often do speak more freely to a female listener—detectives like Bob "Good-Guy" Snyder notwithstanding. Yet even when the squad room was all male and at least as macho as a locker room, there had to be a place for empathy. *Not* just sympathy—too distant to create a link. With women even now only about fourteen percent—some 4,000—NYPD detectives, confessions would be few and far between if only one sex had what it takes emotionally to elicit these all-important statements.

What it takes is the ability to put yourself in the perp's place—without losing your objectivity. This is a delicate balancing act that's especially riveting when performed by someone with the football-lineman build of the Ninth Squad's Billy Cutter. Like Katy Stanton, Cutter says, "It's just a matter of hitting on the right thing that's gonna get them to talk to you."

### Detective Second Grade Bill Cutter:
### Humans

It's like sitting down at a negotiation. Sometimes somebody will say to you, well, I was there but I didn't do anything. Once you get a person to say they were there, if you can continue with them talking to you, you can usually talk them through to the point where they'll tell you, yeah, I did it, why I did it, and everything else.

I think sometimes you can tell in the first five minutes that this guy's gonna be a hard person to get his name out of him. Sometimes you can just tell that the guy, sooner or later, wants to tell you what took place. It's like anything else, the cue is given by the other person.

This was a homicide that took place in Tompkins Square Park. A homeless guy killed another homeless guy in the park, over drugs. We looked for him for a couple of weeks, couldn't find anything, and then somebody told us that they once saw him at a particular location.

So on a Sunday morning we went to 14th Street and First Avenue, and lo and behold, there the guy was, on the street. Get out of the car, and the guy stood there. We said, come with us to the station house—which he did. And ten minutes later, he confessed to the whole thing.

This guy had spent three-quarters of his life in jail—I think he wanted to go back to jail. But I'm sure there have probably been times when people wanted to tell me things and I just didn't hit on the right cue. I think the key thing with him was, when he sat down in here, he started to cry. So I started to cry, and he told the story. You know, whatever works.

It wasn't that difficult—I didn't feel sorry for him at all. He stabbed the guy with a screwdriver. He wanted to tell us what happened; he never took it to trial, he pled guilty.

Sometimes people like to be touched. Other people, they don't want to be touched— sometimes people want to tell you what they did from the other side of the room. Difficult. Everybody is different. It could be a day where I wouldn't care if the guy told me what he wanted to tell me or not. I'm just not in the mood.

Everybody's human. You have to be sensitive to the other person, I guess, even though the other person may be a murderer.

## Partners & Bosses

**Detective Scott Jaffer:** John was a detective for thirteen years in the Two-four, where the undercover Chris Hoban was killed. So we rode up and down Amsterdam Avenue, and we try to speak to everybody we can think of. When John and I came into the squad, there were some people seated on the bench, and there was a woman who John knew from the street.

**Detective Second Grade John Hartigan:** She used to call the squad anonymously about somebody, and then one day I ran into her on the street with this guy who's beatin' her. After we got that taken care of, I said, You're the one who called. . . .

Scotty and I saw her there. Somebody said she's tied in with the drug dealers that killed Hoban. I said, Can we talk to her?

We brought her into the back room. What's going on, you telling these people you're clean? You're dirty. There's a bench warrant out for you, right?

"Oh, maybe they won't look it up; maybe they won't find it. I got a kid . . ."

I said, I'm not gonna tell on you, but come on, tell us.

She won't come across. "I don't know nothin'."

Jack Doyle had looked in and said, "How you makin' out?" I said, Listen, come in in about five minutes and start rantin' and ravin' and play the part. I go back into the room and we're talkin' to her, and Doyle comes in. "What's happenin'? Anything happenin'?"

No, she doesn't—

"Hey, listen! The hell with this crap! She's tied in with this operation! I want everything that can possibly be done, be done to her! And those guys! There's a cop dead here! We're gonna get after these people! We're gonna—" screamin' — "We're gonna hurt them as bad as we can."

Gee, Lieutenant, she's not a bad—

"I don't give a goddamn, John!" He's screamin' and yellin'.

We step outside and I said, Very good—thank you very much. And with that, I give it about five minutes. I walk back in and I said, Listen, you got a kid. The boss is adamant—this is a cop that's dead—he's goin' after *everything*. Those guys are illegal aliens he says, and he's gonna get them deported. He says there's nothin' he can do about you except—he's on the phone now. He's gonna call Child Welfare about you and the kid.

"Please don't! Please!" She's screamin'. Scotty and I were workin' on her for like two hours—we just hit the right nerve.

We were just playin' the part. It was nothin' but a lie. We weren't gonna do anythin' anyway. We didn't even know—we just guessed. Unbeknownst to us, there *was* a warrant out for her. There was two, one was Narcotics and the other was Family Court, Bureau of Child Welfare.

# 12

# ON TRIAL

Courtroom drama. Sometimes, as in this Brooklyn triumph, the gallery is empty, the only audience at the hearing is a young detective, learning his trade. . . .

### Detective Bill Majeski:
### A Good Case

Detective Frawley had to go to preliminary hearings on a trial. The defendant was accused of desecrating a grave—it was mostly allegations. Frawley did an investigation, really came up with very little. So we're in the DA's Squad office that morning; we're sitting and chatting and I say, You know what you're gonna do? What do you have?

"I don't know—it doesn't look too good." He looks over at another desk and he sees a package, like a roll of film. He takes it, he says, "Yeah, that's a good idea."

What's a good idea?

He says, "Hell, if we have pictures of him doing it, we got a good case."

When did you take pictures?

"I didn't take any pictures, but they don't know that."

Walked into court with about four packages of pictures and two tins of eight millimeter movie film. The defense attorney looked at us once, walked over to the judge, and took a plea.

If you've seen to it that the prosecutor has the makings of a great case—if you've even created the illusion of a great case—you probably won't face a defense attorney at trial. A trial is a defendant's gamble: all or nothing, freedom or prison. If the perp has money, he probably decides not to gamble: he plea bargains so he can keep his money rather than pay lawyers' fees. But he loses a chunk of his life. A win for your side, and you may not even have taken the stand.

Bill Majeski's story about Detective Ed Frawley's sleight of hand couldn't happen today—since the Criminal Procedure Law's "discovery" provision of 1982, prosecutors can't legally conceal evidence from the defense. But for Majeski, the moral of the story never changes. Put it this way: Skill at creating illusion gives a detective just as much of an edge over an adversary as would hard evidence—aka, *truth*.

In the course of an investigation, your perp may or may not have what it takes to compete at head games—but a defense attorney can be relied on to blow smoke in the courtroom. Juries thrive on concrete, specific detail; the defense will try most anything to make your answers, and you, look vague.

By watching Frawley and other veteran detectives, the young Majeski absorbed what is for him the essential lesson. Years before *America's Most Wanted*, he used illusion and psychology to recover a shrewd most-wanted fugitive. Jailhouse author Jack Henry Abbott, released from federal prison in 1981 to an East Village halfway house, was the darling of New York literary society before he fatally stabbed a twenty-two-year-old aspiring actor and fled. Phone call by crafty phone call, Majeski pursued Abbott halfway across the country and took him down by proxy.

The tracking feat won Majeski deserved fame, but only five months later the media reported the startling courtroom sequel—a manslaughter verdict. Leave it to a Manhattan jury to buy the defense that Abbott had acted "under the influence of extreme emotional disturbance" in deliberately killing his victim. The sentence for his gratuitous evil—a paltry fifteen years. Nevertheless, Majeski was content. Top-drawer defense counsel Ivan Fisher "was so magnificent," the detective says, "I felt we just squeaked through."

———

The murder rate explodes, but Manhattan juries are still ultra-susceptible to murder defendants' attorneys' masterly "violin solos." And in all five boroughs, juries are affected by the prevailing cloud over police credibility. All too often, the average New York citizen seems less willing to take your word than the word of a Jack Henry Abbott.

When you testify, in squad jargon you're said to be "in court," yet more than ever today, the detective's experience—any police officer's—is sharpened by the sensation that you're the one who's *on trial*. The defense will certainly do everything it can to reinforce that impression in jurors' minds. Any minor investigative misstep is fair game for a defense lawyer, ever ready to paint that misstep in the colors of a major blunder, even a fraud. Counsel's goal is to leave you out there on the defensive, hurt your credibility with a jury unfamiliar with standard courtroom maneuvers. On the other hand, perfection also may rouse suspicion; the occasional honest "I don't know" can win jurors' sympathy.

In real life, courtroom drama often seems muted. Otherwise, why would real-life jurors doze? Nevertheless, an alert juror can have a field day following the dramatic subtext played out before the judge, tuning in to the psychological vibes adrift in the courtroom well. How tense are the players? Just watch their heads swivel when someone they don't know merely steps through the courtroom doors into the gallery.

If you don't want your ace investigation knocked out in the final round, you better know how the game is played. Tommy Ullo, now an investigations supervisor for a major insurance company, was an intense, dedicated young detective on the Upper West Side when he got some practice in state supreme court, Manhattan.

### Detective Tom Ullo:
### How Do You Get to 100 Centre Street?

In the cross-examination, I was always very comfortable because I didn't lie. I knew you weren't gonna trip me up. You could ask me the questions six different ways, upside down, inside out, I'm gonna answer it the same because I knew I wasn't gonna screw myself up by lyin'.

This particular attorney, apparently he realized he couldn't get to me in his normal cross-examination, so he walked by me with his back to the jury and he said, "You're a fuckin' liar." Just like that.

I turned to the judge. "Did you hear what he just said?" The jury looked at me like I was the one losing my composure. Everybody just grimaced and looked at *me* like, "What the hell is this guy doin'?"

At recess, as soon as I got out into the hall, I went to go grab him, and he says, "Hold it, Ullo. When we're in that courtroom, everything is a stage. We're all actors. We're all players, and the audience is the jury." He made me realize he had to do his little acting thing to get me flustered, to try and make his point for the jury.

The lawyers—defense attorneys or prosecutors—even they had to be little detectives in some ways themselves, to try and play devil's advocate—why was this done, why wasn't it done? They did their own detective work too, putting it into the legal pie.

In the investigation, the process, you make sure everything you've done was complete because you knew—when the attorneys got it, they were gonna cut up what you did. By the time you got done with somethin' in the Two-four, you weren't gonna be torn apart, especially in a homicide case. Because the squad had good leadership with Lieutenant Doyle and Sergeant DiChiaro, we knew when we had a finished product, we were satisfied with it. Not only that we felt self-gratification, but we knew between Doyle and DiChiaro, everything was done to the best of our ability. We couldn't do any more.

I was on the stand in a homicide case; Burton Roberts was the judge. His reputation is not exactly Mr. Nice Guy. The defense attorney was asking me specific times and dates regarding the incidents. Every time he asked, I opened up my notepad and I told 'em. After three or four times, Burton Roberts took that big book that he has and picked it up and he slammed it on his desk. I actually jumped, like two feet out of the chair. He just startled me so.

I looked at him and he starts yelling at me because I kept referrin' to my notes. I got up and walked out of the courtroom. I didn't say a word to anybody. He came right out into the hall and he confronted me; asking why I was taking it so personal. More reinforcement for me of what goes on in a courtroom. Made it more interesting—to learn that part of being a detective.

Not only did you have to be knowledgeable as far as what happened in the case, but you had to be an actor when you got into the courtroom.

The courtroom game can be a bruising contest. Even with her nice-girl-from-Queens image at risk, Karen Krizan never lost sight of the goal. She's the daughter of a patrol sergeant ("the greatest person I ever knew"), whose sergeant's shield she wears. She's also the younger sister of an orthodontist and a CPA (both male), the mother of a college-age daughter, the wife of an engineer, the president of the Policewomen's Endowment Association, and the boss of her own squad in Brooklyn North.

To get the sergeant's shield in 1987, Krizan traded in the detective shield she'd worn for nine years. Any minute she'll trade in the sergeant's tin for a lieutenant's. "This was definitely the choice of my life—" says the tall, blond detective boss, "this career. Because I did so many things." There've been no disappointments, she says, other than being laid off for a year in 1975 when she was only a couple of years into her dream.

By 1977, the heyday of Public Morals (PMD), when "pimps were pimps and the department had money to spend on cases," proper, Catholic-educated Krizan was undercover in the sordid sleaze. "I would go on the street and pose as a pross to get the pimps to approach me." Since a white woman with blond hair could command top money from johns, the pimps approached in droves to "make an application" (recruit her)—only to be summarily arrested by the bogus "snowbitch." In PMD, she also learned investigation.

Then she worked in Queens sex crimes for two years, and then, "in a squad doing regular investigations, just like my guys do." Always there were the trials, and no matter how many times you went to the stand, "You were always nervous. I testified in a lot of supreme court trials because of homicide cases. And all those Sex Crimes cases went to supreme court, because we only handled first-degree sex offenses. Major felonies."

And somehow, those sex crimes trials, whose defendants often were child molesters, were the toughest for Krizan. The snowbitch was a role, after all. The well-brought-up Catholic girl from Queens was real.

### Detective Sergeant Karen Krizan:
### Exhibit A

One of the hardest things I ever did—I was testifying in the Queens grand jury. Normally, you get prepped by the DA. He basically tells you ahead of time every question that he's gonna ask, so you review your notes and you know the answers, as far as addresses and things like that. One of the questions he *didn't* ask me in prep was to describe what "Greek" was.

It's anal intercourse, that's all. But I had to describe it. I had to say, The male puts his penis inside the woman's anus. When you're twenty-something years old and you're looking at all these people that look like your aunts and your grandmothers—I think it's twenty-four, twenty-six grand jurors—it's a lot. I was uncomfortable telling *one*.

I'm sittin' there, I live in Queens, and I'm looking at all these people and I'm thinking, I can't believe this, I'm a nice little Catholic girl . . . I have to tell these people what Greek is?! I had to go through the explanation, and I wanted to kill.

Of course, I'd probably already looked at every single face, because I had to go through the whole investigation, how I made the arrest and all that—and now, when I have to describe this, somehow, I can't find a female to look at. The older women are saying, like, they've never heard of this. After I told them that, I wanted to say *I'm really a nice girl from Queens*!

When I got outside, I told the DA, don't ever do that to me again.

————

The complainant in this other case was a young boy, around ten years old. He had been anally sodomized by his cousin. The family found out about it because he developed genital warts, which is sexually transmitted. So I got called to the hospital, I look at the photos, and I had to go to arrest this person. He was Spanish. He spoke some English—broken. I called in a Spanish interpreter, a uniformed cop came from another precinct, to go through the whole thing.

He didn't really want to confess, but I wanted to make sure that he understood his rights. Finally, at the end of the night, he did start to confess to me. He started to tell me how he did it. Basically, what he did was, he pulled the boy down onto him. He was sitting and he pulled the young boy down.

I wanted to make sure that I fully understood. He was sitting down in a chair and he was cuffed at the time and I uncuffed him, and I called the Spanish interpreter and I said, Make sure that I understand this exactly—even though he's showing me, I want to make sure.

Well, when we got to court, all of a sudden, the defendant couldn't speak a word of English. He had this Spanish interpreter sitting next to him, telling him everything that's going on in the courtroom, and I'm saying, this is a bunch of hooey. This guy told me in English. Yes, I did use the Spanish interpreter, but basically I did that because I didn't want to lose this case. When I saw what he did to that little boy, I wanted the cousin to *go* for this.

When his attorney was questioning me, his whole thing was that this guy never understood a word I said, and there was no possible way that I could have understood what he was saying.

In my answer, all of a sudden, I said, But excuse me, he physically showed me how he sodomized him. And the attorney steps back like this, and he goes, "What do you mean?"

He physically showed me.

"How did he do that?"

So now, again, you have the whole jury there. I had to stand up in the little box there, and I had to show them. He put his hands on my hips, I said, and he pulled me down. Which he did physically. Pulled me down onto his lap to show me how he sodomized the little boy. I was such a nervous wreck—but that was it. He was gone. There was no way that the jury would ever believe that I didn't understand him or he didn't understand me, because he physically showed me.

It worked out good.

————

Once Ronnie Waddell left behind his high-tension undercover identity as pimp "Ronnie Love," he went on to the challenges of classic squad detective work in Queens. Not just Queens—the One-o-three Squad in Jamaica. This was where, in the mid and late eighties, the rampant crack trade would explode in the execution of Officer Edward Byrne by drug gangsters, attracting worldwide attention.

By the time that tragedy hit in 1988, Detective Waddell, second grade, would be working for Lieutenant Dan Kelly in Queens Homicide, and Waddell would back up his pal, Detective Richie Sica, the catching detective in the complex investigation that solved the Byrne homicide.

But when Waddell was still pretty new in the One-o-three, back in 1980, Jamaica was still best known for its beautiful, suburban-style Jamaica Estates section. That fall, Waddell's gold shield would come down. Still wearing a white one, he handled every kind of crime on the squad menu, including homicide. And if a just-retired police captain was murdered, the most glorious thing Waddell and his partners could do was solve the case.

Nothing strengthens a detective's reputation like bringing a cop homicide investigation to a successful conclusion. In about a month, Jimmy Counihan, the catching detective, had written the blue Five that closed the O'Connor case. Waddell's coup was recovering the murder weapon. Conviction followed.

Five or six years pass. Waddell is one of Kelly's best-respected homicide detectives. By the time the O'Connor murder case comes up for appeal, Queens is different. Cops battle drug gangs for big chunks of the borough, police credibility declines, and now a good defense lawyer gets another shot. . . .

### Detective Second Grade Ronnie Waddell:
### The Appeal

A week or so after Captain Francis O'Connor retired in 1980—I think March the thirteenth, it was snowing, anyway—him and his wife was returning home from some community function. Walkin' hand in hand. This was up in Jamaica Estates, which is a very nice neighborhood. It was dark that night, snowing, wet. Two knuckleheads decide they're gonna ambush someone and rob them. And they chose O'Connor and his wife.

Instinct, I would imagine, made O'Connor go for his gun and he gets shot in the process. They take his gun too.

Me and my two partners from the One-o-three Squad at the time, Ron Singleton and Jimmy Counihan, we worked as a team. Myself and Counihan respond to the hospital. They got O'Connor in the emergency room, getting ready to open him up and give him heart massage. And we're trying to talk to him at the same time, because we know he's in trouble. Bein' inside an emergency room even when they're opening an individual up—there's no problem, they let us in. But we can't get any information this time.

We start an investigation. Subsequently one of the knuckleheads' brothers—not the actual shooter's brother, the accomplice's—is upset with him, gets in trouble with the police, and starts talkin' about what his brother did. We get him and we roll him over—he gives us the names and we go after 'em. First we take the accomplice and we tell him, we could arrest you for murder. If you cooperate, the crime *could* be robbery. So he decides he's gonna cooperate.

Now we arrest Tyrone Anderson, the guy who the accomplice says did it.

The night we bring Anderson in with his family and everything, we get permission from the family to go to the house—we believe the gun that killed O'Connor is in there somewhere. At the house is his uncle and we ask the uncle if we have permission to come in: we explain that we believe the gun's in the house. The uncle says, "There's no gun in the house. You're welcome to come in."

So we go in, straight to Tyrone's room, attic bedroom. My partner Singleton, he's searching over around by the bed. My partner Counihan, he's searchin' the furniture—looking down, also. The sergeant too, Bob Plansker. I'm just standing in the middle of the room, looking around, where could this knucklehead put a gun? I don't know what made me look up—there's a tile, a ceiling tile, that's just slightly ajar.

It's low enough for me to stick my hands in, and I feel around and the gun is right there. I pull it out. I says to them, *I got the gun.* Just in time, because the mother and father had arrived and they kicked us out of the house.

We get a conviction. Anderson's attorney's name is Lubasch. He appeals. Routine.

On some kind of technicality, he was able to get a retrial. Same evidence, same set of circumstances. Same defense lawyer. Only one thing is different. Lubasch is going to knock my credibility. Him and his daughter, they're a defense team.

Lubasch is a smart attorney. What he did: every detective who got up on the stand, he asked just one or two questions. "Were you watching Detective Waddell in the bedroom?" Of course, they would only have done that if they didn't trust me for some reason.

And Sergeant Plansker, I believe he testified, "I know he didn't have a gun."

"How did you know he didn't have a gun? Did you search him?" Same thing—why would they search me?

"And when did you first realize Detective Waddell found the murder weapon?" Everyone had to say, *After his hand was out of the ceiling.*

They can't confirm what I say. I'm out there by myself.

The jury's sitting there. Lubasch says something like, "Detective Waddell, isn't it a fact that you got promoted shortly after you convicted my client?" Based on the months, yes, that's a fact. I was promoted.

"Is it a fact that you also got a prestigious assignment in the district attorney's office?" It's not quite that prestigious, I said, but, yes, it is a fact. The jury's lookin' like— Then he goes on to say, and I'll never forget this, "Isn't it a fact that you put that gun in the ceiling and planted it on my client, didn't you, 'cause you don't know who the murderer is and wanted to flake my client?! Isn't it a fact?"

Blood pressure was up around my ears and I said, "No, that's not a fact. I didn't flake your client."

The jury bought it hook, line, and sinker—really not much I could do to convince them—Hey, you got to be kidding. Why would I do this to this guy? If you were ever gonna flake somebody, it wouldn't be in a homicide—the stakes are too high and too complex. You'd have to make it fit too.

This is one of the important cases that really upset me, and it was a lesson that justice isn't always served. The jury believed Anderson and they acquitted him. He got out, he walked.

Tony Lombardo wrote a paper on courtroom testimony two-and-a-half decades ago in the Police Academy and was awarded Class Hero for it. He grew up in what he calls "an organized crime environment" on the Lower East Side of Manhattan. "I saw a lot of people I knew—and I grew up with and I went to school with—die. They'd find them in rugs, in backs of cars."

As a kid, he admired the gangsters' street smarts and their attire, but always wanted to be "a detective, not a gangster." Honestly, he has no answer as to why—but thinks the rugs had something to do with it.

The detectives had their own allure. "They were always telling you, 'Hey, that's the best part of the job'—when you sink 'em on the stand. Juries today think the cops lie—" says Tony Lombardo, whose knowledge of ballistics and photography got him a spot among the other committed eccentrics in the unit where death is ever-present—Crime Scene. "Fingerprints, blood, semen, ballistics, hair, fibers do not lie. That's tangible evidence."

No doubt about it, everyone from mystery buffs to jurors loves that physical evidence, just because it is so concrete, so dramatic. Crime Scene detectives sometimes gather something so powerful, the case is over then and there—but the unit's mission normally is to comb the scene, gathering physical clues for the squad detectives who investigate cases.

Defense attorneys, threatened by the unmistakable message of the Crime Scene Unit's product—hoping to divert the jury's attention—attack the messenger. . . .

### Detective Second Grade Tony Lombardo:
### Expert Testimony

Three-to-elevens was a hot tour. We would catch what was left over from the day tour, and we would catch the beginning of the late tours. This was a case I had in The Bronx on a late tour. It involved a dead female Hispanic, a young girl of sixteen, in an abandoned building.

The only access to this burnt-out building was over a steel girder from the next building, which I was not about to do carrying my equipment. I was not a trapeze artist.

Myself and my Crime Scene partner were placed into the building by a Fire Department cherry picker.

We found this girl with a knife sticking out of her back. The wire lathing was off the walls, the windows were gone, the roof was open. Outside of a few garbage bottles and cans, what was there to process for latent finger prints? Nothing. The case came to light because a second female Hispanic who observed her girlfriend being sodomized anally and stabbed repeatedly, proceeded to get away from her captor and dive out the window in this fifth-floor tenement. She laid in an air shaft full of debris a couple of feet high, which broke her fall—but she broke her arms, her legs, her hip. She survived there with the rats running over her for two days. The district attorney's office took this girl and hid her out in Puerto Rico till she was well enough to testify.

The main perp lived next door to the abandoned building. He had just gotten out of jail for the same crime. The mother threw them out of the apartment. She did not want these girls and her son in the apartment, 'cause she knew what her son was. They took them up to the roof, forced them over the girders, into that building where they did their deed.

The squad made multiple arrests, three or five. When I came to testify on this case, I was badgered more than usual because these three or five defendants were sitting there with their three or five attorneys. One defendant had the jailhouse shaved head to change his appearance. He persisted in trying to make eye contact with me, like I was supposed to be fearful. They have a license to be tough and we don't.

In the courtroom there was also a female I didn't know who was taking notes. It was Ann Mathers; she worked for the *East Side Press* at the time, but I thought she was from Internal Affairs, which complicates things too. You want to be perfect.

I was sitting in the box being questioned and my hands were touching the sides. I was nervous, holding my papers. My hands became dirty from the sides of the box being dirty—dusty.

They were eyeballing me. I was inept—that was their theme, I was inept. And I knew I was a good crime scene investigator.

After being badgered and my mind clicking, I couldn't get up and strangle these attorneys; that would be illegal. The bulb lit up. I asked the judge if I may, in my own words, show the court that I am not an inept detective for not processing those dirty walls or windows.

I think it was the most innovative thing I ever did in my life.

Your Honor, your courtroom is a controlled environment with windows, air conditioning, and a cleaning staff. But how come my hands turned black? And could I get my fingerprints off this witness-box? *Zappo!*

No, I couldn't.

I explained the process of dusting for fingerprints and why it would be almost physically impossible to dust and get anything in an uncontrolled environment like that versus a controlled environment like this. Hands would get dirty, like mine are now. Look—

These fingers, with all this dirt, could never make a readable fingerprint. 'Cause fingerprints are salt and water and oils and so on, and in order to get fingerprints, you have to have a surface that's conducive to getting the oils to stay there. In dirt, your oils would be absorbed. Same thing if a surface is porous, the oils are absorbed.

And it won the day. I'm very proud of that.

--------

The ten contented years Patrolman Ken Carlson spent dealing with serious bad guys in Brooklyn also allowed him enough time in the Court Street state supreme courthouse to get really comfortable on the witness stand. An active cop like Carlson, making felony collars on the streets of a neighborhood like East New York, ends up testifying more than average. Quite a bit more, because lesser crimes are plea-bargained; defense lawyers know "when to hold 'em and when to fold 'em." If you don't make a lot of felony arrests, you don't get much chance to testify at trial.

Carlson is a big blond guy, built like that state trooper whose image ominously fills your rearview mirror. He grew up in Coney Island, but one look at him and you might think of a Wyoming state trooper rather than a Gotham detective lieutenant. Thanks to the Army buddy who made law enforcement sound worth a detour from the construction career Carlson had in mind, he *was* for two years a Wyoming state trooper. He came home, though, to join the NYPD in 1974—and since 1989 the one-time Crook County, WY, trooper is—right, a Gotham detective lieutenant.

In between the rewarding street-cop career and the only job he loves more—commanding a squad of detectives—came an assignment as detective sergeant in a precinct with a patrol scandal brewing, a precinct that could best be described as under a dark star. Traffic in the Detective Bureau at the time was all bottlenecks. If he wanted to move, he did have one option: Internal Affairs.

One of those times when you do what you gotta do.

"I really didn't know what to expect, but I was surprised when I went to Internal Affairs that all police officers didn't hate you and everybody in IAD wasn't a pariah. I was shocked. I maintained friendships that I'd had before, and people said, 'Well, if we have to have an Internal Affairs, at least you were a street cop. I'd rather see a street cop there than somebody who had no experience going in.' "

The assignment wasn't "a mission." For Carlson, it was a job and, he did it. "Wherever the chips fell, that's how it happened." Sooner or later, they were bound to fall on Court Street. On the witness stand, where once he'd felt at his best, he now endured "the worst trial . . ."

### Detective Lieutenant Ken Carlson: Cops on Trial

An anonymous call to 911 said there's a man with a gun on the street in the Eight-one Precinct—had a gun in his back pocket. Good clothing description. The call went out over the division radio. A couple of cars acknowledged that they were going, and "Pete," the cop who was working on that foot post, acknowledged that he was going. As it happened, he got there almost immediately. He was the first one there and he put the guy up against the building.

I was in Internal Affairs in Brooklyn and I got called to the Eight-one that day. A man in the station house was under arrest for possession of a gun. The arresting officer, Pete, was a recent transfer to the precinct. He had sixteen years on the job at the time and was given a steady foot post. On the foot post he had worked for probably six months, he met Ramona and became romantically involved.

She went shoppin' one day, grocery shopping, came back, and was takin' the grocery bags out of the car, and he helped her, carried the grocery bags into her apartment for her. That's how they met, and six months later it was true love for both of them.

The problem was, Pete had a wife and kids and a home on Long Island, but he still became romantically involved with Ramona—who had an old boyfriend, "José," living nearby. José wanted to get back with Ramona real bad. He really liked her. But the policeman, Pete—he wanted to stay with his girlfriend.

She was spurning José's further advances. She liked hanging out with Pete while Pete was working, and when he was not working also. Mostly when he was working. José started makin' complaints anonymously to the station house that the cop was spending on-duty time with this girl. Those allegations were unsubstantiated at the time.

No supervisor had actually observed Pete going into the house for the short period that he was under observation.

Pete suspected that José was the one that was dropping the dime on him. After a while, Pete found that he didn't want this guy José around anymore. He was botherin' him.

José ends up gettin' arrested. Pete puts him up against the building and tosses him, comes up with a gun in the back pocket. The radio cars from the other sectors get there, and he says to them, "I just took a gun off this guy—anybody want the collar?" One of the sectors says, "Yeah, I'll take the collar." So they cuffed him up and off they go to the Eight-one.

When they got to the station house, José told the desk sergeant, "The cop flaked me." Internal Affairs was called in and I went. I was a sergeant in Internal Affairs.

I listened to his statement, and I got the paperwork, roll calls—who was assigned to what sectors, whatever. I got all the pedigree information for the Police Department, and then I went out to the scene and did a canvass.

As it happened, I found two independent witnesses who corroborated part of the defendant's story. One guy said he was lookin' out his window and he saw a policeman take something out of his pocket and put it in José's pocket. He didn't know what kind of object it was, but saw it clearly. He said it was a small black object. I felt bad when I heard that. I really did—because it just rang true. He took me up to the window where he saw it from, and yeah—he had a very good clear view of what happened.

The second witness was a female who said that the foot man approached the bad guy in like a casual, lackadaisical way. Nonchalant. That's not the way you approach somebody if you suspect he has a gun. Especially if there's a detailed radio description and you're the only one there. Which, as it turned out, he was. I didn't like the sound of that, either.

The patrolman had some minor infractions in the past, disciplinaries, but nothing serious. He had sixteen years on the job.

I obtained the 911 call, the actual tape. I got a court order forcing the patrolman to read back a verbatim transcript of what the 911 call had said. I sent that for voice analysis and it came back as a positive. It was in all likelihood him. It's not as accurate as a fingerprint, but in the expert's opinion, he was the anonymous 911 caller.

The only problem I wish I had been able to tie up was where he made the call from. He was supposed to be on foot post. It was a busy street, but there were no background noises on the tape. I don't think he made it from a pay phone. I believe he made it from the girlfriend's apartment—but 911 calls don't show up on telephone records because they're not billed.

Eventually, the case went. He was arrested. I was the arresting officer. I didn't like that. There *was* no exchange. The only thing that happened during the arrest processing was I got him in and out of Central Booking and the initial arraignment very quickly. Afterwards he said thank you for that. He appreciated the consideration that he didn't have to wait in line to be processed or to be arraigned. I felt even worse. Here I am, I did the investigation, I locked him up, and he's thanking me for something.

He went to trial in supreme court in Brooklyn. It was very tough testifying. The policeman was sitting right there at the defense table. I couldn't help but look at him. Very tough. I had to remind myself that he was stealing time from the job. He was supposed to be on foot post and he was playing with his girlfriend. Had he done that off duty, that would have been a different story. I don't know what his home life was like.

As far as flakin' the guy, I was totally shocked. I've never seen a police officer flake anybody in all my time on the job. I've heard stories about it, and I imagine that in the past it's probably happened, but all the stories I've ever heard were about police officers flaking really bad people. They knew they were bad people, drug dealers, and—the officers were just frustrated.

I'm not excusing or condoning the behavior, but they were doing something to get a bad guy—or who they believed to be a bad guy—off the street. This was a totally personal reason—he didn't want his girlfriend's ex-boyfriend to try to get back together with this woman. I just couldn't understand doing anything like that for such a ridiculous reason. And then the consequences he suffered—he threw sixteen years away.

I don't know what happened to him after, but between the time he was suspended and the trial, he was drivin' a delivery truck in the City. It wasn't a good delivery truck job. You deliver newspapers, you belong to the union, you can make a good living at that; this was, like, a nothing job.

He was subsequently convicted and fired from this job. He didn't go to jail, but because of the felony conviction, he was automatically fired. I can't imagine what he went home and told his wife. How he faced his kids. Eventually they're going to get older and know that he was a policeman at one time. What do you tell your family, why you did this? I mean, if you tell the truth, you can't even rationalize it like, "I was trying to get a bad guy off the street." I just felt very confused at his reasoning—the motivation. A shock that a police officer would actually do that.

------

Behind-scenes at the thirteen-day trial, some players were invisible to the courtroom audience, like Bill Carreras and Scott Jaffer of the Two-six Squad, key detectives among at least two dozen who investigated the case. Testimony from their witnesses, among other evidence, formed the basis for indicting Jonah Perry for assault and attempted robbery—also for the prosecution theory that Jonah's younger brother Eddie had been shot while acting as accomplice.

In the aftermath of the failed mugging on a summer night in 1985, one alleged mugger was dead. The victim of this one among many hundreds of such crimes in the City survived with more devastating emotional than physical aftereffects, but that is not uncommon among mugging victims.

Eight months later, in January 1986, much was uncommon about the trial. *People* v. *Jonah Perry* would certainly have played to an empty courtroom, as many a homicide trial does, if not for the cast of characters. As it was, spectators and press jammed Justice Eve M. Preminger's court. Front-page articles and a book about the case would result.

Who were the other characters in this tragic piece?

The assault victim: a young plainclothes officer, Lee Van Houten, who'd been on Anti-Crime patrol behind St. Luke's hospital that summer night. The officer—capable, with a clean record—took the stand and testified to many details of his ordeal but was unable to identify his attacker. He also had waived immunity to appear before the grand jury, which found the shooting an act of self-defense and cleared him of wrongdoing.

Accused of the vicious assault and the robbery attempt: Jonah Perry, a black youth with an unusual Harlem background. Jonah and his brother Eddie had prep school and college educations thanks to their mother, the late Veronica Perry, at the time an ambitious, politically connected Harlem figure. Jonah hadn't testified in the grand jury, and he sat out the trial, sporting his red Cornell T-shirt at the defense table. He was now in his sophomore year.

For the defense: high-profile black activist lawyer Alton H. Maddox, successor in the case to the even higher-profile black activist lawyer, C. Vernon Mason. Mason sped to Jonah's side when detectives wanted to interview him just after the fatal shooting by Officer Van Houton of Eddie Perry.

Prosecuting *People* v. *Jonah Perry*: James Kindler, DA Robert M. Morgenthau's Harvard Law School–trained executive assistant, who did not ordinarily prosecute cases but took over *Perry* at Morgenthau's direction.

Fourteen days into the trial, after deliberating four hours, the jury bought in a verdict: not guilty. Next morning the *Times* reported that "troubling questions remain about who did what" on the night of June 12, 1985. Nor did jurors quoted in the article claim a firm grasp of the facts in *People* v. *Jonah Perry.*

Would the promising Eddie Perry, just graduated from Philips Exeter Academy, headed for Stanford University in the fall, have risked everything for a street crime? *That* was the question that provoked the media attention throughout. Jonah Perry's acquittal provided one kind of answer. Journalist Robert Sam Anson's 1987 book, *Best Intentions,* by documenting Eddie's consistent drug use and drug dealing at Exeter, indirectly provided another.

For Detective Scott Jaffer the question was more like, "How could we lose—?" The detective was off duty when the jury came in: "I'm in my car, I hear the verdict on WINS, and I almost drive off the road. I could not believe it. We proved a good case. We were spelling everything out. I was flabbergasted."

Jaffer, a hoop fanatic, was a good competitor, a good sport. On the basketball court or in supreme court, he was prepared to win most and maybe gracefully lose one. But not this one.

Detective Bill Carreras, about to retire, relished as a last big case this unusual assault/attempted robbery. He was impressed by the resources devoted to the investigation: detectives from *both* of Manhattan's homicide squads, a video surveillance van to aid in identifying witnesses—"anything we wanted." Plus, a prosecutor from Morgenthau's inner circle.

Carreras was on restricted duty, "where you're not supposed to leave the squad—I was assigned to this case at the DA's request even though someone else caught it. Of course, I couldn't attend the trial, because I would be called to testify. But I wasn't called. There were a lot of things about this trial. . . ."

There surely *were* "things," among them the failure to call to the stand the lead case detective. Other setbacks damaged the case that once seemed to have everything going for it. The autopsy, Carreras recalls, said Eddie's hand—"his left hand I think"—bore a series of bruises. Forensic dentist Lowell Levine's files are inaccessible, but in Carreras's recollection, Levine identified Lee Van Houten's teethmarks.

"Eddie had apparently yoked Van Houten from behind," Carreras says. "This would have cleared up the jury's doubt that at least one brother had scuffled with the cop." But at the trial, "the judge excluded the teethmarks as inflammatory," Carreras believes. In an acquittal, the case files are sealed. ADA Kindler remembers Dr. Levine being on the case, but not the rest. ADA John Stein, who assisted Kindler, would not comment on this, or any, aspect of the case.

"There's nothing you wouldn't do in a life-threatening fight," says Lee Van Houten, "but did I bite the guy? It didn't happen. Did the guy's hand connect with my teeth, while he was punching me? I don't know."

"Who knows why the judge excluded it?" says Carreras. "In this town . . ." For Billy Carreras, a great theorist, all the "things" added up to a theory about a quid pro quo involving the district attorney race (Morgenthau won) and the Perry case (the other side won).

But for the down-to-earth Jaffer, the answer seemed simpler, more basically human: "The jury wasn't gonna take away the second son." Van Houten says he received two anonymous letters, purportedly from jurors, that told him exactly that.

*Politically correct* was not yet the popular buzz phrase, but Manhattan juries have always understood the concept. Especially against a background of sympathy for a mother who had tried so hard to defeat the Harlem odds, not covering bases at trial spelled doom, Jaffer felt.

Another one of those 'things": "We had some people that were talking," Jaffer says, "who told us Jonah had apparently run down through the park into the area where they live, One Hundred Fourteenth Street, and had told some people his brother was just shot." The detectives sweated to get two of those sensitive, community-tied witnesses on the stand and did. But though neither witness had a record, media accounts confirm that both were unprepared to counter attorney Maddox's sharp, diversionary attacks on their backgrounds and reasons for testifying.

Scotty Jaffer, who started in the NYPD in 1969, is a vivid
example of the paradoxes lived by NYPD detectives. As a kid, he
was big on cop movies. Voluble, charming, well-built, when he
walked away from a junior salesman's spot in wholesale men's
clothing into the physical job you saw in the cop movies, he hadn't
the slightest notion what a salesman you sometimes have to be
with a witness.

Nor could the youthful Jaffer have had an inkling from any
celluloid scenario of the little drama that would one day clarify
how the case that seemed to have everything going for it . . . went
down in flames.

### Detective Second Grade Scott Jaffer:
### Manhattan Jury

Van Houten was fighting with two guys and he was beat up pretty badly. He was all
bruised.

This person that was shot was brought into the Emergency Room. Subsequently
pronounced DOA. So now the investigation begins. Going down into the valley, we're
able to get some information about this guy's background. Eddie Perry: a student at a
famous prep school in New England, accepted as a freshman at Stanford. . . .

Became a very, very political case. Black activists got involved. Lots of pressure
because summer was coming and they were starting to make this a racial thing—"a
white cop shot a black youth in a robbery."

Mrs. Perry, very bright woman. She was in the campaigns of the local congressman,
used to get the kids summer jobs at his office. She utilized her power to better her
children, and I have no problem with that—I commend her for that. She got in touch
with C. Vernon Mason, and now lots of press gets involved.

Eddie Canepa and Bill O'Connor get a call in the squad from a girl, Desiree, who was
in that crowd that night when Jonah Perry comes down from Morningside Heights and
begins to tell his story. Desiree was a friend of his, and she's there. She's the best you
have—not an eyewitness, but she's a witness to a statement that Jonah Perry makes,
that "We had a problem up on the hill"—that's his words—and that his brother was
shot. Jonah ran away and left Eddie laying there—that's one of the worst parts of this.

We're able to get ahold of Desiree and we get her confidence and we get some good
information from her regarding who was there that he told this to. Anybody she mentions
is picked up. Some are cooperating, most of them aren't. But we get enough informa-

tion—through patients at St. Luke's, through Desiree, and through other friends who were there—

The DA gives the case to a person that's very high in the office, Jimmy Kindler. An indictment is handed down; we pick up Jonah Perry. Matter-of-fact, I even printed him. Alton Maddox is there. Perry didn't say much—he has a lawyer. To me, he looked as if he felt guilty about leaving his brother. I think if he'd been alone with us . . .

The real investigation in this case is after the indictment. Because now you have to go to court and you gotta *prove* this case. But we're goin' to trial. . . . Understand, this is a Manhattan jury. A woman just lost her son. Very difficult. So we have a lot against us.

We proceed to go to trial. Desiree, the girl who had given a lot of information and who Jonah had made admissions to, had disappeared! Myself and Bill O'Connor, who's also very good at persuading people—he gives the priest image—we go to her sister's house, her mother's house. No one's cooperating.

But we get information that she's working in Valley Stream, Long Island, at the big department store. Out we go, to Green Acres shopping center. She wasn't comin'. I said to her, We're not gonna walk away; this is a very important case; there's a lot of pressure on us. You read the papers; it's all over the papers. I'm sorry, we're gonna try the best to protect you so that your name is not printed or anything, but I'm not leavin' you here. There's no way.

"I'm not comin'."

Well, there's two ways you can come—I take out my cuffs. You can come on your own, or you're gonna be dragged outta here. She came without the cuffs.

Now, Billy Carreras is drivin' and I'm with her in the back, and I'm talkin' and talkin', and I explain to her exactly the way I felt. Innocent guy's gettin' blamed for somethin' he doesn't deserve to get blamed for—the cop, Van Houten. The press is building this up and makin' this a racial issue. This is nothing about racists; there's nothing about race here. He's an honor student, and they're makin' it that this kid was killed unnecessarily. By the time she got out of that car, she couldn't wait to get into court. She was really, really excited.

So we get to court; the DA spoke to her. I think he put her on that day. And she went in there. They brought out some bad things about her background. I'm not allowed to be in the courtroom, but after the testimony we all walked back to Kindler's office—he hugged me. The DA hugged me. "You found her. You did great."

Now we had another witness problem in this case. It was the defendant's girlfriend, Alicia, who he also had made admissions to. We finally get her and she told me this is not the first time the Perry boys did this. That night, they had a bet or somethin' to go to the movies, had to go get movie money—but they'd been doing' robberies for quite a while. Back and forth from school, that was determined later on.

These guys weren't the Goody Two-shoes everybody was making them out to be. Apparently, Eddie had a background, sellin' drugs up in school.

So this girl was a real hot witness. She kept a diary. What more can you ask for? Coincidentally, she "couldn't find it." She "lost" her diary. We were convinced she was lying. We talked to her father; we went up to her house. She wouldn't produce the diary.

But on a Friday, she is down to testify—she's gonna tell what was *in* the diary. Our last witness, but she's goin' bad. You can see just before she's goin' in: she's in the prep room. "I can't do this, I'm sorry, I'm sorry—" The DA says, "I'm not putting her on the stand in this condition. She has to be prepared to go up there and do a good job and tell the truth."

She could have broken this case wide open.

She's gonna go on, on Monday. She's taken home to her project: "Good-bye, we'll pick you up Monday morning." Very bad move. Terrible. She should have been put in as a material witness, taken out of the neighborhood—put in a hotel.

Monday morning she's brought down. Seems to be okay. Again, we go over everything. She goes in on the stand. They ask her about Jonah Perry, "Do you know him?" "Yeah, not too good." "Is he your boyfriend." "No." "Do you know anything about him?" "No."

Time-out. "Can we get a short recess?" They bring her back in the room.

What are you doing?

"I can't, I can't do this. He's looking at my face. I just can't do it. I just can't *do* this. They'll kill me—" this and that.

Listen, you're here, I said. They all know. You gotta go in and tell the truth.

They smooth it out with the jury; she goes in a second time. Basically, the same thing happens. No good. We just lost the best witness. But we figure with Desiree and other people that were produced—everybody in that conversation confirmed he was there. We think we had a good case. And we did. The DA was happy with it.

Jury goes out. They come back. . . .

I could not believe it. It wasn't just Desiree—believe me. It was a good case, I thought. Apparently, the jury didn't, and they acquitted.

Desiree's upset. "What did I do wrong?"

You didn't do anything wrong. They didn't believe you. They painted a bad picture of you, etc., etc.

Acquitted. Big write-ups.

Maybe a year later—maybe a year and a half, I'm in Manhattan North Homicide. I'm working on 112th Street and Lexington Avenue, in the projects there. A man killed his wife; we're doin' an investigation. I come out of a building and I see a girl. She looks at me, I look at her. "Scotty!"

I walk over to her. It's the girlfriend, Alicia. I'm not fond of her, obviously, for what happened. I said to her, Listen, can I talk to you? What's your *story*?

She says, "You made a mistake. You let me go home. The mother got to me. 'Don't ruin my son's life!' And I was having his baby." She told me this a year, a year-and-a-half later. "I had the diary. I had everything. He was bringin' money home; I was his girlfriend. I was pregnant with his child—"

She had a child in a stroller, right there—his child! Apparently, they weren't together anymore.

I mean, we were sure we had it. It's like I wanted to bring her and open this whole matter up. But you can't.

———

*My whole thing was to become a detective. I had a desire to lock up the bad guy.* Going on twenty-five years now, since Tommy McKenna got his shield, he's been fulfilling his desire not merely to collar the bad guy but to convict him and send him to jail. At the nationally-known 1990 "Central Park Jogger" trial of four teenagers indicted for attempted murder, rape, and other charges, the media had a field day with the ruse the Manhattan North Homicide detective used to try to get a confession from defendant Yusef Salaam on the terrible night of "wilding."

"DETECTIVE: I DID WHAT I HAD TO DO TO GET HIM TO CONFESS . . ." screamed *New York Newsday*'s page one. Without benefit of quotation marks, because of course McKenna was too experienced ever to have testified in such terms. He did readily admit on the witness stand in Judge Thomas Galligan's courtroom to having deceived Salaam. Cross-examining defense attorney Robert Burns started one exchange by accusing the detective of looking the defendant in the eye—"What I'm saying is that when you look at him, you looked at him eyeball to eyeball, isn't that true?"

A. That's the way I like to look at you.
Q. And you weren't smiling, were you?
A. No, sir.
Q. But you weren't laughing or kidding around, is that true?
A. It's a serious matter. No, sir, I was not.

Q. Because you were serious about what you were doing, isn't
   that true?
A. Absolutely true.
Q. You had—Would it be fair to say that you had a no-nonsense
   attitude?

[Prosecutor Elizabeth] LEDERER: Objection.
THE COURT: I'll let him answer.

A. I always have a no-nonsense attitude.
Q. In other words, you weren't fooling around. There's no fooling
   around there, is that right?
A. Business is business, sir.
Q. And your business at that time was to get a statement from
   Yusef, one way or the other, in relation to what happened
   to the female jogger, isn't that also true?
A. My job was to get the truth.
Q. And you had an idea in your mind of what the truth was, isn't
   that true?
A. Yes, sir.
Q. And it was in that context when you told him that if he didn't
   speak to you, he was going to be there all night, is that true?
A. I never said that to him.
Q. Words to that effect.
A. I never mentioned that at all, counsel.
Q. That he had to talk to you?
A. I never said he had to do anything. I advised him of his rights.
   He volunteered to talk to me.
Q. After you lied to him.
A. Pardon?
Q. After you lied to him.
A. I guess, if you want to call it a lie, yeah.

THE COURT: [. . .] This is a courtroom; it is not a forum of some
   kind. [. . .] Let's remember that.
MR. BURNS: May I, Your Honor?
THE COURT: Yes.

Q. Well, the story about getting fingerprints from—from—from
   jogging pants, that wasn't true, was it?

A. I didn't think so.

Q. But you told it to Yusef Salaam like you thought so, didn't you?

A. Yes, sir.

Q. And it wasn't true, am I correct?

A. I find out that it's not true, right.

Q. Oh. At the time when you told him about getting fingerprints from satin pants, you thought that was possible?

A. No, sir. I did not know if it was possible. I didn't know if we had fingerprints.

Q. Well, that's another question. My question is, did you believe that it was possible to get fingerprints from some satiny cloth surface?

A. No, I did not.

Q. So, when you told fifteen-year-old Yusef, who you believed was sixteen, and you told it to him, eyeball to eyeball, he believed you, didn't he?

MS. LEDERER: Objection.

THE COURT: Objection sustained.

Q. Well, you told it to him like it was something that he should believe.

MS. LEDERER: Objection.

THE COURT: I'll let him answer it.

Q. Isn't that true?

A. If was guilty, he would believe it. He would believe it, I guess, if his prints were on the pants.

Q. But his prints are not on the clothes, and we're here to determine whether he's guilty or not, isn't that true?

MS. LEDERER: Objection.

THE COURT: Objection sustained.

MS. LEDERER: I ask that it be stricken.

THE COURT: Strike it. Disregard it.

Q. [. . .] But that was a lie, am I correct?

A. It's a fib. It was a fib, a nontruth.

Q. Intentionally told, is that correct?

A. Yes, sir.

A sidebar to *Newsday* court reporter Emily Sachar's thorough story on McKenna's "fib" testimony quoted legal experts, letting readers in on what McKenna well knew—his tactics were altogether legal. But the jurors—regularly admonished by Judge Galligan to avoid all media exposure to the case, not to discuss it with anyone—were on their own to make what they could of Detective McKenna's fib and his confident demeanor as a witness.

On or off the stand, of course, McKenna would never deny his heartfelt desire to obtain justice for the jogger. Off the stand . . .

"The jogger case was treated as a homicide from the get-go, a homicide with a victim but no witnesses. We didn't think we had any witnesses. What we knew was that we had a girl that was severely beaten and raped and found in Central Park. It's an unusual case for the Homicide Squad because our victims don't usually talk to us. Our victims are usually dead. Sometimes we can interview people before they succumb to their wounds, but our clients are usually dead, and we work from there.

"She was supposed to die—that's why we were involved. Thank God that two guys were going through the park and found her. Why were they there? They always take that route home. Why did they find her? Only God knows why they found her, but they saved her life. They saw her—normal New York attitude would have been, Legs don't fail me now, let me get the hell out of here.

"They didn't. They went to the police, led the police back to where she was. Ambulances. And the girl's life was saved as a result of those two indigent people who cared. There's no ands, ifs, or buts. They cared. They saw a girl who was in deep, dire trouble, and they reacted.

"I had the privilege of dealing with the jogger. I transported her to court and took her from court for both trials. As long as you don't get to know your victim, you can remain aloof, you can remain professional. I still remained professional in the damn thing, but I got to know her.

"Did it mean something to me after meeting her that they were found guilty? It meant something to me that they were found guilty whether I had met her or not, simply because they were guilty, and they deserved to go to jail."

The squad always breaks your balls when you're a media star, and the *Newsday* cover starring McKenna was surely no exception. In-house, McKenna is known for posterity as The Lying Detective. "Don't trust McKenna," warn all those relentlessly truthful homicide detectives. "He lies."

On one level, you remember this as the trial that made you a household name for a New York minute. On a deeper level, it's a long-running, uncommonly intense criminal justice episode, even in a high-intensity city. In the criminal justice life of an NYPD homicide detective, the episodes inevitably blur. Few cases stay with you in detail. Dates and victims' complicated ethnic names materialize as McKenna relates one more that stuck.

### Detective First Grade Thomas McKenna:
### Wrong Man

I put so many people in jail, I forget the numbers. But the only time I ever got somebody out of jail—was that a highlight? Yeah, that sure as hell was.

It was a pattern type of thing, where somebody stole limousines, killed the drivers, left them on the West Side Highway in the Two-four. First victim was Michael Kyriacou, August 21, 1986.

Kenneth Harris was the bad guy, and another guy, "Smith," was doin' his time for sticking up these car service "black cars"—Lincoln Continentals. They're often driven by retired cops.

Chris Heimgartner and I, we were partners at the time; Chris is now a lieutenant. We're workin' the homicide and we get a couple of breaks, and we get a lot of help from people here after the second one went down. Bottom line was, we knew who we were lookin' for, and after the second homicide, we knew who did it. Had we been able to put the case together a little bit quicker, we would have maybe prevented the second homicide. But we weren't able to get enough yet on the individual.

September 10, we collar Harris for the homicides, and when we hit his apartment with the search warrant, we come up with all the proceeds of that robbery—namely, the radio from the car that *Smith* was accused of sticking up and a shitload of other stuff. We just knew the wrong guy was in.

Smith was running a scam on the car services downtown near the World Trade Center. He would take a black car home to Brooklyn and charge it off to a major investment bank with illegal taxi voucher numbers. He was basically set up by a driver, a retired cop who was onto him. The cop picked Smith up and when he gave a bad number, the retired cop locked him up. The Two-four RIP found out about it and put Smith's picture in a photo array. Smith was tentatively identified in the photos by one of the robbery victims, and subsequently picked out in a lineup by a cab driver. *That's him.* Wrong identification.

He doesn't plea bargain: he's innocent. Tried, convicted, and sent to the can.

Thanksgiving he got out. Thanksgiving keeps popping up in my lifetime in the Police Department. Thanksgiving Day I'm working, and he comes through the door with his girlfriend. He got out of jail the day before, and he comes in Thanksgiving to find me, to thank me.

It's wrong when other people are doing the time for something they didn't do. You hear, "Aw, that's one we owed him." This job, we owe the bad guy the time in jail, we owe the good people of the City—I don't want to sound like a holy guy, because I'm not—but we owe the people our pay. We owe them the job that we do.

We do a good job. Lot of people don't think so—bad guys certainly don't think so. But we do the job as best we can.

# EPILOGUE

**Lieutenant Ken Carlson and Detective Second Grade Ralph Blasi:** Sunday morning, September 1989, near LaGuardia airport. Seven-thirty. A car burning on a desolate side street. The fire is all in the interior of the car, and after the firemen get the flames extinguished, they pop the trunk to make sure there's no flames inside. There are none, but there's a dead body in the trunk.

It's a guy—bonked over the head, it turned out. His skull is crushed.

Police are called, naturally; the One-fourteen cops call the squad. My Detective Chris DeLuca catches the case. They run the plate—the car's a rental. Rented by the victim, Conrad, in Oklahoma City. He had ID on him; we notified the Oklahoma police. Sheriff Buck Johnson went and told the victim's wife, Trudy, and she said, "He was here the day before yesterday." She "didn't know" her husband was in New York.

We were fairly certain that the homicide happened or started in Oklahoma. From the rental records and from what the sheriff told us, Conrad was in Oklahoma a couple of days before.

Chris DeLuca had Trudy on the phone long distance before she knew what hit her; think he scared her a bit. Chris and his partner Ralph Blasi left Monday morning to go to Oklahoma.

Prior to their arrival, Sheriff Johnson got a call from a local locksmith. Trudy had called to open up a safe that Conrad had in the house, but she didn't know the combination. The locksmith called the sheriff and the sheriff said, "No, don't bother going over there. I'll come pick up the safe." Small town, Claremore, Oklahoma. Turned out there was a lot of cash—in excess of twenty-five thousand cash—in the safe.

357

**Detective Blasi:** Sheriff Johnson had Trudy in custody when we got there. Very pretty girl from New York, gorgeous girl, like a model. We found she gave in to cocaine and used her looks to get it. For thirteen hours, Trudy had stuck to her story: "I don't know what happened to him."

Chris said, "She's scared shit of me. You talk to her." I asked the sheriff, Mind if I go in there? "Go ahead."

Two hours, she gave up everything. The deputies laughed. All these six-foot-four football-player sheriffs, with .45s. It took me a few minutes to convince 'em that Trudy gave it up.

**Lieutenant Carlson:** Sheriff Johnson obtained a search warrant. They got physical evidence out of the house—hair, blood, fibers, everything. And the weapon too.

What happened? Trudy and Conrad's business partner, Mike, both hated Conrad with a passion, and they ended up talkin' to each other. Mike said in passing, "Jeez, y'know, I can't stand Conrad. He's my partner but I hate his guts." And Trudy says, "Yeah, well, I'm married to him and I hate his guts too."

**Detective Blasi:** She said, "I'll give you five thousand to whack him." They were gonna hook up later, live together. He was in love with her.

**Lieutenant Carlson:** Trudy's husband had some kind of medical condition, asthma, or something like that. He took medication whenever the symptoms bothered him, made him drowsy, *very* drowsy.

They waited till he took his medication next time. Conrad went in and he was layin' on the bed. Trudy called Mike and said her husband was sleeping off the medication. Mike came over and they both bonked him over the head. Killed him.

**Detective Blasi:** Lead pipe—very crude. Made a bloody mess of an absolutely gorgeous house that would cost six hundred thousand dollars on Long Island.

**Lieutenant Carlson:** They wrapped him up and put him in the trunk of a rental car. Not being a really professional type hit guy, the partner didn't know what to do. He drove to the only other place he ever knew in the world, New York City. He was originally from Brooklyn. They had moved to Oklahoma ten years prior, and he was involved in a drug-smuggling ring, we heard.

He drove to Astoria, Queens, by LaGuardia Airport, parked the car on a side street, and went to buy a gallon of gas. Brought the gas back. It was a new type car—only the interior burned.

Then he walked across the street to the airport. We found the ticket clerk who actually sold him the ticket for cash to go back to Oklahoma right after he walked away from the dead body. We were fortunate we were able to interview the people who worked that morning. Early on a Sunday, even LaGuardia wasn't that busy. The clerk remembered him clearly, his demeanor and his clothing and the fact that he had no luggage with him.

When he found out there were two New York detectives in Claremore, Mike flew back here.

**Detective Blasi:** But first we were chasin' him all around Claremore, just missin' him—the football-player deputies and two Italian detectives. The deputies would tell these New York drug-ring types they were lookin' for Mike and, "Y'all should cooperate. We'd sure appreciate that, son."

Then we'd tell 'em to fuckin' give the guy up, and they gave us information. Pretty soon the deputies tried it and it worked for them too. They were great, a million laughs.

**Lieutenant Carlson:** There weren't that many flights coming to New York from Oklahoma. We knew what day he probably left, so we were able to corroborate it that way. LaGuardia to Oklahoma and then back to Brooklyn.

**Detective Blasi:** We were still in Oklahoma. Queens Homicide—Kelly's boys—staked out Mike's mother's house. Six hours, he comes out. They took him to Central Booking. He didn't talk.

**Lieutenant Carlson:** But near the car fire we found the gas can that he used to obtain the gallon's worth of gas, his fingerprints were on the can. We found the gas station. The attendant identified his photo later as the guy who purchased the gas.

The guy must have driven through hundreds of miles of desolate area between Oklahoma and here. Why didn't he dump the body there?

**Detective Blasi:** In Trudy's confession, she said they figured if they dropped it in New York City, nobody would care and nobody would do anything, because there were too many.

**Lieutenant Carlson:** They just didn't think anybody would investigate enough to connect a dead body in a New York City street with Oklahoma.

# THE LAST WORD

Active and retired NYPD detectives were interviewed for *Cop Talk* in 1991, 1992 and 1993. Each narrating detective's rank is given in the text as of the interview date. If a narrator's rank or status had changed by the time the manuscript was completed in September 1993, the change is reflected below.

Dennis Roberts was promoted to second grade in 1992.
Robert Chung was promoted to sergeant in 1993.
Mike Burke was promoted to sergeant in 1993.
Pat Brosnan was promoted to second grade in 1993.
Tom McKenna was promoted to first grade in 1993.
Jack Doyle retired in 1993.

The following narrators were retired by the time they were interviewed. Most of them (better than eight out of ten) still work in law enforcement in either the public or private sector.

Evrard Williams
Tom Ullo
Tom Duffy
Joe Brandefine
Ed Kelly, Jr.

Ron Cadieux
Joe Pepe
Bob Kohler
George Terra
Tony Lotito

Jim Varian
Tom Lane
Jack Donovan
Mike Gerhold
Bob McKnight
Steve Weiner
Dan Kelly
Jack Godoy
Leslie Hinds
Gene Roberts
Ed Howlette
Jim Ziede
John Skala

Sam Skeete
Steve Mshar
Ron Waddell
Joe Sofia
Olga Ford
Tim Byrnes
Terry Quinn
Romolo Imundi
Katy Stanton
Scott Jaffer
John Hartigan
Bill Majeski